Per Jarle Bekken

Paul's Negotiation of Abraham in Galatians 3 in the Jewish Context

Beihefte zur Zeitschrift für die neutestamentliche Wissenschaft

Edited by
Matthias Konradt, Judith Lieu, Laura Nasrallah,
Jens Schröter, and Gregory E. Sterling

Volume 248

Per Jarle Bekken

Paul's Negotiation of Abraham in Galatians 3 in the Jewish Context

The Galatian Converts — Lineal Descendants of Abraham and Heirs of the Promise

DE GRUYTER

ISBN 978-3-11-072192-8
e-ISBN (PDF) 978-3-11-072210-9
e-ISBN (EPUB) 978-3-11-072217-8
ISSN 0171-6441

Library of Congress Control Number: 2021931475

Bibliographic Information published by the Deutsche Nationalbibliothek
The Deutsche Nationalbibliothek lists this publication in the Deutsche Nationalbibliografie; Detailed bibliographic data are available in the Internet at http://dnb.dnb.de.

Printing and binding: CPI books GmbH, Leck

www.degruyter.com

Dedicated to the memory of my late parents, Erna Johanne and Gunnar Bekken

Acknowledgments

There are persons and institutions I owe thanks and acknowledgments for their support during the completion of this book. I am grateful to the Faculty of Education and Arts, Nord University, for having granted me research time to bring this book to an end. Thanks are also due to the librarians at Nord University in Bodø and Levanger, who have provided helpful services. I also thank Tyndale House, that made it possible for me to spend the spring 2016 and two months in 2018 in Cambridge as a Visiting Professor. A special thanks to the library staff of Tyndale House for their kind assistance.

I would also like to thank Professors Sigurd Grindheim, A. Andrew Das, and the members of the "Philo and Early Christianity" seminar, SNTS, for valuable comments on various parts of the work. I am grateful to Professor Thomas Kazen (University College, Stockholm) for inviting me to present a paper in his doctoral seminar in September 2019. I owe special thanks to the Publisher De Gruyter due to the constructive criticism and helpful remarks provided during the peer review process. Any flaws or shortcomings are my responsibility.

I am once again grateful to Dr. Brian McNeil, who has revised my English.

Last but by no means least, I thank Editorial Director Dr. Albrecht Döhnert, for accepting my work for publication in the prestigious series BZNW, and Acquisitions Editor Alice Meroz, for her kind support during the production of this book.

I dedicate this book to the memory of my late parents, Erna Johanne and Gunnar Bekken, for the love and encouragement they always offered.

Levanger, January 2021

Per Jarle Bekken

https://doi.org/10.1515/9783110722109-001

Contents

Chapter 1: Introduction

1 The Thesis of this Study

Samuel Sandmel once wrote about Philo's interpretation of Abraham: "To see what the writer makes of Abraham is often to see most clearly what the writer is trying to say."[1] This statement may be applied to Paul and Philo as well as to other Jewish authors. A presupposition of this study, which justifies it, is that, in spite of the vastness of the secondary literature, the various aspects of Paul's appropriation of Abraham need to be examined further, especially since Philo can provide us with parallels which have not yet been made the subject of a detailed analysis.[2] It is the main thesis of this study that Paul in Galatians 3:6–29 shares aspects of a Jewish referential background,[3] particularly evident in Philo's writings, in which the figure of Abraham was conceived as an authoritative norm relative to the law of Moses. I shall now investigate the constituents of such a Jewish referential background in and behind Galatians 3, and this study leads to the following main conclusions:

1. Gal 3:6–29 provides a small "exegetical treatise", in which words from the main quotation of Gen 15:6 and from other subordinate biblical passages have been given an exegetical paraphrase throughout the passage. Paul follows a conventional method of Jewish exegesis, in which phrases from the biblical quotation may be omitted or replaced and supplemented by other interpretative terms or otherwise combined with various exegetical traditions. Such exegetical traditions may be identified either as exegetical motifs or as a cluster of other biblical passages, i. e., exegetical explanations that deviate from the Hebrew Bible itself, or a conjunction of biblical passages that appear regularly together and can be found to be deployed in different writings by other ancient authors who belong

1 S. Sandmel, "Philo's Place in Judaism," *HUCA* 25 (1954): 237.

2 For the most comprehensive attempts at a detailed comparison of Philo and Paul, see the following monographs: O. McFarland, *God and Grace in Philo and Paul*, NovTSup (Leiden: Brill, 2015); N. Calvert-Koyzis, *Paul, Monotheism and the People of God: The Significance of Abraham Traditions for Early Judaism and Christianity*, JSNTSup (London; New York: T & T Clark, 2004); G.W. Hansen, *Abraham in Galatians: Epistolary and Rhetorical Contexts*, JSNTSup (Sheffield: Sheffield Academic Press, 1989).

3 By "referential background," I have in mind discussions, perspectives, concepts, ideas, and conventions which, without necessarily being explicitly referred to in a text, nevertheless are presupposed in such a way that one should know about this background in order to grasp the implications of the meaning of the text. For such a definition, cf. L. Hartman, *Asking for a Meaning: A Study of 1 Enoch 1–5*, ConBNT (Lund: Gleerup, 1979), 123.

https://doi.org/10.1515/9783110722109-002

to an author's cultural context.[4] Moreover, parallels in Philo and other Jewish data also suggest that Paul has cast his exegetical argument into conventional "forms" in terms of exegetical structures and terminology of his own day.

2. The Galatian converts had experienced that God had granted the Spirit and worked manifestations of power in them when they came to trust in God. At this juncture, Paul applies the exegetical motifs, in which Gen 15:6 is interpreted about Abraham's reception of the Spirit and his experience of being transformed by God in a context in which Abraham is characterized as the paradigmatic proselyte. By comparing the experience of the Galatian converts to this crucial event in Abraham's life, Paul ascribed to the Galatians the status of being approved by God as Jewish proselytes apart from circumcision and a way of life under the jurisdiction of the Law. This assertion was most probably developed in an intramural debate with Paul's opponents, who draw the opposite conclusion from the same exegetical motif and data, namely, that the mode of conversion based on the paradigm of Abraham implied that the Galatian converts needed to be circumcised and become adherents to the commandments of the Law of Moses.

3. Furthermore, the experience of becoming a Jewish proselyte under the same scriptural terms as Abraham meant that Abraham was not merely a model, but was also conceived as the father of the Jewish converts. Thus, Paul insists that the non-Jews as Jewish converts, and not without regard to their conversion, inherit the status of being incorporated into the lineage of Abraham, identified as "οἱ ἐκ πίστεως", that is, the fundamental virtue of piety that defined their father Abraham. As for Paul's conception of the converts as being descended from Abraham, a comparison with Philo and rabbinic data shows they all were sensitive to the converts' foreign lineage, but tried to solve this predicament in different ways. Philo, who never crafts a new genealogy for the proselytes, rather turns to the notions of "spiritual" and "civic" kinship as superior to biological ancestry, in order to claim for the Jewish proselytes the status as "citizens" within the Jewish *politeia*, who thus were ascribed equal rights and could live in fellowship with Jews on the basis of common virtues that the par-

4 For the concept of "exegetical motif," I follow the definition by J.L. Kugel, *Traditions of the Bible: A Guide to the Bible as It Was at the Start of the Common Era* (Cambridge, MA: Harvard University Press, 1998), 27:

> Simply put, an exegetical motif is an explanation of a biblical verse (or phrase or word therein) that becomes the basis for some ancient writer's expansion or other alteration of what Scripture actually says: in paraphrasing or summarizing Scripture, the ancient writer incorporates the exegetical motif in his retelling and in so doing adds some minor detail or otherwise deviates from mere repetition or restatement of the Bible.

ticular laws of Moses are meant to promote. In contrast to Philo, both Paul, and later on, some rabbis resort to a view that considered the converts as adherents of Abraham's God, and therefore already legitimate lineage of Abraham.

4. Paul's exegetical paraphrase of Gen 15:6 is fused together with words from other Genesis passages about God's promise spoken to Abraham and his descendants. Just as the emulation of Abraham's trust in the one God was the means of marking the identity of patrilineal lineage, so too were the patriarchal promises. Thus, we can find that Paul further warrants the identity of the Galatian converts as valid descendants from Abraham by claiming their share in the promise and their blessings. Paul's conjunction of Gen 15:6 with a catena of promises from the Abrahamic narrative presupposes a specific Jewish tradition, which suggests a correspondence between the conduct of Abraham's trust and the very same conduct expected in return from God, in terms of the reward God promised through a solemn oath to Abraham *and* to his descendant Isaac. It is my hypothesis that a particular version of this Jewish thought pattern is evident in Philo's appropriation of Abraham and presupposed by Paul. In Galatians 3, Paul argues that the granting of the Spirit to Isaac's descendants, as well as to Jewish converts, is evidence that God had demonstrated his will to keep his oath of promise; this results from the parallelism of Abraham's trust and the reward of God's trust / faithfulness given in return. In Paul's new perspective, the promised blessing to Abraham and to his descendant is now conferred on the Jews and Gentile converts and comes to fruition as the result of the crucifixion of Christ, who is taken by Paul to be Abraham's ultimate descendant. Just as the oath of promise was originally made to Abraham (Gen 22:16–18) on the ground of his conduct of trust (Gen 15:6), and later was also reiterated to his offspring (Gen 26:3–4), it is now conferred on Isaac's descendants, provided that they manifest the same fundamental quality attributed to their ancestors. Such a line of thought, with an analogy attested in Philo's interpretation of the oath of promise in *QG* 4:180, seems also to be presupposed in Paul's allusions to Gen 26:3–4, i.e., a patrilineal correspondence between Abraham, Christ, and those who belong to Abraham's offspring in terms of their common character of trust. This pattern of thought also resonates with Paul's claim that "those of trust" are Abraham's sons and therefore partakers of the blessings promised to his descendants by oath.

5. Since Philo and Paul coincide in appropriating Abraham as the foundational model of Jews and non-Jewish converts, they seek to explain how the Law of Moses stands in a dynamic relation to Abraham as a legal norm. In a discussion with his interlocutors, Philo modified the view of "some" who interpreted Gen 26:5 about Abraham positioned as an observer of the Law of Moses. According to Philo, Abraham was himself a "law and an unwritten ordinance",

however, so that he read Gen 26:5 about his adherence to the divine Law in Nature achieved through his instinctive words and deeds, and manifested in Abraham's trust in God and His commands. Consequently, it was his observance of the divine Law in Nature, antecedent to the written Law revealed through Moses, that made him worthy to receive the oath of promise. Philo's view, however, seemed to maintain a dynamic between these two "jurisdictions" of the Torah, in that an emulation of Abraham and access to the Abraham-centered divine Law and its promise of blessings were mediated by means of the observance of the Mosaic Laws. The basis for this assumption was the view that the Law of Moses represented a copy of the divine Law in Nature, i. e., that the Law of Moses only sets forth as legislation a record of what Abraham and the other patriarchs did and said (*Abr.* 3–5, 273–276).

In a way that corresponds to Philo, albeit without speaking explicitly about Abraham himself as a "Law", Paul too seems to have operated with a dynamic, temporal, and conceptual distinction in the Torah and Scripture, namely, between, on the one hand, an "Abrahamic jurisdiction", centered on Abraham's trust and God's promise, and, on the other hand, the "Mosaic jurisdiction" revealed later at Sinai. In contrast to Philo, who would preserve the Law of Moses as representing the best proximity to the divine Law in Nature reflected in the "Abrahamic jurisdiction", Paul took the view that the time had now arrived when the constitutional norm inherent in the "Abrahamic jurisdiction" had taken effect exclusively through Abraham's ultimate descendant, "Christ". Unlike Philo, who ties God's promise to the patriarchs as concomitant with living as "citizens" of the Jewish *politeia* and conditional upon the observance of the Law of Moses, Paul no longer made the fulfillment of Abraham's blessing conditional on the jurisdiction of the Mosaic Law. For Paul, therefore, the vicarious death of Christ "*for us*" not only meant that God kept his oath to Abraham to rescue Isaac's descendants from the curse caused by their transgressions of the Law, but even that the Gentile "nations" as Jewish converts might be blessed in the offspring of Abraham, the crucified Christ, and thus apart from observance of the Law of Moses. In the context of such a subtle view of the effects of Christ's death, and in a situation in which the Galatians were on the way to be circumcised and to subject themselves to the jurisdiction of Law, it is all the more understandable that Paul rebukes the Galatians that they should have known better, that is, about the true reality and consequences of Christ's crucifixion as mediating Abraham's blessing to them.

2 Previous Research

In general, the insights offered in this study claim to be fresh answers to some of the questions that have been discussed in Pauline and in Philonic scholarship. Since I am going to survey in more detail the research situation in each chapter of this study, I shall restrict myself at this juncture to commenting on the distinctive contribution of this study under three headings, since they relate to themes concerning Abraham that are intertwined and have received much attention in recent works on Galatians 3. This short survey of previous research will make clear that there is room for further investigation.

2.1 Abraham and Scripture

In which way can expository methods and motifs prevalent in Paul's own day inform his appeal to Abraham, Scripture, and the argument in Galatians 3? In general, Paul's appropriation of Scripture in Galatians 3 has perplexed scholars, since his assertions appear unwarranted by his evidence. For example, T.L. Donaldson has maintained that Gal 3:1–4:7 is a "maze of laboured exegesis, puzzling illustration, and cryptic theological shorthand".[5] Furthermore, J.L. Martyn has characterized Paul's interpretation of Gen 15:6 as a "strange exegesis".[6]

R.N. Longenecker finds that Paul "goes far beyond the rules of historical-grammatical exegesis."[7] Likewise, J.H. Neyrey claims that "Paul construes the Scriptures in his own idiosyncratic way."[8] Moreover, M. Silva perceives "glaring gaps in the argumentation."[9] Against the background of such comments, the main objective of this study is to demonstrate that Paul's exegesis and argument in Galatians 3 become more coherent when we enquire after their referential background in Jewish exegesis such as, for example, is evidenced in Philo's writings.

Paul's scriptural references about and to Abraham in Gal 3:6–29 serve as a warrant for the claim that the Galatian believers were legitimate descendants of

---

5 T.L. Donaldson, "The 'Curse of the Law' and the Inclusion of the Gentiles: Galatians 3.13–14," *NTS* 32.1 (1986): 94.
6 J.L. Martyn, *History and Theology in the Fourth Gospel*, 3rd. ed., NTL (Edinburgh: T & T Clark, 2003), 162.
7 R.N. Longenecker, *Galatians*, WBC (Nashville: Thomas Nelson, 1990), 110.
8 J.H. Neyrey, "Bewitched in Galatia: Paul and Cultural Anthropology," *CBQ* 50.1 (1988): 93.
9 M. Silva, "Abraham, Faith, and Works: Paul's Use of Scripture in Galatians 3:6–14," *WTJ* 63.2 (2001): 254.

Abraham and partakers of the promise. In previous studies of Paul's appropriation of Abraham in Galatians 3, scholars have a tendency to neglect the use of various Jewish exegetical traditions as an explanation for such warrants drawn from the Scripture about and to Abraham.[10] Thus, earlier works that compare Philo's and Paul's appropriations of Abraham have focused more on the contrasts, at the cost of a more detailed scrutiny of how common Scriptures and exegetical motifs are applied within the framework of conventional exegetical methods and terminology.[11] An important aspect that justifies this study is the suggestion that Philo and other Jewish texts might corroborate the hypothesis that Paul builds upon a fabric of Jewish exegetical traditions, in which Gen 15:6 has been paraphrased in conjunction with other passages such as Gen 22:18 and 26:3–4.[12] Thus, the question that should be asked is not whether there is a particular text in Scripture that enables Paul to derive his interpretation of Abraham, but whether there are smaller pieces of an interpreted Scripture or

---

10 Cf., e.g., B.R. Trick, *Abrahamic Descent, Testamentary Adoption, and the Law in Galatians: Differentiating Abraham's Sons, Seed, and Children of Promise*, NovTSup (Leiden; Boston: Brill, 2016), 24–5; J.M.G. Barclay, *Paul and the Gift* (Grand Rapids: Eerdmans, 2015), 415–18; Hansen, *Abraham in Galatians*, 109–39.

11 So, for example, N.A. Dahl (*Studies in Paul: Theology for the Early Christian Mission* [Minneapolis: Augsburg, 1977], 169) claims that the whole hermeneutical procedure shows less affinity with Philo than with a rabbinic midrash: "With respect to hermeneutical terminology and method, Paul is much closer to the rabbis than to Philo. This could be illustrated from many details of Gal 3." *Pace* Dahl, P. Borgen's study (*Bread from Heaven: An Exegetical Study of the Concept of Manna in the Gospel of John and the Writings of Philo*, NovTSup [Leiden: Brill, 1965], 47–51) comes to a different conclusion and shows instead the existence of similarities between Philo, the rabbinic data, and Gal 3:6–29 with regards to Paul's exegetical paraphrase of Gen 15:6. He notes exegetical features such as a correspondence between the opening and closing parts of the exegesis, the use of subordinate biblical passages, and the method of paraphrasing words from the main text cited. Unfortunately, Borgen's observations are brief and thus represent only a fresh start that invites further analysis.

12 At this juncture, I shall build upon an earlier article of mine, which unfortunately has never been available to an international public; see P.J. Bekken, "Abraham og Ånden: Paulus' anvendelse av Genesis 15:6 i Galaterbrevet 3:6 belyst ut fra jødisk materiale," *Tidsskrift for Teologi og Kirke* 71.4 (2000): 265–76. Although published after my initial work, S.-K. Wan ("Abraham and the Promise of Spirit: Points of Convergence Between Philo and Paul," in *Things Revealed: Studies in Early Jewish and Christian Literature in Honor of Michael E. Stone*, ed. E.G. Chazon, D. Satran, and R.A. Clements, JSJSup [Leiden; Boston: Brill, 2004], 209–24) and M. Thiessen (*Paul and the Gentile Problem* [New York: OUP, 2016], 109) have reached similar conclusions to mine, but more attention should be drawn to additional data and the specific issue of Jewish proselytism with regard to the context of Paul's use of Gen 15:6 in conjunction with other exegetical traditions and motifs.

"exegetical motifs", incorporated in his exegetical paraphrasing of the individual text, which might explain the "inferential leap" on Paul's part.[13]

Earlier scholars have disagreed on which texts from the Abrahamic narrative in Genesis are referred to throughout Gal 3:8–29. For example, when Paul obviously cites from Genesis in Gal 3:8b ("ἐνευλογηθήσονται ἐν σοὶ πάντα τὰ ἔθνη"), usually Gen 12:3, 18:8, and also 22:18 are listed as possible sources. So, for example, scholars such as S.W. Hahn, R.B. Hays, and most recently B.R. Trick have identified the citation in Gal 3:8b as a conflation of Gen 12:3 and Gen 22:18, since Paul's reference to Abraham's faithfulness in Gal 3:9 seems to presuppose an allusion to the latter Scripture that the Lord will bless the nations because of Abraham's obedience.[14] On the other hand, Gen 22:18 has been discounted by other scholars as a possible source behind Gal 3:8–9,[15] precisely because it is associated in Jewish expository traditions with Abraham's faithfulness and obedience at the *Akedah* and with his faithful observance of the Law of Moses, rather than with Abraham's trust in the promise.[16] Accordingly, Paul, in contrast to such Jewish interpretative motifs in Second Temple texts, emphasizes Abraham's trust in terms of Gen 15:6 to the exclusion of any references to Abraham's faithfulness at or subsequent to the *Akedah.*[17] Although I concur with the view that Paul is subverting any allusion to Isaac and the *Akedah*, this does not exclude references to Scriptures inherent in Jewish interpretations of the *Akedah*, such as Gen 15:6, 22:16–18, and 26:3–4 spoken about and to Abraham and his descendants. For this reason, Paul's interpretation of Scripture in Gal 3:6–29 seems to depend on such an interpretative tradition, attested in Philo and Jewish traditions, that conceived a parallelism between Abraham's conduct of trust (πίστις) (cf. Gen 15:6) and the conduct expected in return from God, corresponding to God's faithfulness (πίστις) in terms of an oath given in return to

---

13 Even J.L. Kugel (*Traditions of the Bible: A Guide to the Bible as It Was at the Start of the Common Era*; *The Bible As It Was*), who otherwise presents a wealth of data concerning exegetical motifs that have found their way into the writings of authors belonging to the period of Second Temple Judaism, including Philo and Paul, has overlooked instances of such parallels in the case of Paul's appropriation of Genesis passages in Galatians 3.

14 Cf. S.W. Hahn, "Covenant, Oath, and the Aqedah: Διαθήκη in Galatians 3:15–18," *CBQ* 67.1 (2005): 92 n. 64; R.B. Hays, *Echoes of Scripture in the Letters of Paul* (New Haven: Yale University Press, 1989), 106–8; Trick, *Abrahamic Descent*, 67.

15 Cf. D.J. Moo, "Galatians," in *Galatians*, BECNT (Grand Rapids: Baker Academic, 2013), 199–200, who discounts Gen 22:18 for its reference to Abraham's obedience.

16 So, J.D.G. Dunn, *The Epistle to the Galatians*, BNTC (London: A & C Black, 1993), 164–5; A.A. Das, *Paul and the Stories of Israel: Grand Thematic Narratives in Galatians* (Minneapolis: Fortress Press, 2016), 118–9.

17 Cf. Das, *Paul and the Stories*, 119.

Abraham and later reiterated to Isaac and his descendants (cf. Gen 22:16–18 and 26: 3–4).

Furthermore, the allusion to God's promise to Abraham in Gal 3:14 in terms of blessing for the nations "in Jesus Christ", is taken by N.A. Dahl to be an exegetical paraphrase of the phrase "in your offspring" in Gen 22:18, and emphasizes that the death of Christ was interpreted as fulfilling the gifts that God had promised to Abraham by oath.[18] Dahl's observation, however, should be expanded to a more detailed investigation that also includes the descendant-mediated version of the oath of promise reiterated to Isaac according to Gen 26:3–4.[19] This suggestion is supported by the fact that the oath of promise according to Paul was not spoken *only* to Abraham, but also explicitly to Abraham *and to his seed* (Gal 3:16). In Paul's mind, it does not after all refer to the collectivity of the Jewish people as such, but to only one of Isaac's descendants, namely, to Christ as a collective person, even encompassing those of Isaac's descendant among Gentile converts who are party to Abraham's blessing and belong to Christ (Gal 3:14, 29). Such a study will seek to demonstrate that Paul's elaboration of God's promise in Gal 3:8–29 builds upon the composite citation of Gen 12:3, 22:18, and Gen 26:4 in Gal 3:8b.

Most recently, however, T.L. Donaldson has claimed that Paul avoids a "straightforward option available" to him such as is reflected in Gen 22:18 and Gen 26:4, which could be taken to secure the blessing for the "all the nations", without compromising the distinction between the "nations" (ἔθνη) and Abraham's "descendants" (σπέρμα).[20] According to Donaldson, Paul rather rejected "this easier route", i.e., that the *ethnê*-in-Christ represented the fulfillment of

---

18 N.A. Dahl, "The Atonement: An Adequate Reward for the Akedah?" in *Jesus the Christ: The Historical Origins of Christological Doctrine*, ed. D.H. Juel (Minneapolis: Fortress Press, 1991), 137–51.

19 Cf. B. van der Lans, "Belonging to Abraham's Kin: Genealogical Appeals to Abraham as a Possible Background for Paul's Abrahamic Argument," in *Abraham, the Nations, and the Hagarites: Jewish, Christian, and Islamic Perspectives on Kinship with Abraham*, ed. M. Goodman, G.H. van Kooten, and J.T.A.G.M. van Ruiten, TBN (Leiden; Boston: Brill, 2010), 316, who takes Gal 3:16 to refer "more specifically to the descendant-mediated version of the blessing of nations (Gen 22:18, 26:4, and 28:14), continuing the argumentation from Gal 3:8–9." Unfortunately, her suggestion is not supported by a detailed scrutiny of Paul's argumentation in the context of Gal 3:6–29. My study aims to remedy the lack of such an analysis.

20 Cf. T.L. Donaldson, "Paul, Abraham's Gentile 'Offspring,' and the Torah," in *Torah Ethics and Early Christian Identity*, ed. S.J. Wendel and D.M. Miller (Grand Rapids: Eerdmans, 2016), 137; "Paul Within Judaism: A Critical Evaluation from a 'New Perspective' Perspective," in *Paul Within Judaism: Restoring the First-Century Context to the Apostle*, ed. M.D. Nanos and M. Zetterholm (Minneapolis: Fortress Press, 2015), 297–98.

such Scriptures, meaning that they would be blessed *through* Abraham's "seed" – as ἔθνη and not as converts and circumcised proselytes. Therefore, Donaldson claims that Paul represents an anomaly and idiosyncracy in this effort to construct the ἔθνη as legitimate descendants of Abraham, "a project that seems to have no real precedent or analogy within Judaism".[21] A weakness in Donaldson's assertion is that he neglects comparative material that shows that it is precisely Scriptures such as Gen 22:18 and 26:4 which are prevalent in the Jewish discourse of the terms under which one qualifies as Abraham's genuine descendants. Such a referential background may thus explain Paul's application of these texts to include the Galatian converts among Abraham's family as well. Thus, Paul may be seen as participating in a broader Jewish debate on patrilineal descent, attested by Philo, in which the Jewish people, including Jewish converts, has its origin in the character traits of Abraham and the promises given to him and to his descendants. This observation brings me to the next issue to be reviewed.

2.2 Abraham and the Gentile Problem

Another main aspect involved in Paul's scriptural appeal to Abraham in Gal 3:6–29 deals with the so-called Gentile problem and Paul's solution to this problem. The Gentile problem concerns various conceptions of how non-Jews may be included in the Jewish community of those who are party to the blessings of God's promise, since they are not lineal descendants from Abraham.[22] The way scholars have dealt with this issue in Galatians 3 depends mainly on the answers one gives to the intertwined questions concerning the figure of Abraham conceived as a "universal" or ethnocentric figure, that is, whether Paul transcends the distinction between born Jews and non-Jews of a foreign lineage, or if he maintains the ethnocentric position on Abraham and his descendants, as the ancestor and founder of the Jewish people, including Jewish converts. At this juncture, I shall briefly review some scholarly *modi operandi* to the Gentile problem, and then indicate my own endeavour to provide a fresh approach.

A prevalent view in recent Pauline scholarship is represented by the so-called "New Perspective on Paul", which contrasted Jewish particularity and Christian universalism. Thus, Paul's target was national exclusivism or ethnocen-

21 Donaldson, "Paul Within Judaism," 298.

22 For example, the Gentile problem is made explicit in M. Thiessen's recent book *Paul and the Gentile Problem* (Oxford: OUP, 2016).

tricity with a polemic against a presumption on the Torah as the boundary around the Jewish people, which made it ethnically distinct among the other nations.[23] From this perspective, Paul argues that on the ground of faith in Christ, Jews and non-Jews are put on an equal footing before God, with Abraham then seen as a universal father of all nations.[24]

A similar interpretation of the Gentile problem finds expression among scholars who align themselves with the paradigm now known as "Paul within Judaism".[25] Representatives of this paradigm suggest that Paul has solved the Gentile problem through the incorporation of the Gentiles in the patrilineal ethnicity of Abraham. So, for example, a scholar such as C. Johnson Hodge can claim:

> By means of kinship-creation, gentiles are made descendants of Abraham, adopted sons of God and coheirs with Christ. Paul makes a place for the gentiles—the ethnic and religious "other" for the *Ioudaioi*—in the story of Israel, so that they may be made righteous before the God of Israel. Although *Ioudaioi* and gentiles now share a common ancestor, Paul does not collapse them into one group (of 'Christians,' for example). Gentiles-in-Christ and Jews are separate but related lineages of Abraham.[26]

According to Hodge, while Paul does indeed ascribe to the Gentiles a certain "Jewishness", he does not imagine them as "Jews", and therefore still speaks of them as Gentiles.[27]

Objections have been raised against such a view of Abraham and the ethnic perspective involved. According to J.D. Levenson, the problem with a "universal" appeal to Abraham, suggesting that he is conceived as an exemplar of a universal

---

23 Cf. J.D.G. Dunn, *The New Perspective on Paul* (Grand Rapids: Eerdmans, 2008), 187: "It is this very distinction that [Paul] will be going on to question."

24 Cf., e.g, J.D.G. Dunn, *Jesus, Paul and the Law* (Louisville, KY: John Knox, 1990), 215–41; K. Neutel, "'Neither Jew Nor Greek': Abraham as a Universal Ancestor," in *Abraham, the Nations, and the Hagarites: Jewish, Christian, and Islamic Perspectives on Kinship with Abraham*, ed. M. Goodman, G.H. van Kooten, and J.T.A.G.M. van Ruiten, TBN (Leiden: Brill, 2010), 291–305. For a recent review of the "New Perspective on Paul", cf. J.M.G. Barclay, *Paul and the Gift*, 159–65.

25 For recent surveys of how scholars within this paradigm deal with the Gentile problem, cf. H. Moxnes, "Who Are the Children of Abraham in Romans 4? Retelling the Memory of Abraham 'Our Ancestor'," in *The Church and Its Mission in the New Testament and Early Christianity: Essays in Memory of Hans Kvalbein*, ed. D.E. Aune and R. Hvalvik, WUNT (Tübingen: Mohr Siebeck, 2018), 193–210; K.O. Sandnes, *Paul Perceived: An Interactionist Perspective on Paul and the Law*, WUNT (Tübingen: Mohr Siebeck, 2018), 212–14; Donaldson, "Paul Within Judaism"; Neutel, "Abraham as a Universal Ancestor," 294–300.

26 C. Johnson Hodge, *If Sons, Then Heirs: A Study of Kinship and Ethnicity in the Letters of Paul* (Oxford: OUP, 2007), 5.

27 Johnson Hodge, *If Sons, Then Heirs*, 5.

human essence, is "that it dramatically underplays the importance of chosenness or election – both the election of Abraham and the election of the Christian – in Paul's theology."[28] So, for example, if Paul intended an anti-ethnocentric appeal to Abraham, Levenson asks:

> Were Paul truly intent on transcending the difference between Jews and Gentiles, would he have so stressed the man known as the father of the Jewish people? And would he have advanced the claim that those who have faith in Jesus had, by that very act, become nothing short of descendants of Abraham?[29]

Unfortunately, although Levenson objects to the view that a universal appeal to Abraham motivates Paul's recourse to Abraham, he still maintains "that some means other than conversion to Judaism must be found to incorporate Gentiles into the Abrahamic family", which he further takes to mean "that at the end-time, the Gentiles, without ceasing to be Gentiles, would renounce their idolatry and embrace the worship of the God of Israel alongside the people Israel."[30] At this point, Levenson sides with P. Fredriksen, who reaches a similar conclusion and approach to the Gentile problem:[31]

> Pagans-in-Christ are also from Abraham's lineage, since Abraham was the father of many nations (Gen 17:4; Rom 4:17); but they descend from Abraham *alone*, not also from Isaac and Jacob. Because of the Spirit, however, these pagans too are now sons, heirs to the "promise" to Abraham: like Israel, they too can now call God "Abba, Father" [...]. But this new kinship is not tantamount to "conversion," because these Gentiles are adopted

28 J.D. Levenson, *Inheriting Abraham: The Legacy of the Patriarch in Judaism, Christianity, and Islam*, Library of Jewish Ideas (Princeton: Princeton University Press, 2012), 157.
29 Levenson, *Inheriting Abraham*, 157.
30 Both quotations are taken from Levenson, *Inheriting Abraham*, 159. A similar view is taken by C. Hayes, *What's Divine About Divine Law? Early Perspectives* (Princeton; Oxford: Princeton University Press, 2015), 161: "[...] Paul adopts the prophetic vision of an ideal time in which ingathered Israel observes the torah *effortlessly*, and Gentiles, recognizing the one true god, forgo idolatry and immortality, and finally leave Yahweh's people in peace."
31 P. Fredriksen aligns herself with the new paradigm in Pauline scholarship dubbed "Paul within Judaism". She has formulated the paradigm shifts and present-day challenges in Pauline scholarship as follows ("How Later Contexts Affect Pauline Content, or: Retrospect is the Mother of Anachronism," in *Jews and Christians in the First and Second Centuries: How to Write Their History*, ed. P.J. Tomson and J.J. Schwartz, CRINT [Leiden: Brill, 2014], 51):

> The paradigm shifted from Paul *against* Judaism to Paul *and* Judaism. That perspective is shifting yet again, from Paul *and* Judaism to Paul *within* Judaism. A daunting task of re-imagining lies before us. The letters must all be translated. The work books must all be recast. The commentaries must all be redone.

> not into Israel's family, but into God's, made such not *kata sarka* [according to the flesh] but *kata pneuma* [according to the Spirit].[32]

The distinction Fredriksen makes between these "pagans-in Christ," who are considered to be offspring of Abraham (*kata pneuma*), but not of Isaac and Jacob (*kata sarka),* is unconvincing, because it does not suit a passage like Rom 9:7–13, where the genealogical line of Isaac and Jacob is taken as a precedent for that of the believers of non-Jewish origin.[33] Moreover, Levenson and Fredriksen fail to take into account a more flexible conception of "Jewishness" that might be expressed in Jewish debates on the status of a convert, in which an individual proselyte can become an adopted son of both Abraham and God through "conversion".[34] Thus, they operate with too strict a definition of what it meant for non-Jews to undertake a "conversion" to Judaism, and they do not recognize what Levenson argues elsewhere, namely, that there are, in Paul's view, *two opposing modes of conversion* to be included among the children of Abraham, of which trust is "the only means of conversion to Judaism, for the Jewish means—acceptance of the Torah and its commandments, symbolized in men by circumcision—have, in Paul's mind, ceased to be efficacious."[35] I shall return to these concepts of conversion and what it means to become a "Jew" further below, but it is necessary first to review shortly another approach.

In a similar way to Levenson and Fredriksen, other scholars have emphasized that Paul redefines Abrahamic sonship christologically or pneumatically in order to include Gentiles, *as* Gentiles, apart from any conversion to Judaism. With regard to the christological approach, H.D. Betz, for example, claims that Paul held that "sons of the 'believer' Abraham are the Christians who believe like Abraham."[36] Scholars have noted that Paul is not content with presenting

32 Levenson, *Inheriting Abraham*, 158, quoting P. Fredriksen, "Judaizing the Nations: The Ritual Demands of Paul's Gospel," *NTS* 56.2 (2010): 243–4.
33 For this argument, see I. Rosen-Zvi and A. Ophir, "Paul and the Invention of the Gentiles," *JQR* 105.1 (2015): 32 n. 123.
34 Previous scholarship has identified various Jewish strategies for relating non-Jews to the God of Israel, such as sympathization, ethical monotheism, eschatological pilgrimage, and conversion. For these Jewish patterns of thought, cf. T.L. Donaldson, *Paul and the Gentiles: Remapping the Apostle's Convictional World* (Minneapolis: Fortress Press, 2006), 51–78.
35 J.D. Levenson, *The Death and Resurrection of the Beloved Son: The Transformation of Child Sacrifice in Judaism and Christianity* (New Haven; London: Yale University Press, 1995), 216–7.
36 H.D. Betz, *Galatians: A Commentary on Paul's Letter to the Churches in Galatia*, Hermeneia (Philadelphia: Fortress Press, 1979), 31. For a similar view, cf. Johnson Hodge (*If Sons, Then Heirs*, 85), based on a patrilineal ideology in which the descendants are seen as manifestations of the ancestor's character traits.

the ἔθνη as genealogically related to Abraham through the promise that "all nations of the earth will be blessed through you / your seed" (as a conflated citation of Gen 12:3 and 18:18 in Gal 3:8), but rather insists on describing them with designations reserved for Abraham's descendants in Genesis, such as "seed" (Gal 3:29). Against this background, Paul's originality is often emphasized.[37] So, for example, T.L. Donaldson claims that "The truly anomalous aspect is Paul's insistence that uncircumcised *ethnê*-in-Christ are at the same time full members of Abraham's 'seed' (*sperma*)."[38] According to Donaldson, what made it possible for non-Jews to become full members of the Abraham's seed was not proselytism in terms of becoming circumcised Jewish converts under the Torah: "What changed for him [Paul] was the new conviction that Christ had replaced Torah as the means by which such incorporation took place."[39] Hence, Donaldson maintains that Paul's application of Gen 22:16–18 and 26:3–4 to include non-Jews would mean a redefinition of Abrahamic descent and claims to Jewish Abrahamic sonship. Again, the basic weakness of such an approach is that it fails to acknowledge that Paul applies such Scriptures to incorporate non-Jews among Abraham's sons *as* Jewish proselytes, and not *as* Gentiles, irrespective of their conversion.

In a similar way, M. Thiessen argues that Paul's belief that uncircumcised Gentiles can be Abraham's sons is unprecedented in Early Judaism.[40] Building on earlier studies by S.K. Stowers and C. Johnson Hodge,[41] Thiessen seeks to build the case that, since the ontological gap between Jews and Gentiles is in it-

---

37 Cf. L. Bormann, "Abraham as 'Forefather' and His Family in Paul," in *Abraham's Family: A Network of Meaning in Judaism, Christianity, and Islam*, ed. L. Bormann, WUNT (Tübingen: Mohr Siebeck, 2018), 232–3; I Rosen-Zvi, "Pauline Traditions and the Rabbis: Three Case Studies," *HTR* 110.2 (2017): 169–94; M. Goodman, "Epilogue," in *Abraham, the Nations, and the Hagarites: Jewish, Christian, and Islamic Perspectives on Kinship with Abraham*, ed. M. Goodman et al., TBN (Leiden; Boston: Brill, 2010), 512.

38 Donaldson, "Paul Within Judaism," 296. Cf. also I. Rosen-Zvi's statement ("Pauline Traditions and the Rabbis," 188 n. 92) on this anomaly on Paul's part: "I do not know of any pre-Pauline text which promises that much."

39 Donaldson, "Paul, Abraham's Gentile 'Offspring,' and the Torah," 140–1.

40 Thiessen, *Paul and the Gentile Problem*, 129 Most recently, however, Thiessen ("Paul, the Animal Apocalypse, and Abraham's Gentile Seed," in *The Ways That Often Parted: Essays in Honor of Joel Marcus*, ed. L. Baron, J. Hicks-Keeton, and M. Thiessen [Atlanta: SBL Press, 2018], 65–78) argues that a parallel to Paul's assertion that non-Jews can become Abraham's seed is found in 1. En. 90:37–38. Since Thiessen's interpretation of this passage is questionable, it may appear dubious to contend that it anticipated Paul's claims by almost two centuries.

41 S.K. Stowers, "What is 'Pauline Participation in Christ'?" in *Redefining First-Century Jewish and Christian Identities: Essays in Honor of Ed Parish Sanders*, ed. F.E. Udoh et al., CJA (Notre Dame: University of Notre Dame Press, 2008), 352–71; Johnson Hodge, *If Sons, Then Heirs*, 72–6.

self immutable and irrevocable,[42] the Gentiles can be genealogically incorporated among Abraham's descendants, apart from being circumcised and becoming Jews, through receiving the Spirit as Christ's *pneuma:*

> In receiving the *pneuma*, then, the gentiles undergo a material transformation—again, to use a modern analogy, they undergo gene therapy—which addresses their genealogical deficiencies as gentiles. Through the *pneuma,* gentiles become Abraham's sons themselves, albeit sons via lineage that is distinct from, but related to, Abraham's sarkic sons through Isaac and Jacob: gentiles-in-Christ are children of the promise, like Isaac (Gal 4:28).[43]

While Gal 4:6 claims that the Galatians ("we") received Christ's Spirit, more emphasis than Thiessen allows for should be laid on Galatians 3:2–7, in which Paul explicitly compares the Galatian converts' reception of the Spirit by trust with Abraham's corresponding experience as a warrant for the subsequent assertion that they are recognized as Abraham's sons. Thus, whereas Thiessen is aware of the Jewish exegetical tradition based upon Gen 15:6, "preserved in both Philo and rabbinic literature, that faith enables or merits the reception of the *pneuma*",[44] he does not take sufficiently into account that such an exegetical motif can be made in the context of Abraham, who is emphasized as the model proselyte and the founder of the Jewish nation.[45] This circumstance opens the way to a further examination of other Jewish texts and aspects of Jewish identity related to the concept of conversion and Jewish proselytism, according to which Abraham is conceived as the common father of both Jews and converts. I now turn to two recent attempts at such an enterprise.

---

42 For a similar argument that Paul was not a constructivist about Jewish identity, but an essentialist who basically did conceive of the Jew / Goy binary as ontological, see C. Hayes, *Divine Law,* 141–51, and A Ophir and I. Rosen-Zvi, *Goy: Israel's Multiple Others and the Birth of the Gentile* (Oxford: OUP, 2018), 140–78.

43 Thiessen, *Paul and the Gentile Problem,* 117–18. See also his recent studies: "Abraham's Gentile Seed," 71–73; "Paul, Essentialism, and the Jewish Law: In Conversation with Christine Hayes," *Journal for the Study of Paul and His Letters* 7.1–2 (2017): 80–5.

44 Thiessen, *Paul and the Gentile Problem,* 109.

45 In contrast to Thiessen, E. Gruen ("Philo and Jewish Identity," in *Strength to Strength: Essays in Honor of Shaye J. D. Cohen,* ed. M.L. Satlow, BJS [Providence, RI: Brown University, 2018], 179–95; idem, "Paul and Jewish Ethnicity," in *Talmudic Transgressions: Engaging the Work of Daniel Boyarin,* ed. C.E. Fonrobert et al. [Leiden; Boston: Brill, 2017], 351–67) finds that both Philo and Paul redefine Jewish identity and "Jewishness" metaphorically, centering more on Abraham's character traits and spiritual kinship with him than on genealogical descent from him. Although Gruen notes Paul's identification of "the sons of Abraham as the men of faith" in Gal 3:7, he fails to discuss more specifically whether this connotation of belief as constitutive of Abrahamic descent meant that, for Paul, the Galatian converts counted as "Jews".

I. Rosen-Zvi and K. Berthelot have focused their investigations on the search for precedents for Paul's claim about the Gentile converts in rabbinic sources which interpret the motif of Abraham as "the father of many nations" (Gen 17:4–5). Accordingly, both scholars have compared a rabbinic text such as y. Bik. 1:4 (62d) with Romans 4, but they read the texts differently and thus come to opposite conclusions. Rosen-Zvi first cites the text and then comments on some parallels:

> Compare *y. Bikk.* 1:4 (64d): "It was taught in the name of R. Judah: the proselyte himself may both bring (the first-fruits) and recite (the statement in Deut 26:5–10). Why? *For the father of a multitude of nations* (גוים) *have I made thee* (Gen 17:5)—formerly you have been a father to Aram, from now on you are a father to all the gentiles *(גוים)*" (cf. t. Ber 1:14). Both Paul and R. Judah read the verse as referring to individual gentiles, rather than to nations. They also share the inference that if Abraham is the father of the gentiles, then they can be legitimately considered his offspring and thus call him "our father." The rabbis, however, convert the gentiles into proselytes, i.e. former gentiles (compare 1 Cor 12:2).[46]

In contrast to Rosen-Zvi, however, Berthelot suggests that Paul in Romans 4 may anticipate a Jewish tradition attested in the Jerusalem Talmud, in which Gen 17:5, about Abraham as father of the nations, is taken to refer, not to individual Gentiles irrespective of their conversion, but rather to converts. Moreover, according to Berthelot, Romans 4 and y. Bik. 1:4 shared similar patterns of thought: the predicament of their foreign lineage was resolved by resorting to the legal and metaphorical notion of adoption, shaped by the Roman context in which Paul and the rabbis lived. Thus, Abraham is conceived as the father of all non-Jews who convert to Judaism, so that the adopted converts can inherit the status of becoming Abraham's descendants and the promises that go with it.[47]

Berthelot's suggestion is viable and should be advanced in a closer contrast and comparison with all the relevant Pauline and Philonic data. In the first place, since Berthelot (like Rosen-Zvi) mainly offers observations on Romans 4 in the light of the Jewish tradition embedded in y. Bik. 1:4, her study invites a further analysis of the specific points of convergence between this text and Gal 3:6–29 too. My study will remedy the lack of such an examination, and argue, going beyond previous studies, that both texts reflect an intra-mural Jewish debate on the status of the Jewish proselyte, with the shared inference that because Abraham is the father of the proselytes, and not of non-Jews in general,

46 Rosen-Zvi, "Pauline Traditions and the Rabbis," 187 n. 90.
47 K. Berthelot, "Entre Octroi de la Citoyenneté et Adoption: Les Modèles Pour Penser la Conversion Au Judaïsme à l'Époque Romaine," *Pallas* 104 (2017): 37–50.

they can be considered as his legitimate offspring and thus also as valid heirs of the promise.

Secondly, with regard to the fact that conversion to become "Jews" entailed different things to Paul and other Jews of his time, the somewhat unnuanced contrast Berthelot draws between Philo, Paul, and the rabbis needs to be modified, however. I agree with her that Philo, in contrast to Paul and the rabbis, never applies to the converts the designation Abraham's descendants, but *pace* her, I shall argue that Philo's rationale for this is precisely that he, like Paul and the rabbis, is very sensitive to the foreign lineage of the proselytes. Hence, Philo's conception of a genealogical distinction between Jews and converts as ontological is not just the reason why he emphasizes the inclusion of the converts into the Jewish community as "citizens" of the Jewish *politeia* within the jurisdiction of the common laws of Moses. Such an ontological Jew / non-Jew binary also explains the presence in Philo of passages, overlooked by Berthelot, in which he speaks of the process of the conversion in terms of the concept of adoption. Thus, Philo comes close to Paul when he almost compares the conversion of the proselytes to the process of being adopted into Abraham's family, in so far as the adopted children fully share the rank of his family and thus qualify as heirs, in spite of not being natural-born and therefore initially like foreigners. Hence, although this may be implicit in Philo's works, Paul may even have drawn the inference and revised the status of the proselytes as the adopted sons and heirs of God in the light of their model and father Abraham, on the basis that he was the first proselyte. This conjecture receives support from Philo's designation of Abraham as the adopted son of God. Against such a Jewish referential background, Paul's exegesis and his claim that the Galatian converts are the adopted descendants and heirs of both Abraham and God may be situated in a Jewish as well as in a Roman context, and may therefore not be so anomalous.

2.3 Abraham and the Law of Moses

In the context of Paul's negotiation on Abraham in Galatians 3, Paul seems to create the phrase ἐκ πίστεως in contrast to the expression ἐκ ἔργων νόμου (see Gal 3:2, 5, and 11).[48] Is Paul idiosyncratic at this juncture, or were there an-

48 Most scholars hold that the expression ἔργον νόμου refers to the observance of the whole of the Mosaic Law. For a survey of the scholarly discussion, see C.S. Keener, *Galatians*, NCBC (Cambridge: CUP, 2018), 106–8.

tecedents to Paul's discourse? In his commentary on Galatians, Betz deals with this question. He writes:

> Paul separates Abraham's faith in God's promise from his obedience to the Jewish Torah. He denies the existence of the Torah at the time of Abraham on the ground that the Jewish Torah was revealed only 430 years later (cf. Gal 3:17). Therefore, Abraham's faith cannot have been anything but his belief in God's promise. This "faith" is then set up in in opposition to the "works of the law", i.e. the obedience to the Jewish Torah. As a result, Abraham becomes the prototype of the Gentile-Christian believer, as opposed to the Jewish (and Jewish-Christian) observer of the Torah. The question is whether this contrasting of Abraham with the Torah of Moses is Paul's own invention or whether there were antecedents.[49]

In scholarship it is common to claim that the contrast between trust or the promise and the Mosaic Law is counterintuitive among Jews at his time. Hence, it is assumed that such a contrast is unique on Paul's part and in contradistinction to other Jewish traditions about Abraham, from which Paul's opponents presumably took their bearings. So, for example, N. Calvert-Koyzis's monograph on Abrahamic traditions in early Judaism and Paul is a conventional statement of such an opinion:

> In using Abraham to discuss the contrast of faith versus works, Paul is using Abraham in a new way. Previously [*sc.* in earlier Jewish tradition], Abraham's faith and his works have been seen together.[50]
>
> However, as mentioned above, Paul is unique in that he is beginning to define this faith in contrast to works, and this is where the similarity between Paul and other Jewish traditions about Abraham ends.[51]

Several studies have emphasized the contrast between Paul, who underlined Abraham's trust in the promise of God, and Philo, who considered Abraham's trust as an expression of the highest and greatest of virtues encapsulating Abraham's entire life. The premise of such an interpretation is that Paul is seen as separating Abraham's trust from the Law, in contrast to Philo, who depicts Abraham's trust as epitomising his adherence to the Law and thus holds together the continuous parts of the Abrahamic narrative. For example, F. Watson represents this prevalent view of Philo's conception of the Law, when he claims:

---

49 Betz, *Galatians*, 139.

50 Calvert-Koyzis, *Paul, Monotheism and the People of God*, 95.

51 Calvert-Koyzis, *Paul, Monotheism and the People of God*, 96.

> The laws revealed at Sinai were preceded by earlier articulations of those same laws; whether these were written or unwritten, the mode of divine discourse is fundamentally the same before Moses as through Moses.[52]

On this basis, Watson can contrast the reading of Genesis in Paul with the readings which are conveyed by Philo and the author of Jubilees:

> In their different ways, Philo and the author of Jubilees read the Genesis narrative along the lines that Paul rejects. Given the Pauline antithesis, it is possible to place their readings on one side and his on the other. To that extent, the two types of reading are incommensurable: what is affirmed by the one is denied or downplayed by the other.[53]

In a most recent study, K.O. Sandnes reaches a similar conclusion:

> Philo offers extensive testimony to an interpretation of the Abrahamic biography where all parts are coming together, forming a continuum of events that Paul emphatically keeps apart.[54]
>
> In Galatians (and in Romans 4), Paul negotiates the way Abraham was commonly seen on the basis of the biblical evidence by separating or keeping apart what had traditionally become a continuum of the texts that depict Abraham's faith.[55]

At this juncture, Watson and Sandnes fail to take into due consideration the modifications and nuances (referred to by Philo himself) of an intra-mural Jewish debate with his interlocutors. It is noteworthy that Philo's distinction between two "Laws" within the Torah has some affinity with Paul, so we might claim that both Philo and Paul to some extent stand on the same side in opposition to those who interpret Abraham's relation to the Law along the lines of the author of *Jubilees,* Philo's interlocutors, and the later rabbis. So, I shall argue that Philo applies the distinction of two jurisdictions in the Law of Moses in key statements in a context in which Abraham and the other patriarchs are characterized as founders of the Jewish nation. The special prominence that Philo gives to this distinction in the concept of the Law seems to have been twofold, namely, on the one hand, to object to the view of Abraham as obedient to Moses, and on the other hand, to communicate within a broader Hellenized con-

---

52 F. Watson, *Paul and the Hermeneutics of Faith*, 2nd ed. (London: Bloomsbury T&T Clark, 2016), 222.
53 Watson, *Paul and the Hermeneutics of Faith*, 223.
54 K.O. Sandnes, *Paul Perceived: An Interactionist Perspective on Paul and the Law,* WUNT (Tübingen: Mohr Siebeck, 2018), 150.
55 Sandnes, *Paul Perceived*, 153.

text the view of the Jewish ancestor as embodying the adherence to the divine law in nature, before it was revealed as the copy of Abraham's life through Moses.

Correspondingly, the distinction Philo makes in discussion with other Jews, between two distinct jurisdictions in his concept of the Torah, has not been taken into full account with regard to a comparison with Paul's reading of Genesis as a background for his discussion of Abraham in Galatians 3. Thus, previous studies comparing Philo and Paul seem to have neglected this nuance, that is, the complementary and dynamic concepts of both Abraham and the Law, in which a distinction was made between Abraham's trust in the promise and God's reaffirmation of the promise by oath, on the one hand, and the Mosaic jurisdiction revealed at Sinai, on the other hand.[56] So, for example, J.M.G. Barclay states that "Paul appeals to the Abrahamic texts and disjoins them from the Torah",[57] or "The Torah is thus neither integral to, nor a means toward, the fulfillment of the Abrahamic blessing",[58] or that Paul has "removed the Torah from the trajectory of the promise."[59] In opposition to such a unilateral concept of the Torah, I shall claim that Paul, without referring to Abraham as embodying a "Law", nevertheless appeals to the Torah as part of the Scripture as testimonies about Abraham in a manner that suggests he conceived of an "Abrahamic jurisdiction" as

---

56 In the course of this book, I shall refer to several scholars who are aware of either Philo's or Paul's distinction between various jurisdictions at work in the Torah, but who fail to make a careful analysis that compares and contrasts Philo and Paul from this perspective. See, e.g., the studies by E.R. Goodenough, *By Light, Light: The Mystic Gospel of Hellenistic Judaism* (New Haven: Yale University Press, 1935; repr., Amsterdam: Philo Press, 1969); S. Sandmel, *Philo's Place in Judaism: A Study of Conceptions of Abraham in Jewish Literature* (Philadelphia: Hebrew Union College Press, 1971); N.A. Dahl, *Studies in Paul*; Betz, *Galatians*; G. Sass, *Leben aus den Verheissungen: Traditionsgeschichtliche und biblisch-theologische Untersuchungen zur Rede von Gottes Verheissungen im Früjudentum und beim Apostel Paulus*, FRLANT (Göttingen: Vandenhoeck & Ruprecht, 1995); B. Schliesser, *Abraham's Faith in Romans 4: Paul's Concept of Faith in Light of the History of Reception of Genesis 15:6*, WUNT 2 (Tübingen: Mohr Siebeck, 2007); C. Hayes, *Divine Law*; P. Borgen, "Perspectives for Mission: Galatians 3:1–14 in Context," in *The Church and Its Mission in the New Testament and Early Christianity: Essays in Memory of Hans Kvalbein*, ed. D.E. Aune and R. Hvalvik, WUNT (Tübingen: Mohr Siebeck, 2018, 181–92); E. Birnbaum and J. Dillon. *Philo of Alexandria, On the Life of Abraham: Introduction, Translation, and Commentary* (Leiden; Boston: Brill, 2020).

57 J.M.G. Barclay, "Paul, the Gift and the Battle Over Gentile Circumcision: Revisiting the Logic of Galatians," *ABR* 58 (2010): 44.

58 Barclay, *Paul and the Gift*, 404.

59 Barclay, *Paul and the Gift*, 407.

distinct from the "Mosaic jurisdiction" at work in the Torah and Scripture.[60] In their discussions with Philo's interlocutors in Alexandria and Paul's opponents in Galatia, respectively, both authors seem to take part in contemporary Jewish negotiations on Abraham, in which they detach Abraham from his putative observance of the Law of Moses and so associate him with "trust" in God's promise and God's responsiveness in terms of the oath of promise. Unlike Philo, of course, Paul's reshaping of the two jurisdictions at work in Scripture in the light of the Christ event made it clear to him that this event was integral to both jurisdictions when they were conceived in a dynamic interplay and as the means toward the fulfillment of God's promise to Abraham and his descendants.

To sum up this review of previous research, I would suggest that more attention should be paid to the appeals that both Philo and Paul made to the figure of Abraham and the character traits they attributed to Abraham as a legal norm that served to define the identifying marks of Abrahamic kinship and descent from him. In key statements, both Philo and Paul identify Jews and converts in terms of the legal figure of Abraham as the foundational model, characterized by his trust in God and God's promise, before the written Law was revealed through Moses. As we shall observe, however, Philo and Paul are quite different in what they see as the legal and pragmatic consequences of what that meant for Jews and proselytes.

60 This warning against reading Paul's conception of the Torah unilaterally also applies to the paradigm known as "Paul within Judaism". This approach proceeds from the conjecture that Paul in Galatians 3 argues that pagans could become Abraham's descendants without becoming Jews. Such an assumption seems to be far from Paul's argument and does not take seriously the fact that the blessing mediated through Abraham's offspring, Christ, was offered to both Jews and non-Jews, and required that they were Abraham's sons and heirs of the promise, attested by the Torah itself. Thus, it is a paradox that an approach that claims to study "Paul within Judaism" excludes a more intramural perspective, in which Paul's appeal to Abraham and Scripture concerning the Jewish identity of the Galatian converts resonates well in the context of a Jewish debate of his own time. The *a priori* likelihood that Paul's appropriation of Abraham would to some extent have been both cherished and opposed by contemporary exegetes (represented by Philo and his interlocutors) seems to confirm this inference. Throughout this study, I interact with several scholars aligned with the paradigm of "Paul within Judaism", such as Johnson Hodge, Thiessen, and Fredriksen. For a critical assessment of this paradigm, see Donaldson, "Paul Within Judaism"; Barclay, *Paul and the Gift*, 161–2; Sandnes, *Paul Perceived*, 212–4.

3 The Approach, Method, and Course of the Study

I shall round off this introductory chapter by some comments on the approach, methods, and course of the study. The aim of this book involves essentially the use of data that generates fresh perspectives rather than a new approach framed by different methods. Thus, my investigation of the data follows a standard "historical-critical" method, in which various scriptural texts, exegetical motifs, and ideas are traced and situated in the broader cultural context of Jewish and Greco-Roman literature. In particular, my comparison and arguments with regard to how Philo's writings bear on Paul's appropriation of Abraham aim to be a significant and original contribution to the scholarly field. Before I shall present briefly the course of the study, however, certain presuppositions that are of a more fundamental character shall be mentioned.

Philo of Alexandria is a representative of Diaspora Judaism and of Judaism as such in the late Second Temple period. Philo is valuable for understanding the Jewish diversity of his time, not only in Alexandria. As a Jew living before the destruction of the Temple in 70 C.E., Philo offers an abundance of evidence about his Jewish contemporaries and their discussions, beliefs, and practices. Hence, his writings can shed light on both the commonality and the diversity among these Jews.

Philo's writings have been used to illuminate the background and the wider context of the New Testament and the Early Church.[61] Substantial parts of the New Testament and the Pauline letters in particular are dependent on the relationship to the Jewish Diaspora. Thus, we may claim that the New Testament consists of texts which are mainly written by Jews and to addressees, living in a Jewish Diaspora context.[62] In the light of this premise, Philo's writings are not only a major reflection of such a Diaspora Judaism, but perhaps the most important body of material that informs us about the world of the kind of Greek-speaking Judaism that formed the background to the New Testament writings.[63]

---

61 Cf. D.T. Runia, *Philo in Early Christian Literature: A Survey*, CRINT (Assen: Van Gorcum, 1993), 3–7.

62 See P.J. Bekken, "Philo's Relevance for the Study of the New Testament," in *Reading Philo: A Handbook to Philo of Alexandria*, ed. T. Seland (Grand Rapids: Eerdmans, 2014), 226–68.

63 See G.E. Sterling, "'Philo Has not Been Used Half Enough': The Significance of Philo of Alexandria for the Study of the New Testament," *PRSt* 30.3 (2003): 252:

> Are the works of Philo important for our understanding of the New Testament and Christian origins? I suggest they are. In fact, I think the Philonic corpus is the single most important body of material from Second Temple Judaism for our understanding of the development of Christianity in the first and second centuries. [...] the Philonic corpus helps

In searching for parallels to a biblical expression or custom in extra-biblical sources, a basic rule is that caution is required. When one compares texts, one presupposition is, of course, that both texts contain comparable material. One has, moreover, to pay sufficient attention to both the similarities and the differences. One must at least concentrate on the differences. This is important in order to avoid over-bold analogy and identification. But even while looking for differences, the distinctive features must not be exaggerated to such an extent that the genuine similarities become concealed. The resemblances in method, form, content etc., which in fact may exist and are perhaps already presupposed, must not be obscured, although a comparative study always entails the risk of over-emphasizing the analogies and overlooking the divergences.

Some further reflections on the label of "referential background" of a text are in order.[64] The broad notion of such a concept briefly outlined above (cf. n. 3), may include a wide range of traditional background material which, without necessarily being explicitly referred to in a text, nevertheless are presupposed in such a way that one should know about this background in order to grasp the implications of the meaning of the text.[65] The evidence of such background material in terms of similarities and differences between two different authors or in mutually independent literary texts can provide the scholar with help in reconstructing the various "signs" or features of a referential background in a text. In such cases, the parallel texts must comply with the following criteria:

a. It must be possible to situate the referential "signs" in the parallel texts chronologically, historically, culturally, and ideologically, so that it becomes probable that the sender and receiver of the text under consideration are aware of and share the same presuppositions or interpretative "horizon".[66] In

---

us to understand the dynamics of early Christianity more adequately than any other corpus.

64 For the use of this concept, see also my previous study, *The Word is Near You: A Study of Deuteronomy 30:12–14 in Paul's Letter to the Romans in a Jewish Context*, BZNW (Berlin; New York: De Gruyter, 2007), 156.

65 In this sense the notion of "referential background" comes close to the concept of "encyclopaedia" coined by U. Eco. According to Eco, this concept may include various components of cultural knowledge and assumptions inherent in semantic units or markers of a literary text, cf. U. Eco, *A Theory of Semiotics* (Bloomington: Indiana University Press, 1976), 99, 105–125.

66 For the hermeneutical concept of "fusion of horizons" dependent on a commonality of tradition, in which the author and addressees particapate, cf. H.-G. Gadamer, *Gesammelte Werke: Bd. 1: Hermeneutik I: Wahrheit und Methode: Grundzüge einer philosophischen Hermeneutik* (Tübingen: Mohr Siebeck, 2010).

the present study a contemporary and historical context in terms of relevant Jewish texts will be drawn upon in the attempt to specify the "horizon" of Paul's text as far as possible.

b. The referring text must contain "signs", which are meant to bring the referential background to the mind of the reader. This implies that it is reasonable to assume that we can speak of a referential "sign" when it forms a meaningful whole or exhibits a thematic coherence together with other signals in the alluding text. This means that the referential sign must have sufficient volume in terms of verbal correspondences between the referring text and the texts referred to. In the case of referential "signs" in terms of "echoes" or "literary allusions",[67] the frequent references to the Abrahamic narratives in Genesis and the exegetical paraphrase of particular passages throughout the selected texts are indicative of its volume and importance, and will thus receive a special focus in this study.

c. It must be possible to explain and understand the "signs" in a text against the referential background. This means that when such signals might be identified in a text, they interplay and indicate the horizon of understanding. This is a hermeneutical process of thinking, often designated as abductive reasoning, by which we might generate that framework of interpretation that makes the best inference of explanation of what we observe: How good is the coherence and fit between the interpretative framework and our observations?[68] For example, the inter-corroborating of the part and whole relations between the textual factors in Gal 3:6–29 and the accumulative effect of the comparative data may help us to identify the Jewish exegetical tradition and motifs appropriated by Paul, and thus provide a more adequate explanation of the relevant textual data than previous and alternative interpretations. In this respect it should be emphasized that similar traditions need not require direct knowledge or influence between authors, or dependence on particular sources, or some shared reservoir of common exegetical traditions. This is not to deny the possibility that this might have been the case; but our lack of knowledge of influence between the traditional expositions and their applications means that we need to cautious about presupposing any such relation. Rather, the commonalities can simply be the result of shared exegetical presuppositions about how a particular Scrip-

67 For such an understanding of the label "literary allusion", see Z. Ben-Porat, "The Poetics of Literary Allusion", *PTL: A Journal for Descriptive Poetics and Theory of Literature* 1 (1976), 105–128. For its application in New Testament texts, cf. M.J.J. Menken, *Studies in John's Gospel and Epistles: Collected Essays*, CBET (Leuven; Paris; Bristol, CT: Peeters, 2015), 169–173.

68 See on the method of abductive reasoning, S. Paavola, "Abduction as a Logic and Methodology of Discovery: The Importance of Strategies," *Foundation of Science* 9.3 (2004): 267–83.

ture was read and interpreted within related contexts, e. g., those in the variegated Jewish communities in the Diaspora.

In part one and the next three chapters, I explore Philo's appropriation of Abraham in two of Philo's writings, *De Virtutibus* and *De Abrahamo.* Before we undertake a comparison of Philo with Paul or other sources, it is important to interpret the relevant Philonic texts on their own terms within their literary and cultural contexts. Other relevant Philonic texts and sources from Second Temple or rabbinic Judaism are drawn upon when they can complement our understanding of Philo's interpretation of the scriptural texts dealing with Abraham and his descendants.

In chapter two, I seek to demonstrate that Philo's portrayal of Abraham as the paradigmatic model, conceived as the first proselyte and the founder of the Jewish nation respectively, was indeed determinative of his conception of Jewish ethnic identity and what he considered essential for being descended from Abraham and becoming a proselyte. Since Philo is sensitive to the issue of the converts' non-Abrahamic lineage, he emphasizes that the proselytes obtain family bonds, fellowship, and citizenship with Jews within the Jewish *politeia.*

In chapter three, the analysis of *Abr.* 262–273 shows that Philo presupposes an exegetical tradition that reads Gen 15:6 and Gen 22:16–18 as a *continuum* of Abrahamic events that belong together. Thus, Philo interprets Gen 15:6 in conjunction with Gen 22:16–18 from the perspective of a parallel between Abraham's conduct of trust (in the promise) and the conduct of trust / faithfulness to the promise granted Abraham in return from God. This pattern of thought can partly be drawn from the Hebrew Scriptures itself, and conforms otherwise to data in Jewish haggadah.

Chapter four argues that Philo deviates from an exegetical tradition that reads Gen 15:6, 22:15–18, and 26:3–5 in a *continuum* as sequences of the Abrahamic narrative. In contrast to such an interpretation, Philo detaches Abraham's trust (Gen 15:6) from his Law obedience (Gen 26:5) and relates it to God's promise that is reaffirmed to Abraham by oath (Gen 22:16–18), before the Law was revealed through Moses. Philo's separation of Abraham's trust in the promise from the Law of Moses was part of a Jewish discussion about Abraham in his own period, where Philo seems to have made a distinction in his concept of the Law of Moses between the "Abrahamic jurisdiction", centered on Abraham's virtues in accordance to the divine Law in Nature, and the "Mosaic jurisdiction", taken as a later record of what Abraham achieved through what he had instinctively said and done. Philo's appropriation of the Abrahamic story as a legal biography or jurisdiction of its own is thus subservient to his communication of the particular Laws of Moses with regard to their cosmic significance to a wider audience of Jews and non-Jews within a Greco-Roman and Jewish context.

In part two and the main chapter of this study, I take my lead from these observations on Philo's appropriation of Abraham, and seek to shed new light on Gal 3:6–29 against this referential background. My approach differs from earlier works because it offers a comparative study on the basis of the exegetical methods, traditions, and motifs involved. This study seeks to substantiate the thesis that this text is in itself a sample of a small "exegetical treatise", in which words about and to Abraham and his descendants have been given an exegetical paraphrase throughout the passage. The parallels in Philo and other Jewish data show that Paul has fashioned his argument not only according to conventional exegetical methods, structures, and terminology, but also in such details as exegetical traditions and motifs in the context of a wider Jewish negotiation on Abraham. Such a Jewish negotiation on Abraham may provide a cultural context for a corresponding debate that is reflected in Galatians, and it suggests that there were Jewish antecedents and analogies to Paul's kind of reasoning in his own time.

Part One: Philo's Appropriation of Abraham in *De Virtutibus* and *De Abrahamo*

Chapter 2: Abraham as Foundational Model for Proselytes and the Jewish Nation

1 Thesis and Approach

In this chapter, we shall consider how Philo's understanding of Jewish ethnicity pertains to ingredients of Jewish identity and the terms under which non-Jews become "Jews" and the connotations of being part of the Jewish *ethnos*. This study suggests that Philo's portrayal of Abraham was appropriate and indeed determinative of his conception of Jewish ethnic identity and the notion of the Jewish nation as a proselyte nation, that is, what it meant to belong to the Jewish nation and become a proselyte. Thus, I shall argue the thesis that Philo's basic notion of Jewish ethnicity presupposes an ethnic differentiation between the Jewish *ethnos* and other peoples. Accordingly, his basic view is that ethnic identity for both a Jew and a convert is constituted by spiritual kinship in the manner of Abraham *and* living in accordance with the laws of Moses as the constitution of Jewish citizenship. This basic view of the kind of kinship connected to Abraham concerns above all his conceptions of becoming a proselyte and has relevance for a born Jew who may be in danger of apostasy. On the one hand, the ethnic difference and distance that exists because of ethnic origins and lineage means that Philo does not make an ethnic blending of a born Jew and a convert. This is why he never says that the proselytes get a new lineage as Abraham's descendants when they are included in the Jewish people. Hence, a special provision is needed for proselytes who choose to live according to these core values that are exemplified in the life of Abraham as the founder of the Jewish proselyte nation. This means that the family bonds between Jews and proselytes in terms of spiritual kinship are thought of as extending beyond physical lineage. On the other hand, Philo's reservation vis-à-vis nationality and boundaries tied to physical lineage is also related to the fact that there were apostates who had deviated from the spiritual kinship within the Jewish nation and thus the virtues exemplified in Abraham and promoted through the Law of Moses. Such "membership requirements" were maintained by Philo in order to be reckoned as genuine biological descendants of the ancestor.

I shall begin this chapter with a short survey of some aspects of Jewish identity that find expression in Philo's writings. In the next two sections, I shall pay particular attention to Jewish Scriptures and exegetical motifs which give special prominence to the intertwined role of Abraham as the paradigmatic proselyte and founder of the Jewish nation. Finally, I shall explore how the merits of Abraham's piety were expected to confer benefits upon his true descendants. This

https://doi.org/10.1515/9783110722109-003

chapter provides a cultural context for the study of Paul's appropriation and discussions of Abraham within such a Jewish discourse.

2 Introductory Remarks on Jewish Ethnicity and Kinship in Philo

How did Philo understand what it meant to be Jewish? Did he have a notion of Jewish ethnicity? If so, in which contexts did he articulate it? Should Philo's notion of the Jewish race be understood in a concrete sense, or does it refer to a spiritualized concept only? As I shall point out in what follows, these questions have been answered differently along a wide spectrum of viewpoints in earlier scholarship.[1] Broadly speaking, the concept of being "Jewish" has been conceived from the perspectives of nationalism via a spiritualized sense to universalism. In this chapter, I shall not take my starting point in any specific theoretical or more modest angle; instead, I shall provide samples of Philonic texts that may illustrate the principles, connotations, and meanings involved in each of the relevant concepts. As we shall point out in due course, these models were involved in discussions of these issues in other Jewish texts as well, not at least in the Pauline and later rabbinic data.

Although I shall argue that Philo maintains the basic viewpoint of the ethnic distinctiveness of the Jewish nation in relation to the other nations, this does not exclude the possibility of conceiving "Jewish" identity along a wide spectrum of notions, such as a sense of community through a common ancestor, blood-line, common beliefs, characteristic traits or virtues, customs, cultic activity, citizenship, and kinship, whether real or more fictitious in a metaphorical sense. The data seems to allow for a distinction between three basic categories or concepts of ethnicity and kinship that are operative in the Philonic corpus. A brief account of the discussion of each of these concepts forms a useful point of departure for the remaining part of this chapter.

---

1 For a survey of previous scholarship on these issues, cf. N.A. Dahl, *Das Volk Gottes: Eine Untersuchung Zum Kirchenbewusstsein Des Urchristentums*, Skrifter Utg. Av Det Norske Videnskaps-Akademi i Oslo. II. Hist.-Filos. Klasse, 1941.2 (Oslo: J. Dybwad, 1941), 108–13; P. Borgen, *Bread from Heaven*, 115–18; E. Birnbaum, *The Place of Judaism in Philo's Thought: Israel, Jews, and Proselytes*, SPhiloM (Atlanta: Scholars Press, 1996), 30–60; D.T. Runia, "Philo and the Gentiles," in *Attitudes to Gentiles in Ancient Judaism and Early Christianity*, ed. D.C. Sim and J.S. McLaren, LNTS (London: Bloomsbury, 2013), 28–45; G.E. Sterling, "'A Law To Themselves': Limited Universalism in Philo and Paul." *ZNW* 107.1 (2016): 30–47.

The first concept, "genealogical kinship", refers to common bonds through ancestry, blood-line, birth, or genetic makeup. This emphasis on lineage and shared physical origin, through patrilineal descent from Abraham and the other patriarchs, is fundamental for Philo's conception of Jewish identity. We find a typical example of this notion in *Praem.* 57, where Philo describes the Jewish nation and the division of the Jewish *ethnos* into twelve tribes as the lineage of the common ancestor, Abraham:

> For instance the twelve tribes into which the nation (ἔθνος) was divided had the same number of chieftains connected not only by membership of the same house (οἰκία) and kinship (συγγένεια) but by a still more real affinity, for they were brothers with the same father [Jacob], and their grandfather [Isaac] and great-grandfather [Abraham] as well as their father were the founders of the nation (ἀρχηγέται τοῦ ἔθνους).[2]

The expression ἀρχηγέται τοῦ ἔθνους, here applied to the patriarchs, refers both to the founder of an ἔθνος[3] and to the notion of being a founder of a city or a family (γένος).[4] As we shall point out below, a key statement at the end of Philo's biography of Abraham makes use of such an expression and declaration: "Such is the life of the first, the founder of the nation (ἀρχηγέτης τοῦ ἔθνους) [...]" (*Abr.* 276).[5]

Although Philo, as we shall observe, may also place value on "spiritual kinship" ties over against ancestry and blood-line, his basic view seems to come to expression in the following text:

> He does not allow them to exact money from their fellow-nationals (ὁμοεθνής), but does permit the recovery of dues from the others. He distinguishes the two by calling the first by the appropriate name of brethren (ἀδελφοί), suggesting that none should grudge to give of his own to those whom nature has made his brothers and fellow-heirs. Those who are not of the same nation he describes as aliens (ἀλλότριοι) reasonably enough, and the condition of the alien excludes any idea of partnership, unless indeed by a transcendency of virtues he converts even it into a tie of kinship (συγγενικός), since it is a general truth that common citizenship rests on virtues and laws which propound the morally beautiful as the sole good. *Spec.* 2:73

2 For the discussion of this kind of patrilineal ideology inherent in Philo's line of thought, cf. Johnson Hodge, *If Sons, Then Heirs*, 22–3.

3 Cf. *Abr.* 57; *Mos.* 1:7 and this expression applied to Abraham as both the ancestor of "Israel" and of Moses.

4 Cf. LSJ. In *QG* frg. 17.6 and *Virt.* 206, the term refers to the Jewish descendants as the "family" of Abraham.

5 For a discussion of these terms, see most recently S. Pearce, "Notes on Philo's Use of the Terms ἜΘΝΟΣ and ΛΑΟΣ," SPhiloA 28 (2016): 220–22.

At this juncture, Philo refers to the rule laid down in Deut 15:1–3 about cancellation of debts. He seems to defend the Mosaic rule that does not allow one to exact debts from one's fellow-nationals (ὁμοεθνής) and only allows one to do so from foreigners. Thus, Philo makes a differentiation between those of the same nation, i.e. the Jews, whom Moses entitles as brothers (ἀδελφοί), and foreigners (ἀλλότριοι), who are prevented from fellowship by ethnic or national difference, since partnership presupposes common nationality. Such an observation speaks against the view that claims that ethnicity is subordinate in Philo's framing of the nation's identity, so that "Jewishness" was only a negotiable entity, not a fixed and predetermined one.[6] Accordingly, a passage such as *Spec.* 2:73 speaks against scholars who either maintain that Philo denies Jewish particularity and emphasizes virtue over against birth and common nationality, or that racial differentiation was not on Philo's agenda.[7] On the contrary, ethnic distinctiveness and boundaries between the Jewish people and the other nations seem to have been a basic presupposition in Philo's reasoning with regard to Jewish identity. This principle does not give prominence to the idea that the kinship ties between the native-born Jews are grounded in Philo's emphasis on the shared piety with the ancestors that is required in order to sustain genuine patrilineal lineage.[8] In *Spec.* 2:73 we saw an illustration of this concept, which also makes a special provision for foreigners so that Jewish kinship can be offered to outsiders who wish to adopt a Jewish lifestyle and beliefs. This message is repeatedly stated by Philo, not at least in passages in which he addresses Jewish apostates.[9] Another example of such a text is *Virt.* 195–196:

> And, therefore, I think, that if God had so formed nobility as to take a human shape, she would stand to face rebellious descendants and address them thus. "In the court where truth presides, kinship (συγγενής) is not measured only by blood, but by similarity of conduct and pursuit of the same objects. But your practice has been the opposite. [...] You have done your best by your actions to make yourself strangers, why do you hypocritically assume a specious name and call yourself kinsmen (συγγένεια)? [...]."[10]

---

6 For a discussion of this view, cf. Gruen, "Philo and Jewish Identity," 189.

7 For the former view, cf. Dahl, *Das Volk Gottes*, 107–14, and for the latter position, see Gruen, "Philo and Jewish Identity", 192–95, respectively.

8 Cf., e.g., *Mos.* 2:171; *Spec.* 1:317–318; *Spec.* 2:73; *Virt.* 195.

9 Cf. *Mos.* 2:171; *Spec.* 1:317–318; *Virt.* 79, 206; *Praem.* 152.

10 *Virt.* 195–196 is part of the discrete unit, §§ 187–227, "On Nobility", which is introduced by the main thesis in § 189 that the virtuous are noble regardless of their ancestry, and supported by the ensuing two major sections of the treatise (§§ 190–210 and §§ 211–225), rounded off by the conclusion (§§ 226–227). The sub-section §§ 195–197 belongs to Philo's explanation of the second part of the thesis in § 189, i.e., that only the virtuous ones have the right to be entitled "noble". Thus, it is directed against rebellious offspring or apostates, and emphasizes that true

Such a passage, then, makes the general point that the "membership requirements" go beyond being born as a Jew and apply to apostates and proselytes alike. In other words, Jewish identity entails more than physical lineage and blood relationships; it must be supplemented and can be overcome through similarity of behaviour and a citizenship characterized by shared laws. I shall suggest that the ethnic boundary between the Jewish people and other peoples is precisely the reason why Philo does not speak about a new lineage on the part of Jewish proselytes who join the Jewish people, but rather emphasizes the civic metaphor of citizenship and the spiritual ties and kinship over against natural kinships.

Philo's remarks about "spiritual kinship" that can overcome not being born as a Jew are related to the third concept I shall note, which can be designated as "legal kinship" or "kinship in Law", "by which the duties and privileges of kinship may be extended to another individual or group, including aliens."[11] This kind of kinship has a fictitious and metaphorical dimension, and can be mediated through legal means such as the taking of an oath, or adoption whereby a non-kin changes ethnic identity, national allegiance, and political affiliation. In the excursuses on proselytism below, I shall touch in particular on Philo's concepts of adoption, while the ritual of an oath will be mentioned in the context of Philo's exposition of the oath of promise reiterated to Isaac and his descendants, making it clear that its promise of blessing makes only the demand that they resemble the qualities of the ancestor Abraham who was granted the oath of promise.

I shall now investigate how the various aspects of Jewish ethnicity and kinship outlined above emerge in Philo's depiction of Abraham as the founder and role model for the Jewish nation and as the paradigmatic first proselyte.

3 Abraham's Conversion as a Model for Proselytes

In this section, I shall briefly situate Philo's portrayal of Abraham within the context of the complex issue of "conversion" and proselytism in Jewish antiquity. I shall take my lead from various threads in Philo's representations of Abraham in

---

nobility is attained not by ancestry alone, but by practicing the virtues truth, humility and self-restraint. For a survey of how the argument unfolds in §§ 187–227, see W.T. Wilson, *Philo of Alexandria, On Virtues: Introduction, Translation, and Commentary*. PACS (Leiden; Boston: Brill, 2011), 386–8.

11 F.M. Cross, *From Epic to Canon: History and Literature in Ancient Israel* (Baltimore; London: Johns Hopkins University Press, 1998), 8.

the treatises *De Virtutibus* and *De Abrahamo*. These works help us to see how Philo understands Abraham as a foundational model for the special qualities of the Jews, as well as for non-Jews who would imitate Abraham and become proselytes.[12] Moreover, *De Virtutibus* elaborates a picture of Abraham as the default proselyte who on the basis of trust in the one God received the Spirit and became transformed as a person. In Philo's thinking, there are some distinctive features that characterize his key statements about Abraham as the founder of the Jewish nation and as the standard of non-Jews who would imitate him as proselytes and become part of the Jewish *politeia*. Although recent Philonic scholarship has paid attention to this foundational and paradigmatic role of Abraham,[13] more emphasis should be put on the evidence that suggests that these imaginaries involve both kinship ideology and exegetical motifs based on texts such as Gen 12:1–3, 15:6, 22:16–18, and 26:3–5, as well as other passages from the Torah. As we shall observe, Gen 15:6 is in the center of Philo's appropriation of Abraham as the founder of the Jewish "proselyte people".

3.1 Abraham's Conversion from Idolatry to the One God

In *Virt.* 175–182, the various aspects of "conversion" are sketched when a non-Jew makes a transition to the Jewish polity.[14] First of all, "conversion" from polytheism to Jewish monotheism comes to prominence when non-Jews became proselytes. *Virt.* 179 may illustrate this theme:

> So therefore all these who did not at the first acknowledge their duty to reverence the Founder and Father of all, yet afterwards embraced the creed of one instead of a multiplicity of sovereigns, must be held to be our dearest friends and closest kinsmen.

A corresponding formulation by Philo is found in *Virt.* 102–104:[15]

---

12 In Philo's works, the words προσήλυτος (*Spec.* 1:51–53), ἔπηλυς (*Praem.* 152), ἐπηλύτης (*Mos.* 1:7), and ἐπήλυτος (*Virt.* 102–104) are used to describe proselytes. In *Virt.* 182, the word ἐπηλύτης is used. Cf. Birnbaum, *The Place of Judaism*, 195–202.

13 Cf. Birnbaum, *The Place of Judaism*, 202–6; Borgen, *Philo of Alexandria: An Exegete for His Time*, NovTSup (Leiden; New York: Brill, 1997), 217–23; J.M.G. Barclay, *Paul and the Gift*, 231–7; Pearce, "Notes," 220–6.

14 This text is part of the third subtreatise of *De Virtutibus*, entitled "On Repentance" (§§ 175–186), and describes the transformation experienced by proselytes. As to the content of this section, cf. Wilson, *On Virtues*, 20–1, 359–79.

15 *Virt.* 102–104 belongs to the second part (§§ 80–160) of the the section "On Humanity" (§§ 51–174), on how the Mosaic legislation promotes humanity.

> [...], the incomers (οἱ ἐπηλύται) [...] abandoning [...] the temples and images of their gods [...] have taken the journey to a better home, from idle fables to the clear vision of truth and the worship of the one and truly existing God.[16]

The issue of transition from polytheism to monotheism is elsewhere described by Philo by means of the model proselytes Abraham and Tamar. These examples show that to be incorporated in the Jewish community, even when one is not born into a Jewish family and comes from an ignoble background in the first place, means to follow in the manner of its founders and thus to be characterized by the belief in the One God. Thus, for example, Abraham, who is called "the most ancient member of the Jewish nation", is described as growing up as non-Jew, being a Chaldean by birth and the son of an astrologer:

> The most ancient member of the Jewish nation was a Chaldean by birth and whose father was an astrologer, one of those who occupied with its branches of knowledge who believe the stars and entire heaven and universe to be gods, on whose account, they say, things turn out for each person better or worse, [...] *Virt.* 212

> For the Chaldeans were especially active in the elaboration of astrology and ascribed everything to the movements of the stars. They supposed that the course of the phenomena of the world is guided by influences contained in numbers and numerical proportions. Thus they glorified visible existence, leaving out of consideration the intelligible and invisible. But while exploring numerical order as applied to the revolution of the sun, moon and other planets and fixed stars, and the changes of the yearly seasons and the interdependence of phenomena in heaven and on earth, they concluded that the world itself was God, thus profanely likening the created to the Creator. In this creed Abraham had been reared, and for a long time remained a Chaldean. *Abr.* 69–70

Although Philo, unlike other Second Temple Jewish texts and rabbinic traditions,[17] does not explicitly describe Abraham as involved in the worship of idols, he lets Abraham recognize that if he stayed within an idolatrous society, "the delusions of the polytheistic creeds would stay within him and render it impossible to discover the One" (*Virt.* 214). In Philo's estimation, the Chaldeans do not reach the truth of the existence of God, since their way of misconstruing the

---

16 A similar text is also found in Jos. Asen. 13:11–12. See also the development of this theme in *Spec.* 1:309; 4:178. Also in the New Testament and in other early Christian writings, this motif is a basic element in the conversion of the polytheists: Gal 4:8–9; 1 Thess 1:9; Acts 15:19; 1. Pet 4:3–4; Barn. 16:8; Justin, *1 Apol.* 14; 25; 49; *Dial.* 11:4, 30; 83:4; 91:3.

17 Cf., e.g., Jub. 11:3–5; Apoc. Ab. 7:1–12; Mek. Nez. 18:36–40; b. Sukkah 49b; Gen. Rab. 38:13; 39:8; 46:1. On Abraham as the first and model of the proselyte, see further, Keener, *Galatians*, 225; Thiessen, *Paul and the Gentile Problem*, 27–28; B. Begleiter, *Imagining a Patriarch: Images of Abraham in Early Jewish and Christian Exegesis* (PhD diss., Yale University, 2004), 107–47.

world precludes such a reality. This description of the context of the Chaldeans' godlessness, in which Abraham is located, is the immediate backdrop for Philo's paraphrastic allusion to Gen 15:6. Thus, Philo claims that Abraham was "the first person spoken of as 'believing God' (Gen 15:6), since he first grasped a firm and unswerving conception of the truth that there is one Cause above all, and that it provides for the world and all that there is therein" (*Virt.* 216). In *Abr.* 70, Abraham's gradual awakening and recognition of God is described in a similar manner, perceiving the existence of a provident God:

> Then opening the soul's eye as though after profound sleep, and beginning to see the pure beam instead of the deep darkness, he followed the ray and discerned what he had not beheld before, a charioteer and pilot presiding over the world and directing in safety his own work, assuming the charge and superintendence of that work and of all such parts of it as are worthy of the divine care.

Similarly, Abraham is conceived as a model of those "abandoning the ignobility of strange laws and monstrous customs which assigned divine honours to sticks and stones and soulless things in general" (*Virt.* 219). Likewise, Philo describes Tamar as a model proselyte who "became schooled in the knowledge of the monarchical principle by which the world is governed" (*Virt.* 220).

In both *Virt.* 179 and *Virt.* 102–104, Philo describes the various forms of polytheism in a general way. However, in other parts of his "Exposition," Philo offers a criticism of polytheism. Thus, in *Decal. 52*–57 and *Spec.* 1:13–31, Philo characterises a variety of polytheistic cults, such as worship of the creation in the form of the deification of elements within the cosmos[18] and living creatures (animals),[19] and the worship of lifeless images such as sculptural forms of deities.[20]

Philo also sees a close relationship between polytheistic worship and immorality,[21] which is expressed in the social relocation made by a proselyte in order to reconstruct his universe of moral order. In passages about proselytes, Philo describes the moral transformation of the way of life from pagan vices to Jewish virtues, which immediately follows from the worship of the One God in accordance with the Laws of Moses of the Jewish polity. Philo's explicit reference in *Virt.* 180–182 to the passing of the "convert" into "the way of life under

---

18 Cf. *Decal.* 54–56, where Philo refers to several Greek and Roman gods, such as Kore, Demeter, Pluto, Poseidon, Hera, Hephaestus, Apollo, Artemis, Aphrodite, Hermes, and Dioscuri. Cf. also *Spec.* 1:19–20; Wis 13:2; Rom 1:23, 25.

19 Cf. *Decal.* 76–80.

20 Cf. *Decal.* 66; *Spec.* 1:21, 28–29. *Mos.* 2:205.

21 Cf. e.g. *Sacr.* 48; *Post.* 96; *Spec.* 1:21–27; 3:40–42.

the best laws" documents this. Here, Philo applies catalogues of vices and virtues to characterize the pagan life and society the proselytes leave behind and the new life they enter:

> [...] but a man should convert, [...] but also in the other fundamental things of life, by passing, as it were from mob-rule, which is the vilest of misgovernments, into democracy, the way of life under the best laws [...] For it is excellent and profitable to desert without a backward glance to the ranks of virtue and abandon vice, that malignant distress; and where honour is rendered to the God who is, the whole company of the other virtues must follow in its train as surely as in the sunshine the shadow follows the body. The proselytes become at once temperate, content, modest, gentle, kind, humane, serious, just, high-minded, truth-lovers, superior to the desire for money and pleasure [...].[22]

Indirectly, Philo also portrays the life of the proselyte in the context of the Mosaic jurisdiction, when he describes their life in *Virt.* 182 by means of a list of virtues in contrast to the life of those who rebel against the holy laws. Although scholars have been cautious about inferring from Philo's writings the exact legal status of the proselyte,[23] we seem to have sufficient data to identify the legal basis for becoming a proselyte in terms of Jewish "citizenship" within the context of the Jewish community.[24] Thus, it is noteworthy that Philo emphasizes Abraham as the first proselyte as "the most ancient member of the Jewish nation", which indicates that the Jewish identity of the proselytes, although beyond the level of bloodline, is intertwined with the national identity of Abraham as their founding model. This means that the differentiation in ethnicity and lineage can be overcome by the Jewish nationality of common fellowship constituted by the shared belief in the One God, with virtues and piety aligned with Abraham and epitomized in the common jurisdiction of the Law of Moses. Again, Philo's basic view is that fellowship depends on common kinship, nationality and constitution. Even, as in the case of proselytes, when kinship trumps physical lineage, the Jewish identity is anchored in the nationality grounded by their common founder Abraham. As we shall observe in the next section, even when spiritual kinship overcomes family ties, it does not transcend and elude the concept of belonging to a common Jewish community.

---

22 The translation in LCL is modified.

23 Cf. Birnbaum, *The Place of Judaism*, 196; S.J.D. Cohen, *The Beginnings of Jewishness: Boundaries, Varieties, Uncertainties*, Hellenistic Culture and Society (Berkeley; Los Angeles; London: University of California Press, 1999), 157.

24 See K. Berthelot, "Judaism as 'Citizenship' and the Question of the Impact of Rome," in *In the Crucible of Empire: The Impact of Roman Citizenship Upon Greeks, Jews and Christians*, ed. K. Berthelot and J.J. Price, Interdisciplinary Studies in Ancient Culture and Religion (Leuven: Peeters Publishers, 2019), 123–9.

3.2 Abraham's Conversion from his Paternal Home to the Family Kinship with God

In his discussion of Abraham, Philo accentuates his piety and "nobility of birth" (εὐγένεια) as foundational for defining the character of the Jewish ἔθνος. As we shall see in this section, Philo appropriates Greek philosophical ideas in relation to the topic of "nobility" (εὐγένεια) as an interpretative framework for his interpretation of Abraham and as criteria for determining aspects of Jewish identity.[25]

In a section of the treatise *De Virtutibus*, and elsewhere, he emphasizes that kinship (συγγένεια) and nobility (εὐγένεια) are based on the similarity in conduct and character of the ancestor more than on genealogical relationships. Thus, in *Virt.* 212–219, Abraham is situated in the context of Philo's claims about "nobility of birth" (*Virt.* 187–227), defining the patrilineal descent as having its origins in the theological qualities of the founder rather than in noble ancestry *per se*. At this point, it seems that Philo makes use of the topic of "ancestry versus virtue": in other words, the virtuous alone are "noble," regardless of their ancestry. This was a common position taken by the followers of the Stoic school. Thus, the moral alieniation of the proselyte from his polytheistic surroundings and ancestry is exemplified by Philo's portrayal of Abraham. Abraham's trust in the one God (Gen 15:6) is conceived as the culmination of his resocialisation away from the Chaldean godlessness:

> And, therefore, he is the first person spoken of as believing in God, since he first grasped a firm and unswerving conception of the truth that there is one Cause above all, and that it provides for the world and all that there is therein. And having gained faith, the most sure and certain of the virtues, he gained with it all the other virtues [...]. *Virt.* 216

Hence, Abraham's trust in God is conceived as a virtue which generates all the other virtues. As a virtuous "immigrant", who "put his trust in nothing created above the uncreated Father of all" (*Virt.* 217), Abraham's trust and virtues caused him to be considered a king by those among whom he settled. Thus, he showed himself to be of the highest nobility, a man who craved kinship with God, "who rewards the lover of piety with imperial powers to benefit those around him" (*Virt.* 218). At this juncture, Philo seems to be familiar with the Stoic notion that the sage alone is king and thus noble.[26] Inspired by the portrait in Gen 15:6, Philo affirms Abraham as the foundational character of the cross-ethnic

---

25 On the treatment of such aspects of εὐγένεια among Greek philosophers, cf. Wilson, *On Virtues*, 381–8.

26 Cf. *SVF* 3.349–66; Plutarch, *Adul. am.* 58e. See Wilson, *On Virtues*, 383.

community of Jews and converts that emulate him as paradigm: "he is the *first* (πρῶτος) to be spoken of as believing in God, since he *first* (πρῶτος) grasped a firm and unswerving conception [...]" (*Virt.* 216). At this juncture, we can observe how Gen 15:6 not only influenced the structure of these texts to a certain extent, but also furnished Philo with other exegetical motifs in his portrayal of Abraham as the first proselyte. Thus, thanks to his virtues and qualities, Abraham, who himself originated from the worst lack of nobility of birth, was, nevertheless, worthy of emulation and had a good reputation. Despite an unpromising beginning, since "the most ancient member of the nation of the Jews was a Chaldean by birth" (*Virt.* 212), Abraham abandoned his own ancestry and kinship and their ignorance of "the One, the Most Ancient, the Uncreated, the Maker of All" (*Virt.* 213). Instead, Abraham, "without relatives or friends was of the highest *nobility* (εὐγενής), [...] craved for kinship (συγγένεια) with God and strove by every means to be well known to Him" (*Virt.* 218). In a previous passage from *De Virtutibus*, Philo calls kinship with God a characteristic trait of the whole Jewish nation, even more genuine than the characteristic of the bloodline:

> For Moses alone, it is plain, had grasped the thought that the whole nation (ἔθνος) from the very first was akin to things divine, a kinship (συγγένεια) most vital and a far more genuine tie than that of blood, and, therefore, he declared it the heir of all good things that human nature can contain. *Virt.* 79[27]

Although Philo here emphasizes that such a kinship with God belongs to the descendants of Abraham, the formulation and metaphorical notion of this kinship here go beyond ethnic boundaries. Thus, the corollary seems to be that those converts who have the ancestor of the Jewish nation as a model also receive a new kinship with God. The claim that "nobility" lies in sharing the "worth" and virtues of Abraham as the model of both Jews and converts, and is not based on ancestry and genetic disposition *per se*, is the reason why Philo can welcome proselytes and warn Jews not to place their trust in the virtue of their ancestors. Although lineage and kinship in blood indeed matter to Philo, he can even voice reservations about biological kinship in the case of apostates and state that the spiritual and civic aspects of kinship are more fundamental:

> Those whom we call our kinsfolk (συγγενής) or within the circle of kinsmen (συγγενής) our friends are turned into aliens by their misconduct when they go astray; for agreement to practice justice and every virtue makes a closer kinship (συγγένεια) than that of blood,

27 In *Virt.* 195–196, Philo asserts that kinship "is measured not in blood alone but in similarity of actions and pursuit of the same ends."

> and he who abandons this enters his name in the list not only of strangers and foreigners but of mortal enemies. *Spec.* 3:155

> For he assumed with good reason that one who was their fellow-tribesman and fellow-kinsman (συγγενής) related to them by the tie which brings the highest kinship (συγγένεια), the kinship of having one citizenship (πολιτεία εἷς) and the same law (νόμος ὁ αὐτός) and one God (εἷς θεός) who has taken all members of the nation for His portion, would never sin in the way just mentioned. *Spec.* 4:159

The fact that Philo can make the value of spiritual kinship trump the physical and biological ties of bloodline should not be taken to mean that the ethnic differences disappear. As we have seen from passages such as *Spec.* 2:73 and 4:157–158, Philo maintains the ethnic differentiation of Jews and foreigners, including the proselytes. In these passages, Philo seems to presuppose that differentiation in ethnicity and nationality excludes fellowship (cf. the adjective ἀκοινώνητος in *Spec.* 2:73), except when the ethnic boundaries are overcome by virtues or laws. In this instance, he surely has in mind the incorporation of proselytes in the Jewish community when they adopt the Jewish monotheism, way of life, customs, and constitution of the Law of Moses. The understanding that the ethnic boundaries between Jews by birth and proselytes from other nations are not dissolved seems to be corroborated by the fact that Philo never speaks about the proselytes as being Abraham's descendants or lineage, nor says that they enter the Jewish nation, which is described as an ἔθνος (nation), λαός (people), or γένος (class / race).[28] Instead, he speaks about the new kind of spiritual and civic kinship that exists between the two groups of Jews and converts within the constitutional framework of "citizenship", government or constitution (πολιτεία), living according to the jurisdiction of the Mosaic Law.[29] This means that Philo believes that while ethnic differences do not disappear within the Jewish community, they become irrelevant as an ingredient of the Jewish identity on the part of the proselytes. Thus, we may speak of a distinct cross-ethnic Jewish community of Jews and converts, based on the role of Abraham as the progenitor of both groups as a central ingredient of its Jewish identity. As we shall observe in what follows, Philo describes the fellowship between Jews and converts in terms of family bonds and kinship within the Jewish πολιτεία.

---

28 *Pace* Gruen, "Philo and Jewish Identity," 189–95, who in my opinion overstates his case that the ethnic boundaries are dissolved, or play a subordinate role, or even become irrelevant, so that ethnic differentiation was not on Philo's agenda in his description of the relationship between Jews and proselytes.

29 Cf. for such an observation, Berthelot, "Judaism as 'Citizenship'," 123–9; Runia, "Philo and the Gentiles," 36–8; Birnbaum, *The Place of Judaism*, 216–7.

We first turn to another aspect of conversion, which entails the reception of the Divine Spirit. The relevant passage is *Virt.* 212–19, where Abraham, in a context in which he is characterized as the prototype of proselytes (*Virt.* 219: οὗτος ἅπασιν ἐπηλύταις εὐγενείας ἐστὶ κανών), experiences a transformation of his soul and body when he receives the Spirit:

> [...] the divine Spirit, which, having been breathed upon him from on high, made its lodging in his soul, invested his body with singular beauty, his words with persuasiveness,and his hearers with understanding (τοῦ θείου πνεύματος, ὅπερ ἄνωθεν καταπνευσθὲν εἰσῳκίσατο τῇ ψυχῇ, περιτιθέντος τῷ μὲν σώματι κάλλος ἐξαίρετον, τοῖς δὲ λόγοις πειθώ, τοῖς δ' ἀκούουσι σύνεσιν). *Virt.* 217

Philo concludes that Abraham's "nobility" makes him the model to emulate for all proselytes:

> He [Abraham] is the standard of nobility for all proselytes (οὗτος ἅπασιν ἐπηλύταις εὐγενείας ἐστὶ κανών), who abandoning the ignobility of strange laws and monstrous customs which assign divine honours to stocks and stones and lifeless things in general, have come to settle in a better land, in a truly vital and living commonwealth (πολιτεία), with truth as director and president. *Virt.* 219

For Philo, therefore, the concepts of "nobility" (εὐγένεια) and kinship (συγγένεια) are patterned on the image of Abraham, who qualified because of his trust in God (Gen 15:6). This embrace of the true God leads to the reception of the transforming Spirit of God and the social relocation into the Jewish community established by Abraham, the first proselyte and founder of the Jewish nation. In the context of *Virt.* 187–227, that is why proselytes can overcome their foreign lineage and partake in Abraham's true "nobility", and why Jews must be warned not to place their confidence only in their birth into the Jewish nation at the cost of maintaining the true nobility of their ancestry. As we shall see in the next sections, Philo's appropriation of Abraham brings us closer to the meaning it would have for the first readers, who included non-Jewish "outsiders" and potential proselytes.

As we have already observed, the religious and moral change of the proselyte entailed a resocialisation, that is, an ethnic and judicial break with the pagan society and a transfer to another social group, the Jewish community. At this point, it is important to bear in mind that the Jews, as members of the Jewish πολιτεία, were themselves as a kind of "proselytes" or "resident aliens" in the various Diaspora cities of the eastern Roman Empire, forming immigrant associations that received proselytes from various ethnic groups. One could therefore say that, in a multiethnic society in which various ethnic associations were represented, the members of the Jewish association were all "proselytes" *qua* "resident aliens", whether they were native born Jews or incoming proselytes from other ethnic backgrounds. According to W.A. Meeks, this social context had some bearing on the Jewish way of interpreting both their own self-identification and the biblical terminology of being a "resident alien":

> But the Judeans also reinterpreted the biblical injunctions about incorporating resident aliens (*gêrim*) into Israel's cultic life to apply to their new situation now that they were resident aliens themselves. Thus the *prosêlutoi*–the term the LXX translators coined to translate *gêrim*–became those individuals who for whatever reason were drawn from the cosmopolitan environment into the transplanted Judean community.[30]

Unfortunately, with regard to the self-identification of the Jews as "proselytes" themselves, Meeks does not corroborate his suggestion. In fact, both the Greek translation of the Hebrew Bible (LXX) and Philo attest such a designation for both Jews and members drawn from non-Jewish nations. Thus, in *QE* 2:2, Philo interprets the term προσήλυτος in Exod 22:21 LXX ("And a proselyte you shall not mistreat, nor shall you oppress him. For you were proselytes in the land of Egypt"):

> [Scripture] first makes it clearly apparent and demonstrable that in reality the sojourner (προσήλυτος) is one who circumcises not his uncircumcision but his desires and sensual pleasures and the other passions of the soul. For in Egypt the Hebrew nation was not circumcised but being mistreated with all (kinds of) mistreatment by the inhabitants in their hatred of strangers, it lived with them in self-restraint and endurance, not by necessity but rather of its own free choice, because it took refuge in God the Saviour, Who sent His beneficent power and delivered from their difficult and hopeless situation those who made supplication (to Him). [...] But what is the mind of the sojourner if not alienation from belief in many gods and familiarity with honouring the one God and Father of all? *QE* 2:2

Here Philo speaks of a family bond between Jews and the sojourners who are united in the belief in the one God, in order to decide who belongs socially to the Jewish association of "resident aliens", whether they are Jews or non-Jews who have disassimilated themselves from the environment.

In the case of the latter group, the ethnic break with foreign deities and the embrace of the true God entails that "proselytes" have made their kinsfolk into mortal enemies (*Spec.* 4:178). So, in *Virt.* 102–104 Philo says that the proselytes have left their family, their country, and their customs: "[...] because abandoning their kinsfolk by blood, their country, their customs and the temples and images of their gods [...]." Again, Abraham is conceived as the prototype of the proselyte

---

30 W.A. Meeks, "Corinthian Christians as Artificial Aliens," in *Paul Beyond the Judaism / Hellenism Divide*, ed. T. Engberg-Pedersen (Louisville, KY: Westminster John Knox Press, 2001), 134.

who leaves his home in this way: "Perception of these truths and divine inspiration induced him to leave his native country, his race and paternal home, [...]" (*Virt.* 214). Again, the model of the proselytes is Abraham, moving from his own country to a new one:

> He is the standard of nobility for all proselytes, who, abandoning the ignobility of strange laws and monstrous customs which assigned divine honours to stocks and stones and soulless things in general, have come to settle in a better land, in a commonwealth full of true life and vitality, with truth as its director and president. *Virt.* 219[31]

According to Philo, proselytes have entered the Jewish πολιτεία, a term which means the rights of a citizen, body of citizens, government, constitution of a state, or commonwealth. Thus, he can claim that the proselytes have entered a "new and godly commonwealth (πολιτεία)" (*Spec.* 1:51), or "the government (πολιτεία) of the best law" (*Virt.* 180), or "a commonwealth (πολιτεία) full of true life and vitality" (*Virt.* 219).

Leaving the context of family and kinfolk could thus imply putting their lives at risk. For example, Tamar is said to have "deserted to the camp of piety at the risk of her life" (*Virt.* 220). In *Spec.* 4:178, Philo says that the proselytes have made their kinsfolk into mortal enemies:

> For the incomer, because he has turned his kinsfolk, who in the ordinary course of things would be his sole confederates, into mortal enemies, by coming as a pilgrim to truth and the honouring of One who alone is worthy of honour, and by leaving the mythical fables and multiplicity of sovereigns, so highly honoured by the parents and grand-parents and ancestors and blood relations and this immigrant to a better home.

This exposure to the risk of mortal dangers also finds expression in Philo's description of the proselytes as "refugees to the camp of piety" (*Spec.* 1:52). This issue of enmity to family relatives as a consequence of the proselyte's conversion is also described in the novel about Joseph and Asenath: "all people have come to hate me, and on top of those my father and mother, because I, too, have come to hate their gods and have destroyed them [...]. And therefore my father and mother and my whole family have come to hate me and says, 'Asenath is not our daughter because she destroyed our gods'" (Jos. Asen. 11:4–6).[32] In the same way, the historian Tacitus echoes the consequences of a religious and social break with the native background that are implied in the convert's transfer to the Jewish community:

---

31 Cf. *Abr.* 62.

32 Compare also Jos. Asen. 12:7.

Those who are converted to their ways follow the same practice, and the earliest lesson they receive is to despise the gods (*contemnere deos*), to disown their country (*exuere patriam*), and to regard their parents, children, and brothers as of little account (*parentes liberos fratres vilia habere*)." *Hist.* 5:5

Commenting on Deut 23:8–9, Philo's remarks on how the proselytes are incorporated into the Jewish community may possibly echo the Roman custom of granting citizenship to former enemies:[33]

And if any of them should want to cross over to the polity of the Jews (κἂν εἴ τινες ἐθελήσειαν αὐτῶν μεταλλάξασθαι πρὸς τὴν Ἰουδαίων πολιτείαν), they are not to be scorned unyieldingly like the children of enemies, but are to be treated in such a manner that the third generation is invited into the congregation and granted that share of the divine oracles into which the native- and noble-born are also rightfully initiated. *Virt.* 108[34]

Moreover, according to Philo, the proselytes have not only been incorporated as equal citizens into the Jewish community; they are also received and considered by the fellow Jews as close friends and relatives, *Virt.* 102:

[...] they have taken the journey to a better home, from idle fables to the clear vision of truth and the worship of the one and truly existing God. He commands all members of the nation to love the incomers, not only as friends and kinsfolk, but as themselves both in body and soul [...].

From the perspective of the welcoming Jewish fellowship, Philo can also describe the proselytes in the language of friendship and family.[35] Texts which offer good insights in Philo's model of social compensation—i.e., the loss of family caused by conversion was to be compensated by a new kind of citizenship, family, and relationships involving practical responsibilities on the part of the Jews—are *Spec.* 1:51–53 and *Virt.* 102–104:

All of like sort to him [i.e. Moses], all who spurn idle fables and embrace truth in its purity, whether they have been such from the first or through conversion (ἐκ τοῦ μεταβάλλεσθαι) to

33 Cf., e.g., Cicero, *Balb.* 31; *Leg.* 1.23; *Rep.* 1.49. For a comparison of Philo's and Cicero's discourse on citizenship granted to former enemies, and based on the community of common laws, cf. Berthelot, "Judaism as 'Citizenship'," 125–6.

34 Trans. Wilson, *On Virtues*, 65.

35 Cf. also K. O. Sandnes, *A New Family: Conversion and Ecclesiology in the Early Church with Cross-Cultural Comparisons*, SIHC (Bern: Peter Lang, 1994), 41–6. For Philo's description of proselytes, see especially Birnbaum, *The Place of Judaism*, 195–202; P. Borgen, *Paul Preaches Circumcision and Pleases Men and Other Essays on Christian Origins* (Trondheim: Tapir Publishers, 1983), 75–97.

the better side have reached that higher state, obtain His approval, the former because they were not false to the nobility of their birth (εὐγένεια), the latter because their judgement led them to make the passage to piety. These last he calls 'proselytes,' or newly-joined (προσηλύτοι), because they have joined the new and godly commonwealth (πολιτεία). Thus, while giving equal rank (ἰσοτιμία) to all in-comers (ἐπηλύται) with all the privileges which he gives to the native-born (αὐτόχθων), he exhorts the old nobility to honour them not only with marks of respect but with special friendship and with more than ordinary goodwill. And surely there is good reason for this; they have left, he says, their country (πατρίς), their friends (φίλοι) and their kinsfolk (συγγενεῖς) for the sake of virtue and holiness. Let them not be denied other cities (πόλεις), family members (οἰκείοι) and friends (φίλοι), and let them find places of shelter standing ready for refugees to the camp of piety. For the most effectual love-charm, the chain which binds indissolubly the goodwill which makes us one is to honour the one God. Yet he counsels them that they must not, presuming on the equal privilege (ἰσονομία) and equal rank (ἰσοτέλεια) which He grants them because they have denounced the vain imaginings of their fathers and ancestors, [...]. *Spec.*1:51–53

Having laid down laws for members of the same nation, he holds that the incomers (ἐπη λύται) too should be accorded every favour and consideration as their due, because abandoning their kinsfolk by blood and their country (γενεὰν μὲν τὴν ἀφ' αἵματος καὶ πατρίδα), their customs and the temples and images of their gods, and the tributes and honours paid to them, they have taken the journey to a better home, from idle fables to the clear vision of truth and the worship of the one and truly existing God. He commands all members of the nation to love the incomers (ἐπηλύται), not only as friends (φίλοι) and kinsfolk (συγγενεῖς) but as themselves both in body and soul: in bodily matters, by acting as far as may be for their common interest; in mental by having the same griefs and joys, so that they may seem to be the separate parts of a single living being which is compacted and unified by their fellowship (κοινωνία) in it. I will not go on to speak of the food and drink and raiment and all the rights concerning daily life and necessary needs, which the law assigns to incomers as due from the native born, for all these follow the statutes, which speak of the friendliness shown by him who loves the incomer even as himself. *Virt.* 102–104

Thus, Philo emphasizes the social aspect of conversion and also the benefits of belonging to the Jewish immigrant association which the convert has now joined.[36] Already in the introductory paragraph (*Virt.* 175) of the section on conversion (*Virt.* 175–186), we recognize these aspects; conversion offers "membership in the best of commonwealths (πολιτείας κοινωνίαν τῆς ἀρίστης) and of the felicities both great and small which that membership confers." "Proselytes" are so called, Philo says, because "they have come to a new and God–loving commonwealth (πολιτεία)," *Spec.* 1:51. Insofar as the Jewish community is conceived as a *politeia*, the proselytes should be treated with the same honour and enjoy

36 For the social inclusion to be extended to the proselytes by the Jewish community, cf. Wilson, *On Virtues*, 103–4; 368.

the common privileges (ἰσοτιμία) together with the native citizens. Moreover, in *Spec.* 1:53 Philo remarks that the proselytes should also be considered equal to the native Jews as far as the law and the taxes are concerned (ἰσονομία καὶ ἰσοτέλεια), that is, they should be considered as equal citizens in all political respects. Both these citations emphasize not only the ties of common citizenship, friendship and kinship that unite the native Jews and the proselytes, but also the aspect of their common bond in terms of their worship of the one true God. So, the kinship between the native Jews and the proselytes can be considered as both a civic and a spiritual kinship connection. As we shall see in the next section, it is a commonplace in Philo's writings that the real kinship that unites the native Jews themselves is grounded in the same theological conviction and characteristic virtues that they share with their ancestor Abraham. As a corollary, Philo can also warn potential apostates against holding natural kinship and the blood-line as sufficient if they lack the spiritual identifying marks of belonging to the Jewish nation.

Excursus: The Adoption of Proselytes into Abraham's Family in Rabbinic Literature in Comparison with Philo

As we have seen, Philo identified proselytes according to religious, ethical, and social criteria of conversion, so that Jewish proselytes were defined in terms of their spiritual and civic kinship and not according to genetic disposition or physical ancestry. At this juncture, it would be helpful to compare to some extent Philo's conception of Jewish proselytism with rabbinic literature in terms of the idea of the inclusion of the convert into the Jewish community.

Most recently, K. Berthelot has compared Philo's conception of conversion with the rabbinic discussion of this issue. In her opinion, the problem posed by the convert's foreign or ethnic origin seems not to have been an issue for Philo, since there is no need to ascribe a new lineage to the proselytes who have become citizens within the Jewish πολιτεία.[37] We find in the rabbinic literature the idea that the proselytes became Abraham's descendants, but this motif is absent in Philo's statements on proselytes. According to Berthelot, Philo speaks about the new kinship ties of the proselytes, but not in terms of a new lineage. She affirms that Philo holds that, since the proselytes have received Jewish "citizenship," their different ethnic origins and lineage became irrelevant in view of the higher, spiritual ties between them and Israel, based on the virtues

37 Berthelot, "Entre Octroi de la Citoyenneté et Adoption," 37–50.

and piety inherent in the observance of the laws of Moses. Such a view seems somewhat oversimplified, for several reasons.

In the first place, as we have seen at the beginning of this chapter, the ethnic dichotomy and differentiation between the Jewish nation by birth and ancestry and foreigners from other ethnic groups represented a fundamental binary that Philo took for granted. In principle, therefore, the proselytes seem to be a distinctive class from Jews within the Jewish community of citizens (πολιτεία), to such a degree that he pleads that the Jewish community should treat the proselytes with the love they show their own selves. In that sense, the Jewish πολιτεία was a cross-national community of native Jews *and* proselytes of foreign lineage.

Secondly, it seems an exaggeration when Berthelot claims that the spiritual kinship was superior to natural kinship. As we have pointed out above, the emphasis on the "civic kinship" of the proselytes, based on virtues and common laws (*Spec.* 2:73), seems to have been made not only in order to include proselytes, but also to maintain the basic principle among the Jews that spiritual kinship always belongs together with blood-line, not as a replacement for genealogical kinship. This idea emerges clearly from a passage that emphasizes that the most intimate kinship (συγγένεια) of the Jewish nation is based on having a common community of citizens, the same law and one God:

> For he assumed with good reason that one who was their fellow-tribesman and fellow-kinsman related to them by the tie which brings the highest kinship, the kinship of having one community of citizens and the same law and one God (συγγένειά ἐστι πολιτεία μία καὶ νόμος ὁ αὐτὸς καὶ εἷς θεός) who has taken all members of the nation (ἔθνος) for His portion, [...]. *Spec.* 4:159[38]

Such a conception of true natural kinship may equally be the reason why Philo cannot say that proselytes receive Abrahamic lineage and become part of the Jewish nation (ἔθνος).[39]

Thirdly, although lineage was dependent on birth, Philo never claims explicitly that the proselytes had Abraham as their father, in terms of being included in his physical lineage. Berthelot has overlooked, however, that Philo resorts to the concept of adoption in order to define an adopted child as a borderline figure between the family they rank with (and thus legitimate heirs), and being foreigners in terms of not being the actual children of their adoptees. It is noteworthy that this concept of adoption is applied in a context in which Philo elaborates on Hagar as a proselyte. Philo has extensive interpretations of Abraham,

38 The Loeb translation slightly modified.
39 Birnbaum, *The Place of Judaism*, 216.

Hagar, and Ishmael in his commentary series.[40] In the treatise *On the Preliminary Studies* (*De Congressu*), Hagar is described as a figure on the borderline between the Hebrew nation and foreign peoples. Notwithstanding her Egyptian origin, Philo underlines her relationship with Abraham's family. Through the relationship with Abraham and Sarah as their slave-servant, and even having a son together with Abraham, Hagar is closely associated with the Hebrew nation, of which Abraham is the founder. In *Congr.* 22–23, Hagar's place on the borderline is formulated principally in two ways: firstly, by means of an etymological interpretation of her name,[41] Hagar's status, as both a "sojourner" and a "proselyte," makes her a person on the borderline between foreigners and citizens: "The sojourner in so far as he is staying in the city is on par with the citizens, in so far as it is not his home, on par with foreigners." At this juncture, Philo seems to presuppose what we have observed above, namely that a proselyte, on the one hand, receives a "civic kinship" within the Jewish community and the status as an equal "citizen" of the Jewish community, and, on the other hand, that the proselyte and the Jews are "immigrants" on a par with other foreign groups of "resident aliens". Secondly, it is noteworthy that the borderline place of Hagar is then compared to a person who is adopted into a family: "In the same way, I should say, adopted children, in so far as they inherit from their adopters, rank with the family; in so far as they are not their actual children, with outsiders" (*Congr.* 23). Although Philo never claims explicitly that the proselytes became Abraham's adopted "sons" or "descendants", the concept of proselytes as adopted children of God may be implicit in Philo's line of thought, following the model of Abraham as an adopted son of God when searching for kinship with God (cf. the expression "τῆς πρὸς θεὸν συγγενείας" in *Virt.* 218). As we shall observe next, although this notion of adoption is applied to the proselyes and implicit in Philo's work, as in the case of Hagar, this is dealt with quite differently by the rabbis. The rabbinic literature attests to a discussion of the problem posed by the proselytes' foreign lineage for their incorporation into the lineage of Abra-

40 Most of Philo's material on Abraham, Hagar, and Ishmael is found in the commentary series called "The Allegory of the Laws": *Leg.* 3:245; *Cher.* 3, 6, and 8; *Sacr.* 43; *Post.* 130–37; *Sobr.* 8 ff.; *Congr.* 1, 11–14, 24, 71, 81, 88, 121–29, 139, 153–158, 180; *Fug.* 1, 5–6, 202–204, 208–212; *Mut.* 201–263; *Somn.* 1:240. Also in Philo's commentary *QG* there is much material on Hagar and Ishmael, *QG* 3:19–38, 57, 59, 61; 4:147, 245. In the comprehensive collections of books called "The Exposition of the Law", which are a rewriting of the Pentateuch, Hagar and Ishmael are referred to in *Abr.* 247–254.

41 Hagar's name is understood to be derived from גּוּר, to be a stranger, sojourn, dwell, in *piel* to make a proselyte, in *hithpael* to become a proselyte.

ham. Hence, some rabbinic traditions emphasized a legal kinship model and thus a metaphorical concept of conversion that conceived of the Gentile converts as Abraham's descendants in order to legitimate them as included in the promises to the patriarchs and in the recitations to the God of "our" fore-fathers in spite of their foreign genealogical origins. A brief survey of the appropriation of Gen 17:5 in rabbinic texts exemplifies the discussion of this topic.

Scholars such as Cohen, Hayes, and Berthelot have shown that for some rabbinic authorities, the converts enjoy the same privileges and rights as the native-born Jew, including the genealogy that goes back to Abraham.[42] This view is stated explicitly in the Jerusalem Talmud, y. Bik. 1:4 (64a). This passage elaborates on m. Bik. 1:4, which discusses the commandment of Deuteronomy 26:3 to bring the first fruits and recite in front of a priest: "I declare this day to the Lord your God that I have come into the land which the Lord swore to our fathers to give us". The passage in m. Bik. 1:4 reads:

> These may bring the First-fruits but they may not make the Avowal: the proselyte may bring them but he may not make the Avowal since he cannot say: *Which The Lord sware unto our Fathers for to give us.* But if his mother was an Israelite he may bring them and make the Avowal. And when he prays in private he should say, 'O God of the fathers of Israel'; and when he is in the Synagogue he should say: 'O God of your fathers'. But if his mother was an Israelite he may say: 'O God of our fathers'.

According to this Mishnah, the proselyte who does not have Israelite ancestors or a mother is legally inferior to the native-born Jews. Thus, he is not allowed to make the recital according to Deut 26:3, since he does belong to the descent of the Israelite forefathers who received the promise, nor to claim "God of our fathers" in public and private prayers. In the comment on this mishnah in the Jerusalem Talmud, attributed to Rabbi Judah, a Tanna of the third generation, the opposite view emerges. I quote the part of a longer elaboration which draws the discussion to a close:

> It was taught in the name of R. Judah:
>
> A first-generation convert brings and recites. What is the reason? [Because God said to Abraham] *for I have made you the father of a multitude of nations* (Gen 17:5). In the past you were a father to Aram, but from now on you are a father to all the nations.
>
> R. Joshua b. Levi said:

42 Berthelot, "Entre Octroi de la Citoyenneté et Adoption," 37–50; C.E. Hayes, *Gentile Impurities and Jewish Identities: Intermarriage and Conversion from the Bible to the Talmud* (Oxford: Oxford University Press, 2002), 166–7; Cohen, *The Beginnings of Jewishness*, 324–5.

> The law follows R. Judah.
>
> A case came before R. Abbahu and he rendered a decision according to R. Judah.

The legal ruling attributed to Rabbi Judah denies the position of the Mishnah that the Deuteronomic promise does not apply to converts, who cannot claim the patriarchs as "our fathers". Accordingly, a scriptural basis has to be provided, so that the convert has the Israelite ancestors as "our fathers". This is offered in God's promise to Abram in Genesis 17:5 that he shall become "the father of a multitude of nations". Thus, according to Talmud, Scripture itself warrants the converts having Abraham as "our father", since it appoints him as the father of the nations. It is noteworthy that this citation from Genesis is the very same verse used by Paul in order to argue that Gentile converts can become children of Abraham. I shall return later to a discussion of Paul's text against such a background.

The scholarly opinions differ on how Talmud reaches the understanding of Abraham as a father to converts. Thus, e. g., S. Cohen considers the appropriation of Gen 17:5 as "a piece of fanciful exegesis with homiletical intent [...] has become an important proof of in a legal discussion. Converts may say 'our fathers' because Abraham is a (the?) father to all gentiles—or, in the language of the Tosefta, 'father to the whole entire world'."[43]

According to Hayes and Berthelot, however, the words "you are a father to all the nations" in the Jerusalem Talmud should not be taken to mean that Abraham is father to all Gentiles as such, regardless of their conversion.[44] Rather, Abraham seems to be interpreted in a metaphorical sense as the father to non-Jews (*goyim*) who convert to the Jewish community. Thus, the "convert of entirely foreign origin may include himself in the promise to Israel's patriarchs and in prayers to the God of 'our' fathers".[45] This conception of Abraham as the father of proselytes is also attested elsewhere in rabbinic traditions. Moreover, a similar metaphorical understanding of Abraham's fatherhood applied to converts is also evidenced in medieval traditions from the late twelfth century, for example in the manner Maimonides interprets this passage from the Jerusalem Talmud in his letter to Obadiah, the convert. Writing from Cairo, he seems to object to advocates of the Mishnah in Egypt who challenge the legal rights of the converts to say "our God and God of our Fathers" and so also to participate fully

---

43 Cohen, *The Beginnings of Jewishness*, 329.

44 Hayes, *Gentile Impurities and Jewish Identities*, 167; Berthelot, "Entre Octroi de la Citoyenneté et Adoption," 37–50.

45 Hayes, *Gentile Impurities and Jewish Identities*, 167.

in the blessings and prayers of the native Jews. I quote excerpts from the relevant text:

> You [Obadiah] ask me if you are allowed to say the blessings and prayers you offer alone or in the congregation: "Our God and God of our fathers". [...] "You who have given to our fathers to inherit (a pleasant, good, and spacious land)" [...] Yes you may all this in the prescribed order and not change it in the least. In the same way as every Jew by birth says his blessing and prayer, you too, shall bless and pray alike, whether you are alone or pray in the congregation. [...] Thus, Abraham our Father, peace be with him, is the father of his pious prosperity who keeps his ways, and the father of his disciples and of all the converts who adopt Judaism. Therefore you shall pray "Our God and God of our fathers," because Abraham, peace be with him, is your father. And you shall say "You who have given to our fathers to inherit (a pleasant, good, and spacious land)," for the land has been given to Abraham [...].[46]

In the conclusion of the letter, Maimonides quotes the passage from the Jerusalem Talmud, y. Bik. 1:4, and thus emphasizes that Abraham is to be conceived as the father of both native-born Jews and converts with a foreign origin, but not of the Gentiles in general. It seems that the conversion and the metaphorical sense ascribed to Abraham as father of both groups functioned as a sufficiently strong legal fiction to sever the convert's ties to his biological family and at the same time to bear on his connection to his "new" Jewish family. As Bertholet suggests, such a rabbinic conception of conversion may have been shaped by the Roman context and model of adoption, so that the converts are to be considered as Abraham's adoptive sons or daughters, who have abandoned their previous family with its various deities and have become members of Abraham's family, as worshipers of Abraham's God.[47] In any case, as I shall discuss further in chapter five, we must ask whether Paul's view of Abraham as the model and father of the converts already provides a first-century analogy and attestation of an exegetical tradition that is preserved and developed in later rabbinic and medieval Jewish texts.

---

46 The text is taken from Cohen, *The Beginnings of Jewishness*, 331–2, who in turn has modified the translation of F. Kobler, *Letters of Jews through the Ages, 2. vols.* (repr., Philadelphia: Jewish Publication Society, 1978), vol. 1:194–6.

47 Berthelot, "Entre Octroi de la Citoyenneté et Adoption," 37–50; idem, "Adoption as a Conceptual Tool to Think About Conversion: A Study in Philo, Paul, and Rabbinic Literature." Paper presented at the Annual Meeting of the SBL in Boston, 2017.

4 Abraham as the Founder of the Jewish "Ethnos"

In the previous section, I have argued that Philo was sensitive to the ethnic distinction between Jews by birth and the non-Jewish lineage of proselytes of other ethnic backgrounds. Hence, there is reason to identify the Jewish community as a distinct cross-ethnic fellowship of Jews *and* converts. Although Philo implicitly applies the concept of adoption in the framework of his description of Abraham and Hagar as proselytes, it is significant that he never speaks about the proselytes in terms of ethnic language such as Abraham's descendants or *ethnos*. As a corollary of such an ethnic and racial differentiation, Philo can instead speak about the new ties of spiritual kinship, friendship, family and legal fellowship that the proselytes obtain with Jews. Thus, the proselytes, who receive a Jewish identity based upon character traits that they share with Abraham as their model convert, also become "citizens" within the Jewish *politeia*, according to their observance of the Mosaic Laws.

In this section, we shall study how such a paradigmatic function of Abraham applies to his biological descendants of the Jewish nation, who are identified and characterized by their ability to emulate the character and quality of their founder. With regard to the idea of Abraham as "the founder of the nation", we shall particularly explore exegetical motifs (marked in parenthesis below in **bold**) related to texts such as Gen 15:6, 22:16–18, and 26:3–5, which are accentuated, combined, and given a special prominence and shape in Philo's appropriation of Abraham. I begin with a survey of some distinctive exegetical motifs, before I offer in the next two chapters a more detailed study of selected pieces of interpretation, showing how Philo has accentuated and shaped certain exegetical traditions and motifs.

First, interpreting scriptures such as Gen 15:6[48] and Gen 26:5,[49] Abraham is characterized as the first who came to trust in God's promises **(Abraham as the Man of Trust)**, thus manifesting and obeying the unwritten divine Law in Nature that is attested in Abraham's sayings and deeds recorded in the Torah, as distinct from the special laws promulgated at Sinai (**Torah kept by Abraham**). Second, the status of being Abraham's ἔθνος depends on the ability to showcase the virtues and conduct of the founder (**Abraham's Descendants share the main Characteristics of Abraham**). Moreover, this patrilineal idea also bears on

48 Philo quotes or refers to Gen 15:6 in *Abr.* 262, 268, 273, 276; *Virt.* 216, 218; *Praem.* 27; *Leg.* 3:228; *Migr.* 43–44; *Her.* 90, 92, 95; *Mut.* 177, 186; *Deus* 4.

49 A quote or an allusion to Gen 26:5 appears in *Abr.* 275; *Migr.* 130; *Her.* 8; *QG* 4:184.

the interpretation of Gen 22:16–18[50] and Gen 26:3,[51] in which the promised blessings are expected to be conferred upon Abraham's descendants (**Abraham's Virtues and Blessings conferred upon his Descendants**).

Before I present Philo's appropriation of such exegetical motifs, some comments on his use of the Greek designation ἔθνος are in order. In the commentaries, the Allegorical Commentary and the Quaestiones, Philo expounds scripture for an internal audience, i. e. addressees well versed in Jewish traditions and customs.[52] In these two commentaries, there are no references to the Jewish nation, ἔθνος (the remark in *QG* 3:48 is the exception). Instead, Abraham is taken as the ancestor of a broader multi-ethnic category of Jews and non-Jews, called "Israel", a spiritual entity of those "who see God".[53] In his more apologetic works, however, such as the "Exposition of the Law" and the historical treatises, the designation "Israel" is exceptionally rare. The exceptions are found in *Abr.* 56, *Praem.* 44, and *Legat.* 7.[54] In the "Exposition of the Law", in which the addressees and readers are also "outsiders", more or less informed Jews and non-Jews, Philo associates Abraham with the other patriarchs by means of the distinctive designation "founders of the nation (ἀρχηγέται τοῦ ἔθνους)",[55] in which the term ἔθνος is understood exclusively as the Jewish nation.[56] Thus, in a key statement at the end of his biography on Abraham, the patriarch is characterized as follows: "Such was the life of the first, the founder of the nation (τοιοῦτος ὁ βίος τοῦ πρώτου καὶ ἀρχηγέτου τοῦ ἔθνους ἐστίν) [...]" (*Abr.* 276). From a similar passage later in the Exposition of the Law we can infer that Philo here refers to Abraham as the founder of the Jewish nation. Thus, in the opening of the treatise *De Decalogo*, Philo provides an analeptic statement and flashback to his earlier works on the lives of the patriarchs (probably both *De Abrahamo* and the lost

50 A quote or an allusion to Gen 22:16 appears in *Abr.* 273; *Leg.* 3:203, 204, 210; *QG* 4:180.
51 A quote or an allusion to Gen 26:3 is found in *Abr.* 273; *Migr.* 30; *QG* 4:180.
52 Cf. Runia, "Philo and the Gentiles," 36.
53 Cf. Birnbaum's seminal study of "Israel" in *The Place of Judaism*, 224. When Barclay (*Paul and the Gift*, 231 n. 40), most recently, criticizes Birnbaum's "disjuncture between the allegorical, universal 'Israel' and the literal, particular 'Jews' in a way that threatens to separate what Philo conjoins", he fails to take into account the fact that, for Philo, "Israel" appears to include non-Jews as well, such as Persian Magi and sages from Greek and foreign countries. In support of Birnbaum, cf. Runia, "Philo and the Gentiles," 40.
54 For a discussion of these texts, cf. Runia, "Philo and the Gentiles," 36–7.
55 Philo's use of the Greek term ἀρχηγέτης to denote the founder of an ἔθνος, seems to be a Philonic coinage of a term otherwise applied to the founder of a city or a family; cf. LSJ and Pearce, "Notes," 221.
56 Cf. the references to the "the nation of the Jews" in *Decal.* 97; *Spec.* 2:163, 166; 4:179, 224; *Virt.* 212, 226.

treatises on Isaac and Jacob) and characterizes them as "those whom the Sacred books reveal as founders of *our* nation (ἀρχηγέται τοῦ ἡμετέρου ἔθνους) and unwritten laws" (*Decal.* 1). At this point, the use of the possesive pronoun in the first person plural identifies Abraham explicitly as the founder of the Jewish nation of which Philo and his contemporary readers are citizens.[57] Similarly, in *Mos.* 1:7, Abraham is specified as "founder of the whole Jewish nation": "He [Moses] was seventh in descent from the first settler [i.e. Abraham], who became the founder of the whole Jewish nation."

I now turn to the first exegetical motif related to these statements about Abraham as the "founder of the Jewish nation", according to which Abraham is conceived from the perspective of his piety in terms of trust (**Abraham as the Man of Trust**).[58]

In *Virt.* 212, Philo asserts that Abraham was the oldest member of the Jewish nation: "The most ancient member of the Jewish nation (τοῦ τῶν Ἰουδαίων ἔθνους) was a Chaldaean of birth [...]." This text belongs to the exegetical context of *Virt.* 212–219, in which Philo accentuates the exegetical motif of Abraham as the standard of nobility and the first who came to trust in the one God:

> [...] he is the first person spoken of as believing in God (πιστεῦσαι λέγεται τῷ θεῷ πρῶτος), since he first grasped a firm and unswerving conception of the truth that there is one Cause above all, and that it provides for the world and all that there is therein. *Virt.* 216

> [...] he who believed nothing created rather than the uncreated and Father of all [...]. *Virt.* 218

Inspired by Gen 15:6 LXX, Philo portrays Abraham as the most ancient member of the Jews and the foundational model, who rejects his polytheistic surroundings and home and takes his starting point in the commitment to the One God. A parallel to such an exposition of Gen 15:6 about Abraham as the first person who abandoned the false creeds of his surroundings and put his trust in the truth of the one God, is also provided by Philo in *Her.* 90–94. Here, Philo makes use of the same exegetical motif when he describes Abraham, who, in the face of adversity from the delusional surroundings, never ceased to trust in God. Thus, in a conversation with an imaginary interlocutor, Philo gives an exegetical paraphrase of Gen 15:6 (the paraphrastic rendering is underlined) in the *Her.* 90 and 92–94 as follows:

> The words "Abraham believed God" (Gen. xv. 6) are a necessary addition to speak the praise due to <u>him</u> who has <u>believed</u> (*Her.* 90). [...] you will clearly understand that <u>to</u>

57 Cf. Borgen, *An Exegete for His Time*, 222; Runia, "Philo and the Gentiles," 37.
58 J.L. Kugel, *Traditions of the Bible*, 310–1.

trust in God alone and join no other with Him is no easy matter, by reason of our kinship with our yokefellow, mortality, which works upon us to keep our trust placed in riches and repute and office and friends and health and strength and many other things. To purge away each of these, to distrust created being, which in itself is wholly unworthy of trust, to trust in God, and in Him alone, even as He alone is truly worthy of trust—this is a task for a great and celestial understanding which has ceased to be ensnared by aught of the things that surround us." And it is well said "his faith was counted to him for justice" (Gen. xv. 6), for nothing is so just or righteous as to put in God alone a trust which is pure and unalloyed (*Her.* 92–94).

In *Abr.* 275–276, Philo combines two more exegetical motifs, viz. Abraham's trust in God's promise and adherence to the divine Law:

> He did them, not taught by written words, but unwritten nature gave him the zeal to follow where wholesome and untainted impulse led him. And when God gives his endorsement concerning these, what does it befit men to do other than to grant their firmest trust? Such was the life of the first, the founder of the nation, one who obeyed the law, some will say, but rather, as our discourse has shown, himself a law and an unwritten statute.[59]

As we shall see in more detail in the next chapter, commenting on scriptures such as Gen 15:5–8 and Gen 26:5, Philo's line of thought seems to be that the unwritten divine Law manifests itself and is achieved through Abraham's trust in God's promise, not by his putative adherence to the written Law of Moses. Accordingly, the imaginary interlocutors referred to in this citation seemed to have maintained the position that Abraham was a pre-Sinaitic observer of the laws of Moses. Philo himself, however, needs obviously to modify such a position, and claims that this could not have been the case, since they had not yet been set in writing (cf. *Abr.* 5 and 275). Thus, *Decal.* 1 together with *Abr.* 275 might be taken to testify to the following claim made by S. Pearce on the basis of these texts:

> Thus, the characterization of the Patriarchs as "founders of the nation" is given special prominence in a key statement in which Philo sums up the significance of their lives as embodying the observance of the divine law, before it was revealed in written form through Moses.[60]

Pearce, however, does not take sufficiently into account the way in which Philo gives prominence to Abraham's trust in the promise as a manifestation of the unwritten divine Law of the Torah distinct from the written Mosaic Law that was promulgated later. As we shall see in the following chapter, Philo, then, inter-

---

59 The Loeb translation slightly modified.
60 Pearce, "Notes," 221.

prets and gives his own twist to the exegetical motif of Abraham as a "legal" figure (**Torah kept by Abraham**).[61] Thus, by trust in God's promise Abraham manifested the divine Law in Nature, and, as such, embodied the distinct divine Law enshrined in the first book (Genesis) of the sacred Torah of Moses. Moreover, Philo, therefore, also accentuates Abraham's trust in the promise as a paradigm for all human beings to emulate, manifesting the genuine identifying mark of the Jewish nation in terms of the observance of the unwritten Law before the revelation of the written Law at Sinai. I now proceed to the second exegetical motif related to the idea of Abraham as the founder of the Jewish nation, viz. that the genuine nation which has its origin in descent from the founder Abraham might be claimed by those who resemble the conduct and characteristics of Abraham (**Abraham's Kin defined by being genuine Abrahamites**).

In the treatise *De Virtutibus*, Philo proves the thesis that real "nobility" is not based on genetical disposition alone, but on virtue, for example, by adducing in *Virt.* 207–209 the examples of Esau and the half–brothers of Isaac:[62]

> The first was the father of many children, begotten of three wives, not for indulgence in pleasure but in the hope of multiplying the race. But of his many sons, only one was appointed to inherit the patrimony. All the rest failed to show sound judgement and as they reproduced nothing of their father's qualities, were excluded from the home and denied any part in the grandeur of their noble birth. Again, the one who was approved as heir begat two twins, who had no resemblance to each other, either in body or disposition [except in the hands, and in these only for a particular act of policy]. For the younger was obedient to both his parents and won such favour that God, too, joined in praising him, but the elder was disobedient, indulging without restraint in the pleasure of the belly and the lower lying parts. Influenced by these he surrendered his birth-right to his junior, then, at once, repenting of the surrender, sought his brother's life, and all his concern was to act in such a way as would cause grief to his parents. Therefore, for the younger they prayed that he should be blessed above all others, all which prayers God confirmed and would not that any of them should be left unfulfilled. But to the elder in compassion they granted an inferior station to serve his brother [...]

He builds here on the notion in the ancient world that the genuine brother Esau and the half–brothers of Isaac were excluded from the family and house of Abraham because they did not live up to the moral quality of their noble birth. We find a similar argument in *Praem.* 57–60:

---

61 For this exegetical motif, cf. Kugel, *Traditions of the Bible*, 705–9.

62 Philo first adduces in *Virt.* 198–210 a number of negative examples from Scripture: Cain, Ham, Adam, the sons of Abraham (apart from Isaac), and Esau. Then, in *Virt.* 211–227, Philo refers to examples of virtue without noble descent: Abraham, Tamar, and the two concubines of Jacob. Cf. Bekken, *The Word is Near You*, 208–9; Barclay, *Paul and the Gift*, 236.

> For instance the twelve tribes into which the nation was divided had the same number of chieftains connected not only by membership of the same house and family but by a still more real affinity, for they were brothers with the same father, and their grandfather and great-grandfather as well as their father were the founders of the nation. [...] [Abraham] had many children, but all faulty save one to whom he bound fast the cables of the race and there found a safe haven. That son again endued with a nature which learned from no other teacher than itself had two sons. One was wild and indocile, brimful of fierce temper and lust, who to sum him up armed the unreasoning part of the soul to war against the rational. The other was gentle and kindly, a lover of noble conduct, of equality and simplicity, a soldier of the better cause, the champion of reason and antagonist of folly. This is the third of the founders, father of many children and alone among the three blessed in them all, who met with no mishap in any part of his household, like a happy husbandman who sees his whole crop safe and sound, thriving under his hand and bearing fruit.

Praem. 57 describes the division of the Jewish nation into twelve tribes, each founded by a descendant of Jacob, Isaac and Abraham, as the founders of the people. In the following paragraphs, *Praem.* 58–61, Philo goes on to explain that the true descent from Abraham was transmitted through the one lineage of Abraham–Isaac–Jacob, until Jacob's sons became the founders of the twelve tribes of the nation. Abraham's and Isaac's other sons were considered unfit to carry the lineage. The underlying idea is that the virtues and character of the founding ancestor are passed down through the one genuine son in each generation who exhibits these traits and can be appointed to inherit the patrimony. Thus, Philo can say about Abraham that "he was the father of many children but did not deem any of them worthy (ἀξιόω) to be called his sons save one" (*Praem.* 61). Again, the idea is that physical descent must be complemented by qualities of moral character resembling the origin.

The foundational role of Abraham in defining the Jewish nation on the basis of a spritual kinship over against the natural blood-line is also suggested in *Virt.* 79. Here, Philo interprets Deut 33:6–25 and the blessings of Moses on "all the tribes of the nation (τὰς τοῦ ἔθνους φυλάς)." At this point, Philo states that Moses perceived that "the whole nation (τὸ σύμπαν ἔθνος) had from the very beginning (ἐξ ἀρχῆς) a kinship (συγγένεια) to the divine, a most essential relationship and far more genuine than the ties of blood (πολὺ γνησιωτέραν τῆς ἀφ' αἵματος)."[63] This text may suggest that the blessings Moses confers on the Jewish nation have their origin in the piety of Abraham, an exegetical motif to which we now turn.

63 Cf. Pearce, "Notes," 225 n. 69.

5 Abraham's Virtue and Promised Blessings Conferred on the Jewish "Ethnos"

Frank M. Cross has explained how the language of covenant, "kinship-in-law", is taken from the language of kinship, "kinship-in-flesh". Such language of kinship in ancient Near Eastern cultures could also be applied to outsiders, non-kin, who might be incorporated into the kinship group through various legal means such as marriage, adoption, or the ritual of oath and covenant. Thus, for example, the oath established formally the means by which the covenant was extended to others. Cross writes: "Oath and covenant, in which the deity is witness, guarantor, or participant, is also a legal means by which the duties and privileges of kinship may be extended to another individual or group, including aliens."[64] Philo's writings may illustrate the oath as a legitimate means of such a patrilineal ideology of kinship-in-Law. According to Philo, God's oath of promise concerning blessings to Abraham's descendants was dependent on the criterion of being found worthy of Abraham's nobility and virtue, which thus demonstrated the kinship and bond between the ancestor and his descendants. In an exposition of the promise reiterated to Isaac according to Gen 26:3, referring explicitly back to the oath of promise spoken to Abraham in Gen 22:16–18, Philo emphasizes the requirement of reproducing Abraham's qualities in order to safeguard the promised blessings on the part of the descendants:

> [...] He wishes to praise the son as one worthy (ἄξιος) of his father's nobility, for He would not firmly establish the blessings (εὐλογίαι) made to the father with an oath, for the sake of the son, if He did not witness the same virtue in him. [...] For (this passage) clearly teaches us to define and judge and discern the well-born (as being) not those who have sprung from good fathers or grandparents and are content with that alone, but those who are themselves emulators of their (fathers') piety (*QG* 4:180).[65]

Accordingly, the legitimate descendants of Abraham were identified and characterized by their ability to emulate the character and kind of Abraham's life as a foundational model. Thus, on the ground of Abraham's conduct as the identifying mark of the patriarch's genuine descendants, God's promised blessings and providence were expected to be conferred upon Abraham's descendants.

---

64 Cross, *From Epic to Canon*, 8.

65 The Greek words are inserted according to the fragments of Greek text printed in Wendland, 84.

The exegetical motif in *QG* 4:180 (**Abraham's Blessings conferred upon his true Descendants**),[66] derived from passages as Gen 22:16–18 and 26:3–4, presupposes a direct relationship between the virtue of piety and conduct of Abraham living on in the descendants, and God's blessings that are expected to be received by the succeeding generations of the ancestor.

Spec. 4:179–182 and *Praem.* 166–167 are other instances in which this motif of the merits of the founders of the Jewish nation dependent on the qualities of the descendants is elaborated. In the context of the former text, Philo expounds Deut 10:18 (God "does justice for the orphan"), and conceives of "the whole Jewish race (ἔθνος)" as being in the position of an orphan, as compared with all the other nations. On account of its living under exceptional laws, the Jewish nation "is always an object of the pity and compassion of the Ruler of the Universe" (*Spec.* 4:179). According to Philo's reasoning it is because

> it has been set apart out of the whole human race as a kind of first fruits to the Maker and Father. And the cause of this was the precious signs of righteousness and virtue shown by the founders of the race, signs which survive like imperishable plants, bearing fruit that never decays for their descendants, fruit salutary and profitable in every way, even though these descendants themselves be sinners, so long as the sins be curable and not altogether unto death. Yet let no one think that good lineage is a perfect blessing and then neglect noble actions, but reflect that greater anger is due to one who while his parentage is of the best brings shame upon his parents by the wickedness of his ways. Guilty is he who, having for his own models of true excellence to copy, reproduces nothing that serves to direct his life aright and keep it sound and healthy. *Spec.* 4:180–182

Likewise, in the context of *Praem.* 162–172, we meet again the idea that physical descent must be complemented by qualities of moral character resembling the origin. Thus, the potential loss of the promised blessing to the future generations of the Abrahamic peoplehood shows that not all the sons of one father partake in his spiritual nobility and heritage. Philo's section on the restoration of the Jewish nation in *Praem.* 162–172 seems to belong to the category of "Jewish restoration eschatology".[67] It is essential for the understanding of Philo's "escha-

---

66 For this exegetical motif in post-biblical Judaism, see, e.g., A. Marmorstein, *The Doctrine of Merits in Old Rabbinical Literature* (1920; repr., New York: KTAV Publishing House, 1968); S. Spiegel, *The Last Trial: On the Legends and Lore of the Command to Abraham to Offer Isaac as a Sacrifice: The Akedah* (New York: Pantheon Books, 1967); E.P. Sanders, *Paul and Palestinian Judaism: A Comparison of Patterns of Religion* (Philadelphia: Fortress, 1977), 183–98; N.A. Dahl, "The Atonement," 137–51, esp. 141–2.

67 *Praem.* 162–172 is one of several Jewish texts dealing with this theme of restoration, such as Dan 12:1–4; 1 En. 38:4–6; 46:4; 53:2–7; 90: 28–36; 91,12ff.; Jub. 23; 4 Ezra 11:45; 12:31–33; 13:49; 2 Bar. 51:5; 85:4; Apoc. Ab. 31; T. Levi 2:10. While this theme is a commonplace in such Palestinian

tology" to realise that he relates it to his concept of a God–given cosmic law which is made manifest in the laws of Moses. Thus, his "eschatology" is conditional upon human obedience or disobedience to these laws according to the "eschatological" alternatives of blessings and curses based on Leviticus 26 and Deuteronomy 28–30.[68] If those who have strayed away from the ancestral teaching reproach themselves for going astray by confessing their sin, they will find favour with God (*Praem.* 162–165).[69] According to Philo, three factors make "the reconciliation with the Father" (i.e., God) possible:

> Three intercessors they have to plead for their reconciliation with the Father. One is the clemency and kindness of Him to whom they appeal, who ever prefers forgiveness to punishment. The second is the holiness of the founders of the race because with souls released from their bodies they show forth in that naked simplicity their devotion to their Ruler and cease not to make supplications for their sons and daughters, supplications not made in vain, because the Father grants to them the privilege that their prayers should be heard. The third is one which more than anything else moves the loving kindness of the other two to come forward so readily, and that is the reformation working in those who are being brought to make a covenant of peace, those who after much toil have been able to pass from the pathless wild to the road which has no other goal but to find favour with God, as sons may with their father. *Praem.* 166–67

At this juncture, the motif of the patriarchs' "holiness" and its "reward", effecting the reconcilation between God and the "penitents" of the nation, seems to be based on Lev 26:42, in the context of blessings and curses: "And I will remember the covenant of Jacob [...] of Isaac [...] and of Abraham." Hence, the scriptural line of thought behind Philo's reasoning seems to be the dynamic interaction between the Mosaic covenant and the antecedent Abrahamic one, which means that when the former is broken when the Israelites fall into disobedience and incur the curses, whereas the latter covenant remains in effect and offers a reservoir of salvation or restoration to the errant people.[70] Against the background of

---

Jewish apocalypses, it is not limited to these writings as, for example, Sirach 35 and 1QM 13–14 attest. Cf. L. Hartman, *Prophecy Interpreted: The Formation of Some Jewish Apocalyptic Texts and of the Eschatological Discourse Mark 13 Par.*, ConBNT (Lund: Gleerup, 1966), 23–50; J.J. Collins, "Apocalyptic Eschatology in Philosophical Dress in the Wisdom of Solomon," in *Shem in the Tents of Japhet: Essays on the Encounter of Judaism and Hellenism*, ed. J.L. Kugel, JSJSup (Leiden; Boston; Köln: Brill, 2002), 93–108; Bekken, *The Word is Near You*, 217–8.

68 See e.g., Borgen, *An Exegete for His Time*, 261–81.

69 Here, Philo comments that the curses which have befallen them (cf. Deut 28:15–68) serve as a disciplinary warning; they are not intended to destroy them. Cf. 2 Macc 6:12; Wis 3:5; 12:22; Pss. Sol. 13:6–10; 18:4.

70 For a survey of the biblical basis for this line of thought, cf. Levenson, *Inheriting Abraham*, 55–8.

QG 4:180 cited above, it is also possible that Philo has derived this motif of the merits of the patriarchs from other Torah texts too. In addition to texts such as Gen 22:16–18 and 26:3–4, the concept of the merits of the Patriarchs is perhaps derived from such texts as Gen 12:3 (*Migr.* 122), and Exod 32:13 (*Mos.* 2:166).[71] At this point, it seems that Philo belongs to early Jewish traditions which interpret the "salvation" of the Jews as an adequate "reward", not because of their own deeds, but because of the piety of their ancestors. This tradition and trajectory can be traced back to the oath of promise given to Abraham's and Isaac's descendants.[72]

As we shall see in the final chapter of this study, such Scriptures and the exegetical motif of the merits of Abraham conferred upon his true descendants might have some bearing on Paul's texts as well, in terms of a Pauline exegetical twist, so that Paul holds that "those of faith", i. e., those descended from Abraham who have acquired the same trust as Abraham, are blessed together with the faithful Abraham. In the next chapter, I shall study in more detail the passage in *Abr.* 262–273 on how Philo conceives the oath of promise in Gen 22:15–18 as a culmination and continuation of the line of thought already displayed in Gen 15:6, so that the promised blessings that ensued upon Abraham's faithfulness are reaffirmed through the oath of promise spoken to Abraham post-*Akedah*.

6 Conclusions

1. This chapter suggests that Philo's portrayal of Abraham as the paradigmatic model, regarded as the first proselyte and, as such, as the founder of the Jewish nation, was determinative of his conception of Jewish ethnic identity and of what he considered essential for being an Abrahamic descendant and for becoming a proselyte. I have argued that Philo's basic notion of Jewish ethnicity takes as its point of departure an ethnic differentiation between the Jewish *ethnos* and other peoples. On the one hand, the ethnic differenence and distance that exist because of ethnic origins and lineage mean that Philo does not make an ethnic blending of a born Jew and a convert. This is why he never says that proselytes get a new lineage as Abraham's descendants or become members of the Jewish *ethnos*. Hence, a special provision is made for proselytes who choose to live ac-

71 See, for this suggestion, Pearce, "Notes," 223 n. 63.

72 For a recent study of this Jewish tradition, see M. Himmelfarb, *A Kingdom of Priests: Ancestry and Merit in Ancient Judaism* (Philadelphia: University of Pennsylvania Press, 2006), 160–85.

cording to these core values embodied in the life of Abraham as the founder of the Jewish proselyte nation. This means that the family bonds between Jews and proselytes in terms of kinship are envisaged as going beyond physical lineage. On the other hand, Philo's reservation vis-à-vis nationality and boundaries constrained to physical lineage also pertains to the fact that there were apostates within the Jewish nation, who had deviated from the spiritual kinship embodied in the laws of Moses.

2. As a corollary of such an ethnic differentiation, Philo can instead speak about the new spiritual kinship and fellowship ties that the proselytes obtain within the Jewish *politeia*. Thus, the proselytes receive a Jewish identity in terms of character traits they share with Abraham as their model convert, such as receiving the Spirit and transformation as persons, when they have come to believe in the one God. Although Philo applies the concept of adoption to the status of Abraham and Hagar regarded as proselytes, it is significant that he never speaks about the converts in terms of ethnic language such as Abraham's descendants or *ethnos*. Since Philo is sensitive to the issue of the converts' non-Abrahamic lineage, he emphasizes instead that the proselytes obtain family bonds, fellowship, and citizenship with Jews within the Jewish *politeia*.

3. In an exposition of Gen 26:3, referring explicitly back to the oath of promise spoken to Abraham in Gen 22:16–18, Philo emphasizes the requirement of reproducing Abraham's virtue in order to safeguard the blessings promised to Isaac's descendants. The interpretation of these passages presupposes a direct relationship between the piety and conduct of Abraham living on in the descendants and God's blessings that are expected to be received by the succeeding generations of the ancestor. The scriptural line of thought behind Philo's reasoning seems to be the dynamic interaction between God's promise and the Law of Moses, which means that when the latter is broken, the former remains in effect and offers a reservoir of blessings to the errant people.

Chapter 3: Abraham's Trust and God's Oath of Promise: *De Abrahamo* 262 – 273 in Context

1 Thesis

My aim in this chapter is to highlight aspects of the conjunction of Genesis 15:6 and 22:16 – 18 in Philo's treatise *De Abrahamo* 262 – 273. We must investigate the extent to which Philo's version may coincide with, or diverge from, the Jewish scriptures themselves, and in the light of other Jewish and Christian texts that appropriate the same texts. The thesis I shall argue in this chapter is as follows: Philo may illustrate a common thought pattern attested in many variants of the *Akedah* traditions, which was summarized by S. Spiegel as follows: "It may be surmised that all these variations originally had one feature in common: a parallelism between Abraham's conduct at the Akedah and the conduct expected in return from God."[1] Scholars have failed to notice, however, that Philo provides evidence of such a correspondence.[2] Thus, Philo interprets Gen 15:6 in the light of Gen 22:16 – 18 and vice versa from the perspective of a correspondence between Abraham's conduct of trust in God and the reward of trust / faithfulness granted to Abraham in return in terms of an oath that He will keep the initial promise of gifts. This parallelism conforms to data in Jewish haggadah, as Spiegel's study has demonstrated.

The chapter proceeds as follows: Before I analyse the Philonic text in the light of the appropriation of Genesis 15:6 and 22:16 – 18 in other Jewish and Christian texts, I shall survey the relationship between these texts within the Abrahamic cycle in Genesis itself. At this point, I shall include Gen 26:3 – 5, which will be drawn upon in my next chapter. At the end of this chapter, I will present a chart of the constituents of the exegetical motifs and the terminology involved in this exegetical trajectory, which in turn will provide background data for my analysis

1 Spiegel, *The Last Trial*, 93.

2 For Philo's elaborations on the event of the *Akedah* in his treatise *De Abrahamo*, cf. L.H. Feldman, "Philo's Version of the Akedah," SPhiloA (2002): 66 – 86; L.A. Huizenga, *The New Isaac: Tradition and Intertextuality in the Gospel of Matthew*, NovTSup (Leiden: Brill, 2009), 102 – 4. Both authors neglect, however, to comment on *Abr.* 273, which belongs to the final part of the treatise (§§ 262 – 276) about Philo's praise of Abraham's trust and his right to the title of "Elder". The recent commentay by Birnbaum and Dillon (*On the Life of Abraham*, 409), however, observes the reciprocity of trust between Abraham and God, but unfortunately neglects to compare this parallellism with other Jewish data.

https://doi.org/10.1515/9783110722109-004

in my next chapeter as well as the Pauline text. Finally, I will draw together and summarize the observations so far.

2 The Abrahamic Promises in Genesis 12–26: A Survey

It is in order to begin my investigation with some brief comments on the relevant texts Genesis 15:6, 22:16–18, and 26:3–5 themselves, in their own literary context within the Abrahamic narrative in Genesis. It is commonly accepted among scholars that the promissory elements of blessing stated in Gen 12:1–3 are to some extent taken up and expanded in the succeeding covenantal promises reiterated throughout the Abraham cycle in Gen 12–26.[3] As Westermann puts it:

> It is generally agreed that the texts containing the promises cannot be interpreted solely on the basis of their present contexts; they have an extended context also in the group of identical or similar promises in Genesis 12–50 and also beyond Genesis.[4]

Genesis 12 sets out to specify the blessings promised to Abraham, consisting of four elements: (1) great nationhood, including land and descendants; (2) blessing of Abraham; (3) great name; (4) blessing to all peoples.[5] These motifs can be seen as partly reiterated, expanded, and commented on in Genesis 15, 22, and 26.[6] I begin by presenting the relevant passages, with the allusions to the blessings from Gen 12:1–3 onwards marked in bold type, with references to other relevant scriptures placed in parenthesis.

---

3 Cf. C. Westermann, *The Promises to the Fathers: Studies on the Patriarchal Narratives* (Philadelphia: Fortress Press, 1980), 119; R.W.L. Moberly, "The Earliest Commentary on the Akedah," *VT* 38.3 (1988): 311.

4 Westermann, *The Promises to the Fathers*, 119.

5 For a recent interpretation of Gen 12:1–3, see J.S. Baden, *The Promise to the Patriarchs* (Oxford: OUP, 2013), 8–13.

6 Although Genesis 26 conveys the Isaac tradition and thus is not part of the Abraham cycle in Genesis 12–25, the promises to Isaac in Gen 26:3–5 expand on the earlier promises to Abraham. Cf. K.N. Grüneberg, *Abraham, Blessing and the Nations: A Philological and Exegetical Study of Gen 12:3 in its Narrative Context*, BZAW (Berlin; New York: De Gruyter, 2003), 235; C. Levin, "Die Väterverheissungen: Eine Bestandaufnahme," in *The Post-Priestly Pentateuch: New Perspectives on its Redactional Development and Theological Profiles*, ed. F. Giuntoli and K. Schmid, FAT (Tübingen: Mohr Siebeck, 2015), 135–36; R.G. Kratz, "Die Verheissungen an die Erzväter: Die Konstruktion ethnischer Identität Israels," in *The Politics of the Ancestors: Exegetical and Historical Perspectives on Genesis 12–36*, ed. M.G. Brett and J. Wöhrle, FAT (Tübingen: Mohr Siebeck, 2018), 41.

Gen 12:1 – 3:

Now the LORD said to Abram, "Go from your country and your kindred and your father's house to the land that I will show you. I will make of you **a great nation** (1), and I will **bless you** (2), and make **your name great** (3), so that you will **be a blessing.** I will bless those who bless you, and the one who curses you I will curse; and **in you all the families of the earth shall be blessed** (4).

Gen 15:5 – 8:

He brought him outside and said, "Look toward heaven and count the stars, if you are able to count them." Then he said to him, "**So shall your descendants be** (1)." And he believed the LORD; and the LORD reckoned it to him as righteousness. Then he said to him, "I am the LORD who brought you from Ur of the Chaldeans, to **give you this land** (1; Gen 12:7) to possess. And I will give to you, and to your offspring after you, the land where you are now an alien, all the land of Canaan, for a perpetual holding; and I will be their God."

Gen 22:15 – 18:

The angel of the LORD called to Abraham a second time from heaven, and said, "By myself I have sworn, says the LORD: Because you have done this, and have not withheld your son, your only son, I will indeed **bless you** (2; Gen 12:2), and I will **make your offspring as numerous as the stars of heaven** (1; cf. Gen 15:5) **and as the sand that is on the seashore** (1; cf. Gen 32:13). **And your offspring shall possess the gate of their enemies** (3; cf. Gen 24:60), and **by your offspring shall all the nations of the earth gain blessing for themselves** (4; cf. Gen 18:18), because you have obeyed my voice."

Gen 26:3 – 5:

Reside in this land as an alien, and I will be with you, and **will bless you** (2); for to you and to your descendants **I will give all these lands** (1; Gen 13:5), and I will fulfill the oath that I swore to your father Abraham (cf. Gen 22:16). I will make your offspring as **numerous as the stars of heaven** (1; Gen 22:17), and will give to your offspring all these lands (1; Gen 13:15); and **all the nations of the earth shall gain blessing for themselves** (4; Gen 22:18), because Abraham obeyed my voice (cf. Gen 22:18) and kept my charge, my commandments, my statutes, and my laws.

In what follows, the relationship between the last three texts and the main promissory motifs in Gen 12:1 – 3 shall be briefly commented on and highlighted in the light of recent scholarship. In Gen 15:5 – 8, it is only the promise to become *a great nation* (1) that is taken up from Genesis 12. Its context presents a dialogue between Yahweh and Abraham. Gen 15:1 opens with Yahweh's assurance and promise, to which Abraham responds by seeking further assurance (Gen 15:2 – 3). Yahweh's response is given in the form of the promise of nationhood, with two conditions for its materialization, i.e. the twofold reassurance that Abraham's own child will be his heir and that his descendants will be numerous as stars (15:4–5), on which the promise of land depends (15:7).[7] Abraham's conduct of trust (15:6), which is emphasized in this covenant text, is counted as a response to Yahweh's twofold promise of descendants. Yahweh's reassurance of the promise to Abraham of numerous offsprings overcomes the problem that Abraham, at the moment, is childless (15:4–5). Abraham's responsiveness to the divine oracle, that he "trusted Yahweh", is then related to Yahweh's unconditional reassurance of his promise. Thus, we can observe a parallelism between Yahweh's and Abraham's conduct of responsiveness; it was because of Yahweh's reaffirmation of the promises *and* Abraham's faithful response that Yahweh reckoned this to him as righteousness, that is, as the conduct that brought lasting blessing, so that Israel entered into the promised land and into the covenant with Yahweh. Besides this, the perfect verb of "to have trust in" (וְהֶאֱמִן), with a *waw* consecutive, implies "constant continuance in a past state"[8] and seems to emphasize the continuous and regular occurrence of Abraham's trust. As Moberly puts it:

> The most natural meaning of this is that Abraham's faith in Yahweh was his constant response, and therefore the reference in Gen xv 6 constitutes one particular example which represents and summarizes a regular occurrence.[9]

Thus, the point would appear to be that Abraham's trust in God's promise in Gen 15:6 is an illustration of the consistent responsiveness to God that characterised his whole life, which can be evinced already in Gen 12:1–4. Again, this response on Abraham's part "is notable particularly because of God's response in the covenant that follows (Gen 15:7–21), a covenant that becomes the basis for God's relationship with Abraham's descendants."[10] As I will note later, this feature of a link between Yahweh's reassurance of the promise and Abraham's responsiveness which brought lasting blessing in Genesis 15 points forward to Genesis 22 and the analogy of Abraham's response to Yahweh and Yahweh's reaffirmation of the promise of blessings by means of an oath of promise in Genesis 22. We should also notice that the other blessings of Genesis 12 that are left out in Genesis 15 are to be taken up later in Genesis 17. Thus, when Gen 17:6–8 re-

7 Cf., e.g., P.R. Williamson, *Abraham, Israel and the Nations*, JSOTSup (Sheffield: Sheffield Academic Press, 2000), 99; Levin, "Die Väterverheissungen," 130; Kratz, "Die Verheissungen an die Erzväter," 58–62.

8 *GKC* § 112.

9 R.W.L. Moberly, "Abraham's Righteousness (Genesis XV 6)," in *Studies in the Pentateuch*, ed. J.A. Emerton, VTSup (Leiden: Brill, 1990), 105.

10 R.W.L. Moberly, "אמן," in *NIDOTTE*, ed. W.A. Van Gemeren (Carlisle: Paternoster Press, 1996), 432.

iterates the promises of nationhood, i.e. of land and offsprings, the emphasis is on the expansion of the promise of a "great name" from Gen 12:2.[11] Genesis 17 differs from Genesis 15 in respect of its emphasis on these features: the promise of multinational significance, royal offsprings, and divine-human obligations, i.e. circumcision and moral blamelessness. I now proceed to some observations on Gen 22:15 – 18 in its own right in the context of the Abraham cycle.

Within the Abrahamic narrative, Gen 22:15 – 18 delineates the words spoken between God and Abraham as the final words of any sort between them, and thus seems to form an *inclusio* to the communication initiated in Gen 12:1 – 3.[12] Regardless of whether Gen 22:15 – 18 is secondary or functions as a commentary on the preceding vv. 1 – 14, the passage is integral to the narrative as a whole and constitutes the climax of the story of the Akedah. In the following examination of the Gen 22:15 – 18, we shall note the structural features of the reiterated promises, preceding Abraham's obedience, as the ground for the divine reaffirmation of the initial promise of blessings given by the divine oath.

The view that Gen 22:15 – 18 forms an *inclusio* to Gen 12:1 – 3 is also corroborated by the fact that the former is not only the last words in the communication between Yahweh and Abraham in the Abraham cycle, "for nowhere in xxii 20-xxv 11 does either Yahweh speak to Abraham or Abraham speak to Yahweh." Moreover, the *inclusio* is also supported by the fact that Gen 22:15 – 18 is the last promissory text that reiterates all four of the promises of Gen 12:1 – 3. In comparison with the covenant-making episodes in Genesis 15 and 17, two features stand out: First, the promise of 12:3c, "in you all the families of the earth shall be blessed," which has not been referred to in either of the covenant texts in Genesis 15 and 17, and is thus expanded in a slightly different version: "[...] by your offspring shall all the nations of the earth gain blessing for themselves" (Gen 22:18). Second, while neither Genesis 15 nor 17 speaks of a divine "blessing" for Abraham himself, Gen 22:17 takes up this promise from Gen 12:2a: "I will indeed bless you". Since this blessing is described furthermore as having an offspring, we should regard the promise as an all-encompassing phrase, which includes those aspects of the blessings which relate to his posterity. As Grüneberg suggests: "For we must not forget that the promises relating to the descendants

11 Several elements confirm this: 1. The occurrence of the terminology of a "great name" in Gen 17:5; 2. the changing of the names of Abraham and Sarah; 3. the promise of royalty (17:6, cf. also v. 16) connected to the element of a "great name" from Gen 12:2c; 4. the promise of multinational "suzerainty" and fatherhood of Abraham. Cf. Williamson, *Abraham*, 186 – 7; Kratz, "Die Verheissungen an die Erzväter," 54 – 8.

12 Cf. Moberly, "The Earliest Commentary on the Akedah," 322; Grüneberg, *A Philogical and Exegetical Study of Gen 12:3*, 222; Levin, "Die Väterverheissungen," 133.

all stand under the heading of blessing to Abraham. They are not so much boons for the offspring as for Abraham himself in his offspring."[13]

The promise taken up from Gen 15:5 with the simile of "stars of heaven", and which in Gen 22:17 is juxtaposed with the figure of "sand on the seashore", highlights the almost unimaginable number of Abraham's descendants. The unique juxtaposition of these similes in Gen 22:17 emphasizes the promise of a "great nationhood" in Gen 12:2a. Moreover, the final promise in v.17, "and your offspring shall possess the gate of their enemies", is the sole element which is not paralleled in the other divine promises to Abraham. It might, however, be related to the promissory tropes of kingship and multinational suzerainty expressed in Genesis 17, since this promise might be seen to anticipate the military victory over against the surrounding nations under David and Solomon as described in 2 Sam 8:1–14; 10:1–19; 12:23–31; and in 1 Kings 4:20–21 (cf. the juxtaposition of the motif of the sovereignty of Solomon over the kingdoms with the simile that Judah and Israel were "numerous as the sand by the sea").[14]

According to Gen 22:16–18, the promise of blessings is reaffirmed because of Abraham's obedience (cf. "*because* you have done this", v.16, and "*because* you have obeyed my voice", v. 18). These causal clauses have been interpreted to mean that the promise of blessing ensued upon Abraham's obedience was meritorious as a new factor.[15] In contrast, other scholars have emphasized that God's will to bless was not contingent on Abraham's conduct, since it was a reaffirmation of a promise that was already an established fact, but rather grounded in God's faithful responsiveness to Abraham. Thus, the word יען, which one usually translates as "because", is not to be taken in a meritorious sense, but more as an expression of the unity and correspondence that is established between Abraham's conduct of obedient trust in God's promise and the conduct expcted in return from God, that is, God's trustworthiness to carry out what he has promised by an oath.[16] A similar understanding seems to be presupposed by Moberly, when he urges:

> Abraham by his obedience has not qualified to be the recipient of blessing, because the promise of blessing had been given to him already. Rather, the existing promise is reaf-

13 Grüneberg, *A Philogical and Exegetical Study of Gen 12:3*, 229–30.

14 For a discussion of Gen 22:17 in terms of a series of military conquests, cf. Williamson, *Abraham*, 248–50.

15 Thus, e.g., C. Westermann, *Genesis 12–36*, BK (Neukirchen-Vluyn: Neukirchener Verlag, 1981), 445–6.

16 Similarly, the Norwegian Old Testament scholar I.P. Seierstad, *Budskapet: Et utvalg av gammeltestamentlige artikler* (Oslo: Universitetsforlaget, 1971), 100, referring to M. Noth, *Gesammelte Studien Zum Alten Testament* (München: C. Kaiser, 1957), 155.

> firmed but its terms of reference are altered. A promise which previously was grounded solely in the will and purpose of Yahweh is transformed so that it is now grounded *both* in the will of Yahweh *and* in the obedience of Abraham. It is not that the divine promise has become contingent upon Abraham's obedience, but that Abraham's obedience has been incorporated into the divine promise. Hence Israel owes its existence not just to Yahweh but also to Abraham.[17]

Levenson interprets Gen 22:15 – 18 in the same vein as Moberly, and puts it as follows:

> [...] God's amazing promise came as a kind of bolt out of the blue; there was nothing Abram (as he then was called) had done to merit it. [...] What Gen 22:15 – 18 does is to reinterpret those old promises of blessing, descendants and land so that they, though gracious, are no longer arbitrary; they have now become consequences of the Akedah. [...] And no longer is God's election of Abraham a matter of grace alone, which is to say, an act of sheer arbitrariness. For now Abraham has vindicated God's faith in him. In the end, Abraham has proven worthy of the promises God graciously extended to him in the beginning. It is "because you have done this" that God takes a solemn oath—his first in the entire Bible—to fulfill his outstanding promises to Abraham.[18]

Two more comments should be offered: On the one hand, it should be emphasized that in Gen 22:16–18 too, Abraham's trusting behaviour is still contingent upon the divine promises, and not the other way around.[19] Again, as I pointed out above, Abraham's trusting response has characterized his life as grounded in Yahweh's purpose and promises; this is evident in such passages as Gen 12:1 – 4, 13:14 – 17, and 15:4 – 5. On the other hand, as Moberly has also pointed out, there is a striking similarity between Gen 15:6 and 22:15 – 18 with regard to the value of Abraham's trust in the divine promises in order to anchor Israel's existence in both Yahweh's will and Abraham's action of trustful obedience. In addition to the divine approval of Abraham's conduct as an established fact, both texts assert that divine affirmative responsiveness to Abraham brought the bestowal of divine blessing on him ("righteousness" in Gen 15:6 merges with the notion of "blessing" with a parallel in Ps 106:31). Moreover, on the ground of the dynamic between the gracious promises of Yahweh and Abraham's

---

17 Moberly, "The Earliest Commentary on the Akedah," 320 – 1.

18 Levenson, *Inheriting Abraham*, 84.

19 *Pace* B. Ego, "Abraham als Urbild der Toratreue Israels: Traditionsgeschichtliche Überlegungen zu einem Aspekt des biblischen Abrahambildes," in *Bund und Torah: zur theologischen Begriffsgeschichte in alttestamentlicher, frühjüdischer und urchristlicher Tradition*, ed. F. Avemerie and H. Lichtenberger, WUNT (Tübingen: Mohr Siebeck, 1996), 29: "[...] Stand dort [Gen 12] Gottes freie Zusage am Anfang, auf die Abraham *reagierte*, so folgt in der hier vorliegenden Darstellung die göttliche Verheissung auf Abrahams Gehorsam."

trust in Yahweh, Yahweh solemnized an unconditional and promissory relationship with him, in Gen 15:7–19 by the ritual called "the covenant between the pieces", and in Gen 22:16 through the divine oath. At this point, one may ask: What is then the relationship between the earlier promises given to Abraham, the covenant in Gen 15:7–19, and the promises in Yahweh's oath according to Gen 22:15–18? In this regard, it is relevant to mention an important observation made by E. Bickerman in an article which he himself complains has been neglected in scholarship.[20] Here, he argues that there is a clear distinction between a ratified covenant and an oath relative to the promises:

> But it seems that the biblical accounts of the making of the *berith* permit the inference that this act was not ratified by means of an imprecatory oath, as I believe I have shown in this essay. According to the biblical narratives, neither the *berith* of Sinai nor that of Schechem (Jos 24) contained a validation by means of a vow.[21]

The biblical and the extra-biblical evidence on which Bickerman's compelling argument is based makes it clear that an oath is *not* a ratification of a covenant, but rather a distinctive confirmation or reaffirmation of the promise that had already been given, whether inherent in the covenant or not.[22] Accordingly, while the covenant ratifies its underlying promise by means of a certain kind of rite, the characteristic of an oath is to be an additional affirmation and an even stronger way than a covenant to make Yahweh's commitment to the promise indissoluble. In the case of the *berith* cut with Abraham (Gen 15:1–18), this is made in order to emphasize that Yahweh cannot go back on the promise made to Abraham and his descendants, whereas the oath Yahweh later "swears" by himself to Abraham (Gen 22:16–18) strenghtens his positive disposition to fulfill the initial promises.[23] In sum, according to the oath of promise, the future blessings bestowed upon Abraham are grounded in the correspondence between Yahweh's trustworthiness relative to the earlier promise and Abraham's trust in Yahweh,

---

20 Cf. E.J. Bickerman, "'Cutting a Covenant'," in *Studies in Jewish and Christian History: A New Edition in English Including the God of the Maccabees, Volume One*, AJEC (Leiden: Brill, 2007), 26.
21 Bickerman, "'Cutting a Covenant'," 30. Bickerman refers here to the work of M. Weinfeld (*Deuteronomy and the Deuteronomic School* [Oxford: Clarendon Press, 1972], 63), which independently makes a similar argument.
22 *Pace* Hahn, "Covenant," 79–100, esp. 83–6.
23 In very recent scholarship, there are also scholars who blur this distinction between covenant and oath in their interpretation of Gen 15:18; cf., e.g., G.J. Wenham, *Genesis 1–15*, WBC (Waco, TX: Word Books, 1987), 333; B.T. Arnold, *Genesis*, NCBC (Cambridge: CUP, 2009), 160.

that is, trust that Yahweh will accomplish in act what He has promised through the oath of promise first spoken to Abraham and later reiterated to Isaac in Gen 26:2–5, 25.[24] Some observations should be made on the link between the promises reiterated from Gen 22:15–18 and the emphasis on Abraham's obedience in the latter texts. To begin with, it is only in Gen 26:2–5, 24 that Isaac receives divine promises, and both passages go back to the oath of promise to Abraham. Second, both Gen 26:3–5 and 26:24 clearly echo the divine oath of promised blessings in 22:16–18, so that one can almost speak of a citation of this passage.[25] This inference is supported by the references to the oath that God has "sworn" to Abraham (3b, cf. 22:16a), the promises of offsprings as many as the stars (4a, cf. 22:17a), and blessings extended to all nations through Abraham's descendants (4b, cf. 22:18a), respectively, both of which are perceived as an outcome of Abraham's obedience (5a, cf. 22:18b). The latter two elements are found only in Gen 22:18 and 26:4–5. Thus, Gen 26:3–5 supports the understanding that the divine oath of promise incorporates Abraham's obedience as the sole ground for the application of the promises to Isaac. As Grüneberg puts it: "Isaac will benefit from all that God offers not because he has responded faithfully to God, but because Abraham did so."[26] Third, Gen 26:3–5 expands the content of Gen 22:15–18 in two specific ways: (1) the promise of the land from Genesis 12 is incorporated into the list of what Yahweh had sworn to; (2) Gen 26:5 clearly adds to Abraham's way of obedience categories of the law, namely: "kept my charge, my commandments, my statutes, and my laws". Hence, a commentator or later glossator seems to have characterized Abraham's obedience as a model living by Torah. As to the transference of the promised blessing to Isaac's descendants, although Abraham's trusting response to Yahweh's promise is the fountain from which they flow, their fulfillment is dependent on whether Isaac's own obedience resembles that of his father Abraham. Isaac's obedience appears already to be approved by the statement in 26:6 that Isaac, like Abraham, settled in the land that Yahweh showed him. This obedience proves Isaac as the legitimate son of his father Abraham and the worthy recipient and mediator of the promised blessings to his descendants.

To sum up: The promises to Abraham in Gen 12:1–3 as well as the element of Abraham's trusting response have had a cumulative effect on Genesis 15, 22, and 26. The novelty of the oath of promise to Abraham in Gen 22:15–18 and Gen

24 On the discussion of Genesis 26 in the context of the Abraham cycle (Gen 12–25:18) and the Jacob cycle (25:19–35:29), cf. G.J. Wenham, *Genesis 16–50*, WBC (Dallas: Word Books, 1994), 184–8.

25 Thus Levin, "Die Väterverheissungen," 136.

26 Grüneberg, *A Philogical and Exegetical Study of Gen 12:3*, 227.

26:3–4 consists in the reaffirmation of the promise, now grounded both in the divine will *and* Abraham's trusting obedience. Moreover, it is notable that the divine response to Abraham's trusting response to the promise, in terms of both the covenant that follows in Genesis 15 and the oath of promise in Genesis 22 and 26, constitute the basis for God's relationship with Abraham and his descendants and the fulfillment of the promise in the generations to come. Abraham's behaviour and the promises are made the means of marking the identity of the descent from the patriarchs.

3 The Exegetical Tradition of Gen 15:6 and 22:16–18

Our survey in the preceding section on the expansions of the Abrahamic promises in Genesis 12–26 brought out a certain similarity between Gen 15:5–21 and the oath of promise in Gen 22:15–18 and 26:3–5. These passages show a concern for how marking the identity of Israel not only depends on the promise and will of Yahweh, but also on the trusting response of Abraham. This line of thought, already displayed in Gen 15:5–6, in so far as the promise of blessing that ensued upon Abraham's trust is reaffirmed by God's response in the covenant that follows (Gen 15:7–21), is continued in Gen 22:16–18 and 26:3–4 in terms of the oath of promise given to Abraham and his descendants. In this section, I shall further investigate the use of the exegetical tradition of Gen 15:6 and 22:16–18 in *Abr.* 262–273 in comparison with other Jewish and Christian texts which have likewise made use of the same conjunction of texts.

3.1 Abraham's Trust and God's Faithfulness

I now turn to the data in *Abr.* 262–273, where Philo makes use of the exegetical tradition that combines Gen 15:6 with Genesis 22:16–18. This part of *De Abrahamo* belongs to the section 262–276, which concludes the whole treatise. Up to this section, Philo's elaboration has been based upon episodes from Abraham's life. In the conclusion, then, Philo for the most part picks up themes explored earlier, particularly from the introduction §§ 3–6 on his position relative to the Law (cf. my interpretation of *Abr.* 275–276 in the next chapter) and Abraham's separation from Lot (§§ 217–224).[27] In the latter section Philo prefigures and con-

27 On the basic structure of *De Abrahamo*, see now Birnbaum and Dillon, *On the Life of Abraham*, 396.

trasts two distinct soul-types; an elder one represented by Abraham, and a younger one symbolized by Lot. He takes Abraham as a manifestation of the virtues and Lot as representing the external goods. Now, in §§ 263 – 267 Philo focuses on bodily goods in addition to the external ones, and thus emphasizes that such goods are lowly and subordinate and as such not trustworthy and unreliable. In contrast to such a unreliable trust in "human"goods, Philo turns to the the additional praises of Abraham, and especially signifies Abraham's trust in God (cf. Gen 15:6) as the goal towards which the path of the virtues and piety has led him (cf. § 269).[28] Thus, the emphasis on Abraham's trust in God, in general even higher and superior to the virtues,[29] enables Philo to draw upon his discovery of God when he broke up from Chaldea (§§ 60 – 207) as well as his virtues of piety, such as justice, courage, wisdom, moderation, and love of humanity (§§ 208 – 261).

As I mentioned at the beginning of this chapter, it assumes the parallelism that Spiegel pointed to between Abraham's conduct at the *Akedah* and the conduct expected in return from God. Philo provides evidence of such a correspondence at three junctures in his elaborations on the event of the *Akedah*, viz. in *Abr.* 177, 202 – 203, and 273. In *Abr.* 177 and 202 – 203, the congruity between Abraham's and God's conduct finds expression by means of the notion that God gave back to Abraham what he had virtually sacrificed to God. Thus, in *Abr.* 177, Philo states this thought as follows: "So Isaac was saved, since God returned the gift of him and used the offering which piety rendered to Him to repay the offerer [...]". On the basis of Abraham's piety, God correspondingly rewards Abraham not only by saving Isaac, but also by returning the gift of joy, symbolically expressed by Isaac's name and associated with God.[30] The same correspondence is affirmed in *Abr.* 202 – 203:

> This the Sage is said to sacrifice as his duty to God, thus showing in a figure that rejoicing is most clearly associated with God. [...] The frame of mind which has made this true acknowl-

---

28 It is worthwhile that Philo turns to particular scriptures to convey Abraham's additional merits (at this juncture, Philo applies ἔπαινος instead of the related word ἐγκώμιον as in § 217), such as his trust in God (LXX Gen 15:6; §§ 262 – 269), his status as an "elder" in terms of being the first or precedent (LXX Gen 24:1; §§ 270 – 272), the divine trust / faithfulness in terms of the oath of promise given in return to him (LXX Gen 22:16 – 18; §§ 273 – 274), his obedience to the divine Law, and his life epitomizing in itself a "law and an unwritten ordinance" (LXX Gen 26:5; §§ 275 – 276).

29 For the notion of the virtues as a path that leads towards the goal of trust in God, and thus higher than the virtues, cf. Birnbaum and Dillon, *On the Life of Abraham*, 396.

30 Cf. Josephus, *Ant.* 1.13.4 § 234. See H.W. Attridge, *The Epistle to the Hebrews: A Commentary on the Epistle to the Hebrews*, Hermeneia (Philadelphia: Fortress Press, 1989), 335.

> edgement God, Who has banished jealousy from His presence in His kindness and love for mankind, fitly rewards by returning the gift in so far as the recipient's capacity allows.

In § 273, Philo adopts this correspondence to the relationship between Abraham's trust and God's faithfulness and expresses it as follows:

> ὃς τῆς πρὸς αὐτὸν πίστεως ἀγάμενος τὸν ἄνδρα πίστιν ἀντιδίδωσιν αὐτῷ, τὴν δι' ὅρκου βεβαίωσιν ὧν ὑπέσχετο δωρεῶν, οὐκέτι μόνον ὡς ἀνθρώπῳ θεός, ἀλλὰ καὶ ὡς φίλος γνωρίμῳ διαλεγόμενος· φησὶ διάνοιαν ἀκλινῶς καὶ παγίως ἔτι μᾶλλον ἢ πρότερον ἐρηρεῖσθαι.
>
> [God], marveling at Abraham's faith in Him, repaid him with faithfulness by confirming with an oath the gifts which he had promised, no longer conversing with him as God might with man, but as one friend with another. For he says, "By myself have I sworn," by him that is whose word is an oath, in order that Abraham's mind may be established still more firmly and immoveably than before.

Here, the line of thought is that the conduct of Abraham's trust is recompensed by God's corresponding conduct of trust / faithfulness, which is further explicated as God's reaffirmation of the gifts already promised by means of the divine oath, and seen as a token of friendship between God and Abraham. The blessing that Abraham was promised is reaffirmed by the oath of promise, so that it was integrally connected to Abraham's trust that occasioned it. Thus, Abraham is recognized with the gift of God's trust in terms of the divine oath, which means both a divine vindication of Abraham's trust and the existing promises in terms of the oath of promise. The constellation of these motifs will be analysed further in the wider context of Philo's writings and other Jewish and Christian texts below. At this point, I offer some further observations on the former text.

In *Abr.* 273, both Abraham's conduct and that expected in return from God are characterized as πίστις:[31] ὃς τῆς πρὸς αὐτὸν πίστεως ἀγάμενος τὸν ἄνδρα

---

31 For the study of πίστις and its cognates in Philo's writings, A. Sclatter's brief survey (*Der Glaube Im Neuen Testament* [Stuttgart: Calwer, 1927], 575 – 81) is still helpful. Schlatter identifies four categories of meaning: A. Pledge, Security, Proof; B. Trustworthiness or Faithfulness in the execution of a charge; C. Trust, Faith; D. Conviction, Belief. For other useful discussions of the same topic, cf. W. Bousset, *Die Religion des Judentums im Späthellenistischen Zeitalter*, HNT (Tübingen: Mohr Siebeck, 1926), 411 – 31; H. Windisch, *Die Frömmigkeit Philos und ihre Bedeutung für das Christentum: Eine religionsgeschichtliche Studie* (Leipzig: J.C. Hinrichs, 1909), 23 – 9; R. Bultmann, "πιστεύω κτλ," *TDNT* 6: 201 – 202; E. Grässer, *Der Glaube im Hebräerbrief* (Marburg: N.G. Elwert Verlag, 1965), 95 – 146; R. Williamson, *Philo and the Epistle to the Hebrews*, ALGHJ (Leiden: Brill, 1970), 331 – 72; D.M. Hay, "Pistis as 'Ground for Faith' in Hellenized Judaism and Paul," *JBL* 108.3 (1989): 463 – 8; D.R. Lindsay, *Josephus and Faith: Pistis and Pisteuein as Faith Terminology in the Writings of Flavius Josephus and in the New Testament*, AGJU (Leiden: Brill, 1993), 53 – 73; B. Schliesser, *Abraham's Faith in Romans 4: Paul's Concept of Faith in Light of*

πίστιν ἀντιδίδωσιν αὐτῷ, [...] ("[God], marveling at Abraham's trust in Him, repaid him with faithfulness, [...]").[32] I begin with some comments on the content of this particular parallelism. In the first place, *Abr.* 273 attests that Philo stands in the well-attested expository tradition that related Gen 15:6 to the *Akedah*. In its immediate literary context, *Abr.* 273 – 276 represents an *inclusio* and continues the exegetical paraphrase of Gen 15:6a running through *Abr.* 262 – 276. This *inclusio* also attests the association of Gen 15:6a, 22:16 – 18, and 26:3 – 5 and shows how Philo reads these texts cumulatively, forming sequences of the Abrahamic biography. In the opening statement in *Abr.* 262, Gen 15:6a is quoted:

> Ἔστι δὲ καὶ ἀνάγραπτος ἔπαινος αὐτῷ χρησμοῖς μαρτυρηθείς, οὓς Μωυσῆς ἐθεσπίσθη, δι' οὗ μηνύεται ὅτι "ἐπίστευσε τῷ θεῷ," [...] (There is another record of praise attested by words from Moses' prophetic lips. In these it is stated that he "trusted in God," [...])

Thus, in *Abr.* 273 the expression ἡ πρὸς θεὸν πίστις paraphrases and refers back to the quotation of Gen 15:6a in *Abr.* 262.[33] Accordingly, Philo construes Abraham's "trust" in Gen 15:6a as reaching its culmination with God's responsiveness expressed by the words of Gen 22:16 – 18. The notion that Abraham "trusted God" is explicated in *Abr.* 263–269 in contrast to the unworthy trust in "human" goods, such as the external goods "political power", "fame", "wealth", "high birth", and the goods of the body, such as "health", and bodily beauty".[34] In a corresponding way, Philo's interlocutor asks in *Her.* 90 – 95 whether—again the reference is to Gen 15:6— Abraham's trust was unfitting for the tribute of praise, since even the most unworthy would heed the words and promises of God by faith. Ac-

---

the History of Reception of Genesis 15:6, WUNT 2 (Tübingen: Mohr Siebeck, 2007), 203 – 11; T. Morgan, *Roman Faith and Christian Faith: Pistis and Fides in the Early Roman Empire and Early Churches* (Oxford: OUP, 2015), esp. 183 – 4.

32 My own translation.

33 Gen 15:6a is either quoted or alluded to by Philo also in *Virt.* 216, 218; *Praem.* 27; *Leg.* 3:228; *Migr.* 43 – 44; *Her.* 90 – 95; *Mut.* 177, 186; *Deus* 4; *QG* 3:2, 58; *QG* 4:17. Other texts that quote Gen 15:6 include 1 Macc 2:52; Jub 14:6; 4Q225 I:7 – 8; Rom 4:3, 22; Gal 3:6; Barn. 13:7; Justin, *Dial.* 92:3; Mek. Exod 14:15, 31; Tanh. Buber Metsora' 5. Allusions are found in Rom 4:9; Heb 11:2; Barn. 13:7; Justin, *Dial.* 23:4. Cf. M. Dibelius, *Der Brief des Jakobus*, Kritisch-exegetischer Kommentar über das Neue Testament Abt. 15 (Göttingen: Vandenhoeck & Ruprecht, 1956), 168 – 79; F. Hahn, "Genesis 15,6 im Neuen Testament," in *Probleme biblischer Theologie* (Münich: Kaiser, 1971), 90 – 107; M. Oeming, "Der Glaube Abrahams: Zur Rezeptionsgeschichte von Gen 15,6 in der Zeit des zweiten Tempels," *ZAW* 110.1 (1998): 23 – 4; Schliesser, *Abraham's Faith in Romans 4*, 205 – 8; D.C. Allison, *A Critical and Exegetical Commentary on The Epistle of James*, ICC (London: Bloomsbury T&T Clark, 2013), 491.

34 These values refer to the distinction between external, bodily, and goods of the soul, to be found, e.g., in Plato, *Leg.* 697b, and Aristotle, *Eth. nic.* 1.8.1098b. Cf. Birnbaum and Dillon, *On the Life of Abraham*, 394; 399 – 403.

cording to Philo's refutation of his dialogue partner, Abraham is depicted as one who overcame his godless surroundings to have trust in God. Thus, Abraham distrusted created being and trusted in God, who alone is truly worthy of trust (cf. *Her.* 93). At this juncture, Philo defines Abraham's "trust" in God as the mark of being "worthy" (= "righteous") *despite* his past life of being "ungodly". It is precisely the worth of Abraham's trust in God that marks the break between his past life of ungodliness and the establishing of his being recognized with "worthiness" before God. Thus, Gen 15:6 is in *Her.* 92 taken to mean that "trust in God alone and joining no other with Him is no easy matter, by reason of our kinship with our yokefellow, mortality, which works upon us to keep our trust placed in riches and repute and office and friends and health and strength and many other things." This contrast of Abraham's trust in God with the social, cultural, or "symbolic capital" or wealth that humans may value as worthy of their trust implies that πίστις takes on the meaning of trust, equivalent to being faithful.[35] Thus, in *Abr.* 273 too, Philo contrasts Abraham with ordinary men by emphasizing his pre-eminence both as the "first" in the human race and as founder of the Jewish nation in terms of trust in God and of the oath of promise given to Abraham in return. As S. Sandmel put it:

> As the first among men, he surpasses them in endowments and in achievements; and his capacities bring benefits to men. These capacities are the result of his possession of faith. Faith makes Abraham the "first" among the human race. [...] Moreover, that God utilized an oath is a further token of Abraham's eminence, in that God thereby addresses Abraham not as God usually addresses man, but as a friend addresses an acquaintance. Abraham, then, is not only pre-eminent among men, but his eminence is such that God converses with him in familiar terms.[36]

Abraham's trust in God, here expressed by an exegetical paraphrase of Gen 15:6 (ἡ πρὸς θεὸν πίστις), is the most prominent use of πίστις by Philo (cf. Schlatter's category C., classified as "Vertrauen"). The construction ἡ πρὸς θεὸν πίστις appears often in Philo and indicates a trust directed towards God as object, and is found synonomously with πιστεύειν θεῷ as an expository paraphrase of the trust of Abraham in Gen 15:6.[37]

As is well known, the exegetical conjunction of Genesis 15 and Genesis 22 is presupposed in Jewish expository tradition as well as in early Christian literature. Nehemiah 9:7–8 may already convey this coupling:

35 For a similar interpretation, cf. Sandnes, *Paul Perceived*, 150.
36 Sandmel, *Philo's Place in Judaism*, 140.
37 Cf. *Abr.* 268, 270–271; *Her.* 94; *Mut.* 182, 201; *Praem.* 27.

You are the LORD, the God who chose Abram and brought him out of Ur of the Chaldeans and gave him the name Abraham; and you found his heart faithful (נאמן) before you, and made with him a covenant to give to his descendants the land of the Canaanite, the Hittite, the Amorite, the Perizzite, the Jebusite, and the Girgashite; and you have fulfilled your promise, for you are righteous.

According to scholars such as Oeming and Allison, this passage may reflect a *continuum* of Abraham's story that brings together Genesis 12 (the promise of land), Genesis 15 (Abraham's trust and covenant), Genesis 17 (the renaming of Abraham), and Genesis 22 (the sacrifice of Isaac).[38] Levenson, however, has argued that the adjective נאמן here is an interpretive paraphrase of Gen 15:6 rather than a reference to Abraham's willingness to sacrifice Isaac, since there is no specific mention of that incident in the whole passage.[39] Even if it is uncertain whether Neh 9:7 – 8 reflects the association of Gen 15:6 and Gen 22:16 – 18, the authors of 1 Maccabees and Sirach seem to provide the same exegetical paraphrase of Gen 15:6 about Abraham's trust / faithfulness, and relocate this hallmark of Abraham's behavior as tested and approved at the event of the *Akedah*. Unlike Philo, *Abr.* 273, however, the author of 1 Maccabees refers to the binding of Isaac as one of the "works" (ἔργα) of the ancestors (2:51) and paraphrases the protasis of Gen 15:6a with reference to Abraham's faithfulness together with the apodosis of Gen 15:6b: Αβρααμ οὐχὶ ἐν πειρασμῷ εὑρέθη πιστός, καὶ ἐλογίσθη αὐτῷ εἰς δικαιοσύνην; ("Was not Abraam found faithful in temptation, and it was accounted to him as righteousness?"). Hence, the motif of Abraham's trust in God according to Gen 15:6 has been detatched from its immediate narrative context and instead interpreted as a summary interpretation of Abraham's justification by *faithfulness*, which was thought to be pronounced upon Abraham and to apply post-*Akedah*.[40] Like 1 Macc 2:52, also without referring explicitly to Gen 15:6, Sir 44:20 – 21 seems to allude to the same motif that Abraham was found *faithful* (εὑρέθη πιστός) in combination with the binding of Isaac and the subsequent promise given to Abraham by oath (Gen 22:16 – 18):

καὶ ἐν πειρασμῷ εὑρέθη πιστός· (v. 20)
διὰ τοῦτο ἐν ὅρκῳ ἔστησεν αὐτῷ ἐνευλογηθῆναι ἔθνη ἐν σπέρματι αὐτοῦ,
[...] (v. 21)

38 Oeming, "Der Glaube Abrahams," 23 – 4; Allison, *The Epistle of James*, 492.
39 Levenson, *The Death and Resurrection*, 175. For a similar understanding, see also J.L. Kugel, "Exegetical Notes on 4Q225 'Pseudo-Jubilees'," *DSD* 13.1 (2006): 95.
40 Cf. Levenson, *Inheriting Abraham*, 73.

> (and in a trial he was found faithful. [v. 20]
> Therefore he established by means of an oath with him
> that nations would be blessed by his seed, [...] [v. 21])

Jub 17:15–16 ([Mastema proposed the *Akedah* as a challenge to Abraham being] "faithful in everything") and 4Q225 2:8 ([Mastema was testing] "whether A[braham] should not be found *faithful* ") also employ Gen 15:6 and the exegetical motif of Abraham's faithfulness being put to test at the *Akedah.*[41] It is interesting that the same exegetical idiom is found in m. Qidd. 4:14 and Mek. Beshallaḥ 7, in contexts in which a similar cluster of motifs appears to reflect the same expository tradition. The relevant markers that point to such a referential background are emphasized in italics in the following quotation of the texts, which I shall present here at some length:

> [...] R. Nehemiah says: Whence can you prove that whosoever accepts even one single commandment with true faith is deserving of having the Holy Spirit rest upon him. We *find* (מצינו) this to have been the case with our *fathers.* For as a *reward for the faith* (האמנה בשכר) with which they believed, they were considered worthy of having the Holy Spirit rest upon them, so that they could utter the song, as it is said. "And they believed in the Lord [...]. Then sang Moses and the children of Israel." And so also you *find* that *our father Abraham* inherited both this world and also the world beyond only as a *reward for the faith* (אמנה בשכר) with which he believed, as it is said: "And he believed in the Lord, [...] (Gen 15:6). [...] He keeps in remembrance the faith of the *fathers.*[42]

It is noteworthy that the rabbinic text here might have interpreted the conjunction of Gen 15:6 and Gen 22:16–18 in a similar way as *Abr.* 273 about the oath of promise given as a reward for Abraham's conduct of trust in God. Moreover, both Sir 44 and the rabbinic text seem to presuppose an interpretation of Gen 22:16 about Abraham's reward and inheritance of the world on the ground of his trust with reference to Gen 15:6. Early Christian texts evidence the same Jewish exegetical tradition.[43] Thus, also 1 Clem. 10:6–7, Jas 2:21–23, Heb 6:12–15 and 11:11–12 likewise assume this association between Abraham's faithfulness (Gen 15:6), which involved action, and the *Akedah.* The first of these texts cites Gen 15:6 and then immediately passes to the *Akedah:*

> Again it says, "God led Abraham out and said to him, 'Look up into the sky and count the stars, if you are able to number them. So will your offspring be.' And Abraham trusted God,

---

41 Cf. Huizenga, *The New Isaac*, 90; Allison, *The Epistle of James*, 491–2.

42 The italicized words are mine; the translation is Lauterbach's.

43 See the surveys by H. Moxnes, *Theology in Conflict: Studies in Paul's Understanding of God in Romans*, NovTSup (Leiden: Brill, 1980), 127–9; Allison, *The Epistle of James*, 480–96.

> and it was accounted to him as righteousness. Because of his faith and hospitality, a son was given to him in his old age; and in obedience he offered him up as a sacrifice to God on one of the mountains that he showed him. 1 Clem. 10:6 – 7

It is noteworthy that 1 Clem. 10:1 applies the same exegetical motifs about Abraham as in 1 Macc 2:52 and Sir 44:20 on the basis of this conjunction of Gen 15:6 and the *Akedah*, viz. that "Abraham was found to be faithful (πιστὸς εὑρέθη) and called 'The Friend' when he became obedient to God's words." According to Jas 2:21 – 23, Abraham's faith reaches its culmination in his actions at the *Akedah*, attesting the same exegetical motifs on the basis of the conjunction of Gen 15:6 and Genesis 22:[44]

> Was not our ancestor Abraham justified by works when he offered his son Isaac on the altar? You see that faith was active along with his works, and faith was brought to completion by the works. Thus the scripture was fulfilled that says, "Abraham believed God, and it was reckoned to him as righteousness," and he was called the friend of God.

Likewise, Heb 6:12 – 15 seems to resemble the same exegetical tradition:

> [...] so that you may not become sluggish, but be imitators of those who through faith and patience inherit the promises. When God made a promise to Abraham, because he had no one greater by whom to swear, he swore by himself, saying, "I will surely bless you and multiply you." And thus Abraham, having patiently endured, obtained the promise.[45]

In any case, like the author of James, Philo takes it for granted that Abraham's trust in Gen 15:6 required action, as we see from his brief remark in *Abr.* 262 that trust "is a little thing if measured in words, but a very great thing if made good by action."[46] Unlike Philo, however, James may depend on the Jewish ex-

---

44 Cf. Dibelius, *Der Brief des Jakobus*, 168 – 79; Allison, *The Epistle of James*, 481 – 99.

45 Cf. H. Köster, "Die Auslegung der Abraham-Verheissung in Hebräer 6," in *Studien zur Theologie der alttestamentlichen Überlieferungen*, ed. R. Rendtorff and K. Koch (Neukirchen: Neukirchener Verlag, 1961), 95 – 109; H. Attridge, *The Epistle to the Hebrews*, 335.

46 Thanks to Genesis 22:16 – 18, the faithful Abraham is emphasized as an exemplar of obedience, who faithfully obeyed the listened word of God and thus is depicted as someone who accomplished the will of God in in offering up Isaac. This motif can be found in many Jewish and Christian texts with its consistent vocabulary: Gen 22:18 LXX (ὑπήκουσας τῆς ἐμῆς φωνῆς), Gen 26:5 (ὑπήκουσεν Ἀβραάμ ὁ πατήρ σου τῆς ἐμῆς φωνῆς); Jub. 21:2 – 3; Heb 11:8 (Ἀβραάμ ὑπήκουσεν); Josephus, *Ant.* 1:225 (Abraham, deeming that nothing would justify disobedience to God [παρακούειν τοῦ θεοῦ]); 1. Clem. 10:1 (Ἀβραάμ [...] πιστὸς εὑρέθη ἐν τῷ αὐτὸν ὑπήκοον γενέσθαι τοῖς ῥήμασιν τοῦ θεοῦ); Tg. Ps.-J. Gen 22:18 ("you obeyed my word"); Mek. Beshallaḥ 7 ("Whoever accepts one single commandment with true faith [...] Abraham inherited [...] as a reward for the faith with which he believed").

pository tradition in which Gen 15:6 was taken to apply only *after* the Akedah.[47] Moreover, as in *Abr.* 273 ("He no longer talked with him as God with man but as a friend with a familiar"), the authors of 1. Clem. 10:1 and Jas 2:23 have likewise employed the exegetical motif of calling Abraham God's "friend".[48] Thus, Abraham has been called a friend in order to indicate that Abraham's friendship is based on the faithfulness he shares with God. The concept of Abraham as God's friend then goes along with the exegetical motifs of Abraham's faithfulness and the oath granted to him in terms of God's corresponding conduct of faithfulness, probably because of the common exegetical tradition that combined Gen 15:6 and Genesis 22 in various ways.

When compared with the Jewish exegetical tradition that relates Gen 15:6 to the *Akedah*, *Abr.* 273 seems to be idiosyncratic, in that it makes evident the correspondence between Abraham's conduct of trust in God with the conduct of God's trust / faithfulness in terms of the oath given to him in return from God: "ὃς τῆς πρὸς αὐτὸν πίστεως ἀγάμενος τὸν ἄνδρα πίστιν ἀντιδίδωσιν αὐτῷ [...]." The measure of πίστις that is here ascribed to both Abraham and God shows that the two first categories that a scholar like Schlatter operated with, might converge. Both Abraham's and God's πίστις represent the idea of trust or faithfulness in the execution of a charge or a task. Thus, Abraham's trust in God was specifically shown in his faithfulness towards God's promises, while in return for this obedient trust, God rewarded Abraham with His own trust and faithfulness by means of the divine oath as a pledge or guarantee (cf. Sclatter's category A. "Gewähr, Garantie, Beweis" referred to above) that He shall fulfill the promises made to Abraham. In accord with this meaning of faithfulness, Philo calls both Abraham and God "faithful" by means of the adjective πιστός. For example, in *Post.* 173 Abraham is called "the faithful one" ('Αβραὰμ ὁ πιστός). Likewise, God is called "faithful" in giving his oath in *Leg.* 3:204 (πιστὸς δὲ μόνος ὁ θεός) and *Sacr.* 93 (ὁ δὲ θεὸς καὶ λέγων πιστός ἐστιν). In the last text, Philo even says that is not the oath that makes God "faithful", rather it is God who assures the oath (οὐ γὰρ δι' ὅρκον πιστὸς ὁ θεός, ἀλλὰ δι' αὐτὸν

47 For such a reading of Jas 2:20–24, see Levenson, *Inheriting Abraham*, 161. R. Bauckham (*James: Wisdom of James, Disciple of Jesus the Sage* [London; New York: Routledge, 1999], 123) and Allison (*The Epistle of James*, 492) interpret Gen 15:6 as "fulfilled" in the sense that the verdict spoken of in that verse is confirmed, manifested, and vindicated at the *Akedah.*

48 As Sandmel (*Philo's Place in Judaism*, 44–5, n. 130), Jacobs ("The Midrashic Background for James II. 21–3," *NTS* 22.4 [1976]: 463), and Allison (*The Epistle of James*, 495) have suggested, Philo (*Sobr.* 55–56) and James (2:23) may be referring to a version of Gen 18:17, according to which Abraham is called God's friend, an exegetical motif that is also attested in Targum (Frg. Tg. to Gen 18:17) and later rabbinic Midrashim (e.g., Midr. Gen 18:17; Pirqe R. El. 25).

καὶ ὁ ὅρκος βέβαιος). Similarly, Philo claims that God's promises are firm and steadfast by reason of God who promised them.[49] In sum, the notions of trust or faithfulness and steadfastness are closely related, distinguished only by some nuances, if not indeed at times taken as synonomous.[50] I now turn to a further investigation of the correspondence and parallelism of Abraham's trust and the oath of promise, based on the exegetical tradition that combines Gen 15:6 and Gen 22:16 – 18.

3.2 The Congruity between Abraham's Trust and God's Oath of Promise

In his analysis of *De Abrahamo*, Sandmel describes the content of *Abr.* 273 as follows:

> Now Philo proceeds to his climax: God holds Abraham's faith in high esteem, and he repays this faith with divine faith; this consists in God's confirming by an oath the gifts already promised.[51]

Most recently, E. Birnbaum and J. Dillon comment on Philo's exegesis of Gen 22:16 in § 273 with the following words:

> In that biblical verse, God is rewarding Abraham specifically for not withholding his son Isaac (see §§ 177 and 203). Now, however, Philo takes this verse as a response to Abraham's faith in general.[52]

Although I think these scholars have interpreted Philo's line of thought correctly, we must still go beyond such a general characterization in order to determine somewhat more closely the meaning and association of the motifs that appear here. I shall discuss further the correspondence between Abraham's conduct of trust and the oath of promise given in return by God.

In the first place, the text of Gen 22:16 – 18 itself might suggest the congruity of act and adequate reward, that is, a *reward* of an oath on God's part *because of* what Abraham has already done, that is, his behavior at the *Akedah:* "By myself I have sworn, says the LORD: *Because you have done this*, and have not withheld

---

49 *Migr.* 44.

50 Cf. Grässer (*Der Glaube*, 144): "[Die Festigkeit] fanden wir als Strukturelement auch des alttestamentlichen Glaubensbegriffes. Aber niemand hat sich mit solcher Intensität zum eigentlichen Wesenmerkmal der Pistis erklärt wie Philo: Πίστις und βεβαιότης sind synonyme."

51 Sandmel, *Philo's Place in Judaism*, 140.

52 Birnbaum and Dillon, *On the Life of Abraham*, 405.

your son, your only son, *I will indeed bless you* [...]".[53] Similarly, the idea in *Abr.* 273 that God rewarded and "repaid" (ἀντιδίδωμι) Abraham's trust with the gift of divine trust / faithfulness might then be an implied reference to Abraham's faithfulness in terms of his willingness to sacrifice Isaac. However, such an understanding cannot stand unqualified. Some scholars have interpreted Abraham's trust in *Abr.* 262 and 273 as being demonstrated and vindicated by his actions at the *Akedah*,[54] while others are more reluctant to associate this trust with any particular situation.[55] In the context of *Abr.* 167–190 the reference to Abraham's "action" (ἔργον) in *Abr.* 262 most probably refers in general to Abraham's obedience towards God's commands,[56] and not particularly to the *Akedah*, which he omits from the narrative in Genesis 22 (cf. §§ 186, 188, 190, and 191).[57] It is a fact that Philo in this treatise apparently subverts the role and the physical binding of Isaac. Whereas in Gen 22:16–18 God is rewarding Abraham for not withholding his son Isaac, Philo takes this verse (see §§ 262 and 273) as a response to Abraham's trust in general.[58] Instead of regarding *De Abrahamo* as Philo's interpretation of Abraham's biography as a *continuum* of events,[59] it may be appropriate, with L. Feldman, to view this treatise as a "hagiographical biography in which the events of Abraham's life are not chronological."[60] At this point, I shall anticipate a discussion to be taken up in the next chapter, i.e., the association of Abraham's trust in God's promises relative to the divine Law in nature and as distinct from the Mosaic jurisdiction. Thus, the clo-

---

53 Accordingly, as I have pointed out above, the conjunction in Gen 22:16 that we usually render "because" is not to be understood as a meritorious reward on God's part, but rather as a reference to two aspects of responsiveness that stand in conjunction, i.e. the correspondence between Abraham's responsiveness in trust to God and his promise and God's faithful responsiveness in terms of his oath of promise. Again, see for such an interpretation of Gen 22:16–18 Moberly, "The Earliest Commentary on the Akedah," 320–1.

54 D. Lührmann, "Pistis Im Judentum," *ZNW* 64.1 (1973): 30, n. 63; E. Birnbaum, "The Biblical Interpretations of Philo: On the Life of Abraham," in *Outside the Bible: Ancient Jewish Writings Related to Scripture*, ed. L.H. Feldman, J.L. Kugel, and L.H. Schiffman (Lincoln, NE: Jewish Publication Society, 2013), 946; Sandnes, *Paul Perceived*, 152.

55 Dibelius takes *Abr.* 262 and Gen 15:6 as referring to a generalization about Abraham's life rather than to one item from the story of Abraham, cf. Dibelius, *Der Brief des Jakobus*, 164; G. Sass (*Leben aus den Verheissungen*, 110 n. 40) similarly interprets Abraham's faith "weniger um einen individuellen Akt als um eine generelle Einstellung des Menschen zu seinem Gott."

56 For such an understanding, cf. Sandmel, *Philo's Place in Judaism*, 126–9.

57 *Pace* Sandnes, *Paul Perceived*, 152.

58 For a similar understanding of Philo's appropriation of Gen 22:16–18 and Gen 15:6 in *Abr.* 273, see Birnbaum and Dillon, *On the Life of Abraham*, 405.

59 *Pace* Sandnes, *Paul Perceived*, 150.

60 Cf. Feldman, "Philo's Version of the Akedah," 86.

sure of the treatise, *Abr.* 275–276, seems to provide an *inclusio* to the opening part in *Abr.* 262, in which Philo elaborates on Abraham's trust in God's promises, thus indicating how it is to be interpreted in the context of Abraham's relation to the Law of Moses. The relevant passage reads:

> So much for all this, but to these praises of the Sage, so many and so great, Moses adds this crowning saying "that this man did the divine law and the divine commands." He did them, not taught by written words, but unwritten nature gave him the zeal to follow where wholesome and untainted impulse led him. And *when God gives his endorsement concerning these, what does it befit men to do other than to grant their firmest trust?* Such was the life of the first, the founder of the nation, one who obeyed the law, some will say, but rather, as our discourse has shown, himself a law and an unwritten statute.

With regard to the association of Abraham's trust in God's promises and the divine Law, the words in the italic in this quotation are noteworthy. Here, we find that Philo takes Abraham to be the first who did "the divine law and commands" (Gen 26:5) manifested in Nature. Thus, in contradistinction to a Jewish discourse which conceived Gen 26:5 and Abraham's keeping of the commandments of the Torah as inseparable from his faith, Philo instead identified Abraham's trust in God's commands, including His promises, as a manifestation and achievement of the divine law in Nature. Morover, Philo hints at Abraham's trust in God's commands as worthy of emulation ("to grant their firmest trust") supported by the endorsement of these on God's part, most probably referring back to the oath of promise, as an assurance of their trustworthiness (cf. § 273). As I shall point out in the next chapter, in the context of a Jewish discussion of this matter, Philo argues that the oath of promise (Gen 22:16–18) was not contingent on his obedience to the Mosaic Law (Gen 26:5), but was grounded in Abraham's trust in general (Gen 15:6), before the "Mosaic jurisdiction" was set in writing. Accordingly, it is perhaps more reasonable to suggest that Philo's understanding of the conjunction of Abraham's behavior of trust and its corresponding reward of trust on God's part follows the line of thought in Gen 22:16–18 and the logic of God's gift and reward.[61] The same pattern of an adequate reward, albeit

61 With regard to the logic and conjunction of the concepts of God's gift and reward, Barclay's comment (*Paul and the Gift*, 316) seems to be to the point:

> On the logic of the congruent gift, God's grace is not the opposite of recompense, but is *simultaneously* gift and reward. There is no antithesis here between gift and merit; grace and recompence stand in conjunction, not opposition. This is not to make the gift any less a gift or something akin to "pay". Those who deserve gifts are still the recipients of gifts, given voluntarily and without legal requirement. They do not *cause* the gift to

grounded in Abraham's trust manifested at the *Akedah*, in terms of a corresponding action on God's part is also attested in Irenaeus:

> For Abraham, according to his faith, followed the commandment of the word of God, and with ready mind gave up his only and beloved son, as a sacrifice to God, in order that God might be pleased to offer his beloved and only Son for all his offspring, as a sacrifice for our salvation. *Haer.* 4.5.4

In the Armenian version of this text, the idea of reward emerges more explicitly; Abraham is called the one "who also through faith asked God that for the sake of humanity He might *reward him* for his son."[62] The same line of reasoning, without explicitly using the phraseology of Abraham's trust and God's corresponding reward, is articulated also in an anonymous Syriac homily from the fifth century, as well in a sixth-century text by Romanos, a hymn-writer born in Syria to Jewish parents.[63]

As for the condition for God's imparting of the reward to Abraham, however, Philo should be compared and contrasted with much of the literature that has come down to us from Second Temple Judaism. Thus, for example, Sirach 44:19–21 refers to the pattern of an adequate reward in terms of Abraham's faithfulness and God's responsiveness by means of an oath, alluding to the words in Gen 15:6 and 22:16–18 in the following way:

---

be given (that is always a matter of the benefactor's will), but they prove themselves to be its suitable recipients and thus provide the condition for its proper distribution.

62 The translations are taken from N.A. Dahl, *Jesus the Christ: The Historical Origins of Christological Doctrine*, ed. D.H. Juel (Minneapolis: Fortress Press, 1991), 139. Dahl thought that Irenaeus here reflects earlier versions of haggadic traditions about the *Akedah* prevalent in Jewish circles, from which Paul too has drawn, e.g., in Rom 8:32.

63 The fifth-century Syriach homily is translated by S. Brock ("Two Syriac Verse Homilies on the Binding of Isaac," *Le Muséon* 99 [1986]: 61–129) as follows:

> Because you have offered up your son as a whole offering, I too will offer up Mine to the cross; if you have not spared your child, neither will I spare Mine. You have performed as a human an action that is too hard for humans; I, then, as God (will perform) an action even harder than yours.

The sixth-century Romanos reverberates this line of thought in this way: "Just as you did not spare my son because of me, just so, I shall not spare my son because of all men. But I shall give him to be slain for the whole world" (translation by M. Carpenter, *Kontakia of Romanos, Byzantine Melodist: On Christian Life* [Columbia, MS: University of Missouri Press, 1973], 69). See for a further discussion of these texts in the context of the motif of Abraham's conduct as a precedent for God's, K.H. Zetterholm, "Isaac and Jesus: A Rabbinic Reappropriation of a 'Christian' Motif?" *JJS* 67.1 (2016): 102–20, esp. 110 n. 26.

καὶ ἐν πειρασμῷ εὑρέθη πιστός· (v. 20b)
διὰ τοῦτο ἐν ὅρκῳ ἔστησεν αὐτῷ
ἐνευλογηθῆναι ἔθνη ἐν σπέρματι αὐτοῦ [...] (v. 21)
(and in a trial he was found faithful. [v. 20b]
Because of this he established by means of an oath with him
that nations would be blessed by his seed [...] [v. 21])

In a way corresponding to Gen 22:16 – 18, the prepositional phrase διὰ τοῦτο here in v. 20 underscores the idea that Abraham was worthy of receiving the oath of promise because of his faithfulness at the *Akedah*. Like other Jewish texts, the preceeding v. 20a ("Abraham kept the law, and came into covenant with him") conceived of this conduct as a manifestation of his obedience to the Mosaic laws even before they were written and thus as the basic constituent of Abraham's covenant with God.[64]

It seems, however, that Philo differs from this Jewish exegetical tradition in one crucial way, viz., in the manner in which he re-imagines God's trust / faithfulness in the light of Abraham's πίστις and vice versa. In contrast to other Jewish authors, who conceived of Abraham's trust (Gen 15:6) as vindicated after he had passed his great test at the *Akedah*, Philo refrains from attaching the motif of Abraham's testing to the Binding of Isaac. Thus, Philo focuses on Abraham's trust as the mechanism whereby he becomes the recipient of the gifts inherent in the oath of promise. Since the oath is a reaffirmation of the already existing promise, its character of promise and its terms of reference have been changed. The earlier promise is now transformed into an oath of promise and is grounded in the congruity between God's faithfulness to his promise of blessings *and* Abraham's trust. Although this exegetical motif of congruity between Abraham's trust and God's trust / faithfulness in *Abr.* 273 is not treated by Barclay, his general comment on Philo's perfections of God's gift is applicable to the content of this passage as well:

> [...] God's gifts are generally and for good reason *congruous* with the quality of the recipient. [...] It is important to be clear about what this entails. A *congruous* gift is still a gift: it has not been "debased" into a form of payment, "earned" by good works of the recipient.[65]

At this juncture, I shall add some brief remarks on the content of the divine oath of promise. Here the verb for the beneficent action, ἀντιδίδωμι, carries the sense of an adequate responsiveness on God's part that defines the "oath" (ὅρκος) as

64 Cf. B.C. Gregory, "Abraham as the Jewish Ideal: Exegetical Traditions in Sirach 44:19 – 21," *CBQ* 70.1 (2008): 66 – 81, esp. 77.
65 Barclay, *Paul and the Gift*, 237.

such. In *Leg.* 3:203–204, 207 and *Sacr.* 93, Philo similarly uses ὅρκος in reference to God's swearing according to Gen 22:16–17, and writes that God confirmed his promise by an oath. In *Abr.* 273, the oath is conceived of as a congruous "gift of return", not as a "payment" in the meritorious sense of the word, marked by the prepositional prefix ἀντί. For the benefits or gifts themselves, Philo employs a conventional noun related to the verb ἀντιδίδωμι, viz. δωρεά.[66] What is returned as a gift is specified as "the gifts (δωρεά) which were promised (ὑπισχνέομαι)", that is to say, given by God.[67] In the preceding parts of the treatise *De Abrahamo*, the cognates of ὑπόσχεσις refer to Philo's paraphrasing of Genesis 18. Thus, in *Abr.* 110 it is used about the divine promise that Abraham will soon have a son. Since Abraham and Sarah, however, found it difficult to believe the promises (ὑπισχνέομαι) (*Abr.* 111), God reaffirms the pledge (ὑπισχνέομαι) that they shall have a son of their own (*Abr.* 132; cf. Gen 18:3, 10). Since the promises in the immediate context thus focus on the promised offspring, we should probably regard the reference to the gifts inherent in the oath of promise in *Abr.* 273 as an all-encompassing phrase, which includes the blessings of Gen 22:16–18, embracing the blessings of Abraham's posterity and the other nations. In sum, the purpose of Philo's conjunction of Gen 15:6 and Gen 22:16–18 appears to be to link Abraham's trust in God's promises as congruent with the gift returned to him by God's faithfulness in terms of the divine oath of promise. Thus, the word πίστις seems to refer to the corresponding conduct of both Abraham and God, carrying a dual meaning of trust and faithfulness. I believe that in his comment on *Abr.* 273 in conjunction with other relevant Philonic passages on the divine oath conceieved as universal Law, such as *Spec.* 2:13, *Leg.* 3:203, *Decal.* 84, and *Sacr.* 91, Goodenough's understanding is on the right lines:

> As Abraham lives by faith in the λόγος or λόγοι of God he is living in that faith that is the πίστις of God. God has met Abraham's πίστις by giving him the supreme πίστις, the very Law and regularity of the divine Nature. It is in this sense that only God and the friend of God are πιστός, for only they have the fixity of the divine nature that expresses itself in the universal Law.[68]

As a final comment, I would add that *Abr.* 273 may be illuminated by two other Philonic texts in which a Jewish debate on the use of anthromorphic language is applied to God, viz. *Sacr.* 91–93 and *Leg.* 3:203–205. These texts attest a Jewish

---

66 For the various lexemes of "gift" in Greek texts, cf. Barclay, *Paul and the Gift*, 575–9.

67 For the usage of ὅρκος and ὑπόσχεσις in Philo's writings, see most recently the survey by K.P. Conway, *The Promises of God: The Background of Paul's Exclusive Use of 'Epangelia' for the Divine Pledge*, BZNW (Berlin: De Gruyter, 2014), 111–20.

68 Goodenough, *By Light, Light*, 68.

discourse on the question whether it is inappropriate for God to swear an oath that is reminiscent of Genesis 22. In the former text, without referring explicitly to Gen 22:16, Philo takes the position ascribed to other exegetes of his own time, explaining that it is impossible to ascribe to God the notion of an oath, because God cannot appeal to another god as a higher witness than himself; he who bears witness is superior to him to whom the witness is given. Philo supports this line of thought by emphasizing its premise: "there is nothing equal to Him, or even but a little below" (*Sacr.* 92). Accordingly, unlike human beings, who need an oath to prove their trustworthiness, God himself is trustworthy:

> [...] but God is trustworthy (πιστός) in His speech as elsewhere, so that His words in assurance (βεβαιότης) differ not a whit from oaths. And so it is that while with us the oath gives warrant for our sincerity, it is itself guaranteed by God. For the oath does not make God trustworthy (πιστός); it is God that assures (βέβαιος) the oath (*Sacr.* 93).

In *Leg.* 3:203–205, Philo argues again on the basis of the same criterion that God is without equal, but this time he defends the view that it is appropriate to God to take an oath, emphasizing the idea of God's uniqueness vis-à-vis human beings, expressed by the statement in Gen 22:16 that God swears "*by himself*":

> Some have said, that it was inappropriate for Him to swear; for an oath is added to assist faith, and only God and one who is God's friend is faithful (πιστός), even as Moses is said to have been found "faithful in all His house" (Numb. xii. 7). Moreover, the very words of God are oaths and laws of God and most sacred ordinances; and a proof of His sure strength is that whatever He saith cometh to pass, and this is specially characteristic of an oath. It would seem to be a corollary from this that all God's words are oaths receiving confirmation by accomplishment in act (ὅτι πάντες οἱ τοῦ θεοῦ λόγοι εἰσὶν ὅρκοι βεβαιούμενοι ἔργων ἀποτελέσμασι). *Leg.* 3:204

If one puts *Abr.* 273 alongside *Sacr.* 91–93 and *Leg.* 3:203–207, it appears that the similarities of terminology and motifs establish the following thought pattern: (1) All these texts refer to the oath in Gen 22:16. (2) God was trustworthy / faithful (πιστός), and this was manifested and confirmed (βεβαιόω) by the oath of promise. God's trust / faithfulness is almost seen to be synonymous with the firmness, the steadfastness, and the guarantee (βεβαίωσις) inherent in the oath. In *Sacr.* 93, Philo even claims that it is God's faithfulness that assures the oath, not the other way around. (3) As a corollary from these two points, it follows that God's words or promises are conceived like oaths, receiving steadfastness or confirmation. So, God's promise might be characterized as firm, steadfast, sure (βέβαιος). (4) Moreover, the association of oath and action / deed is a recurrent topic that defines the oath as words or promises that reach their accomplishment in action. (5) By receiving the divine oath of promise, one is incorporated into the steadfastness and faithfulness of God. Thus, Philo can say that Abraham's trust mirrors God's trust / faithfulness, "so that his mind might be established more securely and firmly even than it was before" (*Abr.* 273). Thus, as in the rendering of the oath in Gen 22:16 and Gen 26:3, the promises are not conceived as contingent upon Abraham's trust (πίστις), in the sense that Abraham's obedience has qualified him to be the recipient of God's promised blessing. Although the oath can be conceived as a reward, the promised gifts are thus not considered as a "payment" conditioned by Abraham's trust. Rather, the divine oath of promise is an adequate reaffirmation of the promises that were already given, so that Abraham's trust is transformed and incorporated into the divine oath of promise, conceived as grounded in and corresponding to the trust / faithfulness that belongs to God (πιστός), i.e. the kind of trust / faithfulness and steadfastness that only God and the friend of God can have.

It is noteworthy that the same constellation of motifs evinced in these texts also occurs in Heb 6:13–18, indicating a common underlying thought pattern and tradition. As H. Köster has shown, they share the following similarities:[69] (1) In addition to the use of Gen 22:16–18 LXX, both Philo (*Sacr.* 91–93 and *Leg.* 3:204–5) and Hebrews (Heb 6:13) mention that God swears by himself, since he had no one greater by whom to swear. (2) Both authors define the oath as a reaffirmation of the earlier promises. In Heb 6:13, the content of the oath of promise is referred to by the phrase ἐπαγγελία, while Philo employs the verb ὑπισχνέομαι (*Abr.* 273) or the noun λόγος (*Abr.* 273; *Sacr.* 93; *Leg.* 3:204). (3) Philo (*Abr.* 273; *Sacr.* 93; *Leg.* 3:204; cf. *Somn.* 1:12) and Hebrews (6:16) share the notion that oaths have the function of being a confirmation (βεβαίωσις) of the promise. (4) Like Philo, Hebrews seems to presuppose that an oath should strengten human beings' trustworthiness or faith, so that they might become as trustworthy as God. Thus, Philo takes it for granted that "an oath is added to assist faith" (*Leg.* 3:204) or that "men have recourse to oaths to win belief" (*Sacr.* 93), in contradistinction to God, who "is trustworthy in His speech as elsewhere, so that His words in certitude and assurance differ not a whit from oaths" (*Sacr.* 93). Or, as Sandmel put it in terms of Abraham's faith in *Abr.* 273: "God's oath is a measure of faith added to that faith which Abraham antecedently possessed."[70] As we noted above, Philo says here that by receiving the oath, Abraham's trust has reached the level of trust or faithfulness that only God and the friend of God can share. In Hebrews, this thought seems to be presupposed when the author claims in 6:17–18 that when

69 Köster, "Die Auslegung der Abraham-Verheissung," 95–109, esp. 98–102.
70 Sandmel, *Philo's Place in Judaism*, 140.

God desired to show even more clearly to the heirs of the promise the unchangeable character of his purpose, he guaranteed it by an oath, so that through two unchangeable things [that is, both God's promise and the oath], in which it is impossible that God would prove false, we who have taken refuge might be strongly encouraged to seize the hope set before us.[71]

3.3 The Phraseology of the Exegetical Tradition

The foregoing investigation of *Abr.* 262 – 273 suggested that it makes use of an exegetical tradition that associates Gen 15:6 with Genesis 22:18, in terms of a common thought pattern attested in a wide spectrum of Jewish and early Christian texts. Since such a thought pattern consists of a certain constellation of motifs, which is bound to be expressed in words and established phraseology, we should consider how far *Abr.* 262 – 273 and the other texts also have used similar or common terminology. In the light of the preceeding survey of the relevant data, the following observations will not reproduce an exhaustive survey of all the texts and motifs that are referred to above, but only present those texts which provide the greatest number of parallels and thus present features that are immediately obvious. The procedure will be as follows: For each item of the motif constellation, I shall take as my point of departure *Abr.* 262 – 273. I shall then list parallel expressions that occur in the other postbiblical Jewish texts and Christian texts. Next, I shall list parallel expressions that occur in the other postbiblical Jewish texts and Christian texts. Although I run the risk of simplification, this chart of the main vocabulary inherent in the exegetical tradition of Gen 15:6 and Gen 22:16 – 18 (I have put in brackets behind some of the passages instances of similar terminology to that in *Abr.* 273) confirms the impression that the Philonic passage should be placed within the context of a relatively constant set of motifs and fixed words, more or less inspired by the Jewish scriptures and their expositions.

3.3.1 The biblical Phraseology of Gen 15:6 and 22:16 – 18

The first item to be noted is the phraseology reminiscent of the biblical texts with which we are concerned here. In the references below, the passages in question are in brackets. The literary relations between the biblical passages in question and their applications in the Jewish and Christian texts may be variagated.

71 Cf. Köster, "Die Auslegung der Abraham-Verheissung," 100; Moxnes, *Theology in Conflict*, 141 – 2; J.I. Griffiths, *Hebrews and Divine Speech*, LNTS (London: Bloomsbury, 2015), 117.

Hence, I shall distinguish the following three levels: 1. To the degree I am confident that the Hebrew Bible passages to some extent have become a quotation, the "quoting" parts are printed in italics. 2. I shall refer to the terminology that certainly seems to have been influenced by the biblical passages, although differing from the case of "quotation", as at the first level, by being more of an "allusion" or a rephrasing of the Biblical text. These texts are typed in bold. 3. At level 3, I include motifs and terminology which seem to resemble corresponding features in the Hebrew Bible passages. These items are underlined.

Genesis 15:

Neh 9:8: *and you found his heart* ***faithful (πιστός) before you*** [...] (cf. Gen 15:6)

Abr. 262: In these it is stated "*he trusted in God*" *(ἐπίστευσε τῷ θεῷ)* (Gen 15:6)

Abr. 268: **Faith in God** (**ἡ πρὸς θεὸν πίστις**), then, is the one sure and infallible good [...] (cf. Gen 15:6)

Abr. 273: That God marvelling at **Abraham's trust in Him** (**τῆς πρὸς αὐτὸν πίστεως**) [...] (cf. Gen 15:6)

Deus 4: for in this [in the the unwavering steadfastness of the Existent] we are told he **had put his trust** (**πεπιστευκέναι**) (cf. Gen 15:6)

Sir 44:20: and in a trial he was found **faithful** (**πιστός**) (Gen 15:6)

1 Macc 2:52: Was not **Abraam found faithful** (**Αβρααμ [...] πιστός**) in temptation, *and it was accounted to him as righteousness?* (*καὶ ἐλογίσθη αὐτῷ εἰς δικαιοσύνην;*) (cf. Gen 15:6)

Jub. 18:16: that <u>you are faithful to me</u> (Gen 15:6) in everything I have told you

4Q225 2 II, 8: he would be found weak, and whether <u>A[braham] should not be found</u> <u>faithful</u> (כנאם) (Gen 15:6)

Jas 2:23: Thus the scripture was fulfilled that says, "*Abraham believed God, and it was reckoned to him as righteousness*" [...] (Gen 15:6)

Heb 6:12: those who **through faith** (**διὰ πίστεως**) and patience inherit the promises (cf. Gen 15:6)

Heb 11:17: **By faith** (**πίστις**) Abraham, when put to the test, offered up Isaac (cf. Gen 15:6)

1. Clem. 10:1: **Abraham [...] was found to be faithful** (**πιστός**) when he became obedient to God's words. (cf. Gen 15:6)

1. Clem. 10:6–7: *And Abraham trusted God, and it was accounted to him as righteousness.*" Because of **his faith** (**διὰ πίστιν**) [...] (cf. Gen 15:6)

Irenaeus, *Haer.* 4.16.2: *Abraham* without circumcision and without Sabbath observance *believed God, and it was reckoned to him as righteousness* [...] (cf. Gen 15:6)

Genesis 22:

Neh 9:8: [...] *and made with him a covenant* **to give to his descendants the land** [...] you have fulfilled your **promise** [...] (cf. Gen 22:16–17)

Abr. 273: [...] repaid him with trust by confirming with an oath the gifts which he had promised [...]. For He, with Whom a word is an oath, yet says "*By Myself have I sworn* [...]" (cf. Gen 22:16–18)

Deus 4: **He brings to God the dearly loved** [...] named **Isaac.** [...] But **first he bound,** as the law tells us**, the feet of the new strange victim** (Gen 22:2, 9)

Sir 44:19: and in a trial [...] (Gen 22:1)

Sir 44:21: *Therefore he established by means of an oath with him that nations would be blessed by his seed, that he would multiply him as the dust of the earth and like the stars to exalt his seed and to give them an inheritance* **from sea to sea and from the river to the end of the earth** (Gen 22:16–18)

Sir 44:22: And with Isaak he likewise established, **on account of Abraam his father. A blessing for all humankind** [...] (Gen 22:16–18; cf. Gen 26:3–4)

1 Macc 2:52: Was not Abraam found faithful in temptation, and it was accounted to him as righteousness? (cf. Gen 22:1)

Jub. 18:15–16: **He said, I have sworne by myself, says the Lord, because you have performed the command and have not refused me your first-born Son whom you love, and I will indeed bless you [...] because of the fact that you obeyed my command** (cf. Gen 22:15–18)

4Q225 2 II, 4: Isaac said to his father, 'T[ie ...]' (Gen 22:9)

Heb 6:13–14: When God made a promise to Abraham [...] *He swore by himself*, saying, "*I will surely bless you and multiply you*" (Gen 22:16–17)

Heb 11:17: By faith Abraham, when **put to the test, offered up Isaac.** He who had received the promises was ready **to offer up his only son** (cf. Gen 22:2, 9)

Jas 2:21: Was not our ancestor Abraham justified by works **when he offered his son Isaac on the altar?** (cf. Gen 22:2, 9)

1. Clem. 10:7: [...] in obedience **he offered him up as a sacrifice to God on one of the mountains that he showed him** (cf. Gen 22:2, 9)

3.3.2 The Exegetical Motif of Abraham's Trust and God's Adequate Reward

Some of the texts that attest the exegetical tradition that related Gen 15:6 to the *Akedah* contain the motif of a congruity between Abraham's trust and the adequate reward bestowed by God. We find the same interpretation of the oath in the exegetical tradition of Gen 15:6 and 22:16–18.

Abr. 273: [God], marveling at Abraham's trust in Him, repaid him with trust by confirmation (βεβαίωσις) through oath (ὅρκος) of the gifts (δωρεαί) which He promised ὑπισχνέομαι).

Sir 44:20–21: [...] and in a trial he was found faithful. *Therefore* he established by means of an oath with him that nations would be blessed by his seed, that he would multiply him as the dust of the earth and like the stars to exalt his seed and to give them an inheritance from sea to sea and from the river to the end of the earth

Jub. 18:15–16: He said, I have sworne by myself, says the Lord, because you have performed the command and have not refused me your first-born Son whom you love, and I will indeed bless you [...] because of the fact that you obeyed my command. [...] that you are faithful to me in everything I have told you

Mekilta Beshallah 7: And so also you find that our father Abraham inherited both this world and also the world beyond only as a reward for the faith (אמנה בשכר) with which he believed, as it is said: "*And he believed in the Lord*" (Gen 15:6) [...]

Hebr 6:16–17: [...] an oath (ὅρκος) given as confirmation (βεβαίωσις) puts an end to all dispute. In the same way, when God desired to show even more clearly to the heirs of the promise (ἐπαγγελία) the unchangeable character of his purpose, he guaranteed it by an oath (ὅρκος) [...]

Heb 11:17–19: By faith Abraham (Πίστει [...] Ἀβραάμ), when put to the test, offered up Isaac [...]. He considered the fact that God is able even to raise someone from the dead—and figuratively speaking, he did receive him back.

Irenaeus, *Haer.* 4.5.4: For Abraham, according to his faith, followed the commandment of the word of God, and with ready mind gave up his only and beloved son, as a sacrifice to God, in order that God might be pleased to offer his beloved and only Son for all his offspring, as a sacrifice for our salvation.

3.3.3 The Exegetical Motif of Abraham as God's Friend

The exegetical motif of Abraham being called a friend of God (here marked in italics) is one of the interpretative features related to Gen 15:6 and occurs also in the context of the exegetical tradition related to Genesis 22 and the *Akedah*.

Abr. 273: no longer conversing with him as God might with man, but as one *friend* (φίλος) with another [...]

Jas 2:23: Thus the scripture was fulfilled that says, "Abraham believed God, and it was reckoned to him as righteousness," and he was called the *friend* (φίλος) of God.

1. Clem. 10:1: Abraham, who was called "the *friend*" (φίλος) [...]

Irenaeus, *Haer.* 4.16.2: *Abraham* without circumcision and without Sabbath observance *believed God, and it was reckoned to him as righteousness,* and he was called the *friend* of God (*amicus* Dei).

4 Conclusion

My survey of the way in which the Abrahamic promises are expanded in Genesis 12–26 presupposes a certain *continuum* between the events reported in Gen 15:6, 22:15–18, and 26:3–5. These passages show a concern about how Israel's existence as a covenant people of God depends on the divine promise and will of Yahweh *and* the trust / faithfulness of Abraham. My analysis of *Abr.* 262–273 has shown that Philo follows such a line of thought. A closer examination has further displayed a constellation of motifs with the application of a somewhat fixed terminology, which corroborates the assertion that Philo makes use of an exegetical tradition that reads Gen 15:6 and Gen 22:16–18 as a *continuum* of Abrahamic events that belong together. Thus, Philo interprets Gen 15:6 in conjunction with Gen 22:16–18 from the perspective of a reciprocity between Abraham's conduct of trust and the conduct of trust / faithfulness expected in return from God. This correspondence can partly be drawn from the Hebrew scriptures themselves and conforms to data in Jewish tradition.

In the next chapter, I shall go on to argue that Philo deviates from an exegetical tradition that reads Gen 15:6, 22:15–18, and 26:3–5 in *continuum* as sequences of the Abrahamic narrative that belong together. Thus, Philo detaches Abraham's trust (Gen 15:6), usually taken in the Hebrew Bible and Jewish tradition as a conduct that comes to expression in his obedience to the Laws of Moses before they were written (Gen 26:5), and rather one-sidely relates it to the promises given to Abraham (Gen 22:16–18) apart from the Law of Moses. Hence, I shall suggest that Philo has made a distinction in his concept of the Law between an "Abrahamic jurisdiction", in which Abraham's trust in God's promise is conceived of as observing and epitomizing the divine Law in Nature, and the "Mosaic jurisdiction", which reflects a Jewish discussion of Abraham. This conclusion will in due course have some bearing on the last chapter as well, when I investigate further whether Paul's negotiation on Abraham in Galatians 3 resembles a similar Jewish debate and a corresponding distinction in the concept of the Law.

Chapter 4: Philo's Negotation of Abraham between the Divine Law in Nature and the Law of Moses

1 Thesis

Philo's writings attest a rationalization of the relationship between the divine Law in Nature and the Torah of Moses.[1] The Hellenistic context provides a challenge in this regard, since the Greek concept of the Law of Nature was incompatible *a priori* with the idea of a written law of particular polities.[2] The conundrum Philo faced may be formulated as follows: In order to legitimate and authorize the Law of Moses in such a context, how could Philo overcome the view that denigrated the written laws of particular nations and peoples, which might be temporary and supersedible, in favour of the unwritten, general, unalterable, and everlasting Law of Nature?

H. Najman has dealt with this topic in several studies, in search of a conceptual room for Philo's authorization of the Law of Moses in the light of Hellenistic concepts of the Law of Nature.[3] With regard to Philo's hermeneutical maneuvers, Najman claims:

---

1 On the relationship between the Law of Moses and the Law of Nature in Philo, cf. H. Köster, "νόμος φύσεως: The Concept of Natural Law in Greek Thought," in *Religions in Antiquity: Essays in Memory of E. R. Goodenough*, ed. J. Neusner, SHR (Leiden: Brill, 1968), 521–41; Sandmel, *Philo's Place in Judaism*, 107–10, 201–3; V. Nikiprowetzky, *Le Commentaire de L'Écriture chez Philon D'Alexandrie* (Leiden: Brill, 1977), 117–55; R.A. Horsley, "The Law of Nature in Philo and Cicero," *HTR* 71.1–2 (1978): 35–59; D. Winston, "Philo's Ethical Theory," in *ANRW 21.1: Part 2, Principat 21.1*, ed. H. Temporini and W. Haase (Berlin: De Gruyter, 1984), 381–88; P. Borgen, *An Exegete for His Time*, 144–53; D.T. Runia, *Philo of Alexandria: On the Creation of the Cosmos According to Moses: Introduction, Translation and Commentary*, PACS (Leiden: Brill, 2001), 106–7; J.W. Martens, *One God, One Law: Philo of Alexandria on the Mosaic and Greco-Roman Law*, SPhAMA (Leiden: Brill, 2003), 83–101; H. Najman, *Seconding Sinai: The Development of Mosaic Discourse in Second Temple Judaism*, JSJSup (Leiden: Brill, 2003a), 70–107; idem, "A Written Copy of the Law of Nature: An Unthinkable Paradox," SPhiloA 15 (2003): 54–63; Y. Paz, "Prior to Sinai: The Patriarchs and the Mosaic Law in Rabbinic Literature in View of Second Temple and Christian Literature" (Jerusalem: Hebrew University of Jerusalem [Hebrew], 2009); S. Wilf, *The Law Before the Law* (Plymouth: Lexington Books, 2008), 117–23; C.E. Hayes, *Divine Law*, 111–24.

2 See, for example, Sophocles, *Ant.* 450–460; Aristotle, *Eth. nic.* 5.7; Plutarch, *Lyc.* 13.1–2.

3 Cf. H. Najman, "The Law of Nature and the Authority of Mosaic Law," SPhiloA 11 (1999): 55–73; idem, *Seconding Sinai*; idem, "A Written Copy of the Law of Nature"; idem,

https://doi.org/10.1515/9783110722109-005

> So Philo must show–*in opposition to Greek thought on the topic*–that the perfect and authoritative copy of the Law of Nature is to be found, not only in the unwritten law, exhibited by the life of the sage, but also in the written law of Moses, despite its writtenness and despite its apparent particularity.[4]

According to Najman, Philo's rationale for this is the assumption that the divine law in Nature and the Mosaic Law are one and the same: "For Philo the Mosaic law is identical with the law of nature."[5] Against this view, I shall argue that this interpretation blurs the concept of two dynamic jurisdictions at work in the Torah, which Philo is careful to keep apart, i.e., between the divine Law in Nature manifested in Abraham's life, and the written Law revealed through the particular ordinances of Moses. Thus, I shall seek to nuance Najman's position and take a slightly different approach: While there appears to be no room in Greek thinking for a written copy of the laws of Nature, Philo seems to build upon a Roman discourse of Law, attested (for example) by Cicero, that envisages a future eternal and unchangeable Law made valid for for all nations. Thus, Philo solves the conundrum of an unwritten law incompatible with a written law by admitting that the Law of Moses is *not identical* with the divine Law of Nature, but in conformity with it,[6] as the best possible copy of an unchangeable and cosmic Law that one day is to be observed by all nations. This line of reasoning does not differ much from Najman's, but it makes better allowance for the nuanced ways in which Philo claims authority for the cosmic significance of the Law of Moses without compromising its value as the particular constitution of the Jewish people.

This approach takes its point of departure in the observation that Philo presupposes an exegetical tradition that reads Gen 15:6, Gen 22:16–18, and Gen 26:3–5 in a *continuum* of events that belong together in the Abrahamic narrative. In contradistinction to this exegetical tradition, however, Philo argues against

---

Past Renewals: Interpretative Authority, Renewed Revelation, and the Quest for Perfection in Jewish Antiquity, JSJ (Leiden; Boston: Brill, 2010).

4 Najman, "The Law of Nature," 59.

5 Najman, "The Law of Nature," 64. Cf. also the statement in idem, "A Written Copy of the Law of Nature," 61:

> Philo says that the enacted laws – that is to say, the laws given by God to Israel through Moses – may be properly regarded as reminders of the lives of the patriarchs, indeed as nothing else. In other words, if read in accordance with Philo's instruction, the lives of the patriarchs and the laws of Moses turn out to be equivalent.

6 Thus also Winston, "Philo's Ethical Theory," 386–7: "Furthermore, not only does Philo take over the well-known Greek contrast between conventional and natural law, but he explicitly asserts that the Torah is in conformity with the latter [...]."

the view that Abraham was a worthy recipient of the promise because of his observance of the Law of Moses (Gen 26:5) even before it was written. To the extent that Abraham is described as "lawful", I shall argue that Gen 26:5 is rather attributed by Philo to Abraham's adherence to the divine Law in Nature, manifested in his trust in the promise (Gen 15:6).[7] Since Gen 26:5, no less than the other commandments in the Torah, refers to the Law of Moses, Philo would seem here to have made a distinction in his concept of the Torah. Thus, Philo seems to conceive of two dynamic jurisdictions at work in the Torah, i.e., a distinction between an "Abrahamic jurisdiction" and the "Mosaic jurisdiction", which exemplify the very same virtues. This means that the latter jurisdiction reproduces the same kind of virtues that Abraham achieved through his instinctive words and deeds before the Mosaic ordinances were written. Accordingly, we should avoid speaking of the unwritten Law of Nature as more "universal", "higher", or "superior" in contrast to the written Law of Moses, conceived as "particular", "secondary", or "subordinate".[8]

A more elaborate argumentation of this view will be offered in the remainder of this chapter and tested against the available data. I suggest that it might be corroborated by a closer reading of *Abr.* 275–276 in the context of the treatise itself and against the background of Greco-Roman and Jewish data. In order to uphold the Hellenistic contrast between an unwritten Law of Nature and the written Law of Moses, Philo here reflects a Jewish discussion of his own time, in which he engages with other Jews who see Abraham as a "lawful" observer of the Law of Moses. Thus, in contrast to this conventional Jewish position on Abraham, Philo adapts Greco-Roman notions about the Law of Nature to his own interpretation of Law of Moses and vice versa, in order to show how Abraham rather came to be "lawful" in accordance with the divine Law in Nature. Before proceeding to a fresh interpretation of *Abr.* 275–276, we shall take into account previous scholarship on this passage.

---

7 Gen 26:5 clearly adds to Abraham's way of obedience categories of the law, that is: "kept my charge, my commandments, my statutes, and my laws." Hence, a commentator or later glossator seems to have characterized Abraham's obedience as a model of living by Torah. Cf. Moberly, "The Earliest Commentary on the Akedah," 322.

8 *Pace* scholars such as Goodenough, *By Light, Light*, 73–96; Sandmel, *Philo's Place in Judaism*, 109; A. Myre, "La Loi l' Ordre Cosmique et Politique selon Philon d'Alexandrie," *ScEs* 24 (1972): 217–47; idem, "La Loi et la Pentateuque selon Philon d'Alexandrie," *ScEs* 25 (1973): 208–25; idem, "La Loi de la Nature et la Loi Mosaïque selon Philon d'Alexandrie," *ScEs* 28 (1976): 163–81; Martens, *One God, One Law*, 83–130.

2 Previous Research

In the closure of the treatise *De Abrahamo* 275–276, Abraham's trust in God's promises is set in the context of Abraham's relation to the Law of Moses:

> Ταῦτα μὲν οὖν ἐπὶ τοσοῦτον εἰρήσθω. τῷ δὲ πλήθει καὶ μεγέθει τῶν ἐπαίνων ἐπιτιθεὶς ὥσπερ τινὰ κεφαλὴν τοῦ σοφοῦ φησιν, ὅτι τὸν θεῖον νόμον καὶ τὰ θεῖα προστάγματα πάντα ἐποίησεν ὁ ἀνὴρ οὗτος, οὐ γράμμασιν ἀναδιδαχθείς, ἀλλ' ἀγράφῳ τῇ φύσει σπουδάσας ὑγιαινούσαις καὶ ἀνόσοις ὁρμαῖς ἐπακολουθῆσαι· περὶ δὲ ὧν ὁ θεὸς ὁμολογεῖ, τί προσῆκεν ἀνθρώπους ἢ βεβαιότατα πιστεύειν; τοιοῦτος ὁ βίος τοῦ πρώτου καὶ ἀρχηγέτου τοῦ ἔθνους ἐστίν, ὡς μὲν ἔνιοι φήσουσι, νόμιμος, ὡς δ' ὁ παρ' ἐμοῦ λόγος ἔδειξε, νόμος αὐτὸς ὢν καὶ θεσμὸς ἄγραφος.
>
> So much for all this, but to these praises of the Sage, so many and so great, Moses adds this crowning saying "that this man did the divine law and the divine commands." He did them, not taught by written words, but unwritten nature gave him the zeal to follow where wholesome and untainted impulses led him. And when God gives his endorsement concerning these, what does it befit men to do other than to grant their firmest trust? Such was the life of the first, the founder of the nation, one who obeyed the law, some will say, but rather, as our discourse has shown, himself a law and an unwritten statute.[9]

This centrally important passage has given rise to several comments in Philonic scholarship on the various interpretations of both Abraham and the divine Law. The point of departure for the discussion has been the different interpretations of Abraham and the divine Law based on Philo's paraphrase of Gen 26:5 in the clause "that this man did the divine law and the divine commands".[10] A common interpretation is represented by L. Ginzberg and H.A. Wolfson, who assert that Philo anticipates rabbinic traditions which conceived of Abraham as νόμιμος ("lawful") in its *literal sense*. In other words, the reference to Gen 26:5 implies that Abraham observed the Law of Moses even before it was given at Sinai.[11] In opposition to this interpretation, S. Sandmel argued that Abraham observed the divine Law of Nature, *not* the Torah.[12] Thus, Philo and the rabbis use Genesis

---

9 The Loeb translation is somewhat modified.

10 Cf. for a survey of the discussion, Najman, *Seconding Sinai*, 70–107.

11 Cf. L. Ginzberg, *The Legends of the Jews: 7. Vols.* (Philadelphia: The Jewish Publication Society of America, 1968), esp. vol. V, 259; H.A. Wolfson, *Philo: Foundations of Religious Philosophy in Judaism, Christianity, and Islam: 2 Volumes* (Cambridge, MA; London: Harvard University Press, 1947), vol. I, 187–8. See also for a survey of the rabbinic tradition, E.E. Urbach, *The Sages: Their Concepts and Beliefs* (Cambridge, MA: Harvard University Press, 1987), 315–342; Paz, "Prior to Sinai," 5, 50–4; Hayes, *Divine Law*, 331, 342–4. For rabbinic texts, cf. e.g., m. Qidd. 4:14; t. Qidd. 5:17; b. Yoma 28b; Gen. Rab. 61:1; 64:4; 95:3.

12 Similarly, Goodenough (*By Light, Light*, 74) argued that Philo denied that the Patriarchs were "bundles of commands which were written down by Moses" and claimed that "there is no

26:5 to connect Abraham to the divine Law in very different ways. For some rabbis, Gen 26:5 proves that the Torah of Moses was revealed to Abraham and the patriarchs before it was revealed at Sinai. As C. Hayes puts it:

> Abraham may have been a man of faith—indeed, many midrashim celebrate his faithful endurance of repeated trials—but according to certain rabbinic traditions, he was no less a follower of God's commandments, statutes, and laws.[13]

Sandmel put it this way: "The rabbis say that Abraham observed the Law; Philo says that the Law sets forth as legislation those things which Abraham did."[14] Likewise, Sandmel claimed that "Philo is not interested in portraying Abraham as an observer of the Law [...]. Abraham is Philo's proof that there is an antecedent to the Laws of Moses, and that it is possible for a man to live by that Law."[15]

A third interpretation might be seen as a way of combining these two: it assumes that Abraham observed the unwritten Law of Nature, yet this was equivalent to the written Mosaic Law.[16] This position has found support in recent scholarship too. Thus, for example, scholars such as F. Watson, J.M.G. Barclay, and most recently K.O. Sandnes tend to read Philo's interpretation of the Abraham biography as a *continuum* of scriptures and events that belong together, in a way that that conjoins what Philo tries to keep apart. Thus, e.g., F. Watson takes as the point of departure a common view of Philo's conception of the Law:

> The laws revealed at Sinai were preceded by earlier articulations of those same laws; whether these were written or unwritten, the mode of divine discourse is fundamentally the same before Moses as through Moses.[17]

Similarly, Barclay, without taking into due consideration the modifications and nuances referred to by Philo himself in a discussion with his interlocutors, interprets "Abraham's obedience to divine commands, including God's statutes and laws (Gen 12:4; 22:18; 26:5)" as identical with the Law of Moses: "Philo took

---

thought of deducing the specific commands from the incidents of the lives of the Patriarchs." Likewise, J.L. Kugel ("Jubilees, Philo, and the Problem of Genesis," in *The Hebrew Bible in Light of the Dead Sea Scrolls*, ed. N. David, et al., FRLANT [Göttingen: Vandenhoeck & Ruprecht, 2012], 305–8) has pointed out, unlike sources such as Jubilees or rabbinic literature, Philo nowhere says explicitly that Abraham observed any of the laws in the Mosaic legislation.

13 Cf. Hayes, *Divine Law*, 340.

14 Sandmel, *Philo's Place in Judaism*, 108.

15 Sandmel, *Philo's Place in Judaism*, 240.

16 Cf. Borgen, *An Exegete for His Time*, 69; Martens, *One God, One Law*, 108; Najman, *Seconding Sinai*, 128; Hayes, *Divine Law*, 340.

17 Watson, *Paul and the Hermeneutics of Faith*, 222.

these biblical texts to indicate that Abraham (and the other patriarchs) conformed to, and embodied the unwritten laws of nature, of which the written Mosaic law was a copy (*Abr.* 1–6; 276)."[18] Similarly, Sandnes claims that Philo's biography *On Abraham* "is marked by references pointing to Abraham as embodying what a continous reading of his biography conveys, namely obedience to the law."[19] A further representative of this position, J.W. Maartens, reads Gen 26:5 in *Abr.* 275–276 as follows:

> If we agree that Philo is here referring to the law of Moses, and we know that Abraham has done the law of nature, it should be clear that there exists no difference between them. Indeed, Abraham was not νόμιμος, "lawful" according to a legal code, he was a "law" himself and an unwritten law (*Abr.* 276); but being "lawful" and becoming a "law" are not contradictory: Abraham became a law because he did the things which the law required.[20]

The "law" spoken of in the phrase "one who obeyed the law" here is thus taken in recent scholarship as a reference to the ambiguous aspect of the divine Law of Moses that Philo is thought to maintain, i.e., the particular Mosaic laws correlative with the divine Law in Nature. This view is often based on the syllogism imposed on *Abr.* 276: Since the laws of Moses are "copies of the laws of nature", Abraham was *eo ipso* observing the laws of Moses before they were even written, in opposition to the view of the rabbis, who took Gen 26:5 in its literal sense, believing that the Torah was revealed to Abraham before Sinai.[21] Most scholars mentioned above fail to discuss the fact that Philo, in this passage, draws a distinction, on the one hand, between Abraham being a "law himself and an unwritten law", and, on the other hand, the view obviously known to him that Abraham was "one who obeyed the law". Thus, there is no indication that either Philo, or those persons he here explicitly refers to, or the rabbinic traditions ever held the idea that the Torah was identical with the natural law. I believe that, without explicitly referring to *Abr.* 275–276, Hayes encapsulates Philo's modified interpretation of Abraham and the Law, discernible from both the conceptions prevalent in the Jewish community of Philo's own time and the later rabbis on this issue, when she remarks: "none of the rabbinic traditions about

18 Barclay, *Paul and the Gift*, 233.
19 Sandnes, *Paul Perceived*, 150.
20 Maartens, *One God, One Law*, 108; idem, "The Meaning and Function of the Law in Philo and Josephus," in *Torah Ethics and Early Christian Identity*, ed. S.J. Wendel and D.M. Miller (Grand Rapids: Eerdmans, 2016), 27–40.
21 For this position, cf., e.g., Borgen, *An Exegete for His Time*, 61; Najman, *Seconding Sinai*, 70–107; Kugel, "Jubilees, Philo, and the Problem of Genesis," 306; Hayes, *Divine Law*, 340.

the law observed by the patriarchs represents this law as embedded in nature, distinct from the revealed Mosaic Law."[22]

In what follows, I shall revisit and mainly endorse the view of Sandmel that Philo interpreted Gen 26:5 about the divine Law in Nature precisely as an antecedent to the Law of Moses. I shall argue that Sandmel's position on the contrast between Philo and the rabbis is corroborated, albeit it should be nuanced, in view of the fact that Philo himself here explicitly referred to those, who like the rabbis, would claim that Abraham obeyed the Law even before it was revealed through Moses at Sinai. Philo's awareness of a Jewish debate on this issue in his own time has to some extent been neglected, and invites further research. Thus, the question which should be scrutinized somewhat further is whether Philo himself provides more clues about the context and meaning of his paraphrasing of Gen 26:5. The answer seems to be in the affirmative.

3 A Fresh Look at *Abr.* 275–276 in Jewish and Roman Context

To begin with, further examination needs to be made of the echo of a Jewish debate in *Abr.* 276, that is, between Philo's own exposition of Gen 26:5 and the one ascribed to his Jewish "colleagues". Here, Philo most probably refers explicitly to a view held by Jewish "literalists" and "exegetes" in his environment, whom he presents with the formula ἔνιοι φήσουσι ("some will say").[23] Like the rabbis, these persons regarded Abraham as νόμιμος ("lawful"), viz. as someone obeying the commandments of the Mosaic Torah, a view somewhat distinct from the one Philo himself propounds. This contrast has been somewhat neglected in scholarship, and as far as I know, the only exceptions are some brief comments on *Abr.* 276 by a few scholars. Thus, for example, Goodenough remarks:

---

22 Hayes, *Divine Law*, 354.

23 Philo appropriates phrases like these when he explicitly conveys the views of other exegetes; this shows that he was an exegete among other exegetes. Cf. E. Stein, *Philo und der Midrasch: Philos Schilderung der Gestalten Des Pentateuch Verglichen mit der Des Midrasch*, BZAW (Giessen: De Gruyter, 1931), 4–10; M. Shroyer, "Alexandrian Jewish Literalists," *JBL* 55.4 (1936): 261–84; Borgen, *An Exegete for His Time*, 93–95, 151; A. Kamesar, "The Literary Genres of the Pentateuch as Seen from the Greek Perspective: The Testimony of Philo of Alexandria," SPhA 9 (1997): 170–1; M.R. Niehoff, "Homeric Scholarship and Bible Exegesis in Ancient Alexandria: Evidence from Philo's 'Quarrelsome' Colleagues," *CQ* 57.1 (2007): 166–82; idem, *Jewish Exegesis and Homeric Scholarship in Alexandria* (Cambridge: CUP, 2011).

> The last contrast is striking. It was apparently a common thing among the Jews of Philo's day to regard Abraham as one who obeyed the Law, νόμιμος. But Philo is not content with this conservative statement. [...] He says he has proved a position different from that held by others [...][24]

Furthermore, with regard to the affinity between the view known to Philo and the rabbis, Borgen claims: "Philo was, therefore, aware of this rabbinic picture of Abraham, and referred to it explicitly as background for his interpretation."[25] Most recently, the commentary of E. Birnbaum and J. Dillon contains the following remarks:

> In mentioning "as some would have it" (ὡς ... ἔνιοι φήσουσι) Philo appears to be referring to a real, known position, namely, that Abraham followed various laws before they were written down. [...] By contrast with the interpretation maintained by some [...], Philo's own position is that Abraham himself was "a law and an unwritten ordinance."[26]

Such scholarly remarks on the distinction between Philo's own view and that held by others of his day are sketchy, however, and should be taken further by a closer analysis of *Abr.* 275 – 276 in its immediate literary context.

In the first place, to assume, as most scholars do, that Philo's reference to the view of others at this point concurs with his own interpretation fails to take into account Philo's notion of Abraham as "himself a law and an unwritten statute" in contrast (cf. the adversative conjunction δέ) to the sentiment inherent in the phrase "one who obeyed the law".[27] As I shall suggest, at this juncture Philo's disjunction refers rather to a Jewish discourse in which Abraham, on

---

24 Goodenough, *By Light, Light*, 145.

25 P. Borgen, "Philo of Alexandria: A Critical and Synthetical Survey of Research Since World War II," in *ANRW II:21:1* (Berlin; New York: De Gruyter, 1984), 126. See also Sass, *Leben aus den Verheissungen*, 110 n. 41, who refers to Borgen's assumption, but without any further comment. Cf. also Borgen's comment (*An Exegete for His Time*, 69) on *Abr.* 276, with regard to his objection to the contrast Sandmel draws between the views of the rabbis and that of Philo: "Philo indicates himself, however, that he modifies and interprets the view that Abraham obeyed the Law [...]." Watson (*Paul and the Hermeneutics of Faith* [London; New York: T & T Clark, 2004], 251 n. 40) refers to Borgen's observation at this juncture, but seems to neglect its implications, when he states that Philo's interpretation of Gen 26:5 in *Abr.* 276 about the "Law of Nature" is indentical with the Jewish Torah. For a similar interpretation of *Abr.* 276, cf. also Betz, *Galatians*, 166 – 7.

26 Birnbaum and Dillon, *On the Life of Abraham*, 407 – 8.

27 Even Borgen (*An Exegete for His Time*, 149) seems to maintain this view, despite his observation that Philo here explicitly refers to the view of others as the background to his own interpretation.

the basis of Gen 26:5, was conceived as being obedient to the divine Law that was inseparable from the Law of Moses.

Second, it is noteworthy that *Abr.* 275–276 and its exposition of Gen 26:5 follow immediately after the reference in *Abr.* 273 to the correspondence between Abraham's πίστις and God's πίστις granted him in return in terms of the oath of promise. A further corroboration that Abraham's trust is here conceived of as trust in the divine commands, including the promises of God, seems to be found in *Abr.* 275–276: "And when God gives his endorsement concerning these, what does it befit men to do other than to grant their firmest trust? Such was the life of the first, the founder of the nation, one who obeyed the law, some will say [...]." In that case, Philo implicitly ascribes to his interlocutors a view that Abraham's trust in God's commands manifested itself and was achieved through his obedience to the Mosaic Law. This conjecture gains in probability when evidence makes clear that it is in touch with a widely attested Jewish interpretation of Abraham's faith, which conflated two exegetical motifs, namely, Abraham's faithfulness as maintained at the *Akedah* with reference to Gen 15:6 and conceived of as a manifestation of his observance of the Sinaitic Law. As we have seen in the previous chapter, this exegetical tradition is attested in the texts analysed in that chapter, such as Sir 44:19–21 and 1 Macc 2:52. Thus, in contradistinction to the assumption known to Philo, which seems to resemble later rabbinic traditions,[28] Philo interprets Abraham, the founder of the Jewish nation, as someone who was living according to *the divine Law in Nature*, as distinct from the Law of Moses revealed later at Sinai. At this juncture, then, Philo appears to give us a glimpse of a Jewish conception known to him, that Abraham performed the Torah in a literal sense. This conjecture is expressed by Sandmel and seems to support his contentions about the difference between Philo's and the rabbinic view:

> The rabbinic view is completely foreign to Philo. The rabbis take as their norm the Mosaic (and Oral) Law, and they bring Abraham up to the norm by portraying him as an observer. Philo, however, takes Abraham (and the Patriarchs) as the norm, and shows in what way the Law of Moses fits in with the norm. The rabbis say that Abraham observed the Law; Philo says that the Law sets forth as legislation those things which Abraham did. [...] Insofar as he was a lawful man, it was the law of nature which Abraham followed. Since the particular laws, that is, the Mosaic code, are the copy of deeds of men who followed nature, the Mosaic Law is consistent with nature.[29]

---

28 Cf., e.g., m. Qidd. 4:14; b. Yoma 28b. On these texts, see Hayes, *Divine Law*, 340–59.
29 Sandmel, *Philo's Place in Judaism*, 108.

Sandmel's contention that "the rabbinic view is completely foreign to Philo" should be nuanced, however, since Philo's own explicit reference makes clear that he is aware of a Jewish picture of Abraham resembling the conception of the later rabbis.[30] Rather than saying that Abraham lived in conformity with the Law of Moses, Philo seems to have applied this position of other Jewish "exegetes" as the background for his own interpretation of Gen 26:5. Since the Law of Moses (e.g., Gen 26:5) records the virtues of what Abraham instinctively said and did (cf. *Abr.* 4) in conformity with the unwritten divine Law in Nature, anyone who later lives by the Law of Moses lives in mutual accord with the divine Law of Nature. Fresh observations on some clues in *Abr.* 275–276 in the light of a rabbinic conception may provide more nuances to such a conjecture about the cultural context of Philo's own exegetical paraphrase of Gen 26:5.

It is noteworthy that in the rabbinic texts Abraham came to learn the Torah within a schoolhouse setting by one of two modalities,[31] either by a self-taught study of the Torah under the guidance of an internal teacher, or by learning the Torah under tutelage of an external teacher. The former view comes to expression in several rabbinic texts that emphasize Abraham's autonomy. For example, Gen. Rab. 95:3 refers to Abraham's solitary study of the Torah independent of any external teacher: "Abraham learned the Torah from himself, for it is said, 'and a good man shall be satisfied from himself''."[32] In a similar vein, Jub. 12:25–27 holds that Abraham had a written copy of the Law received from his fathers: "And he took his father's books—and they were written in Hebrew—and he copied them. And he began studying them thereafter." Others assumed that Abraham had a written copy of the Law passed down from Enoch (1QapGen ar 19:24b–26a).[33] The latter modality is attested by Gen. Rab. 61:1, which depicts Abraham engaged day and night in the study of the Torah under the tutelage of his kidneys as divinely appointed teachers: "[...] whence did he learn Torah? The Holy One blessed be He made his two kidneys serve like two teachers, and these welled truth and taught him wisdom."[34] As for Philo's picture of Abraham, do we find any signs of a similar understanding in the treatise *De Abrahamo?* Although Philo himself never explicitly elaborates on the view of those who claim that Abraham obeyed the Law of Moses, and how they thought that Abraham came to know the Torah, it is my hypothesis that Philo's emphasis on how Abraham was educated into the divine Law might be read in contradistinction to and

---

30 Cf. Borgen's affirmation, cited above.

31 For these modalities, cf. Wilf, *The Law*, 120; Hayes, *Divine Law*, 342–5.

32 Cf. Urbach, *The Sages*, 282–4.

33 Cf. Gregory, "Abraham as the Jewish Ideal," 72.

34 Cf. Kugel., *Traditions of the Bible*, 706–7.

against the background of the rabbinic modalities. Thus, in the following texts the words in **bold type** mark the protestations as to how Philo envisages that Abraham (and the Patriarchs) did not know and observe the statutes of the Law of Moses, while the words in *italics* explain what kind of law they actually adhered to, i.e. the divine Law in Nature:

> For **they were not scholars or pupils of others, nor did they learn under teachers** what was right to say or do: they **listened to no voice or instruction** *but their own:* they gladly *accepted conformity with nature*, holding that nature itself was, as indeed it is, the *most venerable of statutes*, and thus *their whole life was one of happy obedience to law. Abr.* 6

> Great indeed are the efforts expended both by lawgivers and by laws in every nation in filling the souls of free men with comfortable hopes; but he who gains this virtue of hope fulness **without being led to it by exhortation or command** has been *educated into it by a law* which nature has laid down, *a law unwritten* yet *intuitively learnt. Abr.* 16

> For anyone who contemplates the order in nature and the constitution enjoyed by the world-city whose excellence no words can describe, **needs no speaker to teach him** *to practise a law-abiding and peaceful life* and to aim at assimilating himself to its beauties. *Abr.* 61

> He did them, **not taught by written words**, but *unwritten nature gave him the zeal to follow* where wholesome and untainted impulse led him. And when God gives his endorsement concerning these, what does it befit men to do other than to grant their firmest trust? Such was the life of the first, the founder of the nation, one who obeyed the law, some will say, but rather, as our discourse has shown, *himself a law and an unwritten statute. Abr.* 276

If one reads the words in italics together, the view emerges that Abraham came to know the divine Law in Nature, that is, as one who made a solitary study of the unwritten Law in Nature, not taught by written words and inspired by an external teacher. These protestations about Abraham are emphatic, and the best logical explanation for some of them may be that Philo was aware of the opposite view, corresponding to that of the rabbis, namely that Abraham learnt the Torah alone or by studying the written Torah under a teacher. Since *Abr.* 276 contrasts the notion that Abraham was educated by unwritten nature and not taught by written words (cf. also *Abr.* 6 and 16) with the view explicitly ascribed to those of Philo's day who conceived that Abraham was "lawabiding", Philo may have inferred that the same persons have thought that Abraham came to learn the Torah before it was given by Moses at Sinai. They may have even held the view reported in b. Yoma 28b that Abraham had an obligation to *fullfill* the commandments, suggesting that he was commanded to observe them.[35] If that is the

35 Cf. Najman, *Seconding Sinai*, 128 n. 44.

case, Philo comes close to a text such as m. Qidd. 4:11, which states that Abraham *performed* the commandments, without any hint that he was under order to do so. This may also explain Philo's change of verb in his paraphrase of Gen 26:5 in *Abr.* 275. Here Philo says that Abraham "did" (ποιέω) these laws rather than "fulfilled" (φυλάσσω) them as the LXX translates.[36] Againt such a background, it makes sense that Philo insists on the opposite, *viz.* that Abraham's *paideia* into the Law was independent of any exhortations or commands based on instructions from external teachers (cf. the **bold type** in *Abr.* 6, 16, and 61). Moreover, although Philo in general regarded Abraham as one who did not require formal apprenticeship or teaching from an external teacher,[37] this does not mean that he needed no instruction at all. Instead, Philo gives prominence to Abraham as a *self-taught* person who "did" the divine law under the inspiration of a teacher. Accordingly, Philo asserts that unwritten nature "gave" to Abraham the zeal to follow where wholesome and untainted impulse led him (cf. the *italics* in *Abr.* 276). As a corollary, Philo states that Abraham's life was one of happy obedience to an unwritten law, intuitively learnt – educated by a record

---

36 Martens (*One God, One Law*, 107–8) observes this significant change in the verb, but he is wrong to assume that Philo here refers to the Law of Moses, that is, Gen 26:5 taken in its literary sense. Martens argues on the basis of the allusions to Gen 26:5 in *Migr.* 130, but he fails to take into account the literary context of *Migr.* 128–129, in which Philo argues that the "Law", equivalent to the divine word, is not the Law of Moses, but the injunctions of right reason, that is, the divine reason which is embodied in the physical cosmos and constitutes its immanent Law in Nature. Thus, the actions of Abraham manifest this "Law" and the way he follows God:

> This is the aim extolled by the best philosophers, to live agreeably to nature; and it is attained whenever the mind, having entered on virtue's path, walks in the track of right reason and follows God, mindful of His injunctions, and always and in all places recognizing them all as valid both in action and in speech. *Migr.* 128

> So in another place He says, "Abraham did 'all My law'" (Gen. xxvi. 5): "Law" being evidently nothing else than the Divine word enjoining what we ought to do and forbidding what we should not do, as Moses testifies by saying "he received a law from His words" (Deut. xxxiii. 3f.). If, then, the law is a Divine word, and the man of true worth "does" the law, he assuredly "does" the word: so that, as I said, God's words are the wise man's "doings." To follow God is, then, according to Moses, that most holy man, our aim and object [...]. *Migr.* 130

For such a reading of Philo's paraphrase of Gen 26:5 in *Migr.* 128–130, cf. Sandmel, *Philo's Place in Judaism*, 165–6, 209.

37 Cf. E. Birnbaum ("The Biblical Interpretations of Philo," 947 n. 3):

> Philo does not explicitly address the role of teaching in Abraham's life in this work, possibly because Philo emphasizes that the early figures of Genesis were able to follow the written laws *without* instruction from others (e.g., *Abraham* 6, 16, 61), and it may thus have been awkward for him to highlight Abraham as someone who was taught.

which nature has laid down (cf. the *italics* in *Abr.* 6, 16, and 61). In short, in contradistinction to the views held by later rabbinic traditions and possibly by a contemporary Jewish interpretation known to Philo, which may have attributed to Abraham the external education and obedience to the written Torah of Moses in a literal sense, Philo interpreted the Patriarch's pre-Sinaitic adherence to the divine Law as caused by his solitary study and reasoning of the unwritten statutes, and under the divine instruction laid down in Nature as an *internal* teacher.

Some more comments should be offered, however, on Philo's discourse on Abraham and the divine Law in *Abr.* 275–276. This text has been taken to demonstrate that Philo held the unwritten Law of Nature to be superior to the written Law of Moses.[38] Although the divine Law is conceived of by Philo as the "archetype" or "original", with which the Torah revealed at Sinai is in agreement (cf. *Mos.* 2:52–53), this does not imply that the Law of Moses is to be seen as "inferior" to or identical with the "higher" Law. Both views fail to reckon with two different, though supplementary, aspects that Philo accentuates about these two jurisdictions or legal systems at work in the Torah. First, when Abraham followed the divine Law in Nature, this does not mean that he complied with the Law of Moses in a literal sense. As I have argued above, Philo only mentions the fact that the divine Law Abraham followed was the unwritten statutes in contradistinction to the Law of Moses, as some of the "interlocutors" of Philo's day possibly maintained. According to Philo, the most holy scriptures contain two sets of laws, the unwritten and more general and the written and particular, which exemplify the very same virtues. Thus, as a memorialized record of the unwritten legislation (ἀγράφῳ τῇ νομοθεσίᾳ), it is precisely Abraham's virtues manifested through his words and deeds that have been employed (cf. the use of the verb χράομαι, "make use of", "employ") and recorded in the Law of Moses (*Abr.* 4–5).[39] As Sandmel puts it: "Philo says the Law sets forth as legislation those things which Abraham did."[40] Or as Birnbaum and Dillon, most recently, have explained the relationship between the lives of the patriarchs and the particular Mosaic laws:

> Indeed Philo says that the more general laws are "men who have lived irreproachable and noble lives, whose *virtues* happen to have been recorded in the most holy writings (§ 4, our emphasis). Accordingly, the particular laws replicate the lives of the early figures because

38 Cf. Goodenough, *By Light, Light*, 90; Sandmel, *Philo's Place in Judaism*, 201–9.

39 For a similar emphasis on Abraham's virtues, illustrated throughout the treatise of *De Abrahamo*, as the "linkage" and intersection between Abraham's biography and the Mosaic ordinances, see Birnbaum and Dillon, *On the Life of Abraham*, 398.

40 Sandmel, *Philo's Place in Judaism*, 108.

these laws either reflect or lead to the identical virtues that the early figures achieved in their own "untutored" way.[41]

This statement goes along with the obeservation that Philo in his "Exposition of the Law" elaborates on precily those virtues that Philo in *De Abrahamo* says that Abraham displays.[42] Such a view also coincides with what the author of Jubilees claims, namely, that the patriarchs did spontaneously on their own that would later become Mosaic law.[43]

Second, Philo draws a distinction with regard to the Torah as a *memorial* or copy of the deeds and words of Abraham, who embodied the divine Law in Nature (cf. *Abr.* 3). Since, as Philo himself states in *Praem.* 29, "every copy by its deceptive resemblance falsifies the original", the Law of Moses is not *identical* with the divine Law in Nature, but is rather *consistent* with Nature and the legal normative force of Abraham.[44] In fact, Philo himself nowhere suggests that Abraham was an observer of the Torah in its literal sense – an interpretation at variance with the ideas of Philo's "interlocutors" and later rabbinic traditions that adjusted Abraham to the jurisdiction of the Law of Moses as the basic norm. It is all the more interesting that when Philo paraphrases Gen 26:5, and thus assures that Abraham kept the divine Law, he goes on to explain that Abraham as the founder of the (Jewish) nation was the first who trusted in God's promise. The relevant passage reads:

He did them, not taught by written words [of the Torah], but unwritten nature gave him the zeal to follow where wholesome and untainted impulse led him. And when God gives his endorsement concerning these, what does it befit men to do other than *to grant their firmest*

41 Birnbaum and Dillon, *On the Life of Abraham*, 398. When they further claim (*On the Life of Abraham*, 397), however, "that Philo views Abraham as himself a law because he achieves in his life the very same *virtues* that the particular laws are designed to promote", Birnbaum and Dillon tend to blur the distinction Philo made between the two sets of law in order to show how the Law of Moses fits with Abraham (and the patriarchs) as the legal norm, and not the other way around.

42 Just as Philo in this treatise exemplifies that Abraham exhibits the virtues of justice, courage, wisdom, and moderation (*Abr.* 208–261), so he can argue elsewhere that the written laws of Moses embody and promote the same specific virtues (e.g., in *Spec.* 4:133–135, 143–148; *Mos.* 2:8–11). See Sandmel, *Philo's Place in Judaism*, 105–6; Birnbaum and Dillon, *On the Life of Abraham*, 397–8.

43 Thus, Kugel, "Jubilees, Philo, and the Problem of Genesis," 298–304; Goodenough, *By Light, Light*, 74.

44 *Pace* Najman (*Seconding Sinai*, 99), who goes too far when she maintains that "Philo regards the Law of Moses as a written copy of the Law of Nature [...]."

> *trust?* Such was the life of the first, the founder of the nation, [...] as our discourse has shown, himself a law and an unwritten statute. *Abr.* 275–276

As I argued above, this passage and the phrase in italic may be taken to provide an *inclusio* to the opening part in *Abr.* 262, in which the allusion to Gen 15:6 implied that Abraham had trust in God's commands, including the promises.[45] In *Abr.* 275–276, then, Philo elaborates further on Abraham's trust in God, at this juncture, in the context of the issue of Abraham's adherence to the divine Law in Nature as distinct from the Law of Moses.[46] The line of thought seems to be that when Abraham did what the zeal supplied by the "unwritten nature" prompted him to do, the divine Law manifests itself and is achieved through his trust in God's promise.[47] Instead of saying that Abraham in this way observed written laws of Moses, because they had not yet been set in writing (cf. *Abr.* 5 and 275), Philo emphasizes that God's commands or words of promise are like unwritten commands achieved through the virtue of trust, with Abraham as the first among the humans who manifested this.[48] A parallel to such an exposition of Gen 15:6 about Abraham's trust in God's promise, which manifests itself in conformity with nature, is provided by Philo in *Her.* 90. It is noteworthy that Philo here refers to imaginary interlocutors who reads Gen 15:6a ("Abraham be-

---

45 For a similar reading of this passage in its literary context, see now Birnbaum and Dillon, *On the Life of Abraham*, 407.

46 *Pace* Sass (*Leben aus den Verheissungen*, 110), who claims that *Abr.* 275–276 "wirkt [...] wie ein Einschub und steht auch grammatisch in keiner kausalen Verbindung zu den vorherigen und folgenden Ausführungen zu Verheissung und Vertrauen."

47 In *Migr.* 130–131 and *Her.* 7–14, Philo specifically cites Gen 26:5, without making any explicit reference to what kind of law was involved. In *Migr.* 130–131, he also quotes from Deut 33:3, pointing out that Moses himself testified that Abraham did the law, so that that he became an embodiment of God's words:

> So in another place He says, "Abraham did 'all my law'" (Gen. xxvi. 5): "Law" being evidently nothing else than the Divine word enjoining what we should do, as Moses testifies by saying "he received a law from His words" (Deut xxxiii. 3f.). If, then, the law is a Divine word, and the man of true worth "does" the law, he assuredly "does" the word: so that, as I said God's words are the wise man's doings.

48 *Pace* Sandnes (*Paul Perceived*, 151), who somewhat unnuancedly reads Philo's interpretation of Abraham's trust (Gen 15:6) in the light of Gen 26:5 and his presumed adherence to the Law of Moses:

> This conclusion of the treatise is introduced (275) with a saying by Moses [...] regarding Abraham: "that this man did the divine law and the divine commands" – which is, in fact, a quotation from Gen 26:5 wherein Genesis *sums up* the Abraham biography. [...] This harks back to *Abr.* 262 where Philo starts explaining what Gen 15:6 is about, demonstrated in the fact that 275 picks up on what firm πίστις really is.

lieved God") about trust in God's promise: "When it is God who speaks and promises, who would not pay heed, even though he was the most unjust and impious of mankind?" At this juncture, Philo answers his questioners by taking Gen 15:6b ("his faith was counted to him for justice") as an indictment and reproof of the lack of trust on the part of human beings, since Abraham's trust in God manifested only that he lived in conformity with nature:

> And it is well said "his faith was counted to him for justice" (Gen. xv. 6), for nothing is so just or righteous as to put in God alone a trust which is pure and unalloyed. Yet this act of justice and conformity with nature has been held to be a marvel because of the untrustfulness of most of us. And it is in reproof of us that the holy text tells us, that to rest on the Existent only, [...] is deemed no marvel at the judgement-bar of truth, but just an act of justice and nothing more. *Her.* 94–95

Third, Philo rather concedes a temporal division within the Pentateuch, which pertains to the institution of the Torah in Moses' time and the giving of it at Sinai. This is also reflected in the way the "Exposition of the Law" is organized in the following pattern: Philo begins with the "Creation of the World" (*De Opificio Mundi*), followed by the treatises entitled "Books of the Unwritten Laws", that is, the treatise on Abraham (*De Abrahamo*, with its longer title "The Life of the Wise Man Made Perfect through Teaching, or the First Book on Unwritten Laws"), including the lost treatises on Isaac and Jacob, before he proceeds in *De Decalogo* and *De Specialibus Legibus* to discuss the "written laws" given by Moses at Sinai.[49]

Finally, what is then the pragmatic aim of Philo's argument in this treatise and the distinction he makes between the divine Law and the Torah? A suggestion towards an answer might be provided in Philo's path to Hellenistic Judaism and vice versa. Some more remarks are appropriate in order to explain what I consider to be the connotations of this suggestion.

On the one hand, Philo Hellenizes Judaism by taking Abraham (and the Patriarchs) to be himself a legal figure and norm, a "Law", identical with the divine Law in Nature, with which in turn the Law of Moses is congruent. Thus, instead of depicting these two "Laws" in such a way that one is "higher" or "inferior" to the other, Philo describes them as *distinct* from each other in terms of copies, images, or records that might be easily distinguishable from originals, archetypes, or memories. This conclusion accords well with *Abr.* 4–5 and 11, in

49 For Philo's comments on the organization of the Law of Moses, cf. Borgen, *An Exegete for His Time*, 65–79; Najman, *Seconding Sinai*, 83; G.E. Sterling, "'Prolific in Expression and Broad in Thought': Internal References to Allegorical Commentary and Exposition of the Law." *Euphrosyne* 40 (2012): 55–76, esp. 67–9.

which the laws of Moses are portrayed as "memorials" and legal records of the virtues of the first generations of men epitomizing the unwritten divine Law:

> These are such men as lived lived good and blameless lives, whose virtues stand permanently recorded in the most holy scriptures, not merely to sound their praises but for the instruction of the reader and as an inducement to him to apire to the same;
>
> [...] and Moses extolled them for two reasons. First he wished to shew that the enacted ordinances are not inconsistent with nature; and secondly that those who wish to live in accordance with the laws as they stand have no difficult task, seeing that the first generations before any at all of the particular statutes was set in writing followed the unwritten law with perfect ease, so that one might properly say that the enacted laws are nothing else than memorials of the life of the ancients, preserving to a later generation their actual words and deeds. *Abr.* 4–5
>
> He did well, too, in speaking of the *book* of the coming into being of the true man. The word was appropriate because the hoper deserves a memorial written not on pieces of paper which moths shall destroy but in the undying book of nature where good actions are registered. *Abr.* 11

Philo deduces the rationale for this argument from the premise that the laws of Moses were to be seen as a written records of the "Law" found in the biography of Abraham in Genesis, conceived of as an embodiment of the unwritten Law in Nature. By claiming that Abraham was "νόμος αὐτὸς ὢν καὶ θεσμὸς ἄγραφος (himself a Law and an unwritten statute)" (*Abr.* 276), Philo delineates Abraham as distinct from the written laws of Moses, as one who was not living under the Law of Moses, because his own instincts matched the divine Law in Nature. The Greek concepts of θεσμός and νόμος here applied to Abraham underline Philo's conception of him as a legal figure; θεσμός envisages Abraham as the embodiment of the unwritten Law in Nature sanctioned and legislated by God, while νόμος embodies Abraham as the founder of the Jewish nation and thus as what it should regard as a valid constitution and binding norm.[50] Accordingly, we might imagine the Greco-Roman context as the background for Philo's statement in *Abr.* 4. When Philo here envisages "that the first generations before any at all of the particular statutes was set in writing followed the unwritten Law with perfect ease", he draws the corollary that it was possible for any human being to live by that Law. This is exactly why the life and virtues of Abraham

---

50 For such connotations of these concepts in Greeks texts, see M. Ostwald, *Nomos and the Beginnings of the Athenian Democracy* (Oxford: Clarendon Press, 1969), 12–54; idem, "*Was There a Concept* Agraphos Nomos *in Classical Greece?*" in *Exegesis and Argument: Studies Presented to Gregory Vlastos*, ed. E.N. Lee, A.P.D. Mourelatos, and R.M. Rorty (Assen: Van Gorcum, 1973), 70–104.

and the other patriarchs are recorded in the Scriptures, Philo says, "These are such men [...], *whose virtues stand permanently recorded in the most holy scriptures*, not merely to sound their praises but for the instruction of the reader and as an inducement to aspire to the same" (*Abr.* 4). Philo's deflection from the literal sense of his "interlocutors" and his own modified interpretation of Abraham as "lawful" apart from the Mosaic jurisdiction also served to emphasize the broader significance of Abraham beyond the Jewish nation in relation to an audience of both Jews and non-Jews.

On the other hand, Philo Judaizes Hellenism, claiming the view – unintelligible according to a Greek discourse – that the unwritten divine laws are embodied in the form of Abraham's life as part of the written code of Moses, and thus as congruent, consistent, and in harmony with the norm of divine Law enacted in Nature. As I mentioned above, Najman has argued that Philo appropriates the universal significanse of the divine Law in order to give authority to the written and particular Law of Moses. She argues that the laws of Moses possess authority for Philo as opposed to Greco-Roman thought, since the unwritten law of nature could find expression only in the life of a sage, not in the written laws of a nation.[51] It seems to me, however, that Philo's point of view is more coherent with Roman thought than Najman allows. Thus, he can take advantage of it and claim boldly that the life of the sage represented by Abraham precisely constitutes the authority and legal force of their written record, embodied in the particular laws of the Torah. Hence, Philo can claim that the divine Law in Nature authorizes the laws of Moses as if they were "stamped [...] with the seals of the nature herself" (*Mos.* 2:14). The accessibility of the divine Law in Nature thus does not imply that it is accessible outside and beyond the specific enactments of the Torah of Moses.[52] As a corollary of Philo's distinction between the divine Law in Nature and the Law of Moses, any Jew or non-Jew who wants to live in conformity with Nature must obey the Law of Moses. Inherent in Philo's *Universal* Particularism is then his vision of a *Particularistic* Universalism. Thus, in *Mos* 2:44 Philo envisages an eschatological time when all peoples would abandon their ancestral laws and accept the Jewish laws alone. Such a future *scenario* has a striking parallel in Cicero's concept of the Roman civil Law, conceived of as a shadow of the original Law in Nature:

---

51 Najman (*Seconding Sinai*, 70–100).

52 *Pace* A. Reinhartz, "The Meaning of *Nomos* in Philo's *Exposition of the Law*," *SR* 15.3 (1986): 342, endorsed by Hayes (*Divine Law*, 123): "One might suppose that those capable of accessing the law of nature directly need not trouble themselves with the details of the enacted laws."

> For there is a bond of fellowship—although I have often made this statement, I must still repeat it again and again—which has the very widest application, uniting all men together and each to each. This bond of union is closer between those who belong to the same nation, and more intimate still between those who are citizens of the same city-state. It is for this reason that our forefathers chose to understand one thing by the universal law and another by the civil law. The civil law is not necessarily also the universal law; but the universal law ought to be also the civil law. But we possess no substantial, life-like image of true Law and genuine Justice; a mere outline sketch is all that we enjoy. I only wish that we were true even to this; for, even as it is, it is drawn from the excellent models which Nature and Truth afford. Cicero, *Off.* 3.69

> True law is right reason in agreement with nature; it is of universal application, unchanging and everlasting; it summons to duty by its commands, and averts from wrongdoing by its prohibitions. And it does not lay its commands or prohibitions upon good men in vain, though neither have any effect on the wicked. It is a sin to try to to alter this law, nor is it allowable to attempt to repeal any part of it, and it is impossible to abolish it entirely. We cannot be freed from its obligations by senate or people, and we need not look outside ourselves for an expounder or interpreter of it. And there will not be different laws at Rome and at Athens, or different laws now and in the future, but one eternal and unchangeable law will be valid for all nations and all times, and there will be one master and ruler, that is, God, over us all, for he is the author of this law, its promulgator, and its enforcing judge. Whoever is disobedient is fleeing from himself and denying his human nature, and by reason of this very fact he will suffer the worst penalties, even if he escapes what is commonly considered punishment. Cicero, *Rep.* 3.33

In contrast to and in competition with Cicero, however, Philo could not say that the Mosaic Law was not only a shadow and mere outline sketch of such a true Law. Rather, it is *the* best possible written imitation and authentic source of the divine Law in Nature.[53]

In its cultural context, Philo's interpretation of the Law seems to be addressed both against the Greek view that there is no true earthly representation of the Law of Nature, and against those Jews who might think that the cosmic and primary import of the Law of Moses exempts them from obeying it.[54] Philo's

---

53 Cf. S. Sandmel, "Philo's Environment and Philo's Exegesis," *JBR* 22.4 (1954): 252:

> Moses' law, for example, differs from other written laws, such as enactments in Athens and Sparta, in that the latter are subject to alterations by tyrants, or in this, that written law is different in Athens from what it was in Sparta. But the law of Moses is the same everywhere, and it is not alterable by any usurper of authority.

54 According to Betz (*Galatians*, 166), in *Abr.* 276, "Philo develops his position against Jewish opponents who are altogether hostile to the Torah and abandon it." In referring to *Conf.* 2–3 and *Migr.* 89–93 in support of this assertion, Betz seems to confuse the Jewish opposition from Jewish apostates such as the scoffer (*Conf.* 2) and the antinomian Jewish "spiritualists" (*Migr.* 89–90). The latter group were not hostile to the Law of Moses as such.

writings illustrate how the conception of the cosmic significance of the laws of Moses played a role in intra-mural controversies of the Jewish community in his own time. For example, in *Migr.* 89–93, Philo addresses some "spiritualists" who are in danger of interfering with established customs.[55] Although they were aware of both the literal and the noetic aspects of the laws of Moses, they stressed the noetic meaning and neglected the literal observances. Philo exhorts himself and the (potential) "spiritualists" not to separate the universal meaning from praxis, or intellectual understanding from observances. According to *Migr.* 89–90, the (potential) "spiritualists" had a correct intellectual understanding of the laws, but were tempted to prefer a life-style at the expense of the external observances laid down in the Law of Moses. Thus, their emphasis on the noetic meaning of the laws of Moses and the practical consequences of such a view can be seen as a reversal and the opposite of the stance Philo took, according to *Migr.* 93. In Philo's view, the concrete and the spiritual aspects of the Law belong together. Otherwise, Philo warns that they will be subject to censure and accusation by the Jewish community: "If we keep and observe these, we shall gain a clearer conception of those things of which these are the symbols; and besides that we shall not incur the censure of the many and the charges they are sure to bring against us" (*Migr.* 93).[56]

Against such a background, then, Philo can make the bold claim that these laws of Moses as the copy of Abraham's words and deeds are now the concrete and authentic means to attain these divine laws in Nature. Or, as Sandmel has imagined him saying, Philo exhorts both himself and those he addresses:

---

55 The text of *Migr.* 89–90 reads:

> There are some who, regarding laws in their literal sense in the light of symbols of matters belonging to the intellect, are overpunctilious about the latter, while treating the former with easy-going neglect. Such men I for my part should blame for handling the matter in too easy and offhand a manner: they ought to have given careful attention to both aims, to a more full and exact investigation of what is not seen and in what is seen to be stewards without reproach. As it is, as though they were living alone by themselves in a wilderness, or as though they had become disembodied souls, and knew neither city nor village nor household nor any company of human beings at all, overlooking all that the mass of men regard, they explore reality in its naked absoluteness. These men are taught by the sacred word to have thought for good repute, and to let go nothing that is part of the customs fixed by divinely empowered men greater than those of our time.

56 Cf. P.J. Bekken, *The Lawsuit Motif in John's Gospel from New Perspectives: Jesus Christ, Crucified Criminal and Emperor of the World*, NovTSup (Leiden; Boston: Brill, 2015), 154–5.

> [...] if you and I observe the law of Moses, we are living by nature, unconciously, as it were; if we penetrate to the soul of that law, that is, to the deepest mystery, we live no longer by the literal but, as did the patriarchs, we live consciously by nature itself.[57]

According to Philo, adherence to the divine Law in Nature is no difficult task, because the words and deeds of the patriarchs exemplify the virtues that are preserved in the written Law of Moses (cf. *Abr.* 4):

> [...] those who wish to live in accordance with the laws as they stand have no difficult task, seeing that the first generations before any at all of the particular statutes was set in writing followed the unwritten law with perfect ease, so that one might properly say that the enacted laws are nothing else than memorials of the life of the ancients, preserving to a later generation their actual words and deeds. *Abr.* 5

4 Conclusion

Philo's solution to the Greco-Roman conundrum of the relationship between the unwritten divine Law in Nature and the written Law of a nation was the dynamic interaction he found at work in the Torah between two "jurisdictions" embedded in the narrative of Abraham in Genesis and the special laws of Moses, respectively. In order to legitimate the cosmic validity of the written Law of Moses beyond the restraints of time and place, Philo's concern is to appropriate Abraham and the Law in Nature to its Jewish and Greco-Roman cultural context.

In contradistinction to an application of Gen 26:5 about Abraham that saw him and the Law of Moses as inseparable, a position that he explicitly states is held by some others of his day, it is Philo's task in *Abr.* 275–276 to interpret Abraham in a way that disjoins him from the written Law of Moses, without dissolving the intersection that exists between the divine Law in Nature and the Law of Moses. On the one hand, against the position of a too literal understanding of the Torah and Abraham, Philo *hellenizes* Judaism by advocating that the Law of Moses is not identical with the divine Law in Nature, but that it is nevertheless fully in conformity with the unwritten statutes in Nature. Thus, on the other hand, and in opposition to an antinomian tendency, Philo *judaizes* Hellenism: Since the Law of Moses begins with the record of Abraham's virtue of piety and thus the legislation of what Abraham and the other ancestors achieved through what they said and did, it is, as a written Law code, unlike any other human legislations which operate among Greeks and Romans, the best possible approximation to the divine Law in Nature.

---

57 Sandmel, "Philo's Environment and Philo's Exegesis," 252.

Part Two: Paul's Appropriation of Abraham in Galatians 3:6–29 in the Jewish Context

Chapter 5: The Appropriation of Abraham in Galatians 3:6–29

It is the assumption of this chapter that a specific case has warranted a basic exegetical question based on the quotation of Gen 15:6, which in turn has been elaborated into a smaller exegetical "treatise" in Gal 3:6–29. A fresh study of Paul's treatment of Gen 15:6 on the basis of the method of exegetical paraphrase can not only explain aspects of Paul's rendering of the Jewish Scripture, but also clarify the exegetical reasoning and argument in and behind Gal 3:1–29, and thus to some extent justify his fresh exposition of Gen 15:6 in a Jewish context. Paul's interpretative rendering of Gen 15:6 gives a sample of the exegetical paraphrase of a biblical text, in which words, phrases, and sentences from the Hebrew Bible are given an exegetical explanation in terms of interpretative terms or exegetical motifs, and fused together with other subordinate quotations.[1] Thus, the whole analysis aims at substantiating the thesis that Paul's handling of Gen 15:6 can be placed within a Jewish exegetical context of his day with respect to the wording of the quotation, exegetical methods, motifs, structures, and terminology. This conclusion goes against recent investigations that are inclined to look at Paul's exegetical treatment of Gen 15:6 as an idiosyncratic creation by himself.

1 Literary Organization of Gal 3:1–29: A Survey

J. L. Austin's classic work *How to Do Things with Words* (1962) dealt with what he termed performative sentences, and drew attention to what words do to the hearer(s)—that is, evoking some sort of response.[2] After the publication of Austin's book, it has become common in text–linguistic studies to speak about the syntactic, semantic, and pragmatic dimensions of a text. The surface organization stands for the syntactic aspect (dealing with the relation between sign and signifier); the structure of the contents corresponds to the semantic aspect (concerning the relation between signs and designata); the historical context and the function of the text over against its addressees are ways of speaking

1 This definition of an exegetical paraphrase is deduced from the empirical data provided by the texts themselves. Thus, we have attempted to avoid a definition which can be assumed to be too mechanical and too abstract.
2 J.L. Austin, *How to Do Things with Words: The William James Lectures* (Cambridge, Ma.: Harvard University Press, 1962).

https://doi.org/10.1515/9783110722109-006

of the pragmatic aspect (regarding the relation between signs, designata, and sign–users). Of these aspects the pragmatic one includes the two others, and the semantic aspect includes the syntactic aspect. One has, in fact, not rendered justice to a textual communication unless all these dimensions of a text are taken into account.[3] However, as one tries to reconstruct elements of the supposed historical situation of an ancient text, one gets into trouble, since we often know too little about the external contexts of the textual communication.[4] This regards also the texts we have selected for our investigation, and implies that we have to be cautious. Accordingly, in this study, I shall restrict myself to investigating Gal 3:6 – 29 in the light of a Jewish exegetical tradition in which the *continuum* of texts such as Gen 15:6, 22:16 – 18, and 26:3 – 5 is located within a larger Jewish discourse on Abraham. Then it is imperative to analyse the Jewish texts within which these texts are embedded, with regard to their actual surface organisation and meaning in their own right. Such an investigation is an essential and necessary preliminary step in an exegesis of a text, and will be valuable for the further analyses of the application of the exegetical tradition and the constellation of motifs on which the text is woven.[5]

The analytical tools that will be instrumental for the analysis are taken from the field of text–linguistics. I shall survey some markers on the literary surface of the text that the author provides for the addressees, which may serve as guideposts and be helpful in the task of organizing the text in its hierarchical and sequential structure. I shall first introduce briefly some typical markers before I proceed to point out the bearing of these characteristics on the hierarchical

3 These three components or dimensions correspond to what Austin (*How to Do Things with Words*, 94 – 120) identified as the three distinct elements of the speech act: 1. the locutionary act, saying something which has a certain sense and reference; 2. the illocutionary act, uttering orders, warnings etc., i. e. sentences with a certain conventional force; 3. the perlocutionary act, achieving something *by* saying something, e. g., convincing or deterring.

4 See D. Hellholm, *Das Visionenbuch des Hermas als Apokalypse: Formgeschichtliche und texttheoretische Studien zu einer literarischen Gattung. Band I: Methodologische Vorüberlegungen und makrostrukturelle Textanalyse*, ConBNT (Lund: Gleerup, 1980), 78 – 9; B. Johanson, *To All the Brethren: A Text-Linguistic and Rhetorical Approach to I Thessalonians*, ConBNT (Stockholm: Almqvist & Wiksell, 1987), 7.

5 Cf. D. Hellholm, "Substitutionelle Gliederungsmerkmale und die Komposition des Matthäusevangeliums," in *Texts and Contexts: Biblical Texts in Their Textual and Situational Contexts. Essays in Honor of Lars Hartman*, ed. T. Fornberg and D. Hellholm (Oslo: Scandinavian University Press, 1995), 22 – 3, who remarks:

> Werner Kallmeyer und Reinhard Meyer-Hermann haben mit Recht hervorgehoben, dass "die Gliederung von Texten nach Sinn- oder Funktionsabschnitten immer schon ein Gegenstand der Textwissenschaft und der Rhetorik", und – das muss man als Bibelwissenschaftler hinzufügen – der Exegese "gewesen ist".

structure and text-sequence of Gal 3:1–29.[6] Space does not permit an extensive discussion of text–linguistic technicalities. My observations will be rounded off in a table which summarizes the way I consider the argument to be literally organized.

1. Meta-communicative clauses (abbreviated MC). Such clauses will mostly involve a meta–communicative verb of saying, hearing or writing etc., and the identification of someone speaking, hearing etc. The MC clauses are about the communication at hand, and serve to thematize the communication in a communication situation.[7] Gal 3:1 may be seen as such a clause and as the headline of the following argument. The reference to Christ's crucifixion here elaborates on the preceding reference to his death in 2:19–21. In this way, 3:1 is not an abrupt new beginning,[8] but reminds the addresses of the main point of Galatians, namely, the proper understanding of Christ's crucifixion as an argument applied to them against righteousness based on the Law of Moses.[9] The implied message and meaning of 3:1 in the light of the preceding context could be something like:

---

6 Cf. E. Gülich and W. Raible, *Linguistische Textmodelle*, UTB (München: Fink, 1977), 137–40; Hellholm, *Das Visionenbuch des Hermas*, 80–3. According to Gülich and Raible, text-sequences of a text's macro-structure are often manifested on the surface level of a text by various linguistic signals provided for the addressee by the author. Such markers can be classified according to whether their function is pragmatic, semantic or syntactic, with the pragmatic markers holding the highest rank and the syntactic the lowest. However, such a systematisation of the markers should be used heuristically rather than axiomatically, with sensitivity towards an author's possible idiosyncratic use of such markers. On this, see the deliberations by Johanson, *To All the Brethren*, 25.

7 Cf. D. Hellholm, "Amplificatio in the Macro-Structure of Romans," in *Rhetoric and the New Testament: Essays from the 1992 Heidelberg Conference. FS Wilhelm Wuellner*, ed. S.E. Porter and Th.H. Olbricht, JSNT (Sheffield: JSOT Press, 1993), 124, who remarks:

> The importance of these meta-communicative clauses lies mainly in the fact that they serve as signals for changes between various levels of communication, that is for distinguishing between text internal and text external communication levels and between text internal communication levels. Consequently they also signalise different dialogue phases and dialogue structures in a text.

8 *Pace* Hartman ("Galatians 3:15–4:11 as Part of a Theological Argument on a Practical Issue," in *The Truth of the Gospel [Galatians 3:15–4:11]*, ed. J. Lambrecht, MSBen.BE 12 [Rome: Benedictina, 1993], 132), who rightly highlights Gal 3:1 as the main theme of Galatians, but who emphasizes that Gal 2:11–21 "receives a clearcut end by the abrupt new beginning in 3:1."

9 Both the intense use of direct address ("You, foolish Galatians") and the second person ("who has bewitched you?") in 3:1 show that Paul applies the argument in 2:19–21 to his readers in a special way in order to influence them to take a practical stand. It is only to be expected that the readers get the impression that Paul is here at a kernel point in the communication at hand. Cf. Hartman, "Galatians 3:15–4:11," 129.

> If you insist on living by the righteousness of the Law, it would mean nullifying the impact of Christ's death (2:21). Do not pay attention to those who try to entice you away from the true gospel I proclaimed to you, in which Jesus Christ had died for your benefit, as he was publicly placarded before your eyes as an accursed "criminal" who was sentenced and found liable to the punishment of impalement.

2. Thematic markers (abbreviated ThM).[10] Another type of marker that appears particularly in an argumentative text is words, clauses, or sentences that in different ways signal the theme or sub-theme to be dealt with. When the communication at hand is established, a major ThM can introduce larger or smaller sequences (1.ThM; 2.ThM; 3.ThM etc.), within which a subordinate ThM (1.1. ThM; 2.1. ThM; 3.1. ThM etc.) may in turn mark out subordinate sequences of a text or an argument. Often, a ThM is introduced by an expression on a meta-level as related to the clause indicating the theme. Such explicit semantic expressions are constituted by what can be labelled a 'Meta-propositional Base' (abbreviated MB).[11] Gal 3:2, 7, 15, 19 are examples of ThMs introduced by a MB, although the last text lacks the MB that may be implied by the question asked:

> 3:2: The only thing I want to learn from you is this (MB): Did you receive the Spirit by doing the works of the law or by believing what you heard?
> 3:7: [...] so, you see (MB), those who believe are the descendants of Abraham.
> 3:15: Brothers and sisters, I give an example from daily life (MB): once a person's will has been ratified, no one adds to it or annuls it.
> 3:19: (I ask,) Why then the law? (MB) It was added because of transgressions, until the offspring would come to whom the promise had been made; and it was ordained through angels by a mediator.

In Gal 3:2–29, such examples of both major and subordinate ThMs have a text-delimiting function which organizes the argument of the text in hierarchical text-sequences. For example, the questions in Gal 3:2–5 function to set up the major ThM for the whole sequence of Gal 3:6–4:7.[12] The MB ("The only thing I want to learn from you is this") signals that Paul and the readers agreed on these questions, with their only possible answer in the affirmative. The questions may be conceived as equal to statements which suggest an answer as follows: the (promised gift of the) Spirit is contingent on hearing the gospel on the basis of trust, not on the ground of works of the Law of Moses. This topic consists of three components, the first of which is the reception of the Spirit. This fact relates to the

---

10 Cf. E.U. Grosse, *Text und Kommunikation: Eine linguistische Einführung in die Funktionen der Texte* (Stuttgart: Kohlhammer, 1976), 95–100; Johanson, *To All the Brethren*, 29–30.

11 See Grosse, *Text und Kommunikation*, 95.

12 It is indubitable that the Spirit argument in Gal 3:2–5 reaches its conclusion in Gal 4:6–7.

other two components, i.e. the circumstances of its giving by faith and the function of the Law of Moses. As I shall argue in the subsequent sections of this chapter, Paul's task is to shed light on the legitimacy and interrelation of these components in the light of Christ's crucifixion and the legal warrant given in the Scriptures. In the argument of the text-sequence of Gal 3:6–29, 3:7 may be seen as the 1. ThM, which runs on to 3:29, while 3:8–14 (1.1 ThM) and 3:15–29 (2. ThM) may be regarded as subordinate sequences.

3. Shift of person. Seen from a pragmatic point of view, the shift in person often signals that the author will make an application of an argumentation to the readers, e.g., when an author makes a transition from third person to second person, or when an author argues that the addressee should take a practical stand or move, and pursues his argument from third person to second person, and then returns to third person. This shift in person has a certain delimiting text-organising effect, which we should observe and note.[13] Gal 3:1, 7, 15, 26 provide examples.

4. Shift of style. Shifts of person can also involve a shift of style, and have in general a text-organising effect. "Style" refers here generally to different types of sentences, such as rhetorical questions and answers, reproaches, Hebrew Bible (HB) quotations and allusions, the use of the vocative at the beginning of a new text-sequence, and the occurrence of *inclusio*.[14] Here are some examples of this style from Galatians 3:

For the rhetorical questions and answers and the use of reproaches, I have already mentioned Gal 3:2–5. Further examples of the same style are found in the questions in Gal 3:19 and 3:21 about the Law and the rationale for its giving.

In the nest section, I shall argue that Gal 3:6–29 is to be styled as an exegetical paraphrase of various HB quotations, providing a kind of warp on which the structure of the text is woven.

Gal 3:15 begins with a renewed address in the vocative (ἀδελφοί). As a device for appealing to their common bond and maintaining their relationship, it has a phatic function and may occur at the transition to a new sub-theme, as is the case here.[15]

Moreover, stylistic markers as an *inclusio* make a special contribution to our observations of the textual organisation of the text. This characteristic serves to indicate text-delimitation, and involves phrases or clauses that occur at the

---

13 Cf. Hartman, "Galatians 3:15–4:11," 129–30.

14 If not otherwise specified, the designation Hebrew Bible (HB) also refers to its Greek translation, the Septuagint (LXX).

15 The use of the vocative ἀδελφοί is quite characteristic of Paul's style; cf. Johanson, *To All the Brethren*, 32.

opening of a text-sequence and are repeated in the closing part, often with the function of summarizing a central point in the sequence. Gal 3:7 and 3:29 provide examples of an *inclusio:*

> Opening staement (v. 7): "[...] so, you see, those who believe are *the descendants of Abraham.*"
>
> Closing and conclusive statement (v. 29): "And if you belong to Christ, then you are *Abraham's offspring*, heirs according to the promise."

Here the point made about the question of who belongs to the kinship of Abraham in v.7 is identified in the conclusive statement of v. 29 as those who have a relationship to Christ. At the same time, this inclusio may be read as a syllogism. In other words, it is those who believe and belong to Christ that are the true descendants of Abraham.

5. Temporal markers may indicate a change of time with regard to a sequence of actions or events in a text, and may have a text-delimiting function in the organisation of the argument. Thus, in Gal 3:8, 19 – 21, 23 Paul makes use of the temporal prepositions such as πρό, ἄχρις, and μετά in order to argue that Abraham actually was the first who knew the gospel of Christ and that the time of the promise and faith therefore has a rank and priority before the Law which came later.

The markers mentioned above from 2 to 5 are markers of the text-semantic type and hold a middle position in the task of classifying the markers in a hierarchical order according to their predominant function.[16]

6. The connectors are markers of various types, and help to relate clauses in different ways to each other. Within a taxonomy of connectors, items such as sequential, additive, concessive, inferential, comparative, specifying and illustrative connectors may be included. These markers are often conjunctions, particles etc., that relate both larger text-units to each other within the text's macro-structure, and smaller clauses to each other, often in a logical relationship. In Galatians 3, conjunctions and particles such as καθώς, δέ, ἀλλά, γάρ, εἰ, or ὅτι function as connectors of this kind. Often, the connectors co-operate with other text markers such as those mentioned above, e.g., a ThM: when the author's aim is reached, a conclusion can be explicitly introduced by conjunctions such as οὖν, ἄρα, ὥστε, or ἵνα. For example, Paul reaches the conclusion of his arguments in Gal 3:7 – 9 and 3:23 – 29 as follows: "[...] thus (ὥστε), those out of faith are blessed with the faithful Abraham" (3:9); "And if you belong to Christ, then (ἄρα) you are Abraham's offspring, heirs according to the promise" (3:29). Such connectors de-

16 See Hellholm, *Das Visionenbuch des Hermas*, 78 – 95; Hartman, "Galatians 3:15 – 4:11," 130.

serve extra attention, because they mark logical structures of the text, and serve to delimit larger or smaller units of a text.[17] The connectors belong to the predominantly text-syntactic markers and are of the lowest rank.

A Table of the Argument in Galatians 3

The following table summarizes a survey of some of the textual markers that may be found to organize the argument of Galatains 3 as a hierarchical and sequential structure. It should be emphasized that such a chart involves the risk of simplifications. The literary structure suggested at this stage of the research process needs therefore to be tested by subsequent analyses of the exegetical methods and the referential background involved in Paul's argument. This will be the task in the remaining sections of this chapter.

Literary context: 3:1–4:11
3:1 Statement of the practical main theme
(2nd pers.; shift of style; keep to the "gospel" of the crucified Christ)
3:2–4:7 Argument in favor of 3:1

- 3:2–5 Thematizing questions (ThM; MB; the promised Spirit given by hearing of trust, not by works of Law)
- 3:6–29 Exegetical warrant for the ThM in 3:2–5 (God kept the oath in faithfulness to Abraham)
  - 3:6–7 Thesis (1. ThM; MB; Scriptural quote; καθώς – ἄρα; just as Abraham who believed, those of faith are the sons of Abraham)
  - 3:8–9 Argument for 1. ThM (1.1 ThM; Scriptural quote; ὥστε; those of faith are blessed with the faithful Abraham)
    - 3:10–14 Argument for 1.1ThM (γάρ; Blessing is given through Christ out of faith)
    - 3:10–12 Argument *e contrario* (Law brings curse, but trust leads to justification)
    - 3:13–14 Christological argument (Christ's redemption from the curse of the Law mediates Abraham's blessing)
      - 3:13 Basis and application (Christ became a curse for "us"; shift to 1st p.pl.)
      - 3:14 Consequences in regard to 3:8–9 and 3:2–5 (ἵνα; Abraham's blessing in terms of the promised Spirit is given to the nations and Jews *in Jesus Christ* on the ground of trust)
  - 3:15–24 A new argument for the ThM in 3:2–5 (2.ThM; shift to 3rd p.; the superiority of the oath of promise to Abraham over against the function of the Law)

17 See Hartman, "Galatians 3:15–4:11," 129–30.

3:15 Argument from human analogy (2.1 ThM; MB; shift of style: vocative; 3rd p.; no one can interfere with a ratified covenant)
3:16 Application of the argument (The covenantal promise concerned Abraham and his offspring Christ)
3:17–18 Argument from divine analogy (2.2 ThM; MB; the Law cannot interfere with the promise to Abraham)
3:19–24 Argument for the relationship between Law and promise (2.3 ThM, shift of style; the Law had a subordinate function integral to the realization of the promise)
3:25–29 Application of the argument of 3:6–22 to the readers (inclusio; shift to 2nd p.; conclusion)

2 The Exegetical Treatise of Gal 3:6–29: Exegetical Methods and Forms

In the previous section, I have investigated the textual organization and argumentative line of thought in Gal 3:6–29 in its literary context. This study of the syntagmatic aspects serves as a basis for the focus of this section, the appropriation of the figure of Abraham and Scripture in Gal 3:6–29. In what follows, I shall pay special attention to Paul's interpretation of Scripture in terms of his use of the method of exegetical paraphrase as well as of exegetical forms and terminology.

2.1 Exegetical Method of Paraphrase

It is the thesis of this section that Paul's interpretative rendering of Gen 15:6 is the main quotation which carries much of Paul's argument throughout Gal 3:6–29.[18] Thus, the recurring wording of Gen 15:6 in this passage illustrates Paul's exegetical paraphrase of this text.[19] It thus represents techniques of adapt-

18 *Pace* K. Kujanpää (*The Rhetorical Functions of Scriptural Quotations in Romans: Paul's Argumentation by Quotations*, NovTSup [Leiden; Boston: Brill, 2019], 67 n. 17), who claims: "Paul devotes little attention to its wording […]." This conclusion is the corollary of the fact that her comparison of the use of Gen 15:6 in Galatians 3 and in Romans 4 fails to pay sufficient attention to Paul's use of exegetical paraphrase throughout these chapters.

19 The technique of exegetical paraphrase employed in Gal 3:6–29 seems to bear some resemblance to the features of "lemmatic exegesis" to be found in Philo's exegetical works, in which comments on a word or phrase from the main biblical lemma can be expanded by adducing secondary biblical lemmata that were linked by common words or themes. Unlike "lemmatic exe-

ing and conforming a biblical text to various themes and contexts, including the practice of selective citation, omissions, alteration, and additions, in which a biblical phrase has been replaced by interpretative terms and supplemented with other subordinate citations of the Hebrew Bible.[20] The procedure of exegetical paraphrase helps us to delineate the exegetical motifs and the language involved in the exposition. Thus, e. g., the words Ἀβραάμ, πίστις, and δικαιοσύνη from the quotation of Gen 15:6 are repeated and expounded alongside other words and phrases such as πνεῦμα, υἱοί, ἐπαγγελία, εὐλογία, and κληρονομία, and juxtaposed and contrasted with words such as νόμος, ἔργον, κατάρα, etc. This language gives a hint of the problem that Paul refers to, namely, the relationship between the jurisdictions of πίστις and νόμος in view of the Christ-event. Moreover, the flexibility of conventinal methods and techniques display a complexity and variety of exegetical forms, such as *inclusio*, subordinate questions, direct exegesis, questions and answers, paraphrasing of words, cited and composite quotations, confirmation of a correct reading, and exegetical phrasology. In what follows, analogies in Philo and other data relevant to Paul's appropriation of this exegetical method, will be explored further.

First of all, the method of exegetical paraphrase helps us to delineate and identify the unit to which the paraphrase or exposition of the Hebrew Bible quotation (HBq) belongs. Parts of the quotation are repeated and given an exposition throughout the unit. The unit may be demarcated by examining how far the paraphrase of the HBq goes, often indicated by the similarities in the opening and closing statements of the expository unit.[21] The outline and structure of the paraphrase could vary. Sometimes, as for example in units such as *Leg.* 3:162 – 168, *Mut.* 253 – 263, or John 6:31 – 58, the HBq is divided into parts

---

gesis", however, Paul does not interpret the primary biblical lemma word by word or phrase by phrase, as it is typical in Philo's use of this exegetical technique in the Allegorical commentary and *Questions and Answers*, which both are running commentaries on Genesis 2:1 – 18:2. For Philo's *modus operandi* and exegetical treatments in these treatises, cf. D.T. Runia, "The Structure of Philo's Allegorical Treatises. A Review of Two Recent Studies and Some Additional Comments," *VC* 38.3 (1984): 209 – 56; idem, "Further Observations on the Structure of Philo's Allegorical Treatises," *VC* 41.2 (1987): 105 – 38; idem, "The Structure of Philo's Allegorical Treatise *De Agricultura*," SPhA 22 (2010): 87 – 109; G.E. Sterling, "When the Beginning is the End: The Place of Genesis in the Commentarties of Philo," in *The Book of Genesis: Composition, Reception, and Interpretation*, ed. C.A. Evans et al. (Leiden: Brill, 2012), 427 – 46.

20 This definition of an exegetical paraphrase is deduced from the empirical data provided by the texts themselves. Thus, we have attempted to avoid a definition which can be assumed to be too abstract. For previous comparisons between Philo and Paul with regard to this method, cf. Bekken, *The Word is Near You*, 53 – 81.

21 Cf. Borgen, *Bread from Heaven*, 46 – 51.

and paraphrased in a successive sequence. In other passages, as in Philo's paraphrase of Gen 15:6 in *Her.* 90–94, most of the words and phrases are paraphrased in the same sequence as in the HBq. In other places, as in Rom 4:1–22 and Gal 3:6–29, the paraphrase does not follow the sequence in which words occur in the quotation. Instead, the words from Gen 15:6 are here drawn upon when they can throw light upon the problem that is discussed. Also, the second "exegetical treatise" in Galatians, i.e., Gal 4:21–31, is relevant for a brief comparison with Gal 3:6–29, since they both follow to some extent the same exegetical outline: a) The main biblical lemma introduced by an exegetical question; b) A paraphrastic rendering of the biblical lemma; c) Exegetical paraphrase and "commentary" on the primary lemma, adduced with secondary biblical lemmata(s); and d) Expository application and conclusion. Thus, Gal 4:21–31 can be displayed as follows:

a) 4:21: The question: Λέγετέ μοι, οἱ ὑπὸ νόμον θέλοντες εἶναι, τὸν νόμον οὐκ ἀκούετε;
b) 4:22: A paraphrase of the basic scriptural "quotation": γέγραπται γὰρ ὅτι <u>Ἀβραὰμ δύο υἱοὺς ἔσχεν, ἕνα ἐκ τῆς παιδίσκης καὶ ἕνα ἐκ τῆς ἐλευθέρας</u> (a summary of LXX Gen 16:15; 21:2–3, 9)
c) 4:23–27: Exegetical paraphrase and "commentary" (words from the HBq are underlined):

1) 4:23: Description of the different kinds of the two sons of Abraham:

ἀλλ' <u>ὁ μὲν ἐκ τῆς παιδίσκης</u> κατὰ σάρκα γεγέννηται, <u>ὁ</u> δὲ <u>ἐκ τῆς ἐλευθέρας</u> δι' ἐπαγγελίας

2) 4:24: The deeper, typological meaning:

ἅτινά ἐστιν ἀλληγορούμενα [...]

4:25–27: The interpretation of the two sons, born to slavery and freedom, and representing two distinctive covenants respectively, corroborated by a secondary biblical lemma:

τὸ δὲ Ἁγὰρ Σινᾶ ὄρος ἐστὶν ἐν τῇ Ἀραβίᾳ· συστοιχεῖ δὲ τῇ νῦν Ἰερουσαλήμ, δουλεύει γὰρ μετὰ τῶν τέκνων αὐτῆς

ἡ δὲ ἄνω Ἰερουσαλὴμ ἐλευθέρα ἐστίν, ἥτις ἐστὶν μήτηρ ἡμῶν

secondary biblical lemma (Isa 54:1):

γέγραπται γάρ· [...]

d) 4:28–31: Expository application

Further evidence of the same exegetical structure is found in Rom 4:1–25:

a) 4:1: Thematizing question (What did Abraham find as our ancestor, i.e. for Jews as well as for converts?): Τί οὖν ἐροῦμεν εὑρηκέναι Ἀβραὰμ τὸν προπάτορα ἡμῶν κατὰ σάρκα;

b) 4:2–3: Introductory paraphrase and quotation of the basic scripture (Gen 15:6; Abraham's reward by trust, not by deeds): εἰ γὰρ <u>Ἀβραὰμ</u> ἐξ ἔργων <u>ἐδικαιώθη</u>, ἔχει καύχημα, ἀλλ' οὐ πρὸς θεόν. Τί γὰρ ἡ γραφὴ λέγει; *ἐπίστευσεν δὲ Ἀβραὰμ τῷ θεῷ καὶ ἐλογίσθη αὐτῷ εἰς δικαιοσύνην*.

c) 4:4–22: Exegetical paraphrase and "commentary" of Gen 15:6 (words from the quotation are underlined), and addition of a secondary biblical lemma (Ps. 31:1)

4:4–12: Arguing of sub-theme (Abraham's reward from trust, not deeds):

τῷ δὲ ἐργαζομένῳ ὁ μισθὸς οὐ λογίζεται κατὰ χάριν ἀλλὰ κατὰ ὀφείλημα, τῷ δὲ μὴ ἐργαζομένῳ πιστεύοντι δὲ ἐπὶ τὸν δικαιοῦντα τὸν ἀσεβῆ λογίζεται ἡ πίστις αὐτοῦ εἰς δικαιοσύνην· καθάπερ καὶ Δαυὶδ λέγει τὸν μακαρισμὸν τοῦ ἀνθρώπου ᾧ ὁ θεὸς λογίζεται δικαιοσύνην χωρὶς ἔργων· *μακάριοι ὧν ἀφέθησαν αἱ ἀνομίαι καὶ ὧν ἐπεκαλύφθησαν αἱ ἁμαρτίαι· μακάριος ἀνὴρ οὗ οὐ μὴ λογίσηται κύριος ἁμαρτίαν.*
Ὁ μακαρισμὸς οὖν οὗτος ἐπὶ τὴν περιτομὴν ἢ καὶ ἐπὶ τὴν ἀκροβυστίαν; λέγομεν γάρ· ἐλογίσθη τῷ Ἀβραὰμ ἡ πίστις εἰς δικαιοσύνην. πῶς οὖν ἐλογίσθη; ἐν περιτομῇ ὄντι ἢ ἐν ἀκροβυστίᾳ; οὐκ ἐν περιτομῇ ἀλλ' ἐν ἀκροβυστίᾳ·καὶ σημεῖον ἔλαβεν περιτομῆς σφραγῖδα τῆς δικαιοσύνης τῆς πίστεως τῆς ἐν τῇ ἀκροβυστίᾳ, εἰς τὸ εἶναι αὐτὸν πατέρα πάντων τῶν πιστευόντων δι' ἀκροβυστίας, εἰς τὸ λογισθῆναι [καὶ] αὐτοῖς [τὴν] δικαιοσύνην,καὶ πατέρα περιτομῆς τοῖς οὐκ ἐκ περιτομῆς μόνον ἀλλὰ καὶ τοῖς στοιχοῦσιν τοῖς ἴχνεσιν τῆς ἐν ἀκροβυστίᾳ πίστεως τοῦ πατρὸς ἡμῶν Ἀβραάμ.

4:13–22: Arguing of new sub-theme (Abraham's reward from promise and trust, not Law)

Οὐ γὰρ διὰ νόμου ἡ ἐπαγγελία τῷ Ἀβραὰμ ἢ τῷ σπέρματι αὐτοῦ, τὸ κληρονόμον αὐτὸν εἶναι κόσμου, ἀλλὰ διὰ δικαιοσύνης πίστεως. εἰ γὰρ οἱ ἐκ νόμου κληρονόμοι, κεκένωται ἡ πίστις καὶ κατήργηται ἡ ἐπαγγελία· ὁ γὰρ νόμος ὀργὴν κατεργάζεται· οὗ δὲ οὐκ ἔστιν νόμος οὐδὲ παράβασις. Διὰ τοῦτο ἐκ πίστεως, ἵνα κατὰ χάριν, εἰς τὸ εἶναι βεβαίαν τὴν ἐπαγγελίαν παντὶ τῷ σπέρματι, οὐ τῷ ἐκ τοῦ νόμου μόνον ἀλλὰ καὶ τῷ ἐκ πίστεως Ἀβραάμ, ὅς ἐστιν πατὴρ πάντων ἡμῶν, καθὼς γέγραπται ὅτι *πατέρα πολλῶν ἐθνῶν τέθεικά σε*, κατέναντι οὗ ἐπίστευσεν θεοῦ τοῦ ζῳοποιοῦντος τοὺς νεκροὺς καὶ καλοῦντος τὰ μὴ ὄντα ὡς ὄντα. Ὃς παρ' ἐλπίδα ἐπ' ἐλπίδι ἐπίστευσεν εἰς τὸ γενέσθαι αὐτὸν πατέρα πολλῶν ἐθνῶν κατὰ τὸ εἰρημένον· *οὕτως ἔσται τὸ σπέρμα σου*,καὶ μὴ ἀσθενήσας τῇ πίστει κατενόησεν τὸ ἑαυτοῦ σῶμα [ἤδη] νενεκρωμένον, ἑκατονταετής που ὑπάρχων, καὶ τὴν νέκρωσιν τῆς μήτρας Σάρρας· εἰς δὲ τὴν ἐπαγγελίαν τοῦ θεοῦ οὐ διεκρίθη τῇ ἀπιστίᾳ ἀλλ' ἐνεδυναμώθη τῇ πίστει, δοὺς δόξαν τῷ θεῷ καὶ πληροφορηθεὶς ὅτι ὃ ἐπήγγελται δυνατός ἐστιν καὶ ποιῆσαι. διὸ [καὶ] ἐλογίσθη αὐτῷ εἰς δικαιοσύνην.

d) 4:23–25: Expository application and conclusion of the argument of 4:1–22 to the readers (continued paraphrase of Gen 15:6)

Οὐκ ἐγράφη δὲ δι' αὐτὸν μόνον ὅτι ἐλογίσθη αὐτῷ ἀλλὰ καὶ δι' ἡμᾶς, οἷς μέλλει λογίζεσθαι, τοῖς πιστεύουσιν ἐπὶ τὸν ἐγείραντα Ἰησοῦν τὸν κύριον ἡμῶν ἐκ νεκρῶν, ὃς παρεδόθη διὰ τὰ παραπτώματα ἡμῶν καὶ ἠγέρθη διὰ τὴν δικαίωσιν ἡμῶν.

As a point of departure for the analysis of Gal 3:6–29, I shall present the NA[28] version of its Greek text in analogy to the organization of Gal 4:21–31 and Rom 4:1–25 laid out above. Two kinds of markings have been included: the underlining indicates allusion to the LXX texts and the exegetical paraphrase of words or phrases based on these texts; *italics* refer to the citation of Gen 15:6 and the secondary biblical lemmas.

a) The paraphrastic rendering of the main biblical lemma introduced by an exegetical question:

3:5 – 6: ὁ οὖν ἐπιχορηγῶν ὑμῖν τὸ πνεῦμα καὶ ἐνεργῶν δυνάμεις ἐν ὑμῖν, ἐξ ἔργων νόμου ἢ ἐξ ἀκοῆς πίστεως; Καθὼς Ἀβραὰμ *ἐπίστευσεν τῷ θεῷ, καὶ ἐλογίσθη αὐτῷ εἰς δικαιοσύνην·*

b) The introductory exegetical paraphrase of the biblical lemma:

3:7 – 9: γινώσκετε ἄρα ὅτι οἱ ἐκ πίστεως, οὗτοι υἱοί εἰσιν Ἀβραάμ. προϊδοῦσα δὲ ἡ γραφὴ ὅτι ἐκ πίστεως δικαιοῖ τὰ ἔθνη ὁ θεός, προευηγγελίσατο τῷ Ἀβραὰμ ὅτι *ἐνευλογηθήσονται ἐν σοὶ πάντα τὰ ἔθνη·* ὥστε οἱ ἐκ πίστεως εὐλογοῦνται σὺν τῷ πιστῷ Ἀβραάμ.

c) Subsequent exegetical paraphrase of the primary lemma, adduced with secondary biblical lemmas:

3:10 – 14: Ὅσοι γὰρ ἐξ ἔργων νόμου εἰσίν, ὑπὸ κατάραν εἰσίν· γέγραπται γὰρ ὅτι *ἐπικατάρατος πᾶς ὃς οὐκ ἐμμένει πᾶσιν τοῖς γεγραμμένοις ἐν τῷ βιβλίῳ τοῦ νόμου* τοῦ ποιῆσαι αὐτά. ὅτι δὲ ἐν νόμῳ οὐδεὶς δικαιοῦται παρὰ τῷ θεῷ δῆλον, ὅτι *ὁ δίκαιος* ἐκ πίστεως ζήσεται· ὁ δὲ νόμος οὐκ ἔστιν ἐκ πίστεως, ἀλλ' *ὁ ποιήσας αὐτὰ ζήσεται ἐν αὐτοῖς*. Χριστὸς ἡμᾶς ἐξηγόρασεν ἐκ τῆς κατάρας τοῦ νόμου γενόμενος ὑπὲρ ἡμῶν κατάρα, ὅτι γέγραπται· *ἐπικατάρατος πᾶς ὁ κρεμάμενος ἐπὶ ξύλου*, ἵνα εἰς τὰ ἔθνη ἡ εὐλογία τοῦ Ἀβραὰμ γένηται ἐν Χριστῷ Ἰησοῦ, ἵνα τὴν ἐπαγγελίαν τοῦ πνεύματος λάβωμεν διὰ τῆς πίστεως.

3:15 – 18: Ἀδελφοί, κατὰ ἄνθρωπον λέγω· ὅμως ἀνθρώπου κεκυρωμένην διαθήκην οὐδεὶς ἀθετεῖ ἢ ἐπιδιατάσσεται. τῷ δὲ Ἀβραὰμ ἐρρέθησαν αἱ ἐπαγγελίαι καὶ τῷ σπέρματι αὐτοῦ. οὐ λέγει· καὶ τοῖς σπέρμασιν, ὡς ἐπὶ πολλῶν ἀλλ' ὡς ἐφ' ἑνός· *καὶ τῷ σπέρματί σου*, ὅς ἐστιν Χριστός. τοῦτο δὲ λέγω· διαθήκην προκεκυρωμένην ὑπὸ τοῦ θεοῦ ὁ μετὰ τετρακόσια καὶ τριάκοντα ἔτη γεγονὼς νόμος οὐκ ἀκυροῖ εἰς τὸ καταργῆσαι τὴν ἐπαγγελίαν. εἰ γὰρ ἐκ νόμου ἡ κληρονομία, οὐκέτι ἐξ ἐπαγγελίας· τῷ δὲ Ἀβραὰμ δι' ἐπαγγελίας κεχάρισται ὁ θεός.

3:19 – 22: Τί οὖν ὁ νόμος; τῶν παραβάσεων χάριν προσετέθη, ἄχρις οὗ ἔλθῃ τὸ σπέρμα ᾧ ἐπήγγελται, διαταγεὶς δι' ἀγγέλων ἐν χειρὶ μεσίτου. ὁ δὲ μεσίτης ἑνὸς οὐκ ἔστιν, ὁ δὲ θεὸς εἷς ἐστιν. ὁ οὖν νόμος κατὰ τῶν ἐπαγγελιῶν [τοῦ θεοῦ]; μὴ γένοιτο. εἰ γὰρ ἐδόθη νόμος ὁ δυνάμενος ζῳοποιῆσαι, ὄντως ἐκ νόμου ἂν ἦν ἡ δικαιοσύνη· ἀλλὰ συνέκλεισεν ἡ γραφὴ τὰ πάντα ὑπὸ ἁμαρτίαν, ἵνα ἡ ἐπαγγελία ἐκ πίστεως Ἰησοῦ Χριστοῦ δοθῇ τοῖς πιστεύουσιν.

d) Expository application and conclusion:

3:23 – 29: Πρὸ τοῦ δὲ ἐλθεῖν τὴν πίστιν ὑπὸ νόμον ἐφρουρούμεθα συγκλειόμενοι εἰς τὴν μέλλουσαν πίστιν ἀποκαλυφθῆναι, ὥστε ὁ νόμος παιδαγωγὸς ἡμῶν γέγονεν εἰς Χριστόν, ἵνα ἐκ πίστεως δικαιωθῶμεν· ἐλθούσης δὲ τῆς πίστεως οὐκέτι ὑπὸ παιδαγωγόν ἐσμεν. Πάντες γὰρ υἱοὶ θεοῦ ἐστε διὰ τῆς πίστεως ἐν Χριστῷ Ἰησοῦ· ὅσοι γὰρ εἰς Χριστὸν ἐβαπτίσθητε, Χριστὸν ἐνεδύσασθε. οὐκ ἔνι Ἰουδαῖος οὐδὲ Ἕλλην, οὐκ ἔνι δοῦλος οὐδὲ ἐλεύθερος, οὐκ ἔνι ἄρσεν καὶ θῆλυ· πάντες γὰρ ὑμεῖς εἷς ἐστε ἐν Χριστῷ Ἰησοῦ. εἰ δὲ ὑμεῖς Χριστοῦ, ἄρα τοῦ Ἀβραὰμ σπέρμα ἐστέ, κατ' ἐπαγγελίαν κληρονόμοι.

Gal 3:5b–9. I shall first discuss the introduction and wording of Gen 15:6 in Gal 3:6. With regard to the wording of the quotation itself, apart from a minor variation in Abraham's name (Abraham instead of Abram),[22] Paul follows LXX Gen 15:6 *verbatim:*

> Ἀβραὰμ ἐπίστευσεν τῷ θεῷ, καὶ ἐλογίσθη αὐτῷ εἰς δικαιοσύνην.
> Gal 3:6
>
> καὶ ἐπίστευσεν Αβραμ τῷ θεῷ, καὶ ἐλογίσθη αὐτῷ εἰς δικαιοσύνην.
> Gen 15:6 LXX

It is not clear, however, whether or not Gen 15:6 in Gal 3:6 is to be regarded as a marked quotation. For example, M. C. de Boer claims: "Paul's way of introducing the citation remains peculiar and without parallel, however, and it is thus unclear whether Paul actually intends to mark the words from Gen 15:6 as a quotation, as he does in in Rom 4:2 [...], or simply weaves them into his own text [...]."[23] Fresh light is thrown upon this problem, if we take Gal 3:6 to be an exegetical paraphrase of Gen 15:6 rather than a marked self-contained citation. *Pace* de Boer, it should be argued that the rendering of the HBq in Gal 3:6 represents no idiosyncracy, and indeed has some instructive parallels. Some observations on the text of Gal 3:5–7 and the parallels of this kind of exegetical paraphrase in Philo, *Mut.* 253–255, *Somn.* 2:17–21, and Rom 4:1–2 seem to corroborate such a view. In the first place, Paul does not unequivocally mark the words from Gen 15:6 as a quotation. For example, the edition of NA[28] regards καθὼς Ἀβραάμ as introducing the citation of Gen 15:6 (with its words in italics): Καθὼς Ἀβραὰμ *ἐπίστευσεν τῷ θεῷ, καὶ ἐλογίσθη αὐτῷ εἰς δικαιοσύνην*. This reading might suggest that the phrase καθὼς Ἀβραάμ should be taken to refer both backwards to the "expository preface" introduced in Gal 3:5–6 and forwards to the exegetical paraphrase of Gen 15:6 that continues in Gal 3:7 and runs to Gal 3:29.[24] Some further observations on the surface level of the text seem to support this. Since the ancient Greek manuscripts of the New Testament in general contain little punctuation, it is possible to interpunctuate Gal 3:5–6 as follows: "the bestower of the

---

22 For a discussion of the placement of Abraham's name as part of the citation or an introduction to Gal 3:6, cf. C.D. Stanley, *Arguing with Scripture: The Rhetoric of Quotations in the Letters of Paul* (London: T & T Clark, 2004), 235. In favor of the view that Paul adapts the quotation of Gen 15:6 because the phrase καθὼς Ἀβραάμ is a transitional statement, Stanley fails to take into account that it functions as part of an "exegetical preface" which is closely linked to the subsequent quotation. For this view, see my argument further below.
23 M.C. de Boer, *Galatians: A Commentary*, NTL (Louisville, KY: Westminster John Knox Press, 2011), 189.
24 So, e.g., Hartman, "Galatians 3:15–4:11," 134 n. 16.

Spirit [...] did he supply you with the Spirit and work miracles among you by your doing the works of the law, or by trusting what you heard just as Abraham? 'He trusted God, and it was reckoned to him as righteousness'." Moreover, in Gen 15:6 LXX the the name Αβραμ follows the verb ἐπίστευσεν, while Paul has both changed the name to Ἀβραάμ and presented a reversed order in Gen 15:6. This has caused scholars to interpret the phrase καθὼς Ἀβραάμ as an introductory statement, so that the meaning is taken to be somewhat like "as was the case with Abraham",[25] "and so it was with Abraham",[26] "take Abraham as the example",[27] or "things were the same with Abraham".[28] However, we must go beyond the view that Abraham is here introduced as a historical example,[29] and search for the specific reason why Paul does so.

It is fortunate that Philo provides an example of such an exegetical motif. In the context of his appropriation of Abraham as a a paradigm for subsequent proselytes, Philo explained Gen 15:6 in terms of Abraham's reception of the Spirit by trust (*Virt.* 219). Thus, an interpreted Scripture about Abraham seems to have been adduced in order to bolster the legal authority of the experience of the Galatians. It is also noteworthy that an event in Mattathias's life is likewise seen as comparable (καθώς) with a biblical event, *in casu* with Phinehas' killing of Zambri, according to 1 Macc 2:24 – 26.[30]

Thirdly, with regard to the reading of Gal 3:5 – 6a as a brief expository "preface" to the following citation of Gen 15:6, this has parallels in Philo, *Mut.* 253 – 255; *Somn.* 2:17 – 21, and Paul's introduction of the same scripture in Romans 4:1 – 3. The similarity in the structure of these texts can be displayed as follows:

Mut. 253 – 255:
(1) HBq: He said to him, we read, "*Yes, Sarah thy wife shall bear a son*" (Gen. 17:19).

25 F. Mussner, *Der Galaterbrief*, HThKNT (Freiburg im Breisgau: Herder, 1974), 214.
26 J. B. Lightfoot, *Saint Paul's Epistle to the Galatians: A Revisited Text with Introduction, Notes, and Dissertations* (London; New York: Macmillan and Co., 1896), 136.
27 Longenecker, *Galatians*, 112.
28 J.L. Martyn, *Galatians: A New Translation with Introduction and Commentary*, AB (New York: Doubleday, 1997), 296.
29 For recent iterations of this position, cf. D.A. deSilva, *The Letter to the Galatians*, NICNT (Grand Rapids: Eerdmans, 2018), 277 n. 34; F.D. Tolmie, *Persuading the Galatians: A Text-Centred Rhetorical Analysis of a Pauline Letter*, WUNT 2 (Tübingen: Mohr Siebeck, 2005), 112; B. Witherington III, *Grace in Galatia: A Commentary on St Paul's Letter to the Galatians* (Edinburgh: T & T Clark, 1998), 217; Martyn, *Galatians*, 296.
30 Cf. Mussner, *Der Galaterbrief*, 213.

(2) Exegetical "preface": How significant is that answer "*Yes*," fraught as it is with inner meaning. For what can be more befitting to God than to grant and promise His blessings in a moment and with a sign of assent? [...]
(3) ThM introduced by a MB: Learn then, soul of man, that *Sarah* also, that is virtue, *shall bear thee a son*, as well as Hagar, the lower instruction. For Hagar's offspring is the creature of teaching, but *Sarah's* learns from none other at all than itself.

<u>Somn. 2:17–21</u>:
(1) HBq: "'*Methought*'", says he, "*that we were binding sheaves*" (Gen 33:7).
(2) Exegetical "preface": The very first word, "*methought*," is the utterance of one at a loss, hesitating, dimly supposing, not seeing steadily and distinctly. For "*methought*" is a word which becomes those waking up out of deep sleep and still in dreamland, not those who are thoroughly awake and see things clearly. You will not find the Practiser Jacob saying "*methought*," but "behold a stairway firmly fixed, whose top reached to heaven" (Gen 28:12) [...]
(3) ThM introduced by a MB: Now, when I listen to him who is telling the dreams I marvel at his deeming that they were *tying up sheaves, not reaping* them. The former is the work of unskilled underlings, the latter the business of masters and of those thoroughly well versed in farm work.

<u>Rom 4:1–3</u>:
(3) ThM introduced by a MB: What then are we to say was gained by *Abraham*, our ancestor according to the flesh?
(2) Exegetical "preface": For if *Abraham* was justified by works, he has something to boast about, but not before *God*.
(1) HBq: For what does the scripture say? "Abraham believed God, and it was reckoned to him as righteousness."

<u>Gal 3:5–7</u>:
(2) Exegetical "preface": Does God supply you with the Spirit and work miracles in you by the works of the law, or by receiving the message with *trust*, just as *Abraham?*
(1) HBq: *"He trusted God, and it was reckoned to him as righteousness"* (Gen 15:6).
(3) ThM introduced by a MB: Accordingly, you must realize, those of *trust* are the descendants of *Abraham*.

These texts display a similar outline, except that in the Philonic texts the HBq (1) is first rendered, and then an interpretation of words from the HBq is given as an expository "preface" (2), followed by a thematic marker (ThM) introduced by a "meta-propositional base" (MB) (3). Thus, in *Mut*. 254–255a a brief expository "preface, which interprets the word "yes" from the citation of Gen 17:9 rendered in *Mut.* 253, is followed by the thematic statement in *Mut.* 255b. The same outline is applied in *Somn.* 2:17–21, in which an expository "preface" in terms of an interpretation of the first word, "methought", from the preceeding quoation of Gen 37:7 (in § 17), is followed by the opening statement in § 21. In the Pauline discourses, however, the order of (1) and (2) is reversed, so that the expository "preface" in Rom 4:2 and Gal 3:5–6a rather serves as an introductory statement to the quotation of Gen 15:6 which follows. Thus, the expository "preface" in Rom 4:2 anticipates the exegetical elaboration of the phrases "Abraham" and "God" from the quotation of Gen 15:6. Likewise, Gal 3:5–6a can be read as presenting an exegetical paraphrase of the two words "Abram" and "believed" from the citation of Gen 15:6. Thus, the verb ἐπίστευσεν has been interpreted about Abraham's trust in God in terms of the promise that was heard with faith (cf. the expression ἀκοῆς πίστεως in Gal 3:5, pointing forward to the comparison with Abraham in Gal 3:7 and 3:9), and the name Αβραμ has been changed to Ἀβραάμ in Gal 3:6a. A more detailed argument in favour of this reading will be offered in our content analysis of Gal 3:6–9 below. As we also shall point out in the next section, there are some noteworthy similarities between these texts with regard to their exegetical.

At this juncture, I shall also argue that Gal 3:7–9 can be seen as a further comment on the authoritative event of Abraham, centered on an exegetical paraphrase of Gen 15:6 in conjunction with the "composite citation" of Gen 12:3 and 22:18 / 26:4. I shall offer some suggestions about various aspects of the methods applied in these verses. Again, Paul's use of this exegetical tecnique seems to corroborate the impression that it is an argument from Abraham himself as the legal norm and foundational model, based on an interpreted Scripture.

Firstly, the phrase οἱ ἐκ πίστεως and the reference to Abraham in both Gal 3:7 and 3:9 represent an elaborate exegetical paraphrase of words from Gen 15:6, and indicate the similarity in kind and nature with the forbear Abraham, viz. the identifying mark of trust which serves as a warrant for the legitimacy of the Galatian converts as Abraham's descendants and partakers of the oath of promise. Thus, in Gal 3:7b, Paul makes use of the exegetical technique of deictic or "direct" exegesis, in which a phrase is explained by another word, phrase, or sentence.[31] Thus, the phrase "those of trust" (οἱ ἐκ πίστεως) is explained (οὗτοι [...] εἰσιν) as Abraham's sons (υἱοί [...] Ἀβραάμ), so that Abraham's trust is conceived of as the foundational identity characteristic of his descend-

31 For the use of this method in Jewish exegesis and with parallels in Greek literature, cf. Bekken, *The Word is Near You*, 79–80.

ants. The same is true in Gal 3:9. Furthermore, on the basis of the exegetical paraphrase of words from Gen 15:6 (οἱ ἐκ πίστεως and τῷ πιστῷ Ἀβραάμ respectively) and the conflated citation Gen 12:3, 22:18, and 26:4 (εὐλογοῦνται σὺν), Paul draws the conclusion about the blessing promised to Abraham and his descendants. Accordingly, Abraham's theological conviction and the promise are the means of marking the identity of Abraham's descendants.

Thirdly, the exegetical paraphrase of Gen 15:6 results in *a refashioning of God in the image of Abraham and vice versa.*[32] Four observations will be briefly offered here in support of this suggestion; the next sections below will argue this in more detail. (1) If we see Gal 3:8 – 9 as a further elaboration of the exegetical paraphrase of Gen 15:6 cited in v.6, Paul draws a parallel between God's justification of Abraham and of the nations as follows:

> v. 6 Καθὼς Ἀβραὰμ *ἐπίστευσεν τῷ θεῷ, καὶ ἐλογίσθη αὐτῷ εἰς δικαιοσύνην·*
> v. 8 προϊδοῦσα δὲ ἡ γραφὴ ὅτι ἐκ πίστεως δικαιοῖ τὰ ἔθνη ὁ θεός, προευηγγελίσατο τῷ Ἀβραὰμ ὅτι *ἐνευλογηθήσονται ἐν σοὶ πάντα τὰ ἔθνη*
> v. 9 ·ὥστε οἱ ἐκ πίστεως εὐλογοῦνται σὺν τῷ πιστῷ Ἀβραάμ.

Thus, by rephrasing the reference to God's "justification" (from *δικαιοσύνη* to δικαιόω) and replacing "Abraham" *(αὐτός)* with the word "nations" (*τὰ ἔθνη*), Paul emphasizes that as Abraham was *justified*, so "God would *justify* the nations". (2) In the paraphrase of Abraham's trust from Gen 15:6 in v. 8, Paul constructs a reenvisioning of God in the image of Abraham and vice versa. Thus, he argues that God acts in a way that corresponds to Abraham's conduct: As Abraham *trusted* (*ἐπίστευσεν*) God, so "God would justify the nations *out of his trust*" (ἐκ πίστεως). (3) In Gal 3:8 – 9 Paul makes evident what is presupposed in Gal 3:6; as Abraham *trusted* in *the promise* (cf. Gen 15:5 – 6), so "God out of his *trust* / *faithfulness*" spoke *the oath of promise* to Abraham: "In you (Abraham / Isaac) shall all the nations (*πάντα τὰ ἔθνη*) be blessed". The scriptural basis for this exposition is, then, the composite quotation of Gen 12:3 and 22:18 / 26:4, as I have stated above. (4) Furthermore, v. 9 elaborates the correlation between Abraham and God from v. 8. At this juncture, however, Paul reverses the parallelism, so that Abraham instead is conceived of in the image of God. Paul interprets Abraham's trust in Gen 15:6 in the light of Gen 22:18 and the exegetical motif of God's trust / faithfulness granted as an adequate reward corresponding to Abraham's trust. Having received God's trust, interpreted in terms of the oath of promise from God, Abraham himself is affirmed as trustworthy or faithful (πιστῷ Ἀβραάμ).

32 Levenson (*The Death and Resurrection*, 220 – 32) has shown that a similar thought pattern, in which God supplants the role of Abraham, lies behind Rom 8:28 – 32.

Thus, God rewards the trust that Abraham antecedently possessed (Gen 15:6) in terms of the oath of promise (Gen 22:16 – 18). In sum, Paul has validated the Galatian believers as legitimate descendants of Abraham on the basis of both Abraham's initial trust in the promise *and* in God's responsiveness to Abraham's trust, expressed through the oath of promise and thus the additional measure of divine trust given to Abraham. As I shall substantiate below, this supposition of Paul's exegetical paraphrase in Gal 3:8 – 9 gains probability since it conforms to the Jewish exegetical tradition that we examined in chapter three, which interprets Gen 15:6 in *continuum* with Gen 22:18 and 26:3 – 5. Moreover, this proposal receives further support from Paul's exegetical paraphrase of Gen 22:18 / 26:4 in Gal 3:14, 16, 29.

Gal 3:10 – 13. The proposition in 3:11a is an exegetical paraphrase of Ps. 142:2 LXX, "for *no one* living is *righteous before you*". According to Paul's reading of this scripture, this statement cannot be taken in an absolute way, because those of trust are justified (cf. Gen 15:6; Hab 2:4). Thus, the exegetical clarification ascribed to the Psalm passage by Paul is that it should be interpreted in a more resticted sense about the jurisdiction of the Law, that is, "because in the Law *no one* (living) *is justified before God.*"[33] I shall return to Paul's exegetical treatment of Ps. 142:2 LXX below.

In Gal 3:12, another exegetical technique and corresponding terminology can be seen. One explanation of a text may be abandoned in contrast to the proper meaning. An example is provided by Philo, *Leg.* 1:1. Here, Gen 2:1 is quoted: "And the heaven and the earth and all their world were completed". In the exposition, Philo discards one interpretation in favour of the proper one: "He [Moses] does *not* (οὔτε) say that either the individual mind or the particular sense perception has reached completion, *but* (ἀλλά) that the originals have done so".[34] An analogy is found in Paul's interpretation of Lev 18:5 in Gal 3:12, in which he discards the idea that the jurisdiction of the Law of Moses is based on the principle of trust rather than on the principles of the actions that need to be performed: ὁ δὲ νόμος οὐκ ἔστιν ἐκ πίστεως, ἀλλ' ὁ ποιήσας αὐτὰ ζήσεται ἐν αὐτοῖς. In my comments on Gal 3:16 below, I point out that a more specific application of the same method is used.

In addition to v. 7b and v. 9, v. 14 (ἵνα εἰς τὰ ἔθνη ἡ εὐλογία τοῦ Ἀβραὰμ γένηται ἐν Χριστῷ Ἰησοῦ, ἵνα τὴν ἐπαγγελίαν τοῦ πνεύματος λάβωμεν διὰ τῆς πίστεως) provides another example of the exegetical technique, in which a compo-

33 Thus Dahl, *Studies in Paul*, 170 n. 18.

34 For Philo's usage of exegetical method and terms in this passage, see Borgen, *An Exegete for His Time*, 155.

site citation is further interpreted by adding a final clause to it in order to indicate its meaning. Moreover, Gal 3:14 illustrates further the method of exegetical paraphrase, in which one or more words from the quotation are replaced by other interpretive words. Thus, for example, N.A. Dahl suggested that the various component parts of Gal 3:14a were a paraphrase of God's oath to Abraham in Gen 22:18 LXX, in that the expression τὰ ἔθνη was sourced from Gen 22:18 LXX and that the phrase ἐν τῷ σπέρματί σου ("in your offspring") from the same verse was replaced by the words ἐν Χριστῷ Ἰησοῦ ("in Jesus Christ"). Moreover, Dahl surmised that the phrase ἡ εὐλογία τοῦ Ἀβραὰμ was borrowed from Gen 28:4 LXX.[35] Several scholars have concurred with his observation.[36] Dahl's suggestion may also be supported by Paul's elaboration and paraphrase of the oath of promise to Abraham, already initiated in Gal 3:8–9. My proposal (see next section), however, that Gen 26:4 may already be invoked in the composite citation in Gal 3:8b, should be brought more into the interpretation of v. 14. A comparison of the relevant Greek texts may help to display this (the words are underlined):

> Gal 3:14a: ἵνα εἰς τὰ ἔθνη ἡ εὐλογία τοῦ Ἀβραὰμ γένηται *ἐν Χριστῷ Ἰησοῦ*
> Gen 22:18: καὶ ἐνευλογηθήσονται *ἐν τῷ σπέρματί* σου πάντα τὰ ἔθνη τῆς γῆς
> Gen 26:4: καὶ ἐνευλογηθήσονται *ἐν τῷ σπέρματί* σου πάντα τὰ ἔθνη τῆς γῆς
> Gen 28:4: καὶ δῴη σοι τὴν εὐλογίαν Αβρααμ τοῦ πατρός μου, σοὶ καὶ τῷ σπέρματί σου μετὰ σέ

According to this comparison, all the motifs and elements in Paul's allusion to and exegetical paraphrase of Gen 22:18, 26:4, and 28:4 may be incorporated in v. 14, that is, "Abraham", "blessing", "in your offspring", and "the nations". Given that this suggestion has some plausibility, this exegesis is given further force by Paul's explicit analogy and interpretation of the "offspring", identified as Christ in Gal 3:16, to which I shall turn next.

With regard to Paul's interpretation and identification of the collective singular, "offspring", with the specific singular, "Christ", the first question which needs to be raised is to which scripture Paul refers. Various answers have been offered. The most relevant HB citations that have been suggested are Gen

35 For this exegetical device of paraphrase, cf. Bekken, "Philo's Relevance for the Study of the New Testament," 234–5.

36 Cf. M. Wilcox, "'Upon the Tree' – Deut 21:22–23 in the New Testament," *JBL* 96.1 (1977): 99; D.H. Juel, *Messianic Exegesis: Christological Interpretation of the Old Testament in Early Christianity* (Philadelphia: Fortress Press, 1988), 86; Levenson, *The Death and Resurrection*, 213; R.B. Hays, *The Faith of Jesus Christ: The Narrative Substructure of Galatians 3:1–4:11*, 2nd ed., BRS (Grand Rapids: Eerdmans; Dearborn, MI: Dove Booksellers, 2002), 180.

13:8; 15:18; 17:8; 22:18. In the sections below (5.2 and 6.1), I shall argue that Gen 26:3 – 4, not hitherto fully appreciated, may fit in the immediate context as an appropriate candidate. This means that the link Paul draws between Gal 3:8b, 14, 16, 29 is supplied by his exegetical paraphrase of words from Gen 22:18 and Gen 26:3 – 4, viz. the oath of promise first spoken to Abraham (Gen 22:18; cf. Gal 3:8, 14a), and then reiterated to Isaac (Gen 26:3 – 4; cf. Gal 3:16), Abraham's specific singular offspring, which is the only promise given to Isaac. This hypothesis gains in probability because it satisfies the following conditions: 1. These promises must refer primarily to the oath of promise, which contains the only promises directed to both Abraham and his descendant, Isaac (cf. v. 16); 2. The phrase *καὶ τῷ σπέρματί σου* must be part of the citation (cf. v.16); 3. It must conform to the coherent argument in the immediate context of Gal 3:6 – 29, in terms of the exegetical paraphrase of the oath of promise in Gal 3:8 – 9, the phraseology about Abraham's blessing to the nations fulfilled "through his offspring" (ἐν τῷ σπέρματί σου) (v. 14a), and the interpretation of this in v. 16 as referring to the specific singular of Abraham's offspring ("as of one, Christ"). Thus, the "seed" envisioned in Gen 22:18 / 26:3 – 4 was never meant to refer to the generic singular of all of his offsprings ("as of many"), pointing to the subsequent generations of Isaac and Jacob. 4. Moreover, Paul's twist to the tradition in vv. 17 – 18, i.e., the priority and independence of the promises over against the Law of Moses, conforms to the context of a Jewish discussion of Abraham in which the oath of promise was conceived of in *continuum* with motifs such as Abraham's covenant, circumcision, descendants, and his adherence to the Law of Moses. It is also significant that Gen 26:3 – 5, with the exegetical motif of **the Torah kept by Abraham,** was embedded in such an exegetical tradition and context. In sum, these considerations point in favor of Gen 26:3 – 4, which is the only reference which satisfies these conditions. The implication of Gal 3:16 – 18 is, then, Paul's claim that the oath of promise associated with the covenant of Abraham was fulfilled in Christ apart from the Law. Thus, Isaac prefigures Christ, and this means that the oath of promise comes to fruition through Christ. Furthermore, those converts who belong to Christ can *eo ipso* be understood as Abraham's legitimate heirs and partakers of the promises, prefigured and warranted by the oath of promise spoken to Abraham and then reiterated to Isaac in Gen 26:3 – 4 (cf. Gal 3:29). In order to bolster his argument, it seems clear that Paul in Gal 3:16 deployed the same exegetical techniques as in Gal 3:12, namely the philological method of discarding a certain reading of a text in favor of its proper meaning: "[...] *οὐ* λέγει· καὶ τοῖς σπέρμασιν, ὡς ἐπὶ πολλῶν *ἀλλ'* ὡς ἐφ' ἑνός [...]" ("[...] 'and to his offspring'; it does *not* say 'and to offsprings', as referring to many, *but*, referring to one, 'and to your offspring' [...]". Philo's exegetical writings offer examples of this method. For example, in *Migr.* 43, the contrast indicates a confirmation of the reading of the text of Gen 12:1, "[...] εἰπὼν *οὐχ* ἣν δείκνυμι *ἀλλ'* ἣν σοι δείξω, [...]" ("[...] into the land that I will show you He says *not* which I am shewing, *but* which I will shew thee, [...]"). Such a philological confirmation of one particular reading of a text is also used in rabbinic exegesis, as in Mek. Exod 15:11: "Doing wonders: It is *not* (אין) written here 'Who did wonders,' *but* (אלא) 'who does wonders', that is, in the future."[37] Such an observation on the method applied in Gal 3:16 should, however, be supplemented. Two other exegetical features are also employed in Gal 3:16, and these have not hitherto been fully appreciated. In the first place, just as a philological confirmation of the correct reading could be developed in a paraphrasing exegesis of the HBq, so Paul's way of elaborating on a phrase from the HBq, "'and to your offspring', which is Christ", is another example of what might be labelled "direct exegesis", which we have observed in Gal 3:7 too.[38] In my observations on exegetical terminology below, I shall point out that Paul has used a typical phrase in such an exegetical operation.

Next, Gal 3:16 illustrates an exegetical reasoning prominent in Paul's own time, which might be classified as the problem-solving method. For example, the specific problem of numbers in scripture, such as the binary singular-plural contrast in the grammatical forms used, seems also to be presupposed in Paul's exegetical paraphrase in Gal 3:16. Further examples of such contrasts are presented and discussed by Philo, e.g., in *Dec.* 36, *Opif.* 72 – 75, and *Conf.* 169.[39] In the last text, the exegetical problem refers to the application of the plural in contrast to the singular about God in Gen 3:22:

> καὶ πάλιν "εἶπεν ὁ θεός· ἰδού, γέγονεν Ἀδὰμ ὡς εἷς ἡμῶν, τῷ γινώσκειν καλὸν καὶ πονηρόν." τὸ γὰρ "ὡς εἷς ἡμῶν" *οὐκ* ἐφ' ἑνός, *ἀλλ'* ἐπὶ πλειόνων τίθεται.
>
> (And once more, "God said, 'behold Adam has become as one of us by knowing good and evil." Here the "as one of us" is said *not* of one, *but* of more than one.)[40]

Although these examples and other rabbinic analogies do not display direct parallels to Paul's change of a collective singular to a specific one, they nevertheless

37 Cf. Borgen, *An Exegete for His Time*, 155; idem, *Bread from Heaven*, 64.
38 Another example of this method is Rom 10:6 – 8, in which a paraphrase of Deut 30:12 – 14 LXX is elaborated by means of "direct exegesis". Cf. Bekken, *The Word is Near You*, 72 – 3.
39 Cf. also *QG* 1:15. See Borgen, *An Exegete for His Time*, 82.
40 The Loeb translation is slighly modified. At this juncture, Philo also applies the common expository method and formula of repeating a phrase from the text ("ὡς εἷς ἡμῶν") by means of the neuter definite article τό, which places the phrase in quotation marks. See, for other examples, Philo, *Leg.* 1:65, 67; *Migr.* 7; *Congr.* 172; *Mut.* 27, 29; *Opif.* 27; *QG* 1:1, 55, 93, 100; 2:54; 3:23, 40; 4:73, 99, 188. For Paul, see Gal 4:25; Eph 4:9.

illustrate a similar kind of problem-solving exegesis, such as the question of grammatical numbers that may be raised on the basis of certain phrases or scriptures in the Pentateuchal narrative.[41] Two other observations may support, at least in an indirect way, the claim that Paul plays on other issues of numbers in his problem-solving approach. Firstly, Gal 3:20 reflects the problem of contrast between the number of years referred to in Gen 15:13 (400 years) and Exod 12:41 (430 years). At this point, Paul invokes an exegetical explanation and tradition attested later in the rabbinic literature, when he refers to the latter number of 430 years reckoned from God's "covenant between the pieces" with Abraham.[42] As I shall point out below (section 6.1), such a "covenantal" framework of the divine oath to Abraham and his seed is corroborated by the evidence in the Hebrew Bible and in post-biblical Jewish literature, where the distinct notions of "oath" and "covenant" can be associated with each other and almost function as synonyms. Thus, although the concept of the "covenant" does not explicitly appear in Gen 22:15 – 18 and 26:3 – 4, Second Temple Jewish interpreters as well as modern scholars have interpreted these texts to mean that the divine oath reaffirms the covenantal promises to Abraham and his descendant.

Secondly, another kind of binary contrast between numbers is found in Gal 3:19c–20, where Paul makes a distinction between the agency of "not one / of one", i. e. the agency of an intermediary, numerically representing a multiplicity of parties, in contrast to the agency of the one God: "Now a mediator involves more than one party; but God is one." Below, I shall suggest that Paul applies such a binary plural-singular contrast to say that the Law at Sinai was mediated by an intermediary, who acted on behalf of other angels / messengers and the people, because of the purpose of the Law, namely, to incriminate the law breaker.[43] In the next section, I shall turn to some observations on exegetical forms and terminology in Paul's argument, particularly in dialogue and juxtaposition with Philo.

---

41 On the problem of grammatical numbers in rabbinic exegesis, cf. D. Daube, *The New Testament and Rabbinic Judaism* (Peabody, MA: Hendrickson, 1994), 440 – 4; A. Samely, *Rabbinic Interpretation of Scripture in the Mishnah* (Oxford: OUP, 2002), 290 – 1.

42 On Paul's use of rabbinic exegetical traditions in Galatians 3, cf. Dahl, *Studies in Paul*, 169 n. 17.

43 For analogous discussions of binary singular-plural contrasts in rabbinic litterature, cf. Samely, *Rabbinic Interpretation of Scripture in the Mishnah*, 290 – 1.

2.2 Exegetical Forms

In this section, I shall succinctly discuss the exegetical forms involved in the larger and smaller units of the expository paraphrase. With regard to the notion of "form", I have found F. de Saussure's linguistic distinction between "form" on the levels of "langue" and "parole" useful in the assessment of exegetical forms appropriated by Paul and his contemporaries.[44] The phenomenon of "langue" implies that such features as words, grammatical forms, syntactical constructions, literary conventions etc. are sociologically conditioned. Accordingly, grammatical features, "patterns" and language structures are deposited in our memories, where they can remain constantly at our disposal. This psychological aspect of "langue" can thus provide substantiation for the impression that classical authors, such as Paul and Philo, were not conscious of employing a certain form as a form. They simply expressed and steeped their message in conventional, traditional forms, and had hardly any independent interest in form as such. Thus, as with exegetical methods, so too exegetical conventional forms developed. A similar view was, for example, taken by R. Le Déaut and D. Daube, according to W.D. Davies:

> The authors were conscious of writing in tradition rather in a certain form (R. Le Déaut, 270–1). [...] Professor Daube long ago taught me that form, unlike substance, tends to be fastened by instinct rather than deliberation.[45]

In what follows, we shall see how Gal 3:6–29 displays some characteristic types of exegetical forms in the larger and smaller units of the expository paraphrase.

2.2.1 The Dialectical Structure of Questions and Answers

In terms of J.L. Austin's approach to see what words do to the hearer(s) or reader(s), it would be useful simply to observe and describe how Paul conducted "theology" in the form of "questions and answers". It seems to me that more attention should be given to this mode of communication in Paul's letters.[46]

The problem-solving method and form of "questions and answers" is a feature common to both Philo and Paul. So, for example, in his first commentary

44 F. de Saussure, *Cours de Linguistique Générale* (Paris: Payot, 1916), 23–54.

45 W.D. Davies, *Jewish and Pauline Studies* (London: S.P.C.K., 1984), 176.

46 N.A. Dahl has written an important article on this subject. It is unfortunate that it has not yet been made available to an international public; cf. his essay, "Når Paulus spør," in *Kirken i Tiden; Troen i Folket*, ed. N.K. Lie (Oslo: Verbum, 1993), 47–59.

series, *The Questions and Answers on Genesis and Exodus*, Philo works sequentially through Gen 2:4 – 28:9 and Exod 12:2 – 28:24 posing questions followed by a citation of the biblical text accompanied by an answer, both on a literal and allegorical level.[47] Philo's writings in general make evident that such a form is appropriate when reporting from a learned school setting in Alexandria such as the Synagogue.[48] Thus, Philo testifies to the use of questions and answers and problem-solving exegesis as part of the teaching activity in the Synagogue, as is suggested by his report on the expository activity among the Therapeutae: "[…] the President of the company […] *discusses* (ζητέω) some questions arising in the Holy Scriptures or *solves* (ἐπιλύω) one that has been propounded by someone else" (*Contempl.* 75). The same Greek cognates are used elsewhere in Philo's writings too, when an exegetical question is raised, and answers and solutions are given.[49] Moreover, in *Contempl.* 79, the leader is said to have conversed with (διαλέγω ["hold converse with"; "discuss"]) his audience, and since questions and answers were part of the discourse, the verb most probably means in this context "discuss". Again, we should remind ourselves of the plausibility that exegetical motifs and explanations arose from the public reading, exposition, and discussion of Scripture in a context like those described here by Philo and also alluded to in his remarks on the educational activity that took place in Jewish family life, his own communication of Scripture, and discussions with other exegetes.[50] Against such a background of variegated forms of discussions of Scripture that took place in learned Jewish settings, learned authors such as Philo[51] and Paul would themselves probably draw on the form of exegetical "questions and answers" as a rhetorical or literary device in their own exegetical "treatises" of smaller or larger kinds. As S.D. Fraade rightly observes,

> The question and answer structure, even if wooden, at least creates the impression of dialogue between the author and Scripture, as well as between the author and the readers. It opens the lemma to interpretation and draws the reader into that activity. It is of course a

---

47 On this series, cf. G.E. Sterling, "The Place of Genesis in the Commentaries of Philo," 427 – 46, esp. 429 – 31.

48 Cf. *Spec.* 1:214; *Leg. All.* 1:33, 48, 91; 2:103; *QG* 1:62. On the attempt to situate Philo's exegetical commentaries within a school tradition, cf. G.E. Sterling, "The School of Moses in Alexandria: An Attempt to Reconstruct the School of Philo," in *Second Temple Jewish Paideia in Context*, ed. G. Boccaccini and J. Zurawski, BZNW (Berlin: de Gruyter, 2017), 141 – 66.

49 Cf. Borgen, *An Exegete for His Time*, 100 – 1.

50 See, e.g., Kugel, "Jubilees, Philo, and the Problem of Genesis," 310; idem, *In Potiphar's House: The Interpretive Life of Biblical Texts* (San Francisco: Harper, 1990), 266.

51 Cf. D.T. Runia, "The Structure of Philo's Allegorical Treatises," 209 – 56; Niehoff, "Homeric Scholarship and Bible Exegesis in Ancient Alexandria: Evidence from Philo's 'Quarrelsome' Colleagues," *CQ* 57.1 (2007): 166 – 82.

common rhetorical device in Greek philosophical literature, as in early rabbinic commentary.[52]

The following questions appear in Galatians 3:

Ironic questions:

Gal 3:1: Ὦ ἀνόητοι Γαλάται, τίς ὑμᾶς ἐβάσκανεν, οἷς κατ' ὀφθαλμοὺς Ἰησοῦς Χριστὸς προεγράφη ἐσταυρωμένος;

Gal 3:2: τοῦτο μόνον θέλω μαθεῖν ἀφ' ὑμῶν· ἐξ ἔργων νόμου τὸ πνεῦμα ἐλάβετε ἢ ἐξ ἀκοῆς πίστεως;

Gal 3:3: οὕτως ἀνόητοί ἐστε, ἐναρξάμενοι πνεύματι νῦν σαρκὶ ἐπιτελεῖσθε;

Gal 3:4: τοσαῦτα ἐπάθετε εἰκῇ;

First exegetical question related to the case:

Gal 3:5: ὁ οὖν ἐπιχορηγῶν ὑμῖν τὸ πνεῦμα καὶ ἐνεργῶν δυνάμεις ἐν ὑμῖν, ἐξ ἔργων νόμου ἢ ἐξ ἀκοῆς πίστεως καθὼς Ἀβραάμ;

Basic answer:

Gal 3:7: γινώσκετε ἄρα ὅτι οἱ ἐκ πίστεως, οὗτοι υἱοί εἰσιν Ἀβραάμ.

Second exegetical question:

Gal 3:19: Τί οὖν ὁ νόμος;

Answer:

Gal 3:19 – 20: τῶν παραβάσεων χάριν προσετέθη, ἄχρις οὗ ἔλθῃ τὸ σπέρμα ᾧ ἐπήγγελται, διαταγεὶς δι' ἀγγέλων ἐν χειρὶ μεσίτου. ὁ δὲ μεσίτης ἑνὸς οὐκ ἔστιν, ὁ δὲ θεὸς εἷς ἐστιν.

Third exegetical question:

Gal 3:21: ὁ οὖν νόμος κατὰ τῶν ἐπαγγελιῶν [τοῦ θεοῦ];

---

52 S.D. Fraade, *From Tradition to Commentary: Torah and Its Interpretation in the Midrash Sifre to Deuteronomy* (Albany: State University of New York Press, 1991), 7.

Answer:

> Gal 3:21–22: μὴ γένοιτο. εἰ γὰρ ἐδόθη νόμος ὁ δυνάμενος ζῳοποιῆσαι, ὄντως ἐκ νόμου ἦν ἡ δικαιοσύνη· ἀλλὰ συνέκλεισεν ἡ γραφὴ τὰ πάντα ὑπὸ ἁμαρτίαν, ἵνα ἡ ἐπαγγελία ἐκ πίστεως Ἰησοῦ Χριστοῦ δοθῇ τοῖς πιστεύουσιν.

This outline has identified four ironic questions initially raised in vv. 2–4 and three exegetical questions posed in vv. 5–6, 19, and 21. The ironic questions should be distinguished from the exegetical ones. The note of irony in the former questions ask for information that both the sender and the addressee already know in order to draw attention to the unreasonableness of the fact that the latter acts contary to such knowledge.[53] Thus, the ironic questions are not directly answered, while the exegetical questions are of a more learned kind and receive their answers in order to explain from the Torah the Galatians' experience of having received the Spirit on the basis of trust apart from the jurisdiction of the Law of Moses. Hence, on the ground of a specific case, a basic exegetical question has been raised in relation to the quotation of Gen 15:6, which in turn Paul has elaborated into a rather condensed argument involving further questions, such as the relationship between the memories centered on Abraham and the Sinaitic events in the Torah. Together, these exegetical questions and answers construct the structure of the small exegetical "treatise" in Gal 3:6–29. It is noteworthy that an analogy to such exegetical questions and answers is to be found in Philo's discussion of Gen 15:6 in the context of *Her.* 90–95. Different from Philo, however, who explicitly refers to a dialogue with an imaginary interlocutor ("it may be asked"; "To such a questioner we will answer", *Her.* 90), Paul appropriates the similar exegetical form for the purposes of argumentation and instruction to recipients well known to him.

The ironic question in Gal 3:2, in terms of a "meta-propositional base" (MB) introducing the main theme (ThM), "The only thing I want to learn from you is this (MB): Did you receive the Spirit by doing the works of the Law or by believing the message you heard?" (ThM), is further picked up and elaborated in the exegetical question posed in Gal 3:5–6, "Does God supply you with the Spirit and work miracles among you (MB) by your doing the works of the Law, or by receiving the message with *trust*, just as *Abraham* [...]?" (ThM). A preliminary answer in terms of a ThM, again introduced by an MB, is reached in Gal 3:7: "Accordingly, you must realize (MB), those of *trust* are the descendants of *Abraham*

53 N.A. Dahl (*Paul's Letter to the Galatians*, 26–9) has drawn attention to parallels to such a function of the ironic questions in Gal 3:2–5 from other ancient sources, such as the letters of Cicero (*Att.* XIII 21a, 54a) and Pliny the Younger (*Ep.* III 17; VIII 3).

(ThM)." The italicised words that are common to Gal 3:7 and 3:5–6 and the use of a MB with a conclusive particle (γινώσκετε ἄρα ὅτι) indicate that Paul has reached the aim for which he set out, namely to provide a preliminary answer and conclusion to the ironic questions posed in Gal 3:2, 5–6. This conclusion demonstrates that the trust-event of the Galatian believers has its very foundation and model in the authoritative trust-event of Abraham.

In Gal 3:19 and 3:21, Paul asks exegetical questions regarding the relationship between parts of the Torah, viz. the intention and function of the Sinaitic event of giving the Mosaic Law in relation to the promise given to Abraham (ὁ οὖν νόμος κατὰ τῶν ἐπαγγελιῶν [τοῦ θεοῦ];). The first question (Τί οὖν ὁ νόμος;) is raised on the preceding elaboration in Gal 3:15–18, in which Paul insists that the Law is not given as a legal codicil that was meant to regulate the conditions for the validity of the covenant with Abraham and its accompanying promises. Philo makes a similar use of the form of exegetical questions and answers in the reasoning of *Mos.* 2:45–51. Here, he too raises the question why the Law of Moses is introduced by the narratives of the creation and the patriarchs, as distinct from the subsequent legislative part with its commands and prohibitions: "We must now give the reason why he began his lawbook with the history and put the commands and prohibitions in the second place (*Mos.* 2:47)."

2.2.2 Exegetical Terminology

It is noteworthy that similar constructions of the verb γινώσκω in Gal 3:7a occur in Philo, *Mut.* 186 and *Her.* 90–95. In all three cases, it functions as exegetical terminology applied in an exegetical paraphrase of Gen 15:6.[54] In the latter text we have a parallel to exactly the same exegetical terminology, viz. γινώσκω + ὅτι, as in Gal 3:7a:[55]

> Καθὼς Ἀβραὰμ *ἐπίστευσεν τῷ θεῷ, καὶ ἐλογίσθη αὐτῷ εἰς δικαιοσύνην·* **γινώσκετε** ἄρα **ὅτι** οἱ ἐκ πίστεως, οὗτοι υἱοί εἰσιν Ἀβραάμ. (Just as Abraham "believed God, and it was reckoned to him as righteousness," therefore you know that those who believe are the descendants of Abraham.) Gal 3:6–7

> "πεπίστευκεν οὖν Ἀβραὰμ τῷ θεῷ," ἀλλ' ὡς ἄνθρωπος πεπίστευκεν, ἵνα τὸ ἴδιον τοῦ θνητοῦ **γνῷς** καὶ μάθῃς οὐκ ἄλλως αὐτῷ γενέσθαι, εἰ μὴ ἐκ φύσεως, τὴν τροπήν. (Abraham therefore believed in God; but he believed as a man; that you may know the peculiar attrib-

54 It has been recognized in previous scholarship that γινώσκω is a common Hellenistic disclosure formula (see R.N. Longenecker, *Galatians*, WBC [Nashville: Thomas Nelson, 1990], 114; Witherington III, *Grace in Galatians*, 226), but its function as exegetical terminology, however, seems to have been neglected.

55 See also *Leg.* 2:79; *Mut.* 186; *Det.* 22; *Post.* 143.

ute of mortals, and may learn that his fall did not happen to him in any other way than in consequence of the ordinances of nature.) *Mut.* 186

βαθυτέραν γὰρ εἰ βουληθείης ἔρευναν καὶ μὴ σφόδρ' ἐπιπόλαιον ποιήσασθαι, σαφῶς **γνώσῃ, ὅτι** μόνῳ θεῷ [...]. (For if you should be willing to search more deeply and not confine yourself to the mere surface, you will clearly know that to trust in God alone [...].) *Her.* 92

Moreover, in Gal 3:9 and 14, Paul makes use of the conjunctions ὥστε and ἵνα, respectively, as exegetical formulas to explain the reception of the Spirit as the outcome of the Christ event and as a fulfillment of the oath of promise to Abraham. A similar exegetical function and usage of these conjuntions can be found in Philo's writings.[56]

As we have already seen, Gal 3:16 illustrated the method of discarding a certain reading of a scriptural text in favor of its proper meaning. Thus, two alternative meanings can be set in opposition by means of the contrast form "not-but." The form ὡς – ἀλλ' ὡς is also to be found in *Decal.* 36 (ὡς οὐχὶ πρὸς πλείους ἀλλ' ὡς πρὸς ἕνα [...]) and *Opif.* 72 (οὐχ ἑνὶ δημιουργῷ καθάπερ τἆλλα ἀνέθηκεν, ἀλλ' ὡς [...]). In Gal 3:16, Paul offers another example of the same form: "[...] 'and to his offspring': It does not say 'and to offsprings', as referring to many, but, referring to one (οὐ λέγει· καὶ τοῖς σπέρμασιν, ὡς ἐπὶ πολλῶν ἀλλ' ὡς ἐφ' ἑνός·), 'and to your offspring', which is Christ." As in Gal 3:16, the discussion of number used in the quotations from the Hebrew Bible between plural and singular forms is relevant to the parallels in *Decal.* 36 and *Opif.* 72–75. Moreover, the epexegetical clause "ὅς ἐστιν Χριστός" in Gal 3:16 is an example of direct exegesis, without an exegetical paraphrase of the biblical text, which has close analogies in Philo's writings.[57]

In Gal 3:19, Paul is faced with a new problem which requires an answer: "Τί οὖν ὁ νόμος; τῶν παραβάσεων χάριν προσετέθη [...]." The question is introduced here by the formula τί οὖν and the answer is introduced in the form of the conjunction χάριν, "for the reason of". Similarly, in his problem-solving interpretation of Gen 3:8 in *Leg.* 3:6, Philo states the problem and provides the answer by means of the same phrases: "Why then (τί οὖν) does it say 'they hid themselves'? The bad man thinks that God is in a place, not containing but contained; and for this reason (χάριν) he imagines that he can hide from Him [...]". *Mut.* 255 and Rom 4:1 provide other examples of the use of the form of the question τί οὖν in Philo and Paul.

56 For ὥστε, cf. *Migr.* 49 and *Her.* 231. For the use of ἵνα, cf. *Her.* 312; *Mut.* 21, 186.

57 Cf. *Op.* 34, 118, 159. See the formulaic phrases for "direct exegesis" listed in Borgen, "Philo of Alexandria: A Critical and Synthetical Survey of Research," 138.

While this section has paid attention the method of exegetical paraphrase of the Scriptural passages as well as to exegetical forms and terminology employed in Gal 3:6–29, the next sections of this chapter aim at substantiating the thesis that Paul's exegetical appropriation of Abraham is inscribed within a Jewish exegetical context and discourse of his day. This cultural context will, then, shed fresh light on the kinds of hermeneutical principles and presuppositions which we can imagine lie behind Paul's interpretation of the biblical texts.

3 Gal 3:1–6a: The Ironic Questions concerning the Crucified Jesus Christ and the Spirit

3.1 The Public Exhibition of the Crucified Christ

From the introductory passage Gal 3:1–5, we learn that Paul is pointedly critical of the Galatians: "You foolish Galatians! Who has bewitched you [...]?" (3:1). "Are you so foolish?" (3:3). "Have you experienced such things in vain? If so, it really was in vain!" (3:4). The words "Who has bewitched you" probably allude to the opponents, who had come to the Galatian converts and troubled them (cf. Gal 1:7).[58] The reference to Christ's crucifixion in Gal 3:1 emerges from the implication of Christ's death relative to the Mosaic Law in the preceding verse in 2:21: "[...] for if justification comes through the law, then Christ died for nothing." Thus, Paul's emphasis on the crucified Christ, its worth and meaning, shows that he places it in the center of what is at stake in his engagement with the Galatian converts: "You foolish Galatians! Who has bewitched you? It was before your eyes that Jesus Christ was publicly exhibited (προγράφω) as crucified!" In order to understand the full implication of Paul's statement, the meaning of the verb προγράφω is crucial and should be investigated. The connotation "to set forth or exhibit publicly"[59] has received unanimous support,[60] and it is thus customary to take it figuratively in the sense "to portray publicly". For example, its meaning in Gal 3:1 is rendered by M.C. Boers as follows: "a vivid, verbal portrait of the event

---

58 For recent discussions of the term βασκαίνω, translated here as "bewitch", cf. Keener, *Galatians*, 207–8; deSilva, *The Letter to the Galatians*, 266–68.

59 Cf. LSJ.

60 For recent scholarship, cf. H. Wendt, "Galatians 3:1 as an Allusion to Textual Prophecy," *JBL* 135.2 (2016): 372–7; S. Muir, "Vivid Imagery in Galatians 3:1—Roman Rhetoric, Street Announcing, Graffiti, and Crucifixions," *BTB* 44.2 (2014): 76–86; B.S. Davis, "The Meaning of ΠΡΟΓΡΑΦΗ In the Context of Galatians 3.1," *NTS* 45.2 (1999): 194–212.

of Jesus' crucifixion before an audience, however small or large".[61] With regard to the specific occasion behind such a vivid portrait, the educational and legal sense of the verb may be relevant and should briefly be mentioned. On the one hand, the papyrological works of R. Cribiore might point to an educational context and the model of a *praescriptum* as the referential background for the verb in Gal 3:1. Thus, the implied metaphorical communication on Paul's part may be that the Galatian converts should not forget the elementary *praescriptum* of "Christ crucified" that Paul as a teacher had mediated (on a school tablet, as it were) for his students to copy and imitate.[62] Although such an educational meaning of προγράφω is highly probable and fits the terminology of pedagogy and teaching in the immediate context, it does not account for the full implications of the portrait of Christ as crucified relative to the jurisdiction of the Mosaic Law, which is hinted at in its immediate context in Gal 2:21 and 3:13. Thus, one should pay more attention to what its legal sense might have invoked in its literal and judicial context in Galatians.[63] Although the educational and legal senses of προγράφω are not mutually exclusive and can very well have been combined by Paul, I shall suggest that the particular meaning of προγράφω as "publicly exhibit" is appropriate to the legal application of the Christ event in its immediate literary context. In a Jewish context, the Roman crucifixion of Jesus Christ is interpreted by Paul (and probably by those who executed Jesus) in the sense of one who suffered the penalty of being impaled, and was thus exposed in terms of publicising the punishment of a cursed criminal. Such a public exhibition was meant to deter others who might fail to to observe the commandments and incur the curse of the Law. When Paul wrote the letter to the Galatians, this message might have served as a warning of the consequences if the Galatian converts were foolish enough to submit to the "works of the Law". The inference would then be that Christ only deserved to be publicised as a cursed criminal, who had breached the Law, and that the Galatians themselves would incur the curse of the Law if they failed to keep all of its commandments.

---

61 de Boer, *Galatians*, 171; Martyn, *Galatians*, 283; Betz, *Galatians*, 131; Hays, *The Faith of Jesus Christ*, 167; T.R. Schreiner, *Galatians*, Zondervan Exegetical Commentary Series: New Testament (Grand Rapids: Zondervan, 2010), 181–2.

62 Cf. for the model of a *praescriptum*, R. Cribiore, *Writing, Teachers, and Students in Graeco-Roman Egypt*, American Studies in Papyrology (Atlanta, GA: Scholars Press, 1996), 122–3.

63 E.D.W. Burton, albeit without any comments on the judicial connotations of προγράφω, suggests that this meaning is the most suitable in the immediate context, and understands thus Paul "as describing his preaching to the Galatians under the figure of public announcement or placarding of Jesus before them" (E.D.W. Burton, *A Critical and Exegetical Commentary on the Epistle to the Galatians*, ICC (Edinburgh: T & T Clark, 1921), 144–5).

In the legal papyri, προγράφω can refer to various measures of legal procedure. For example, "proscription" could be taken to refer to persons who had been publicly "wanted" or "registered", with the implication of being regarded as guilty.[64] From the Roman period, the verb is employed in this sense, for example, in the edict of Tiberius Julius Alexander dated to 69 CE, in the inscription *OGIS* II 669.[65] More instances of this phenomenon have been recently documented by the publication of *P.Oxy.* 4060, which contains correspondence to the *strategos* of the Oxyrhynchite from 161 CE. As R.A. Coles, the editor, notes in the introduction to the transcription of the papyri, "The bulk of the correspondence is concerned with searching (negative in all cases!) for wanted persons".[66] For example, *P.Oxy.* 4060 characterizes various types of fugitives, among them eight who were wanted on criminal charges. Lines 73–74 describe two of them as "having disappeared on being proscribed (προγραφέντας) and not having been seen." N. Lewis comments on these lines as follows: "[...] the men vanished, were proscribed, and did not reappear. Now they were outlaws, and the order that they be searched for followed automatically, inexorably."[67] In any case, to be "proscribed" was damaging to the criminal's case.[68] It seems that to be "publicly displayed" or "outlawed" as a fugitive (the implied sense of the verb, as E.J. Bickerman suggested) gave the impression of being guilty or condemned already at this stage of the due process.[69]

Another aspect of the legal procedure of being publicly exhibited referred to the death sentence that had been imposed as a penalty. Plutarch and Polybius provide evidence for this kind of "proscription":

---

64 Several Ptolemaic documents contain notices of proscription, created after a person was summonsed but failed to appear. Cf. *SB* V 7609; 7610; *BGU* VIII 1774. See R. Taubenschlag, *Opera Minora: II. Band* (Warsaw: Panstwowe Wydawnictwo Naukowe, 1959), 125–31.

65 The text is translated by N. Lewis and R. Meyer, *Roman Civilization: A Sourcebook: Roman Empire Vol. 2*, Records of Civilization Sources & Study (New York: Columbia University Press, 1990), 295–8.

66 R.A. Coles, "4060. Official Correspondence," in *The Oxyrhynchus Papyri: Volume LX* (London: The British Academy, 1994), 127.

67 N. Lewis, "Notationes Legentis," *BASP* 33 (1966): 65.

68 Cf., e.g., *P. Oslo* II 17 (136 CE), *P.Berl.* II 372 (154 CE) and *P.Tebt.* II 411 (2nd century CE). See also the recent study by B. Kelly, *Petitions, Litigation, and Social Control in Roman Egypt* (Oxford: OUP, 2011), 103.

69 According to Bickerman, this Greco-Roman administrative measure attested by the legal papyri would also apply to the denunciation of Jesus according to John 11:57: "[...] his name [Jesus] was put on the register of the 'wanted'", since he was apparently perceived by the Jewish authorities as guilty of the charges against him. Cf. E.J. Bickerman, "Utilitas Crucis," in idem, *Studies in Jewish and Christian History, Volume 2*, AJEC (Leiden: Brill, 2007), 768.

> [...] After this, the three men, Octavius, Antony, and Lepidus, were reconciled with one another, distributed the provinces among themselves, and sentenced to death by proscription (προγραφή) two hundred men. Among these put to death was Cicero. Plutarch, *Brut.* XXVII

> After they had stripped them all, both men and women, to the utmost of their power, they nevertheless brought all the proscribed (προγράφω) before the popular assembly. The people of Phoenice by a majority, either terrorized or seduced by Charops, condemned all the accused not to exile, but to death as enemies of Rome. Polybius, *Hist.* XXXII.6

One conclusion might be drawn from such examples of the legal connotations of what it meant to be "proscribed" in a Greco-Roman cultural context, namely, that a person who had been subjected to such a legal procedure would be considered to be either a guilty criminal or indeed one who was liable to be executed, or one who was "publicly exhibited" as the result of being sentenced to death. The latter aspect might provide a referential background for Gal 3:1 and thus the implicit meaning of προγράφω when Paul attached this verb to the event of Christ's crucifixion. Hence, the meaning of Gal 3:1 may be paraphrased as follows: when Jesus Christ had been exhibited publicly as a crucified criminal, this penalty comes on top of the execution. In a Jewish context, the implication was that Christ suffered the punishment of one who is already cursed, since the enormity of being a cursed lawbreaker merits this penalty of being publicly hanged according to the jurisdiction of the Law. Accordingly, I interpret ἐσταυρωμένος as an adverbial participle, communicating the accomplished circumstance that is coordinate with the action of the finite verb προγράφω.[70]

Such an interpretation of Gal 3:1 accords well with Paul's application of Christ's crucifixion in Gal 3:13. Since I shall comment further on the latter verse below, only the following observation will be offered at this point. Here, the curse manifested at the crucifixion of Christ Jesus is interpreted as his being hanged according to the legal evidence in Deut 21:23: "And if a man has committed a crime punishable by death and he is put to death, and you hang him the same day, for a hanged man is accursed by God [...]."[71] It is noteworthy

70 Cf. Burton, *Galatians*, 145.

71 I take Paul's exegesis of Deut 21:23 in Gal 3:13 to mean that hanging is the punishment of one who is already being cursed from God, that is as a subjective genitive, with parallels in LXX, Targum Neofiti, and the Temple Scroll (11QT 64:6 – 12). For a comparison of these three sources on this point, see, most recently, M.J. Bernstein, *Reading and Re-Reading Scripture at Qumran: Volume 2*, STDJ (Leiden: Brill, 2013), 592 – 613. On impalement as a form of publizicing the penalty for the sake of deterrence in Deut 21:23 in the context of the cultural milieu of ancient Israel, cf. N. Wazana, "'For an Impaled Body is a Curse of God' (Deut 21:23): Impaled Bodies in Biblical Law and Conquest Narratives," in *Law and Narrative in the Bible and in Neighbouring Ancient*

that Philo applies this scripture to the added penalty of the impalement of the body of murderers after their suffering the death penalty.[72] Philo says that since it was not possible to put them to death more than once, Moses adds another punishment, namely by ordering the murderers to be gibbeted:

> Since there are no bounds to the iniquities of evil natures, and they are ever committing a superabundance of enormities and extending and exalting their vices beyond all measure and all limit, the lawgiver would, if he could, have sentenced them to die times beyond number. But since this was impossible he ordained another penalty as an addition, and ordered the manslayers to be hanged up (τιμωρίαν ἄλλην προσδιατάττεται κελεύων τοὺς ἀνελόντας ἀνασκολοπίζεσθαι). *Spec.* 3:151

Although Deut 21:23 did not contemplate death by crucifixion, Paul's application of it was legitimate. Thus, the rhetorical force of considering the crucifixion as referring both to the execution and to the publicly exposure of the body as a cursed criminal is more comprehensible against the background that a Roman crucifixion *per se* would not necessarily require such a perception.[73] It is also noteworthy that early Christian writers such as Victorinus, Ambrose, and Augustine understand the crucifixion of Christ with *proscriptus* in Gal 3:1 in the technical sense of being both "publicly exhibited" and condemned to death.[74]

In the light of this evidence, I would suggest that προγράφω in Gal 3:1 is employed figuratively as part of Paul's message to the Galatians, in which the cru-

---

Cultures, ed. K.-P. Adam, F. Avemarie, and N. Wazana, FAT (Tübingen: Mohr Siebeck, 2012), 69–98.

72 *Pace*, e.g., Borgen ("Openly Portrayed as Crucified: Some Observations on Gal 3:1–14," in *Christology, Controversy and Community: New Testament Essays in Honour of David R. Catchpole*, ed. D.G. Horrell and C.M. Tuckett, NovTSup [Leiden: Brill, 2000], 348), who has suggested that Philo here speaks of crucifixion as a mode of being executed. For such an interpretation as a mistake, since Philo here refers to the impaling bodies after death, see already the comments on *Spec* 3:151–152 by Lightfoot, *Galatians*, 154.

73 For example, from a Jewish perspective, innocent persons, heroes, and martyrs too could be crucified; cf. most recently, D.W. Chapman and E.J. Schnabel, *The Trial and Crucifixion of Jesus: Texts and Commentary*, WUNT (Tübingen: Mohr Siebeck, 2015), 666–9; J.G. Cook, *Crucifixion in the Mediterranean World*, WUNT (Tübingen: Mohr Siebeck, 2014), 238–39; P. Fredriksen, *From Jesus to Christ: The Origins of the New Testament Images of Jesus*, (New Haven; London: Yale University Press, 1988), 147.

74 Cf. Ambrose, "*Quorum ante oculos Christus Jesus proscriptus est, et in vobis crucifixus. Manifestum et quia stultorum oculis Christus proscriptus videtur, id est, exspoliatus vel condemnatus* [...]" (cf. J.P. Migne, *Commentaria in Epistolae Ad Galatas*, PL, Paris, 1844–64], 352). See furthermore E. Plumer, *Augustine's Commentary on Galatians* (Oxford: OUP, 2003), 162. For Victorinus, cf. CSEL 83.2:126. 10–13. Also, the Vulgate transcribes: "*O, insensati Galatae quis vos fascinavit ante quorum oculos Jesus Christus proscriptus est crucifixus.*"

cifixion of Jesus Christ had been publicized vividly before their eyes as the ultimate penalty meted out to a cursed "criminal", after he had been sentenced to death by the Roman authorities. Thus, Gal 3:1 follows the line of thought in Gal 2:21, where Paul makes clear that if the jurisdiction of the Law of Moses was still valid as the condition for righteousness, the effect of Christ's death would be considered to be nill. Thus, in order to bolster this inference, Paul makes the pointed statement in Gal 3:1 about Christ as being set forth before their eyes and publicly exhibited (so to speak) as being hanged as one who suffered the ultimate punishment. The message on Paul's part could not be made clearer; the vivid proscription of Christ's crucifixion made manifest that he died as a cursed criminal in order to deter all who would operate within the jurisdiction of the Law. The reading of Gal 2:21 along with 3:1 in such a way may be paraphrased as follows:

> You must be foolish and bewitched since you still consider the Law as a viable way forward. If justification is attained through the jurisdiction of the Law of Moses, then, Christ suffered the ultimate penalty of being proscribed and hanged as a cursed criminal in vain. So, if you, Galatians, choose to live within the Law of Moses, it means to accept and function within the jurisdiction according to which Jesus Christ was publicly executed and condemned as a cursed criminal by being hanged on a cross! How could you even be thinking about the possibility of going so far?

In Gal 3:2–14, Paul begins to unfold and clarify his teaching about Christ as a crucified "criminal" in relation to the two dynamic, but mutually exclusive "jurisdictions" within Scripture, which might be characterized as the "Mosaic jurisdiction" in terms of doing the "works of Law", and the "Abrahamic jurisdiction", centered on the conduct of Abraham's trust and God's trust in terms of the oath of promise given in return to Abraham and his descendants.[75] According to the former jurisdiction, Jesus Christ died as a cursed criminal, which implies that he was thought to have been punished in the form of impalement or crucifixion *for his own crimes* (an idea implicit in Gal 2:21, if the Law and the "Mosaic jurisdiction" was still valid, and also explicated in Gal 3:10 and 3:13 as applied to Christ). When Christ's execution was interpreted as a vicarious death, however, his impalement on the cross meant that he became a curse "*for us*", that is, "*for our crimes*" (cf. Gal 1:4). In what follows, I shall go on to argue that Paul shapes

75 The interpretation of the crucified Christ in relation to the forensic issue of justification, the antithesis of "blessing" and "curse", the contrast between "works of Law" and "faith", and the differentiation in Scripture between Gen 15:6 / Hab 2:4 and Deut 27:26 / Deut 21:23 / Lev 18:5 in Gal 3:2–14 also fit with the distinction drawn between these two "jurisdictions" that Paul found to be operative in Scripture.

his interpretation of Christ's crucifixion as a cursed "criminal" within the dynamic of both the "Mosaic jurisdiction" *and* the "Abrahamic jurisdiction". Thus, the Christ event pertains to the redemption from the curse of the Law, in order to fulfill God's oath of promise to Abraham and his descendants, encompassing the Galatian converts. I shall first draw attention to what I shall argue is a premise for this view, viz. Paul's consideration of the Galatian converts as legitimate Jewish proselytes after the foundational model of Abraham, the first proselyte.

3.2 The Reception of the Spirit and God's Power Manifestations in the Context of Abraham as the Model of the Jewish Proselyte

The genealogical differentiation between Jews and non-Jews is presupposed in the immediate context of Gal 2:15 and Paul's statement about his controversy with Peter in Antioch: "we who are Jews by birth and not sinners from the ethnē".[76] This biological and ethnic gap between Jews and Gentiles has been taken as relevant to the so-called Gentile predicament: How could Paul solve the problem of the Gentiles' integration into Israel and the Abrahamic family? As I wrote in the introductory survey of recent research, it is frequently argued that Paul links the converts to Abraham's seed as *Gentiles*, and not as Jewish proselytes to the Jewish community.[77] This position fails to take into account, however, the differentiation Paul made between the two jurisdictions at work in the Torah and Scripture, the "Abrahamic jurisdiction" and the "Mosaic jurisdiction". I suggest, contrary to this position, that the key to understanding the reasoning in Gal 3:6–14 is the acknowledgment that Paul interprets Gen 15:6 to include non-Jews among Abraham's sons, precisely as Jewish proselytes and not as Gentiles *qua* Gentiles, i. e. regardless of their conversion. Accordingly, Paul seems to distinguish between two stages or modes of conversion with regard to what it might have meant to become a proselyte in a Jewish context. Thus, on the one hand, Paul seems to maintain a conception similar to that

76 Since this contrast concerns a discussion of dividing missionary work to the "circumcised" and to the "uncircumcised", respectively, it may refer to those born as Jews and those who were Gentile converts to Judaism; this may imply that "Jewishness" embraced both groups. For such an interpretation of Gal 2:7–9, cf. Gruen, "Paul and Jewish Ethnicity," 357–8; Dunn, *Galatians*, 132–3.

77 Cf., e.g., Thiessen, "Paul, the Animal Apocalypse, and Abraham's Gentile Seed," 65–78, esp. 71–5; idem, *Paul and the Gentile Problem*, 12–6; Donaldson, "Paul, Abraham's Gentile 'Offspring,' and the Torah," 142–3.

held by, for example, Philo, that non-Jews became fully proselytes after the model of Abraham, who believed in the one true God, and thus received the Spirit and experienced God's transformation.[78] On the other hand, and quite differently from Philo, Paul did not require the proselytes to follow up on this proselyte status by submitting to the jurisdiction of the Mosaic Law, understood as "nothing else than memorials of the life of the ancients, preserving to a later generation their actual words and deeds" (*Abr.* 5). According to Philo this meant that the particular laws of Moses replicate the lives of the patriarchs since these laws lead to the identical virtues that they achieved instinctively in their own way.

As I shall argue in the next sections, Paul's conception is based on the following two premises: 1. The promise to Abraham pertains to the crucified and cursed Christ, Abraham's true descendant, through whom both Jews and converts were party to the promised blessing. 2. For this reason, Paul infers that the curses still apply to those subject to the jurisdiction of the Law, while the reward and blessings in terms of the reception of the Spirit apply to those who belong to the "Abrahamic jurisdiction", in terms of trust in God and what God promised by oath.

The conflict in Galatia can be conceptualized on the ground of the pointed questions arising from the experience of the Galatians that centers on their reception of the Spirit by trust and its powerful manifestations. Thus, the questions posed in Gal 3:5–6a and the comparison with Abraham go to the inner core of the issue at stake in the letter:

> *Well then, does God supply you with the Spirit and work miracles in you by your doing the works of the law, or by receiving the heard message with trust just as Abraham?*

As we have suggested above, such an interpunctuation of Gal 3:5–6 in its immediate literary context means that an authoritative event in Abraham's life, such as his reception and transformation by the indwelling of the Spirit when he became the first proselyte, is referred to as a pattern for the Galatian converts. Although scholars have observed Paul's reference to the historical precedent and example of Abraham's story for the Galatians's experience,[79] they have found it difficult to connect this scriptural precedent with the text cited in 3:6 (Gen 15:6), although this scripture in its original literary context says nothing explic-

---

78 *Pace* M.F. Bird (*An Anomalous Jew: Paul Among Jews, Greeks, and Romans* [Grand Rapids: Eerdmans, 2016], 80), who contends, on the basis of Galatians 3 and Romans 4: "In this way, Abraham is not the prototype of the ideal proselyte; he is the paradigmatic pagan who believes in the divine promises fulfilled in Jesus Christ."

79 Cf. most recently, Keener, *Galatians*, 221; deSilva, *The Letter to the Galatians*, 277.

itly about Abraham's reception of the Spirit. For example, J.M.G. Barclay and S.K. Williams claim:

> Despite his considerable ingenuity in adapting the Genesis text to his purposes, even Paul could not find a text which connected Abraham with a central aspect of Christian identity – the Spirit. We have just noted the importance of the Spirit in Paul's argument and we may here observe how he endeavors to associate it with the Abrahamic motif even though he has no text to cite in support.[80]

> [...] and the correspondence Paul is stressing would be neater if he had quoted a scripture affirming that Abraham received the Spirit. That he could not do, though, for the very good reason that Scripture includes no such statement.[81]

Hence, both these scholars have overlooked the question whether or not an exegetical motif is involved at this juncture. The question is not whether there is a particular text in Scripture that enables Paul to make this association between Abraham and the Spirit, but whether there is an interpretation of Gen 15:6 in Jewish exegesis at Paul's own time which might affirm this correspondence. Thus, I shall propose that the comparison of the Galatians' experience with Abraham's story is affirmed by Paul's use of the exegetical motif based on an interpreted Gen 15:6 in terms of Abraham's reception of the Spirit by faith.[82] As we shall observe next, Philo and other Jewish texts provide samples of such an exegetical motif which might corroborate the suggestion that Paul builds upon Jewish expositions of Gen 15:6.[83]

In chapter two, I noted that the Philonic passage in *Virt.* 212–219, in a context in which Philo emphasizes Abraham as the founder of the Jewish nation and

80 J.M.G. Barclay, *Obeying the Truth: A Study of Paul's Ethics in Galatians* (Edinburgh: T & T Clark, 1988), 88.

81 S.K. Williams, *Galatians*, ANTC (Nashville: Abingdon Press, 1997), 86.

82 One may wonder how far the first readers have known such an exegetical tradition. It is imaginable that a non-Jew associated with the synagogue could have aquired such a scriptural competence. As I have pointed out above (cf. 5.1), Paul have guided the readers towards an interpretative framework of the text which seems to be presupposed as a theme the author and the readers agree on (cf. the introduction offered by means of the meta-propositional base in Gal 3:2: "this one thing I want to learn from you [...]"). On the scholarly discussion of the audience's scriptural knowledge in Paul's letters, cf. Stanley, *Arguing with Scripture*, 42–52; Kujanpää, *The Rhetorical Functions of Scriptural Quotations in Romans*, 27–9.

83 Cf. P.J. Bekken, "Abraham og Ånden," 265–76, esp. 273–4. Most recently, Thiessen (*Paul and the Gentile Problem*, 109) has pointed to parallels to Paul in Philo and rabbinic literature "that faith enables or merits the reception of the *pneuma*", but more attention should be drawn to additional data and the specific issue of Jewish proselytism as the context of Paul's elaboration of this exegetical motif.

the paradigm of proselytes, speaks of Abraham's reception of the Spirit and his transformation in body and soul. Philo first tells how Abraham turned from astrology and polytheism to the One God, the Creator, drawing on Gen 15:6:

> And therefore, he is the first person spoken of (λέγω) as 'believing God' (πιστεῦσαι [...] τῷ θεῷ), since he first grasped a firm and unswerving conception of the truth that there is one Cause above all, and that it provides for the world and all that there is therein. *Virt.* 216[84]

Having acquired this trust in God, as Philo states, the most certain of the virtues, he possessed all other virtues (*Virt.* 216). Furthermore, although the Abraham narrative makes no reference to the divine Spirit having been breathed upon him, Philo's text suggests that his trust in God led immediately to Abraham's reception of the Spirit. Thus, whenever he was possessed by the Spirit,

> [...] everything in him changed to something better, eyes, complexion, stature, carriage, movements, voice. For the divine spirit which was breathed upon him from on high made its lodging in his soul, and invested his body with singular beauty, his voice with persuasiveness, and his hearers with understanding (ὁπότε γοῦν κατασχεθείη, μετέβαλλε πάντα πρὸς τὸ βέλτιον, τὰς ὄψεις, τὴν χρόαν, τὸ μέγεθος, τὰς σχέσεις, τὰς κινήσεις, τὴν φωνήν, τοῦ θείου πνεύματος, ὅπερ ἄνωθεν καταπνευσθὲν εἰσῳκίσατο τῇ ψυχῇ, περιτιθέντος τῷ μὲν σώματι κάλλος ἐξαίρετον, τοῖς δὲ λόγοις πειθώ, τοῖς δ' ἀκούουσι σύνεσιν). *Virt.* 217

Philo then concludes:

> He (Abraham) is the standard (κανών) of nobility for all proselytes, who abandoning the ignobility of strange laws and monstrous customs which assign divine honours to sticks and stones and lifeless (ἄψυχος) things in general, have come to settle in a better land, in a truly vital (ἔμψυχος) and living (ζάω) commonwealth (πολιτεία), with truth as director and president. *Virt.* 219

It is significant that Abraham's conversion as a proselyte is described as a "pneumatic" and spiritual journey, in which he was finally transformed as a person by the divine Spirit. As J.R. Levison has shown, Philo's portrait of Abraham as a king and a man with rhetorical skills has qualities that are paralleled in Greco-Roman writings, attested among Greek and Roman authors such as Plato, Dio Chrysostom, and Cicero:

---

84 The use of λέγω functions to introduce Gen 15:6, and the same cognate is elsewhere applied in a similar vein in Philo's writings, cf., e.g., *Deus* 52. The word form πιστεῦσαι [...] τῷ θεῷ is found in other renderings of Gen 15:6 in *Abr.* 262, *Migr.* 44, and *Mut.* 186. For Philo's use of Gen 15:6, cf. Schliesser, *Abraham's Faith in Romans 4*, 203 – 15.

> With almost no biblical precedent, Philo's portrayal of Abraham as an extraordinary king mirrors Greco-Roman discussions of rhetoric and rule. Consequently Abraham is characterized as a king who displayed unassailable virtue, resplendent rhetorical skill, and incomparable physical beauty.[85]

The Hellenistic Jewish work Joseph and Aseneth provides an analogy to Philo's description of how Jewish proselytes may receive the Spirit and be transformed by this event. Joseph and Aseneth narrates how various aspects of the Spirit were transmitted to Aseneth as part of her conversion as a proselyte. In the following extractions, the reception of the Spirit meant that Aseneth received blessings such as life, wisdom, and truth:

> Lord God of my father Israel,
> the Most High, the Powerful One of Jacob,
> who gave life to all (things)
> and called (them) from the darkness to the light,
> and from the error to the truth,
> and from the death to the life;
> you, Lord, bless this virgin,
> and renew her by your spirit,
> and form her anew by your hidden hand,
> and make her alive again by your life,
> and let her eat your bread of life,
> and drink your cup of blessing,
> and number her among your people [...]. Jos. Asen. 8:9

> Happy are you, Aseneth, because the ineffable mysteries of the Most High have been revealed to you, and happy (are) all who attach themselves to the Lord God in repentance, because they will eat from this comb. For this comb is (full of the) spirit of life. Jos. Asen. 16:14

> And Joseph kissed Aseneth and gave her spirit of life, and he kissed her the second time and gave her spirit of wisdom, and he kissed her the third time and gave her spirit of truth. Jos. Asen. 19:11

In the Jewish source *De Sampsone*, probably going back to a homiletic composition from the Hellenistic Jewish Synagogue, there is a noteworthy analogy to Philo's application of Gen 15:6 about Abraham's reception of the Spirit. *De Sampsone* 25 describes how Abraham's trust in God led to his justification in terms of receiving the Spirit, characterized as the "the Spirit of Righteousness". This reference to Abraham occurs in a context in which the author lists biblical exam-

85 J.R. Levison, *The Spirit in First Century Judaism*, AGAJU (Leiden; New York: Brill, 1997), 96.

ples of how persons, like Sampson, can be empowered by various aspects of the Spirit. The relevant passage reads:

> Wie (die Sache sich verhält, darüber) können wir uns anhand von Beispielen überzeugen. Unser Urvater ABRAHAM erhielt den Geist der Gerechtigkeit. (Dieser) liess ihn augenscheinlich voller Güte sein, den er glaubte an den Lebendingen (vg. Gen. 15,6). *De Sampsone* 25[86]

Although from the third century CE, Mekhilta de-Rabbi Ishmael makes use of the same exegetical motif as *De Sampsone*, and connects Gen 15:6 with Abraham's trust and righteousness in terms of his reception of the Spirit:

> R. Nehemiah says: Whence can you prove that who so ever accepts even one single commandment with true faith is deserving (זכן) of having the Holy Spirit rest upon him? We find this to have been the case with our fathers. For as a reward for the faith with which they believed, they were considered worthy of having the Holy Spirit rest upon them, [...] And so also you find that our father Abraham inherited both this world and the world beyond as a reward for the faith which he believed, as it is said: "And he believed in the Lord". Mek. Beshallaḥ 134 – 36

It is noteworthy that the verb זכה, "to be right", shares the same root as the noun זכן, "merit", which, for example, the Targumim use to render צדקה from Gen 15:6. This indicates that the idea of the reception of the Spirit can be connected to righteousness and be interpreted in terms of the merit Abraham and the fathers received because of their trust in God.[87] Such an interpretation of Gen 15:6 and צדקה about the "merit of the Fathers" has been made by many Jewish interpreters, who render Gen 15:6 as follows: "And because he [Abraham] put his trust in the Lord, He reckoned it to his merit."[88] Thus, Mekhilta de-Rabbi Ishmael associates the virtues of righteousness and faith with Abraham in his reception of the Spirit, in a way similar to both Philo in *Virt.* 212 – 219 and Paul in Galatians 3. A main difference between Paul, Philo, and the author of Mekhilta de-Rabbi Ishmael, however, is that the last text interprets Abraham's faith as an expression of his adherence to the commandments of the Torah.

---

86 The translation follows the edition of F. Siegert, *Drei hellenistisch-jüdische Predigten I. Ps.-Philon, "Über Jona", "Über Simson" und "Über die Gottesbezeichnung, wohltätig verzehrendes Feuer": Übersetzung aus dem Armenischen und sprachliche Erläuterungen*, WUNT (Tübingen: Mohr Siebeck, 1980).

87 Cf. Thiessen, *Paul and the Gentile Problem*, 109.

88 For such a translation of Gen 15:6 and a discussion of it, cf. Moberly, "Abraham's Righteousness," 109; Levenson, *Inheriting Abraham*, 152 – 3.

At this juncture, a sharper distinction needs to be made between Paul's references to what happened to the Galatians when Paul brought them the Gospel, and the implied criticism of the intruding opponents who had come to the new converts and troubled them. The pointed questions in Gal 3:2–6a seem to presuppose a contrast between two different modes of conversion that Paul believes ought not to be combined:

> Did you receive the Spirit by doing the works of the law or by believing what you heard? Are you so foolish? Having started with the Spirit, are you now ending with the flesh? [...] Well then, does God supply you with the Spirit and work miracles in you by your doing the works of the law, or by receiving the heard message with trust just as Abraham?

The main question at stake here is whether God supplies the gift of the Spirit and works miracles in them through their hearing the message with trust, that is, based on the jurisdiction of trust centered in Abraham, or on the condition of the practice of the Law? If the latter option was not an option, and not the actual state of things, this meant in Paul's eyes that the experience of the Spirit happened apart from the Law and thus was not conditional on a life within the jurisdiction of Law. Thus, the intruders most probably understood the one mode of conversion on the basis of an interpretation of Abraham as one who was circumcised and who was taken to be adherent of the commandments of the Mosaic jurisdiction of Law. Such a debate has an antecedent and affinities with corresponding inner-Jewish discussions involved in Philo's appropriation of the legal figure of Abraham. As we shall observe below (6.2), both Philo and Paul set Abraham's trust in God in contradistinction to the Law of Moses and thus challenge such a view in a discussion with interlocutors of their own day.

In addition to the the appropriation of Abraham as a precedent for the reception of the Spirit on the part of the Galatian converts in 3:6, Paul makes three other explicit references to what happened when he worked as a missionary among them. These passages contain data consonant with basic Jewish proselyte motifs.[89] In the first place, by means of an exegetical paraphrase of Gen 15:6, Paul seems to presuppose that the Galatians had the experience of becoming proselytes, after the model of Abraham, by their hearing with trust and by receiving the Spirit and its powerful manifestations (Gal 3:1–5). Next, consonant with the proselyte motif of a religious conversion, Paul states that the Galatians formerly did not know God and were in bondage to beings that by nature are no gods, and that they had then come to know God (Gal 4:8–9). Moreover, in Gal

89 Cf. chapter two above.

5:19 – 21, Paul states explicitly that he repeats points from his preaching to the Galatians:

> Now the works of the flesh are obvious: fornication, impurity, licentiousness, idolatry, sorcery, enmities, strife, jealousy, anger, quarrels, dissensions, factions, envy, drunkenness, carousing, and things like these. I am warning you, as I warned you before: those who do such things will not inherit the kingdom of God. By contrast, the fruit of the Spirit is love, joy, peace, patience, kindness, generosity, faithfulness, gentleness, and self-control. There is no Law against such things.

In his preaching, therefore, Paul has listed both the pagan vices from which they ought to abstain, and the contrasting virtues which characterized their new ethical life. In Jewish proselyte texts, we can find a a similar ethical contrast drawn between the immoral pagan past the proselytes leave behind and the new ethical life aquired as proselytes within the Jewish community.[90] Moreover, also the love command, Lev 19:18, which Paul cites in Gal 5:14 can probably be situated in the context of a proselyte setting.[91] Furthermore, it is noteworthy that Paul, not unlike Philo, seems to conceive the virtues promoted by the Spirit to exemplify a way of life achieved by the converts that may be consonant with the Law of Moses. The cumulative weight of such observations may support the conclusion that Paul presented the Gospel to the Galatians in the context of ideas and practices related to Jewish proselytism and in particular to Abraham as the model of the proselytes.

To sum up so far: We have considered how Abraham's reception of the Spirit can be conceived as an exegetical motif based on an exposition of Gen 15:6. We have also seen that the transformation by the indwelling Spirit can be part of becoming a Jewish proselyte, such as was the case with Abraham and Aseneth. Moreover, Abraham's trust in God was accounted to him as "righteousness" and "blessing", which in turn can be interpreted in terms of the reception of the Spirit (cf. 3:14). Against this backdrop, I turn to a closer analysis of Gal 3:6 – 9.

---

90 For similar proselyte motifs in Philo's writings, cf. Borgen, *Paul Preaches Circumcision and Pleases Men*, 75 – 99; Birnbaum, *The Place of Judaism*, 195 – 202; Bekken, *The Word is Near You*, 83 – 94.

91 The reference to the love command in Gal 5:14 points forward to the virtue of love in 5:22. A parallel is the use of the Golden Rule by Hillel in b. Šabb. 31a, applied to a non-Jew whom he accepted as a proselyte. The Jerusalem Targum associates in turn the Golden Rule with the love commandment, so that both are paraphrased together in the rendering of Lev 19:18. Thus, there is reason to think that, just as the Golden Rule was used within a proselyte setting, so too was the love commandment. For this suggestion, cf. Borgen, *Paul Preaches Circumcision and Pleases Men*, 99 – 114.

4 Gal 3:6 – 9: Legitimate Descendants of Abraham and Heirs of the Promise

Scholars have wondered why sonship of Abraham and a share in his promises were at stake in Galatians.[92] The following examination of Gal 3:6 – 9 in its Jewish context may provide some indications towards a fresh answer. As we have noted in section 2, Paul not only draws upon the Septuagint in itself, but also applies the scriptural texts to his own time according to conventional hermeneutical techniques and exegetical motifs with analogies in contemporary Jewish exegesis. Hence, the remainder of this study of Gal 3:6 – 29 will argue that Philo and Paul presuppose an exegetical tradition, in which Gen 15:6 is interpreted in conjunction with other passages in terms of a *continuum* of the Abraham narrative in Genesis. In other words, both authors depend on a constellation of exegetical motifs associated with Abraham's trust (Gen 15:6) and the responsiveness on God's part, in which God rewards Abraham with His corresponding trust confirmed by an oath of promise to bless Abraham and his descendants (cf. Gen 22:18; 26:3 – 4). These motifs appear in a context of Jewish discussions in which the authoritative figure of a Law-observant Abraham was conceived as serving as an authoritative legal norm (cf. Gen 26:5).

In Gal 3:7 – 29, Paul provides an argument for the legitimacy and sufficiency of the experience explicated in Gal 3:2 – 6a. In other words, as converts the Galatians inherit the status of lineal descent from Abraham and are thus party to the promise spoken to Abraham and his descendant. The catena of texts in Scripture spoken about and *to* Abraham himself (cf. Gen 15:6; Gen 12:3; 22:16 – 18) and *to* his descendant (cf. Gen 26:3 – 4) serves as the scriptural and legal warrant for Paul's discussion of this experience. In terms of logical analysis, the experience that the Spirit was granted by trust is the data: God supplied the Spirit and worked power manifestations on the basis of trust (Gal 3:2,5). Accordingly, the best explanation of this observation is that the converts qualified as Abrahamic descendants—as a sign of God's approval—and consequently as partakers of the promised blessing.

As a warrant for the legal authority and sufficiency of the converts' experience, Paul applies an exegetical tradition based upon texts such as Gen 15:6, 22:16 – 18, and Gen 26:3 – 4 about and to Abraham and his descendants. Thus,

---

92 For the discussion of this issue, see, e.g., B. van der Lans, "Belonging to Abraham's Kin: Genealogical Appeals to Abraham as a Possible Background for Paul's Abrahamic Argument," in *Abraham, the Nations, and the Hagarites: Jewish, Christian, and Islamic Perspectives on Kinship with Abraham*, ed. M. Goodman, G.H. van Kooten, and J.T.A.G.M. van Ruiten, TBN (Leiden; Boston: Brill, 2010), 307 – 18, esp. 317; Dunn, *Galatians*, 16.

Paul makes use of the various cognates of πίστις inherent in this exegetical tradition, namely, πίστις in terms of both emulating Abraham's promiseworthy behavior and the divine trust confirmed by oath that secured the blessing promised to Abraham and his descendants. Hence, the succinct formula ἐκ πίστεως expresses the legal ground for becoming the lineal descendants of Abraham and party to the promise by emulating Abraham's πίστις, in opposition to the view that believers were legitimate descendants and heirs of the promise posited on circumcision and adherence to the Law of Moses as an emulation of Abraham's promiseworthy conduct.

In the following two subsections, I shall examine the following interrelated questions: What is the implication of the reference ἐκ πίστεως as it delineates the descendants of Abraham, justifies the non-Jews, and determines the ground of those who receive the promised blessings? My suggestion is that ἐκ πίστεως is a shorthand for three meanings in this text: in 3:6 – 7, it is paraphrasing Gen 15:6 and refers to those who emulate Abraham's trust in God as the basis of being considered legitimate descendants from Abraham, including non-Jews who become Jewish proselytes after the model of Abraham; in 3:8, it may be taken to refer to God's own trust, which comes to expression in the oath of promise rewarded Abraham, encompassing the justification of the ἔθνη; and in 3:9, the aspects of God's and Abraham's πίστις are fused together: "those of trust" are those natural-born Jews and Jewish converts who emulate the promiseworthy behavior of Abraham, and therefore share the blessing together with the "trustful" Abraham, which was guaranteed in terms of the corresponding reward of God's trust when Abraham and his descendants received the oath of promise.

4.1 Abraham's Sons ἐκ πίστεως (Gal 3:6 – 7)

Several questions have been raised about Paul's argument in Gal 3:6 – 7. Paul's exegesis and appropriation of Gen 15:6 about Abrahamic sonship have been characterized as "strange exegesis".[93] When Paul, on the basis of Gen 15:6, identifies those who are ἐκ πίστεως as Abraham's descendants, the problem is only, as Williams has expressed it, "that neither his quotation nor anything in its Genesis context claims that Abraham's descendants are 'faith people'."[94] But is Paul's claim in 3:7 idiosyncratic when seen in a Jewish context? What is the function of the comparative connector καθώς in Gal 3:6, introducing the paraphrase

93 Cf. Martyn, *History*, 162; Williams, *Galatians*, 86.
94 Williams, *Galatians*, 86.

of Gen 15:6? Is this citation referring backwards to 3:1–5 or forwards to 3:7? Is 3:7 identifying everyone who is ἐκ πίστεως as Abraham's descendants, allowing the inclusion of non-Jews, or is ἐκ πίστεως emphasized as an essential marker of the Jews who claim Abrahamic sonship for themselves? Assuming an affirmative answer to the former part of this question, how, then, does the reception of trust make non-Jews into sons of Abraham? B.R. Trick, for example, has recently argued that Gal 3:6 does not look backward to the experience of the Galatians' faith, since that "would redefine Abrahamic sonship to allow the inclusion of Christian gentiles."[95] Rather, he assumes a traditional Jewish understanding of Abrahamic sonship, and suggests that 3:6 represents a break in Paul's argument in favor of an exclusively Jewish claim of Abrahamic sonship in 3:7, in which "justification by faith constitutes an essential component of Jewish claims to that sonship."[96] Although Paul might build on a conventional trust-based Jewish claim of Abrahamic sonship, Trick does not take sufficiently into account the arguments in favor of also a backward meaning of 3:6. Thus, he has failed to pay attention to the linguistic details and technique of exegetical paraphrase as well as to the exegetical motif involved in Paul's argument. Thus, as I have argued above, although the linguistic border between Gal 3:5 and 3:6 is very thin, the interpunctuation between 3:5 and 3:6, the conclusive connector ἄρα, and the meta-propositional base in 3:7 intimate that the conclusion is drawn on the basis of the analogy about Abraham referred to in Paul's paraphrasing rendering of Scripture ("just like Abraham [...], so you should know that those of trust are the sons of Abraham"). These observations indicate that 3:6 has both a backward and a forward meaning. Thus, it is typical that a verse or a section in the Pauline texts can function both as a conclusion of what precedes and as an introduction to what follows.

M. Thiessen maintains, like Trick, that Paul's use of Gen 15:6 fails to explain the genealogical connection between non-Jews and Abraham. Thiessen remarks: "In light of Abraham's concern for a son in Genesis 15, were Paul to use Gen 15:6 to argue against the importance of genealogical descent, he would have a difficult time convincing his readers."[97] Thus, Paul's claim that Gentiles *qua* Gentiles had even become sons and seed of Abraham has been considered without parallel and anomalous in the context of Second Temple Judaism. As Donaldson concludes, "the truly anamalous aspect is Paul's insistence that uncircumcised *ethnē*-in-Christ are at the same time full members of Abraham's 'seed' (*sper-*

95 Trick, *Abrahamic Descent*, 54.
96 Trick, *Abrahamic Descent*, 54.
97 Thiessen, *Paul and the Gentile Problem*, 108.

ma)."[98] Hence, these scholars maintain that Paul's application of Gen 15:6 to include non-Jews would mean a redefinition of Abrahamic descent and claims to Jewish Abrahamic sonship. The basic weakness of such an approach is that they fail to acknowledge the presupposition in terms of an exegetical motif at stake at this juncture of Paul's argument about the inclusion of non-Jews as Jewish proselytes among Abraham's descendants. I suggest that the key to understanding Paul's reasoning in Gal 3:6–9 is the acknowledgment that Paul applies Gen 15:6 to include non-Jews among Abraham's sons, i.e., as Jewish proselytes, not as Gentiles *qua* Gentiles, regardless of their conversion.

If we set out Paul's reasoning in terms of logical analysis in abductive reasoning,[99] it could be displayed as follows:

1. The surprising fact C (= The reception of the Spirit by trust on the part of the Galatian converts) is observed.
2. But if A (= God's approval of the Galatians as Abraham's sons) were true,
C would be a matter of course.
3. Hence, there is reason to suspect that A is true.

Accordingly, if we presuppose that Paul follows the implied logic in such a reasoning, the analogy to Abraham's reception of the Spirit and its power manifestations by means of trust in God amounts to the solution to the problem of the terms under which they were made legitimate proselytes. My proposal is that Paul provides the following main answer: They do so under the same terms and scriptural norms whereby Abraham became the "first" proselyte and the founder of the Jewish nation, i.e., by the trust in God, not through observance of the commandments of the Law, which was not yet given. Thus, like Abraham, it is by reception of the Spirit on the basis of the conviction that affirms trust in God that the Galatian proselytes aquire their identity of becoming "Jewish". At this juncture, we must review such an understanding of Gal 3:6–7 in the light of recent discussions of conceptual models that underlie the ways the "Christian" non-Jews have been conceptualized.

In my introductory review of previous research, I referred to Levenson, who argues against the view that a universal appeal to Abraham motivates Paul's recourse to Abraham. Unfortunately, he still maintains "that some means other than conversion to Judaism must be found to incorporate Gentiles into the Abra-

98 Donaldson, "Paul Within Judaism," 296.

99 The theory of abductive reasoning was developed by C.S. Peirce. For the succinct reasoning outlined below, see C.S. Peirce, *Collected Papers of Charles Sanders Peirce*, ed. C. Hartshorne and P. Weiss (Cambridge, MA: Harvard University Press, 1960), vol. 5, 189.

hamic family." Thus, he quotes Paula Fredriksen, who, in Levenson's view, "puts it well":

> Pagans-in-Christ are also from Abraham's lineage, since Abraham was the father of many nations (Gen 17:4; Rom 4:17); but they descend from Abraham *alone*, not also from Isaac and Jacob. Because of the Spirit, however, these pagans too are now sons, heirs to the "promise" to Abraham: like Israel, they too can now call God "Abba, Father" [...]
>
> But this new kinship is not tantamount to "conversion," because these Gentiles are adopted not into Israel's family, but into God's, made such not *kata sarka* [according to the flesh] but *kata pneuma* [according to the Spirit]. Put differently: redeemed Israel and the pagans-in-Christ together share the same heavenly Father *kata pneuma*, but *kata sarka* they remain distinct.[100]

There are several weaknesses with this reasoning. In the first place, both Levenson and Fredriksen refer to the citation of Gen 17:5 about Abraham as "the father of a multitude of nations" rather than Abraham as the father of Isaac / Israel on whom Paul focuses, and into whose lineage the Gentiles are grafted. The distinction Fredriksen makes between these "pagans-in Christ" who are considered to be offspring of Abraham (*kata pneuma*), but not of Isaac and Jacob (*kata sarka),* fails to convince, because it does not suit passages like Gal 4:28 and Rom 9:7–13, where the genealogical line of Isaac and Jacob is taken as a precedent for that of the believers of non-Jewish origin. If Paul was not intent on maintaining the distinction between Jews and Gentiles, why would he then emphasize Abraham claimed as the father of Jewish people, into whose lineage the non-Jews are both adopted and blessed as Abraham's sons?

Second, *pace* Fredriksen, Paul never refers to the distinction κατὰ σάρκα and κατὰ πνεῦμα in his discussion of Abram. Rather, in Rom 4:1 he refers to Abraham as "our forefather in accordance to the flesh", which is taken to refer to Abraham as the ancestor of the Jews. Likewise, Paul elsewhere emphasizes that biologically he is as an Israelite from *the seed of Abraham.*[101] Furthermore, as I shall argue in section 6 of this chapter, the Galatian converts are regarded as the offspring promised to Abraham and to his "seed" Isaac, not just descendants from Abraham *alone*, but including descendants from Isaac, among whom Christ is seen as the ultimate "seed" and fulfillment of the promise.

Third, both Fredriksen and Levenson fail to take into account a more flexible conception of "Jewishness" and "conversion". Thus, they operate with too strict

---

100 See Levenson, *Inheriting Abraham*, 158, citing from Fredriksen, "Judaizing the Nations," 243 – 4.

101 Cf. Rom 11:1: καὶ γὰρ ἐγὼ Ἰσραηλίτης εἰμί, ἐκ σπέρματος Ἀβραάμ, φυλῆς Βενιαμίν, and 2 Cor 11:22: Ἑβραῖοί εἰσιν; κἀγώ. Ἰσραηλῖταί εἰσιν; κἀγώ. σπέρμα Ἀβραάμ εἰσιν; κἀγώ.

a definition of what it meant for non-Jews to undertake a "conversion" to Judaism, and do not recognize what Levenson in fact argues elsewhere, viz. there are in Paul's view two distinct modes of conversion to the status of becoming included among the children of Abraham, of which trust is "the *only* means of conversion to Judaism, for the Jewish means—acceptance of the Torah and its commandments, symbolized in men by circumcision—have, in Paul's mind, ceased to be efficacious."[102]

In sum, a more nuanced and coherent approach to Paul's reasoning in Gal 3:7 and his conception of Abrahamic sonship would be the inference he draws from Gen 15:6. Consequently, as I have argued in the preceding section, Paul presupposes that non-Jews had already gained the status of converts by trust in the One God, approved by their reception of the Spirit and its powerful manifestation, just as Abraham himself experienced when he became the first proselyte apart from the Law of Moses, and thus "before any at all of the particular statutes was set in writing" (cf. Philo's statement on the temporality of the Law of Moses in *Abr.* 5). Hence, Paul presupposed that Abrahamic sonship meant that Abraham is the common father of Jews and converts, not of the non-Jews in general nor of those who become proselytes on the condition of compliance with the law of Moses. Moreover, by paraphrasing Gen 15:6 in Gal 3:7, Paul defines the foundational character of Abraham's descendants, among whom the converts have been included, as having its origin in the trust in God shown by Abraham as its founder. As I shall now point out, this interpretation of Gal 3:7 is perfectly coherent within a Jewish context.

As I pointed out in the excursus of chapter two, both Philo and the rabbis presupposed the natural distinction between the Jewish nation and other peoples with regard to the question of lineage, and this made them sensitive to the problem posed by a proselyte's non-Jewish lineage. But then, how could one fully endorse the idea that a non-Jew could become a "Jew"? It seems that the issue of "Jewishness" allowed for various answers. According to Philo, "spiritual kinship" in terms of a religious and ethical "conversion" after the model of Abraham, and "civic kinship" with native Jews centered on the laws of Moses constitute the fellowship of the Jewish *politeia,* viz. a community of "citizens" of Jews and converts. Although Philo (as far as I know) never claims that the proselytes became descendants of Abraham, because of the genealogical distinction between the proselytes as a separate class of their own and the Jews, the rabbinic literature attests the existence of a discussion of the problem posed by the foreign lineage of the proselytes with regard to their incorporation into

---

102 Levenson, *The Death and Resurrection*, 216–7.

the lineage of Abraham and becoming sharers of the promise. On the one hand, therefore, as we have observed in chapter two, some rabbis claimed that the proselytes, because of the natural fact of being born as non-Jews, could never claim physical descent from Abraham, and so were not permitted to call Abraham "our father" and become partakers of the promise that God had sworn to the ancestors. On the other hand, some rabbinic traditions emphasized a legal kinship model as well as a metaphorical concept of conversion that regarded the converts as Abraham's descendants and thus as included in the promises to the patriarchs. This status enabled them to speak of the God of "our" forefathers in spite of their foreign genealogical origin. As I shall show, the negotiations on Abraham attested in Philo and the later rabbis provide a Jewish context for Paul's discussion in Galatians of Abraham as the father of Jews and of converts.

The two sides of the rabbinic debate mentioned above as a context for Paul's discourse in Galatians have not been given sufficient acknowledgement in scholarship. For example, A.E. Harvey refers only to the rabbis who thought it inconceivable that, merely by being proselytes, the converts could share in Abraham's sonship and the promises. From this, Harvey draws the conclusion that Paul's opponents could hardly have argued a similar position:

> The fatal objection to this is that his opponents cannot have been contending any such thing. They could perhaps have said that there is an advantage in being circumcised and becoming a proselyte: it conferred a definite status (though a humble one) in the Jewish community [...]. But one thing it could never do was to make a man who was not physically a Jew into a son of Abraham.[103]

Similarly, F.F. Bruce maintains that proselytes, although they were circumcised and regarded by some rabbis as Abraham's children by adoption, were not entitled to call Abraham "our father", and thus share in God's promises to Abraham and his descendants.[104] Correspondingly, Berthelot suggests that Paul was facing opponents "who stuck to a genealogical definition of Israel, those who inherit God's promises, as the descendants of Abraham, Isaac and Jacob."[105] Such a view, then, attested in Mishnah, Tosefta, and the Babylonian Talmud, implied a status that only Jews could claim for themselves, excluding proselytes from the privileges to which those of Abrahamic lineage were entitled.

---

103 A.E. Harvey, "The Opposition to Paul," in *The Galatians Debate: Contemporary Issues in Rhetorical and Historical Interpretation*, ed. M.D. Nanos (Peabody, MA: Hendrickson, 2002), 327.
104 F.F. Bruce, *The Epistle of Paul to the Romans: An Introduction and Commentary* (London: Tyndale Press, 1963), 111.
105 Berthelot, "Adoption," 5.

But what if the other side of the rabbinic debate is considered, that is, if Paul has presupposed a counter-message that urged the Galatians to become proselytes in the full sense, which involved circumcision and adherence to the jurisdiction of the Law of Moses, so that they would thus be regarded as descended from the patriarchs and heirs of the promise in spite of their foreign lineage? It is impossible to determine whether Paul's opponents actually argued such a case, but this conjecture is not implausible in the light of the rabbinic data, and might provide a Jewish context for the stance Paul himself took as a response to objections he had to expect. Some details in Gal 3:7 and the backing provided in Gal 3:10–25 seem to corroborate this position, on the basis of the text itself. As I shall suggest, Paul's own stance might represent a distinct variant of the position that non-Jews became Abraham's children and heirs to the promises when they, as proselytes, emulated Abraham's promise-worthy behavior. In contrast to the rabbis, who posited obedience to the Law of Moses as this kind of emulation, Paul centers this emulation of Abraham in the virtue of trust. Thus, they became proselytes, legitimate descendants, and party to the promise in the the context of the "Abrahamic jurisdiction" attested by the narrative part of the "Law" in Genesis.

Several features in Gal 3:7 may add cumulative weight to highlight Paul's own stance in relation to other Jewish positions on Abrahamic sonship and inheritance. To begin with, the ἄρα in v. 7 indicates the connection to the preceding argument in Gal 3:2–6. Thus, the ἄρα indicates that the meaning of what follows as a thesis can be inferred from on the analogy to Abraham and what Gen 15:6 tells about him.[106] Moreover, the expression οἱ ἐκ πίστεως in 3:7a should be understood as an exegetical paraphrase of Gen 15:6 (cited in v.6), indicating a designation of those who have a trust having its origin in Abraham ("those of faith", with the implicit meaning "those who are emulating Abraham by trust") and are therefore defined as Abraham's sons in 3:7b.[107] The problem is that Paul's asser-

106 For such an understanding of ἄρα, cf. Hartman, "Galatians 3:15–4:11," 134 n. 16; F.F. Bruce, *The Epistle of Paul to the Galatians: A Commentary on the Greek Text*, NIGTC (Grand Rapids: Eerdmans, 1982), 153.

107 The phrase οἱ ἐκ πίστεως is usually taken primarily to refer to the believer and translated in its literal sense as "those who believe", cf., e.g., Longenecker, *Galatians*, 114: "those who rely on faith", and Martyn, *Galatians*, 299: "those whose identity is derived from faith". The absence of a verb, however, has elicited a number of other translations among scholars. For exampe, Hays (*The Faith of Jesus Christ*, 171) and Trick (*Abrahamic Descent*, 60–61) argue that it refers to those who are justified out of Christ's faith, and takes it as an allusion to Hab 2:4 quoted in Gal 3:11. Likewise, de Boer (*Galatians*, 191–92) takes it to point to Christ's own faith, and takes it to mean "those from/on the basis of [Christ's] faith", influenced by Paul's use of the phrase ἐκ πίστεως Χριστοῦ in Gal 2:16 and 3:22. Scholars such as Johnson Hodge (*If Sons,*

tion appears unwarranted by his evidence, since "neither his quotation nor anything in its Genesis context claims that Abraham's descendants are 'faith people'."[108] Again, we should ask whether such an exegetical paraphrase has some affinity to Jewish interpretation of Gen 15:6? Fortunately, evidence suggests an answer in the affirmative. If we acknowledge that an exposition of Gen 15:6 in Paul's contemporary Judaism may serve as the scriptural basis for marking the identify of Abraham's descendants, including the proselytes who follow in the footsteps of the patriarch, his exegesis may not seem so "strange". Accordingly, we have observed in chapter two how Philo in key statements can accentuate the character of the Jewish nation and the subsequent proselytes as originating in the theological conviction of Abraham. Such a portrait of Abraham was influenced by Gen 15:6 LXX (cf. the underlined words in common in the citations below):

> And Abraham believed in God (καὶ ἐπίστευσεν Αβραμ τῷ θεῷ). Gen 15:6 (LXX)
>
> [...] he is the first person spoken of as believing in God (πιστεῦσαι λέγεται τῷ θεῷ πρῶτος), [...], that there is one Cause above all, and that it provides for the world and all that there is therein. *Virt.* 216

The Philonic evidence, then, provides a context for Paul's analogy between Abraham's affirmation of trust in God and the thesis stated in 3:7: "Just as Abraham [...], so you should know that those of trust are the sons of Abraham". Although it is a later exegetical tradition based on Gen 15:6, it is noteworthy that b. Šabb. 97a contains the same exegetical motif of the Jewish people as the people of faith and the descendants of people of faith, with its origins in Abraham as the first believer : "[...] They are believers, [and] the descendants of believers, whereas thou wilt ultimately disbelieve. They are believers, as it is written, and the people believed; the descendants of believers: and he [Abraham] believed in the Lord."[109]

Although we cannot be certain that the Galatians have known such an exegetical motif in advance, Paul offers some interpretative signs which indicate such an assumption. In the first place, since the thesis of v. 7 ("those of faith

Then Heirs, 80) and Thiessen (*Paul and the Gentile Problem*, 110 – 1) render it "those who are born out of faith", on the basis of Paul's implied reference to Gen 15:4 LXX. These renderings, however, have failed to take seriously the fact that it is part of Paul's exegetical paraphrase of Gen 15:6, so that it refers both to Abraham's own trust (3:6) and to the trust of believers, whether they are Jews or believing converts, who derive their origin and identity from a trust like Abraham's, and who on this basis are defined as descendants of Abraham.

108 Cf. Williams, *Galatians*, 86.

109 For a comment on this rabbinic text, see Levenson, *Inhereting Abraham*, 27.

are the sons of Abraham") can be implied from the exegetical paraphrase of Gen 15:6 and the verb γινώσκω in v .7 also can function as exegetical terminology introducing the following interpretation, it seems best to take γινώσκω as an indicative ("you know" or "realize") rather than as an imperative ("recognize" or "consider").[110] Thus, as ἄρα too indicates, this means that Paul in v. 7 draws a logical "inference of best explanation" from the data and analogy between Abraham's and the Galatians' experience in vv. 5 – 6 and what Paul assumes that they already should know from Paul's own teaching about Abraham and his progeny. Furthermore, the ironic statement in v. 2 ("The only thing I want to learn from you is this"), makes the rhetorical point that Paul needs to learn nothing from the Galatians, since he has already been *their* teacher and has taught them what he now reminds them about. What they should know is emphasized in v. 7 by two more features. With regard to the delimitation of the true descendants of Abraham, identified as "those of faith", we find an emphatic "they" (οὗτοι).[111] Moreover, Paul's way of accentuating "sons" (υἱοί), by placing it before the verb and separated from Abraham, points in the same direction.[112] Such an emphasis could be meant to highlight Abraham's true descendants, over against both those who stuck merely to a genealogical definition based on physical descent and those who may posit circumcision and "works of Law" as a way of emulating Abraham's behavior except for the shared trust in God. At this juncture, Paul seems to create the phrase ἐκ πίστεως ("those emulating Abraham on the basis of trust") in contrast to the expression ἐξ ἔργων νόμου ("those emulating Abraham on the basis of works of Law"). This antithesis is explicitly expressed in vv. 2, 5, and 11, and seems to be implied here in v. 7 too. Since the thesis in v. 7 is based on the analogy from Abraham in vv. 5 – 6, it is likely that Paul here takes his place in the Jewish debate and negotiation on Abraham and the Law. Again, the discussion attested in Philo's writings of such a negotiation may provide a context for a corresponding debate reflected in Galatians, and suggest the existence of Jewish analogies to Paul's reasoning in his own time.

As I pointed out in chapters two and three above, in a key statement on Abraham as the most ancient member of the Jewish nation (*Virt.* 212), Philo characterizes him as the foundational model as the first who came to trust in God, inspired by Gen 15:6 LXX (*Virt.* 216). Moreover, we have observed how Philo is involved in Jewish negotiations on the understanding of Abraham as the founder

110 So also Hartman, "Galatians 3:15 – 4:11," 134; Witherington III, *Grace in Galatia*, 226; Trick, *Abrahamic Descent*, 55.

111 Cf. Williams, *Galatians*, 86; Trick, *Abrahamic Descent*, 55.

112 Cf., e. g., deSilva, *The Letter to the Galatians*, 281 n. 44; Tolmie, *Persuading the Galatians*, 113.

of the Jewish nation. Thus, in *Abr.* 275–276, Abraham is given special prominence as an observer of the divine Law in terms of trust in God and his promise, before the Law was revealed through Moses. On the other side of the negotiation on Abraham and the Law, the imaginary interlocutors referred to by Philo have maintained a position similar to the author of *Jubilees* and the later rabbis, based on the secondariness of the Sinaitic Law, namely that the Law of Moses was identical with the divine Law in Nature. As a corollary, Abraham was conceived as a pre-Sinaitic observer of the jurisdiction of Moses. Philo, himself, however, clearly needs to correct and modify such a position, and he claims that this could not have been the case, since the Sinaitic laws had not yet been set in writing (cf. *Abr.* 5 and 275). These modifications indicate that Philo operates with a distinction in his concept of the Torah between two jurisdictions, in which Abraham's trust in God and the promise is taken as a manifestation of his adherence to the unwritten divine Law in Nature antecedent to, and distinct from, the special Laws of Moses that were promulgated at Sinai. According to Philo, the Mosaic legislation only sets forth as legal system the archetypical divine Law that came to expression in Genesis and the narrative about the virtues of Abraham and the patriarchs, regarded as a separate jurisdiction and legal part of the Torah.

The distinction Philo makes in discussion with other Jews, and in the context of a Greco-Roman discourse, between two separate, although intersected, jurisdictions in the Torah, has not been taken fully into account in its relevance to a comparison with Paul.[113] Thus, for example, F. Watson, holds the traditional view of Philo's conception of the Law:

> The laws revealed at Sinai were preceded by earlier articulations of those same laws; whether these were written or unwritten, the mode of divine discourse is fundamentally the same before Moses as through Moses.[114]

On this basis, Watson draws a contrast between the reading of Genesis in Paul and that by Philo and the author of Jubilees:

> In their different ways, Philo and the author of *Jubilees* read the Genesis narrative along the lines that Paul rejects. Given the Pauline antithesis, it is possible to place their readings on one side and his on the other. To that extent, the two types of reading are incommensurable: what is affirmed by the one is denied or downplayed by the other.[115]

113 For previous research on this subject, see the introductory chapter (2.3).
114 Watson, *Paul and the Hermeneutics of Faith*, 222.
115 Watson, *Paul and the Hermeneutics of Faith*, 223.

As I have pointed out in the survey of earlier works (chapter one), at this juncture Watson and others fail to take into due consideration the modifications and nuances referred to by Philo himself in a discussion with his interlocutors. *Pace* Watson, we might claim that both Philo and Paul to some extent stand on the same side, in opposition to those who interpret Abraham's relation to the Law along the lines of the author of *Jubilees*, Philo's interlocutors, and the later rabbis. For Philo, both proselytes and Jews by birth should adhere to the jurisdiction of the Jewish *politeia*, i.e., the community of "citizens" centered on the Law of Moses. Although Philo maintains that the particular Law of Moses is not identical with the divine Law of Nature, which is unwritten and universal, but in conformity with it, since it has universal dimensions, he claims authority for the Law of Moses as a valid testimony and the best way to get access to the unwritten Law of Nature. Thus, Philo is emphasizing two distinct, though supplementary aspects of Abraham and Law. Since the Law of Moses replicates and leads to the same virtues exemplified in what Abraham and the ancestors achieved through their instinctive words and deeds, it is, as a written and particular Law, the best possible approximation to the unwritten and cosmic Law in Nature. Although Philo posits the biography of Abraham as the legal norm, he nevertheless demonstrates a dynamic relation between the Law of Moses and Abraham's "Law" with regard to how the former fits with latter. Thus, Philo can even compare the obedience of Abraham to the divine Law and adherence to the Mosaic Law. He tells us that it is "those who wish to live in accordance with the laws as they stand have no difficult task, seeing that the first generations before any at all of the particular statutes was set in writing followed the unwritten law with perfect ease [...]" (*Abr.* 5).

It is noteworthy that the distinction in the concept of the Torah Philo made between two jurisdictions of Law has some affinity with Paul. Like Philo, Paul maintained a legal distinction between two concepts of the Torah, but unlike Philo, he separated the Abraham-centered jurisdiction based upon trust in the promise from obedience to the Law of Moses. Thus, as I shall argue, from the perspective of the Christ event Paul posited Abraham's trust in God and the promise (rather than the jurisdiction of Moses) as the valid jurisdiction for an emulation of Abraham's promiseworthy virtue of piety. In the context of Gal 3:6 – 7, I hold that this is a premise in Paul's portrait of Abraham as the archetype of any believers, whether they are born as Jews or as non-Jews who had become Jewish proselytes. Thus, like Philo, Paul construes Abraham and his virtue of trust in God's promise, as opposed to a Abraham who was a Jewish observer of the Mosaic Law, as the basic figure of emulation and thus as that which constitutes their status as Abrahamic descendants and partakers of the promise (cf. the implied questions concerning Abraham's reception of the Spirit in contrast to obedience to the "works of Law" in Gal 3:2, 5, and the exegetical argument in Gal 3:10 – 25 regarding the relationship between Abraham's trust in the promise and the Law of Moses, in order to counter anticipated objections to his basic warrant and provide further backing for it).[116] Thus, as we shall point out below (section 6), Paul comes close to Philo (and forms a contrast to Philo's interlocutors, Jubilees and the rabbis) on a distinction between two jurisdictions attested in the Torah and Scripture, seeing Abraham as not subject to the Law of Moses, since he lived before the institution of the Law in Moses' own time.

With regard to the characterization of Abraham's ethnicity, and despite differences, Philo provides an analogy to Paul at another point too. F.M. Cross has explained how legal kinship in ancient Israel was based on the covenant and sealed by the act of swearing an oath: "Oath and covenant, in which the deity is witness, guarantor, or participant, is also a legal means by which the duties and privileges of kinship may be extended to another individual or group, including aliens."[117] Philo's appropriation of the oath of promise to Abraham and Isaac in Gen 26:3 is relevant here as an example. According to Philo, the oath of promise to Abraham's descendants was a means of marking identity, dependent on the emulation of Abraham's virtues. In order to be party to the oath of promise, his descendants had to demonstrate the virtues and piety of the patriarchs:

> He wishes to praise the son as one worthy of his father's nobility, for He would not firmly establish the promises made to the father with an oath, for the sake of the son, if He did not witness the same virtue in him. Cease, therefore, now from praising nobility separately by itself and learn from the divine Scriptures what true (nobility) is, and repent. For this (passage) clearly teaches us to define and judge and discern the well-born (as being) not those who have sprung from good fathers or grandparents and are content with that alone, but those who are themselves emulators of their (fathers') piety.
> *QG* 4:180

In a manner similar to this thought pattern, Paul maintains that the sons and heirs of Abraham are defined by spiritual kinship and the emulation of his trust in God's promise, rather than by physical lineage or Jewish citizenship centered upon the jurisdiction of the Law of Moses. Scholars have overlooked the fact that Paul, not unlike Philo, appropriates the oath of promise in Gen 22:18 and Gen 26:3 – 4 as an identity marker for such a claim on descent from Abraham. Since Abraham was the founder of the Jewish nation and the first prose-

---

116 *Pace*, Donaldson ("Paul Within Judaism," 298), who states that Paul's position on the identity of the *ethnê*-in-Christ has no real precedent and analogy within Judaism.
117 Cross, *From Epic to Canon*, 8.

lyte, he was the model of character for his descendants. Hence, Abraham's descendants were those who shared in his main characteristics and the promise: trust in the one God and the oath of promise given in return by God. Accordingly, those who belong to Abraham's seed, Christ, and who like him emulate Abraham's trust, are considered Abraham's offspring and thus inherit the blessings together with Abraham:

> "All the Gentiles shall be blessed in you." For this reason, those who believe are blessed with Abraham who believed. Gal 3:8–9
>
> [...] so that what was promised on the basis of the faith of Jesus Christ might be given to those who believe. Gal 3:22b
>
> And if you belong to Christ, then you are Abraham's offspring, heirs according to the promise. Gal 3:29

I shall now take a closer look at Gal 3:8–9, which further suggests that Paul takes his place in the same discourse as Philo about how to read the *continuum* of the Genesis narrative about Abraham, centered on their conjunction of Gen 15:6 and Genesis 22:18 / 26:3–4 about Abraham's trust and God's responsiveness of trust in terms of the oath of promise.

4.2 The Oath of Promise ἐκ πίστεως (Gal 3:8–9)

In the prevous two sections, I have argued that an exegetical paraphrase of Gen 15:6 served to highlight the character of Abraham as the foundational model of his descendants, including the Galatian non-Jews viewed as Jewish proselytes. In the first place, Paul compares the experience of the Galatian converts and their reception of Spirit to Abraham's experience in terms of his authoritative role as the norm and paradigm for proselytes. Thus, in Gal 3:2–6, the Galatian converts are viewed as valid proselytes apart from the "works of the Law". Moreover, in Gal 3:6–7 Paul emphasizes that Abraham's descendants are defined by the same kind and nature that characterized Abraham, namely, his trust in the One God.

In this section, I suggest that Paul anchors the status and identity of the Galatian converts by an additional proof from the Abrahamic narrative. Departing from the idea that lineal descent from Abraham and his descendant makes one party to the promise, Paul sees the Galatian converts as valid descendants of Abraham, since they already are partakers in what God promised by oath to Abraham and to his descendant, i.e., the blessings provided to them on the ground of their emulating Abraham's trust and of God's responsiveness of trust that is expected in return. My main thesis is that Paul sees the oath of promise (Gen 22:16 – 18; 26:3 – 4) as ensuing upon Abraham's trust (Gen 15:6), and not as contingent on his putative obedience to the Law of Moses (Gen 26:5). Thus, like Philo, but unlike Jewish tradition, Paul takes the oath of promise to be separate from Abraham's obedience to the Law of Moses and grounded wholly in Abraham's trust in God and His promise. Abraham's πίστις in the promise, then, here means living in the same trust that is the πίστις of God, viz. being faithful (πιστός), by virtue of which he shared God's own faithfulness. In Paul's view, it was this correspondence of conduct on Abraham's *and* on God's part that enabled the promise of blessing to reach Isaac's descendants, encompassing "those of trust" among the "nations" (cf. Gal 3:8 – 9). This thesis rests upon the suggestion that Gal 3:7– 9 can be seen as a further exegetical paraphrase of Gen 15:6 in conjunction with the promises of Gen 12:3, 22:18, and 26:3 – 4.

The technique of "composite citation" can be seen in Gal 3:8b, in which words from Gen 12:3 (*ἐνευλογηθήσονται ἐν σοί*) and 22:18 / 26:4 (*καὶ ἐνευλογηθήσονται ἐν τῷ σπέρματί σου πάντα τὰ ἔθνη*) might be conceived as the potential source behind Gal 3:8b (προευηγγελίσατο τῷ Ἀβραὰμ ὅτι *ἐνευλογηθήσονται ἐν σοὶ πάντα τὰ ἔθνη·*).[118] Following scholars such as C.D. Stanley and M.J.J. Menken, we should distinguish between two sorts of composite citations: "combined citations" (a marked quotation, in which two passages are joined together to form one new citation) and "conflated citations" (an unmarked quotation, in which one word or a few words from one passage have been inserted into a quotation from another passage).[119] Although the citation seems to qualify as a marked quotation, in the sense that it is introduced by reference to the Scripture, I take Gal 3:8b to be an example of the latter kind of citation. However, Gen 12:3, 18:8, and 22:18 are usually listed as sources behind Gal 3:8b.[120] In the quotation of Gen 12:3 (*ἐνευλογηθήσονται ἐν σοί*), Paul has replaced the words *πᾶσαι αἱ φυλαὶ τῆς γῆς* with πάντα τὰ *ἔθνη*. Scholars disagree about whether the latter

---

118 I employ the definition of "composite citation" suggested by S.A. Adams, ("Composite Citations in Antiquity," 2016), 4: "A text may be considered a composite citation when literary borrowing occurs in a manner that includes two or more passages (from the same or different authors) fused together and conveyed as though they are only one."

119 C.D. Stanley, "Composite Citations: Retrospect and Prospect," in *Composite Citations in Antiquity: Volume One*, ed. S.A. Adams and S.M. Ehorn (London: T & T Clark, 2016), 204 – 5; M.J.J. Menken, "Composite Citations in the Gospel of Matthew," in *Composite Citations in Antiquity: Volume Two*, ed. S.A. Adams and S.M. Ehorn (London: T&T Clark, 2018), 35.

120 Cf. Hahn, "Covenant," 92 n. 64; Trick, *Abrahamic Descent*, 67; Hays, *Echoes of Scripture in the Letters of Paul*, 106 – 8, who all identify the citation in Gal 3:8b as a conflation of Gen 12:3 and Gen 22:18.

wording is derived from Gen 18:18 or from Gen 22:18. The reference to Gen 18:8 can be eliminated, however, since it employs the phrase *ἐν αὐτῷ*, and is a promise not directly spoken *to* Abraham.[121] Furthermore, the emphasis in the immediate context that the promised blessings are a corollary of both God's *and* Abraham's trust / faithfulness (3:8–9), encompassing the blessings of the nations mediated "in Christ Jesus" (3:14a), who is the ultimate offspring of Abraham (3:16, 19, 22b), and through whom Jews and converts alike become Abraham's offspring and heirs of the promise (3:29), speaks in favor of the oath of promise as the additional source in Gal 3:8b that best fits the immediate context in Galatians.[122] This suggestion is also supported by the fact that Paul states that this promise was spoken not just to Abraham (in Gen 22:18), but *to* Abraham *and to* his descendant (according to Gen 26:3–4). It is noteworthy that the same composite citation of Gen 12:3, 22:18, and 26:4 also appears in Acts 3:25.[123]

Unlike Gen 18:18, both Gen 22:18 and 26:4 pay attention to how Abraham's blessings shall continue to bear not only on his descendants, but more specifically on the ἔθνη mediated through Abraham's descendants, similar to God's initial promise of blessing in Gen 12:3. This might explain why Paul in Gal 3:8b paraphrases the expression *ἐν σοί* from the citation of Gen 12:3 in two ways: (1) about the blessings that shall be bestowed on Abraham and his descendant,

---

121 Although Gen 18:8 can be seen as a narrative recap of Gen 12:3 (cf. Wenham, *Genesis 16–50*, 50), and thus as speaking *about Abraham* in third person, the fact that the reception of the motif about the blessings of the nations "in Abraham" is hardly mentioned in other Jewish texts makes it unlikely that this is the primary scripture referred to in Gal 3:8. Despite Dunn's claim that Gen 12:3 and Gen 18:18 indicate that the promise had "a universal aspect from the first" (*Galatians*, 164), Paul was obviously constrained to to identify the Galatian converts in ethocentric Jewish terms as Abraham's sons and Abraham's offspring, who had received this status in connection with Christ as Abraham's seed.

122 Albeit scholars pay attention to Gen 22:18, Gen 26:4 is almost neglected as a scripture alluded to already in Gal 3:8b, on which Paul elaborates further in the ensuing verses. Hays hints at its relevance for Paul when he he refers to J. Van Seter's comments on Gen 26:3–5 in terms of Abraham's obedience conferring blessings on the subsequent generations: "Although Van Seters does not address the question of Paul's use of the Abraham stories, his remarks provide a significant background for understanding the way in which Paul deals with this material". Cf. Hays, *The Faith of Jesus Christ*, 174 n. 36, refering to J. Van Seter, *Abraham in History and Tradition* (New Haven: Yale University Press, 1975), 272–8. van der Laans ("Belonging to Abraham's Kin," 316) suggests that the promises in Gal 3:16 "refer more specifically to the the descendant-mediated version of the blessing of nations (Gen 22:18; 26:4; 28:14) continuing the argumentation from Gal 3:8–9." Unfortunately, she does not spell out in more detail what such a proposal would entail for the reading of Gal 3:16 in context.

123 See C.R. Holladay, *Acts: A Commentary*, NTL (Louisville, KY: Westminster John Knox Press, 2016), 121.

σὺν τῷ πιστῷ Ἀβραάμ (Gal 3:9), and (2) as mediated to the "nations" in "Jesus Christ", ἡ εὐλογία τοῦ Ἀβραὰμ γένηται ἐν Χριστῷ Ἰησοῦ (Gal 3:14a), where the phrase "ἐν Χριστῷ Ἰησοῦ" has replaced "ἐν σοί " as the means by which the blessings are conferred. As I shall maintain below, there is cumulative evidence in favor of seeing Gen 12:3, 22:18, and 26:3–4 as the warp on which much of Paul's arguments in Gal 3:8–29 are woven. Thus, I shall seek to show how the exegetical paraphrase of Gen 22:18 / 26:3–4 in Gal 3:14, 16, 19, 22b, and 29 might elaborate upon such a conjectural reading of Gal 3:8–9. In this context, it suffices to say that Paul's conjunction of these scriptures suggest that the blessings due to Abraham's trust in God and God's oath of promise given him in return accrue to the Abrahamic descent centered in Christ, through whom the oath of promise *to* Abraham *and to* his "seed" is confirmed.

In what follows, I shall suggest that the exegetical paraphrase of Gen 15:6 results in a refashioning of God corresponding to the image of Abraham. To support such a conjecture, four observations will first be briefly offered. (1) If we see Gal 3:8–9 as a further elaboration of the exegetical paraphrase of Gen 15:6 cited in v. 6, Paul draws a parallel between God's justification of Abraham and of the ἔθνη as follows:

> v. 6 Καθὼς Ἀβραὰμ <u>ἐπίστευσεν</u> τῷ <u>θεῷ</u>, καὶ ἐλογίσθη <u>αὐτῷ</u> εἰς <u>δικαιοσύνην</u>·
> v. 8 προϊδοῦσα δὲ ἡ γραφὴ ὅτι ἐκ <u>πίστεως</u> <u>δικαιοῖ</u> <u>τὰ ἔθνη</u> ὁ <u>θεός</u>, [προευηγγελίσατο τῷ Ἀβραὰμ ὅτι *ἐνευλογηθήσονται ἐν σοὶ πάντα τὰ ἔθνη*]
> v. 9 ·ὥστε οἱ ἐκ <u>πίστεως</u> <u>εὐλογοῦνται</u> σὺν τῷ <u>πιστῷ</u> <u>Ἀβραάμ</u>.

Thus, by rephrasing the reference to God's "justification" (from *δικαιοσύνην* to δικαιοῖ) and replacing "Abraham" (*αὐτῷ*) with the words "the nations" (τὰ ἔθνη), Paul emphasizes that, as Abraham was justified, so "God would justify the nations". Thus, Paul argues that God's conduct of responsiveness corresponds to Abraham's: As Abraham *trusted* (*ἐπίστευσεν*) God, so "God would justify the nations *out of his trust*" (ἐκ πίστεως). (2) In Gal 3:8–9, Paul makes clear what is presupposed in Gal 3:6. Just as Abraham *trusted* in *the promise* (cf. Gen 15:5–6), so "God out of his *trust / faithfulness*" spoke the oath of promise to Abraham: "In you (Abraham / Isaac) shall all the nations (*πάντα τὰ ἔθνη*) be blessed". The scriptural basis for this exposition is, then, the composite quotation of Gen 12:3 and 22:18 / 26:4, as I have stated above. (3) Furthermore, v. 9 elaborates the correlation between Abraham and God that was presupposed in v. 8a. At this juncture, however, Paul reverses the correspondence between God and Abraham, so that the designation of Abraham corresponds to image of God. Paul interprets Gen 15:6 about Abraham's trust in God and his promise in the light of the oath of promise attested in Gen 22:18 / 26:4 and thus highlights the correspondence of God's faithfulness *and* Abraham's faithfulness. Accordingly, God has confirmed Abraham's trust in God (and the promise) that he antecedently possessed (Gen 15:6) with the added measure of faithfulness (πιστός) embedded in the oath of promise. Having received the oath of promise, Abraham's conduct in terms of his trust in God is affirmed as being "faithful" (πιστῷ Ἀβραάμ) corresponding to God's own conduct of faithfulness. It is in this sense that the promise previously given to Abraham (such as the promise that comes to expression in Gen 12:3, cited by Paul) can be said to be anchored not only in God's supreme faithfulnes towards his promise, but now also in Abraham's trust / faithfulness as its terms of reference. In sum, I propose that Paul's argument in Gal 3:8 – 9 basically follows the line of thought inherent in the oath of promise as it is expressed in Gen 22:16 – 18 and Gen 26:3 – 4. Moberly's exposition of the oath of promise in the latter texts can be said to be relevant for our interpretation of the reasoning undergirding Gal 3:8 – 9 as well:

> Abraham by his obedience has not qualified to be the recipient of blessing, because the promise of blessing had been given to him already. Rather, the existing promise is reaffirmed but its terms of reference are altered. A promise which previously was grounded solely in the will and purpose of Yahweh is transformed so that it is now grounded *both* in the will of Yahweh *and* in the obedience of Abraham. It is not that the divine promise has become contingent upon Abraham's obedience, but that Abraham's obedience has been incorporated into the divine promise.[124]

As I shall point out next, this emphasis on the correspondence between God's and Abraham's faithfulness in Gal 3:8 – 9 accords with a common thought pattern attested in many variants of the *Akedah* traditions, which was summarized by S. Spiegel as follows:

> It may be surmised that all these variations originally had one feature in common: a parallelism between Abraham's conduct at the Akedah and the conduct expected in return from God.[125]

As I pointed out in chapter one, several scholars have already drawn attention to the background of the *Akedah* in Paul's reasoning in Galatians 3. According to Hays, "Paul has introduced a crucial new emphasis into this traditional way of thinking by claiming, on the basis of the scriptural text, that Abraham's faithfulness was 'reckoned' by God to the benefit not only of Israel (as in the Jewish

---

124 Moberly, "The Earliest Commentary on the Akedah," 320 – 1.
125 Spiegel, *The Last Trial*, 93.

exegetical tradition) but also of the Gentiles."[126] Thus, Hays presupposes that Gen 22:18 lurks in the background of Paul's mind in Gal 3:6 – 9:

> "The faithful Abraham" (3:9) receives from God a blessing that carries with it a promise that the Gentiles will be blessed "in" Abraham and/or "in his seed". This blessing is not said to be contingent upon anything that the Gentiles might do in the future. It cannot be said to be contingent upon anything at all, other than God's grace, it is contingent, in the Genesis story, upon Abraham's obedient faith. That is why the Gentiles are to be blessed, in the words of the promise Paul quotes, "in you".[127]

Hays's observations are helpful, but should be taken further through a comparison with Philo. While Hays draws attention to the use of πίστις and its cognates in *Abr.* 273 as "the most interesting parallel to Paul's discussion of Abraham's faith" in Gal 2:16,[128] he overlooks the Philonic evidence as a significant parallel to the content structure undergirding Gal 3:8 – 9, viz. the correspondence between Abraham's πίστις and God's πίστις rewarded Abraham through the oath of promise. In what follows, I shall offer a comparison between *Abr.* 273 and Gal 3:6 – 9 which may corroborate such a proposal.

Abr. 273 attests that Philo stands in the well-attested expository tradition that related Gen 15:6 to the *Akedah*. In the opening statement in *Abr.* 262, Gen 15:6a is quoted:

> Ἔστι δὲ καὶ ἀνάγραπτος ἔπαινος αὐτῷ χρησμοῖς μαρτυρηθείς, οὓς Μωυσῆς ἐθεσπίσθη, δι' οὗ μηνύεται ὅτι "ἐπίστευσε τῷ θεῷ" [...] (There is another record of praise attested by words from Moses' prophetic lips. In these it is stated that he "trusted in God [...]")[129]

Philo construes Abraham's "trust" in Gen 15:6a, commented on in *Abr.* 262 – 272, as reaching its culmination in God's responsiveness expressed by the oath of promise in Gen 22:16 – 18. Accordingly, in *Abr.* 273, Philo draws the following parallel between Abraham's and God's conduct in terms of πίστις:

> ὃς τῆς πρὸς αὐτὸν πίστεως ἀγάμενος τὸν ἄνδρα πίστιν ἀντιδίδωσιν αὐτῷ, τὴν δι' ὅρκου βεβαίωσιν ὧν ὑπέσχετο δωρεῶν, οὐκέτι μόνον ὡς ἀνθρώπῳ θεός, ἀλλὰ καὶ ὡς φίλος γνωρίμῳ διαλεγόμενος· φησὶ διάνοιαν ἀκλινῶς καὶ παγίως ἔτι μᾶλλον ἢ πρότερον ἐρηρεῖσθαι.

---

126 Hays, *The Faith of Jesus Christ*, 175.

127 Hays, *The Faith of Jesus Christ*, 176.

128 Hays, *The Faith of Jesus Christ*, xlv-lxi, 176 n. 42.

129 Gen 15:6a is either quoted or alluded to by Philo also in *Virt.* 216, 218; *Praem.* 27; *Leg.* 3:228; *Migr.* 43 – 44; *Her.* 90 – 95; *Mut.* 177, 186; *Deus* 4; *QG* 3:2, 58; *QG* 4:17. Other texts that quote Gen 15:6 include 1 Macc 2:52; Jub 14:6; 4Q225 I:7 – 8; Rom 4:3, 22; Gal 3:6; Barn. 13:7; Justin, *Dial.* 92:3; Mek. Exod 14:15, 31; Tanh. Buber Metsora' 5. Allusions are found in Rom 4:9; Heb 11:2; Barn. 13:7; Justin, *Dial.* 23:4. Cf. Schliesser, *Abraham's Faith in Romans 4*, 205 – 8.

> [God], marveling at Abraham's faith in Him, repaid him with faithfulness by confirming with an oath the gifts which he had promised, no longer conversing with him as God might with man, but as one friend with another. For he says, "By myself have I sworn," by him that is whose word is an oath, in order that Abraham's mind may be established still more firmly and immoveably than before.

Here, the line of thought is that God rewards Abraham's trust in terms of His own trust or "faithfulness" by means of the divine oath. Whereas in Gen 22:16 – 18, God is rewarding Abraham specifically for not withholding his son Isaac, Philo, however, takes this passage as a divine response to Abraham's trust in general. Thus, Philo takes this to mean both God's affirmation of Abraham's trust as promise-worthy and His reaffirmation of the existing gifts which He had already promised. Since *Abr.* 275 – 276 and its exposition of Gen 26:5 follow immediately after the reference to the oath of promise in Gen 22:16 – 18 (*Abr.* 273), the preceding verses Gen 26:3 – 4 about the oath of promise reiterated to Isaac may also have been implicit as part of the *continuum* of events which sums up Abraham's biography. Since both Gen 22:16 – 18 and 26:3 – 5 link the promised blessings with Abraham's obedience, Philo's interlocutors probably interpreted both texts about the promise-worthy behavior of Abraham, posited on his observance of the Law of Moses. Philo's emphasis in the context of *Abr.* 273 – 276 that God's oath of promise to Abraham was grounded in Abraham's trust in general (Gen 15:6), rather than in his keeping of the Law of Moses (Gen 26:5), corroborates this assumption.

Correspondingly, Gal 3:8 – 9 can be read as deploying the same exegetical tradition and pattern of thought, based on the conjunction of Gen 15:6 and 22:16 – 18 / 26:3 – 4. Thus, the *continuum* of divine promise of blessings, which structures the Abraham story from the outset (Gen 12:3) is renewed in the climactic statement of the oath of promise (Gen 22:18 / 26:3 – 4). In Gal 3:8 – 9, this *continuum* finds expression in two significant ways: In the first place, Abraham's trust in God, implying at the same time trust in the promise of blessing, is confirmed. The adjective πιστός about Abraham's promiseworthy conduct, centered on his faithful trust in Gal 3:9, can thus be taken to continue Paul's exegetical paraphrase of Gen 15:6 from 3:6 onwards as the terms of reference for the renewed promise of blessings.

Second, God's will to bless is no longer grounded solely in his promise (such as Gen 12:3), but is also confirmed in his responsiveness to Abraham's promise-worthy trust in terms of the oath of promise that renews the promise to Abraham and his descendants (Gen 12:3 / 22:18 / 26:3 – 4). At this juncture, I suggest that Paul adopts the Jewish pattern of thought that saw a parallel between Abraham's conduct of trust and the conduct expected in return from God. The prepositional phrase ἐκ πίστεως in Gal 3:8a can thus be taken to refer to God's faithfulness in terms of keeping his promise to Abraham by an oath, that is, a guarantee or assurance of His support. Abraham, by trusting in God, is already living in that trust which contains the πίστις of God, that is, trust in the divine promise of blessings. Hence, God has met Abraham's initial πίστις by giving him this supreme πίστις, God's own faithfulness by oath, which secures and reaffirms the gifts already promised. Like Philo, Paul, then, indicates that Abraham's trust is affirmed as promise-worthy by his receiving the oath of promise, as a measure of divine faithfulness added to that trust which Abraham antecedently possessed. Such a reference to Abraham's promise-worthy trust, inherent in the oath of promise, may be hinted at and emphasized in the phrase πιστῷ Ἀβραάμ in Gal 3:9.

Such readings of the prepositional phrase ἐκ πίστεως in Gal 3:8a and the adjective πιστός in Gal 3:9 are not without objections. The former represents an interpretative crux. It can be taken to mean: 1) that God justifies the ἔθνη on the basis of their trust,[130] 2) that God justifies on the basis of Abraham's trust in the promise,[131] or 3) it can be read about God's own faithfulness.[132] The two first options focus wholly on the trust of human beings in Gal 3:7–9, by referring to the trust either of the ἔθνη or of Abraham, and thus regard the implied syllogism in these verse as fixated on the inclusion of the ἔθνη on the same basis of trust as Abraham. If we take v. 7 as the first premise, v. 8 as the second premise, and v. 9 as the conclusion, the syllogism goes like this:

v. 7. Those of trust (οἱ ἐκ πίστεως) are Abraham's sons.
v. 8. On the basis of trust (ἐκ πίστεως), God justifies the ἔθνη.
v. 9. Therefore, those of faith (οἱ ἐκ πίστεως, including the ἔθνη) are *blessed* with the believing Abraham.

Such a reading of 3:7–9 fails to take into account an alternative interpretation of the syllogism in which ἐκ πίστεως in Gal 3:8a can be taken to refer both to Abraham's promiseworthy conduct of trust *and* to God's own conduct of faithfulness by virtue of the oath of promise expected in return, reflected in the composite citation rendered in Gal 3:8b, and with an analogy in *Abr.* 273. In favour of this reading, that Paul in Gal 3:8a equates the performance of justifying the ἔθνη (ἐκ πίστεως) with the promise to Abraham that they would be blessed by

130 Thus most commentators; see, most recently, deSilva, *The Letter to the Galatians*, 284, and A.A. Das, *Galatians*, ConcC (St. Louis, MO: Concordia Publishing House, 2014), 255.
131 Thus, de Boer, *Galatians*, 193.
132 Cf. Hays, *The Faith of Jesus Christ*, 176.

God, that is, apart from any "faith" on the part of the "nations".[133] Thus, the issue of justification here possibly refers to the way God manifests His righteousness, that is, by keeping the oath of promise spoken to Abraham according to Gen 22:18 and Gen 26:3 – 4.[134] Accordingly, if 3:7– 9 form a syllogism, it may be thought of as taking the following form:

v. 7. Those of trust (οἱ ἐκ πίστεως) are Abraham's sons.

v. 8. On the basis of Abraham's trust and God's faithfulness (ἐκ πίστεως), God justifies the "nations" according to the oath of promise of blessings that is renewed to Abraham.

v. 9. Therefore, those of faith (οἱ ἐκ πίστεως) are *blessed* together with the faithful Abraham (πιστῷ Ἀβραάμ), that is, according to the measure of divine faithfulness given to Abraham through the oath of promise on the basis of his initial trust in the promise.

The emphasis on Abraham's obedience posited on his promise-worthy faithfulness in Gal 3:9 makes evident the polemical nature of Paul's statement. As I have already pointed out, Paul seems to refer to the authoritative figure of Abraham as the foundational model for Jews and proselytes, i. e. those who, like Abraham, embraced the promise out of trust (ἐκ πίστεως) in contradistinction to "those working the Law of Moses" (ἐξ ἔργων νόμου). The same antithesis seems to be implied here in v. 9 too. Thus, it is likely that Paul participates in the Jewish discourse on Abraham's relationship to the Law of Moses. As we have seen in chapter four, the discussion attested in Philo's writings on such a negotiation may provide a context for a corresponding Jewish debate reflected in Galatians. The idea attested in Sir 44:20, from which also Philo's interlocutors in *Abr.* 275 – 276 and most probably Paul's rivals in Galatians took their bearings, saw the oath of promise posited on Abraham's faithful obedience to the Law of Moses (Gen 26:4 – 5). Philo interpreted the Genesis texts about and to Abraham (Gen 15:6 and Gen 22:16 – 18) as a fulfillment of the divine Law in Nature (Gen 26:5), in contradistinction to his interlocutors, who interpreted the same *continuum* of texts as a biography of Abraham portrayed as compliant with the Law of

---

133 Thus Hays, *The Faith of Jesus Christ*, 176 – 7. *Pace* Watson (*Paul and the Hermeneutics of Faith*, 186), who understands "faith" in Gal 3:7– 9 as "the human acknowledgment of the divine saving action announced in the gospel and, in anticipatory form, in the promise," Watson himself seems almost to contradict such a view, when he admits that Paul's expository reading of the promise in Gal 3:8 is first of all a statement about God and His action.

134 Cf. Rom 3:3 – 4 for a similar equation of God's faithfulness and the manifestation of God's righteousness, i. e., that God vindicated Himself as being righteous by keeping his words. Cf. H. Ljungman, *PISTIS: A Study of Its Presuppositions and Its Meaning in Pauline Use*, Acta: Skrifter Utgiven Av Kungl. Humanistiska Vetenskapssamfundet i Lund (Lund: Gleerup, 1964), 37– 47.

Moses. Paul, not unlike Philo, dissociates the faithful Abraham (πιστῷ Ἀβραάμ, 3:9) from Law-obedience (ἐξ ἔργων νόμου, cf. 3:2, 5).Thus, the oath of promise (3:8b) is not seen as contingent upon Abraham's obedience to the Law of Moses, as suggested by Gen 26:4–5, that the Lord will bless others *because* of Abraham's adherence to the Law. Rather, it was the particular kind of Abraham's responsiveness, when he previously heard the "gospel" (προευαγγελίζομαι) of promise with trust (cf. Paul's use of the expression ἐξ ἀκοῆς πίστεως in 3:5–6, referring back to this faith-event), that made him worthy of receiving the oath of promise.

To sum up: The purpose of Paul's conjunction of Gen 15:6 and Gen 22:18 / 26:3–4 appears to be to link Abraham's faithful piety of trust with the promised blessing and with God's promise in a way reminiscent of the divine oath of promise spoken to him and his descendant. Thus, like Philo, Paul seems to regard the existing promise of blessing as secured and reaffirmed as an oath of promise because of Abraham's promise-worthy trust in God. Thus, the oath of promise, ensuing upon Abraham's trust (Gen 15:6 followed by Gen 22:18 / 26:4), is a reaffirmation of an already existing promise of blessing (Gen 12:3), but its terms of reference have been altered. The blessing of the "nations" is now grounded in the correspondence between Abraham's trust and God's faithfulness by oath. As a corollary, "those of trust" are blessed together with the faithful Abraham; this is regarded as an emulation of Abraham's promise-worthy conduct and as a confirmation of God's faithfulness to keep his promise, Gal 3:9. Thus, unlike other Jewish expositions of the oath of promise, it is not seen as contingent upon Abraham's obedience to the Law, but rather as grounded in the correspondence between God's faithfulness *and* Abraham's faithfulness.

As I have argued, despite differences, Paul is close to Philo in several ways. Both Paul and Philo maintain a distinction within the concept of Torah, between what we can call an "Abrahamic jurisdiction", centered on Abraham's trust in God and his promise, attested by the Torah's own report about Abraham, and antecedent to the "Mosaic jurisdiction" later revealed through Moses at Sinai. Furthermore, both authors seem to participate in an intramural Jewish discussion of Abraham's relation to the Law of Moses, in which they separate Abraham's trust in the promise from his obedience to the Law. Thus, both authors take the figure of Abraham as representing the foundational and authoritative legal model and norm. Moreover, despite differences, both Paul and Philo try to show how the Law of Moses stands in a dynamic relationship to the legal figure of identification represented by Abraham as the archetype of the believers. According to Philo, it was possible for human beings to live by the "Law" of Abraham, since the the Law of Moses was a written record of Abraham's virtues achieved through his instinctive words and deeds (cf. *Abr.* 4–5). Hence, the access to the earlier Abrahamic divine Law was then mediated through the observance of the Mosaic Law. Paul, however, draws the opposite conclusion on the dynamic relationship between the two distinctive jurisdictions attested by the Torah and Scripture. In the light of the Christ-event, Paul reconceptualizes the dynamic of the "Abrahamic" and "Mosaic" jurisdictions for Jews and converts. As I shall argue below, Paul applies both "jurisdictions" to Christ, in order to make clear the ground on which the descendants from Abraham are heirs of the promise through having received the blessing of the Spirit by trust. As we may surmise from the literary context of Galatians, Paul at the least had to expect a potential objection, namely that believers were legitimate descendants and partakers of the promise of blessing only on condition that they emulated Abraham's promise-worthy behavior posited on circumcision and obedience to the Law of Moses. Paul backs his view by proceeding to a further argument in Gal 3:10 – 14, to which I now turn.

5 Gal 3:10 – 14: The Event of the Crucified Christ in the Light of the Two Jurisdictions at Work in the Torah and Scripture

In this section, I argue that Paul's "figural interpretation"[135] of the event of Christ's crucifixion pertains to the dynamic of the two conceptions he sees at work in the Torah and Scripture, i. e., the "Mosaic jurisdiction" and the "Abrahamic jurisdiction", summarized in the short phrases ἐξ ἔργων νόμου and ἐκ πίστεως, respectively. The referential background for such an interpretive move also runs through the whole chapter of Gal 3:1– 29, namely, the connection Paul establishes between the two figures and events of Abraham and Christ that he finds inherent in Scripture, so that they are reciprocally enlightening: the first imparts a more profound signification to the second, and vice versa. Or, in the

135 The concept of "figural interpretation" derives from E. Auerbach, who describes it as follows: "Figural interpretation establishes a connection between two events or persons in such a way that the first signifies not only itself but also the second, while the second involves or fulfils the first" (quoted from E. Auerbach, *Mimesis: The Representation of Reality in Western Literature*, trans. W.R. Trask (Princeton: Princeton University Press, 1953), 73. *Pace* R.B. Hays, *Reading Backwards: Figural Christology and the Fourfold Gospel Witness* (Waco, TX: Baylor University Press, 2014), 2 – 3, who maintains that the figure of correspondence is primarily retrospective rather than prospective. Thus, he seems to underestimate the process of figural interpretation as reciprocal, in which the significance of the events flows both ways.

terms of E. Auerbach, we may say that "the first signifies not only itself but also the second, while the second involves or fulfils the first".[136]

As I shall further elaborate below, the "figural reinterpretation" of the Christ event relative to God's promise to Abraham and the Law of Moses accords well with Paul's reasoning in the preceding verses in Gal 3:1–9.

5.1 The Crucified Christ interpreted within the Context of the "Mosaic Jurisdiction"

In section 3.1 above, I argued that the legal sense of προγράφω relative to the event of Christ's crucifixion in Gal 3:1 draws on Paul's reasoning in 2:21: if the Galatians still insist on living by the righteousness of the Law, they risk placing themselves within the jurisdiction that brought Christ to be crucified, that is to say, executed and publicly hanged as a cursed criminal. In Gal 3:10 – 14, Paul continues to argue why the crucified Christ manifested that the curse of the Law was in fact operative on those who failed to observe the commandments within the jurisdiction of the Law. With regard to this position, more attention should be paid to how the thematic statement of Gal 3:1 on Christ's crucifixion is explicated further in Gal 3:10 and 3:13 and pertains to redemption from the curse of the Law .

Gal 3:10 reads: "For all who rely on the works of the law are under a curse; for it is written, 'Cursed is everyone who does not observe and obey all the things written in the book of the law'." Paul's implied reasoning in Gal 3:10 has been difficult to unravel.[137] On the surface of Paul's citation of Deut 27:26 here, one would think that the words "all who rely on the works of the Law" means that they would not incur the curse, since Paul affirms that the curse falls on those who *fail to do* the Law. What exactly Paul meant by the citation of Deut 27:26 in Gal 3:10 is a conundrum that has led to various interpretations by scholars. I shall briefly present some of the solutions which have been posed. First, one solution has been to assume the implied premise under Paul's reasoning that no one is able to do "all the things written in the book of the Law."[138]

136 E. Auerbach, *Mimesis*, 73.

137 For a survey of research on Gal 3:10 – 14, see R.B. Matlock, "Helping Paul's Argument Work? The Curse of Galatians 3.10 – 14," in *The Torah in the New Testament: Papers Delivered at the Manchester–Lausanne Seminar of June 2008*, ed. M. Taites and P. Oakes, LNTS (London: T & T Clark, 2009), 154–79.

138 Thus, e. g., R. Bultmann, *Theology of the New Testament: Volume 1*, trans. K. Grobel (New York: Scribners, 1951), 263.

The problem with this interpretation of the law's "unfulfillability" is that such a notion seems to have been bewildering in a Jewish context.[139] Moreover, in Phil 3:6, Paul claims the opposite, viz. that he, as a Pharisee, was blameless with regard to the law.[140]

Second, another solution is to attribute to Paul the view that Israel was in the same position as when the book of Deuteronomy itself was written, i.e., in exile because they were accursed. Thus, Paul's message to the Galatians was that to live by the Law meant to place themselves under the curse alongside Israel.[141] This solution is unconvincing, since Paul nowhere in Galatians indicates such a view of a collective accursed Israel. Rather, he seems to argue in 3:11 in an individualizing manner that "no one is justified before God by the law."

Third, another and more attractive solution is that Paul quotes a *dictum* made by his opponents and applies it for his own purposes. The assumption is that the opponents have quoted Deut 27:26 as a threat in order to impose upon the Galatians the importance of keeping the Law. Accordingly, if they do not follow the path prescribed by them, they will be cursed by the Law, and so also be deprived of the blessing of Abraham, which is the promised Spirit, that depends on being circumcised and keeping the Law.[142] A weakness with this "mirror-reading" of Paul is that it presupposes that the Law has universal applicability, so that the curse of the Law is operative on both its observer and its non-observer. This interpretation runs counter not only to the actual wording of the citation of Deut 27:26, but also to Paul's explicit application of it. The citation in itself then refers to the curse incurring on those who fail to do the Law. As such, the citation concerns those who live under the jurisdiction of the Law, not those who have not yet placed themselves under it.

Fourth, another approach is to understand Gal 3:10 in the light of the reference to the crucifixion of Jesus Christ in v. 1 and in v. 13. So, when Deut 21:23 ("Cursed be every one who hangs on a tree") is applied in Gal 3:13 to Christ

---

139 Cf. Matlock, "Helping Paul's Argument Work," 156–7; M. Cranford, "The Possibility of Perfect Obedience: Paul and an Implied Premise in Gal 3:10 and 5:3," *NovT* 36.3 (1994): 243; R.B. Hays, *The Letter to the Galatians: Introduction, Commentary, and Reflections*, NIB (Nashville: Abingdon, 2000), 257.

140 The reference to Phil 3:6, as invoking Paul's view of the possibility of obeying the law, is associated with K. Stendahl, *Paul Among Jews and Gentiles* (Philadelphia: Fortress Press, 1976), 80–81.

141 For this position, see N.T. Wright, *The Climax of the Covenant: Christ and the Law in Pauline Theology* (Edinburgh: T & T Clark, 1991), 138, 140, 142, 145–8.

142 Thus, e.g., C.K. Barrett, "The Allegory of Abraham, Sarah, and Hagar in the Argument of Galatians," in *Essays on Paul* (London: SPCK, 1982), 159; Martyn, *Galatians*, 325.

Jesus, the premise is that he is thought of as a lawbreaker. This implication concurs with the legal statement about a lawbreaker expressed in Deut 27:26 and the portrait of Jesus Christ as publicly crucified in 3:1, which in turn presupposes that he is presented as one who was liable to be punished as a criminal.[143] If we read the citation of Deut 27:26 in Gal 3:10 in isolation, it applies to Christ Jesus and came into force as in the following paraphrase: "Cursed be Christ Jesus who did not abide by all things written in the book of the law to do them." In its present context, however, and from Paul's new perspective, he further interprets the event of the crucified Christ as a cursed law breaker as taking place "*for us*" (Gal 3:11), and this made it evident that "those who rely on the law are under a curse" (Gal 3:10a).

A more suggestive approach would be to combine the latter solution with Paul's distinction in the concept of the Torah of two jurisdictions at work in a dynamic that proves separate points in a consecutive and coherent argument. As I shall argue, this proposal also indicates that Paul takes part in a broader negotiation on Abraham in his own days (see above and section 6 below), in which Abraham's trust in God's promise can both be separated from and associated with his alleged observance of the Law of Moses. As we have seen, the discussion attested, for example, in Philo's writings on such a negotiation may provide a Jewish context for a corresponding intramural debate that is reflected in Galatians.

Since Paul argues *e contrario* that "those of trust", who emulate Abraham and embrace the promise, are justified and blessed by God (Gal 3:8b–9), he seems to presuppose that the oath of promise given to Abraham applies to those who live under the jurisdiction of the Sinaitic Law.[144] It is noteworthy that this understanding and the same cluster of motifs and their implicit scriptures referring to a *continuum* of the Abrahamic events in Genesis recur in Sirach and Philo. The conception of Abraham attested in Sir 44:20 – 21 is particularly relevant as a comparative referential background for Paul:

20 He kept the law of the Most High,
and entered into a covenant with him;
he certified the covenant in his flesh,
and when he was tested he proved faithful.
21 Therefore the Lord assured him with an oath
that the nations would be blessed through his offspring [...]

143 Cf. P. Borgen, "Openly Portrayed," 349 – 51; T.A. Wilson, *The Curse of the Law and the Crisis in Galatia: Reassessing the Purpose of Galatians*, WUNT 2 (Tübingen: Mohr Siebeck, 2007), 55.
144 For a similar reasoning, see Dahl, *Studies in Paul*, 170.

At this juncture, parts of Abraham's story, such as his trust in God (Gen 15:6), the covenant God made with him (Gen 15:9 – 18), his circumcision (Gen 17:10), and the oath of promise (Gen 22:18, Gen 26:4) are interpreted by the author of Sirach as in a *continuum.*[145] Sir 44:20 – 21 thus attests a solid exegetical tradition (based on Gen 15:6, 22:16 – 18, and 26:3 – 5), from which also Philo's interlocutors in *Abr.* 275 – 276 and most probably Paul's rivals in Galatians took their bearings, that held that the oath of promise given to Abraham was contingent on his obedience to the Law of Moses (cf. Gen 26:5). Hence, Paul's statements in Gal 3:10 – 25 may presuppose a reasoning along these lines and provide a backing for his own view that would be controversial. So, for example, Dahl conjectures: "He had to expect the objection that believers were legitimate descendants of Abraham and partakers of the promise only on the condition that they were also circumcized and kept the Law."[146]

In Gal 3:10, Paul explicitly aligns "works of Law" with the issue of a "curse" that takes effect when the laws are transgressed. Hence, Paul presupposes in Gal 3:10 that those living within the jurisdiction of the Law, only incur punishment and curse, and not blessing, and he quotes from Deut 27:26 as evidence: "for it is written, "Cursed is everyone *who does not observe and obey all the things* written in the book of the law." In this way, Paul makes it explicit that the jurisdiction of the Mosaic Law is not a means toward the fulfillment of the Abrahamic blessings. Furthermore, Paul seems to have distinguished the promise of blessing conferred on Abraham in Genesis from the Deuteronomic conditional promise. According to Gen 22:16 – 18 and 26:3 – 5, Abraham's faithful obedience is not seen as conditional for the blessings, but is only incorporated as the ground for the oath of promise as a reaffirmation of an existing promise of blessing.[147] Thus, the obedience that brings blessing is already an established fact in the past, while the Deuteronomic promise of blessing is a future possibility conditioned on observance of the Law.

Previous research has failed to note that both Philo and Paul say that the oath of promise was grounded in Abraham's and God's πίστις, not in the *Akedah* and Abraham's obedience to the Law of Moses. The precedent and parallel in Philo's appropriation and discussion of the same exegetical tradition demonstrates that Paul's line of thought would have resonated in the context of a Jewish debate on Abraham relative to the law of Moses. In a way that corresponds to Philo, then, Paul separates the oath of promise (3:8b) from the *Akedah* and Abra-

145 Cf. Sandnes, *Paul Perceived*, 148 – 54; deSilva, *The Letter to the Galatians*, 280 – 1; Sass, *Leben aus den Verheissungen*, 223 – 5.

146 Dahl, *Paul's Letter to the Galatians*, 56.

147 Cf. Moberly, "The Earliest Commentary on the Akedah," 320.

ham's obedience to the Law, as suggested by Gen 22:16 and 26:3 – 5. Rather, similar to Philo, Paul takes the oath of promise as a response to Abraham's trust in general. Thus, it was the general kind of Abraham's responsiveness, when he embraced the "gospel" (προευαγγελίζομαι) of promise with trust (ἐξ ἀκοῆς πίστεως, cf. 3:5 – 6), that secured his reception of the oath of promise. Thus, Paul, unlike both the author of Sirach and Philo's interlocutors, highlights the promised blessings (3:8 – 10) apart from circumcision (3:3), Law-obedience (ἐξ ἔργων νόμου, 3:2, 5, 10), and the covenant associated with the Law (3:15 – 18). In chapter 4 above, we have also shown that rabbinic sources too might be cautiously taken to attest a corresponding inner-Jewish debate, where it is claimed that Abraham received the promise of blessing prior to and apart from his circumcision and observance of the Law.

In support of the view that "those of trust" (οἱ ἐκ πίστεως) are blessed and "those who are of the works of the Law" (Ὅσοι γὰρ ἐξ ἔργων νόμου) can only incur its curse, Paul provides another proof from Scripture, i.e., Hab 2:4 and Lev 18:5, respectively. Scholars have tended to interpret Paul's appropriation of these scriptures in terms of a contradiction of passages in Scripture, or as a opposition of "faith" and "Law", or as expressing a supersession of the Mosaic legislation caused by the Christ event, or as a contrast between Torah and promise.[148] I shall suggest that they rather represent an effort on Paul's part to elaborate in more fundametnal terms the juxtaposition and dynamic interaction of the two distinctive jurisdictions and their basic principles that are at work in Scripture and are now manifested as operative in the Christ event. This means that Paul interprets the event of the crucified Christ in the light of both the "Mosaic jurisdiction" (centered on "works" in accordance with the Law) and the "Abrahamic jurisdiction" (centered on Abraham's trust and God's promise) and of the dynamic relationship that exists between them, which contributed to the realization of the promise of God.

In an essay on "Contradictions in Scripture", Dahl claimed that Paul's interpretation of Hab 2:4 and Lev 18:5 was to be considered in the light of the treatment of conflicting scriptural passages in contemporary Jewish hermeneutics. According to Dahl, the basic rule in terms of the 13th middah of R. Ishmael most probably went back to rabbi Hillel's famous resolution of antinomies in Scripture, namely that "two scriptural passages contradicting each other should

148 For a review of scholarship on Gal 3:11 – 12 and the relationship between these passages of Scripture, cf. P. Sprinkle, *Law and Life: The Interpretation of Leviticus 18:5 in Early Judaism and Paul*, WUNT 2 (Tübingen: Mohr Siebeck, 2008), 8 – 14.

be upheld with the help of a distinction in the interpretation of the two contexts."[149] So, Dahl suggested:

> The whole train of thought in Gal 3:1–12 rests on the presupposition that Hab 2:4 and Lev. 18:5 contradict one another, and that the corresponding principles "by faith" and "by (works of) the law" mutually exclude one another as qualifications for justification and life.[150]

Dahl held that the problem of two contradictive scriptures is solved by Paul himself in his words in Gal 3:22:

> "Scripture consigned all things to sin, that what was promised to faith in Jesus Christ might be given to those who believe" (v. 22). Thus, Paul finds no contradiction here. Rightly understood, the Law is in harmony with the promises. It had a subordinate function which contributed to the realization of the promise.[151]

Against Dahl, Betz argues that Paul is not concerned with the rabbinic problem of passages that contradict each other. Thus, the scriptures of Hab 2:4 and Lev 18:5 represent opposite principles of "faith" and "law" in the context of a coherent argument:

> According to Pauline theology, Scripture says that the *concepts* of "faith" and "law" are opposites. This is different from the rabbinic problem of two Scripture *texts* opposing each other. For Paul, Hab 2:4 and Lev 18:5 do not contradict each other, but prove separate points in a consecutive argument.[152]

Other scholars have interpreted Paul's reference to Hab 2:4 as played off against Lev 18:5, because of the temporal fact that the Mosaic legislation has come to an

---

149 N.A. Dahl, *Studies in Paul*, 164. Dahl's essay is a variation of a hypotesis that Paul made use of Ishmael's 13th middah, set forth by H.J. Schoeps, *Paul: The Theology of the Apostle in the Light of Jewish Religious History*, trans. H. Knight (Philadelphia: The Westminster Press, 1961), 177–83. In a response to Dahl's article, J. Vos ("Die Hermeneutische Antinomie bei Paulus [Galater 3.11–12; Römer 10.5–10]," *NTS* 38.2 [1992]: 254–70) claims that Paul's reasoning has a close affinity with Hellenistic rhetoric, and that Paul was primarily concerned to resolve the tension between law and promise, rather than to resolve an apparent contradiction between two passages of Scripture.

150 Dahl, *Studies in Paul*, 170.

151 Dahl, *Studies in Paul*, 173–4.

152 Betz, *Galatians*, 138 n. 8.

end and has been replaced by Christ, who has ushered in a new era of faith.[153] A variant of this temporal argument, where the era of the Christ event has superseded the Torah, has been presented most recently by J.M.G. Barclay. In his view, the "Torah was neither integral to the story of the promise nor effective in securing its fulfillment".[154] Thus, Torah has been removed from the trajectory of promise, since it was not capable of fulfilling the promise, which is accomplished only by faith when Christ comes. This contrast between the Torah and the promise relative to the Christ event then provides the framework for Barclay's reading of Hab 2:4 and Lev 18:5:

> The compressed argument in 3:11–12, contrasting Habakkuk 2:4 with Leviticus 18:5, reinforces the incapacity of the Torah. Because no one is found "righteous" in the sight of God within the terms of the Torah, righteousness is promised (in Habakkuk) on the basis of faith; and the Torah concerns not faith but the practice of its own commandments. Thus the Torah cannot produce the conditions (faith) in which the promise can be fulfilled, and in which it would be fulfilled when "faith arrived" at the coming of Christ (3:14, 25).[155]

A more viable understanding of Hab 2:4 and Lev 18:5 would take these scriptures together with several other scriptural references in Gal 3:1–14 as representing two distinctive jurisdictions[156] attested in the Law and Scripture.[157] Thus, rather than taking Hab 2:4 and Lev 18:5 to be passages portraying either contradiction, opposition, or contrast between faith and the promise, or between faith and the Law, more attention should be paid to their function within the dynamic interaction of two distinctive and juxtaposed jurisdictions at work in Scripture (Gal 3:11–12) and in the context of Paul's interpretation of the Christ event (Gal

---

153 So, e.g., Wright, *The Climax of the Covenant: Christ and the Law in Pauline Theology*, 148–52; K.A. Morland, *The Rhetoric of Curse in Galatians: Paul Confronts Another Gospel*, Emory Studies in Early Christianity (Atlanta, GA: Scholars Press, 1995), 224–5.

154 Barclay, *Paul and the Gift*, 404.

155 Barclay, *Paul and the Gift*, 405–6.

156 As I mentioned in chapter one, a terminology of two legal entities seen at work in Gal 3:1–14 has been applied by various scholars. So, e.g., Vos ("Antinomie," 257) takes Hab 2:4 and Lev 18:5 as representing two opposing halachot, put forward by two rivals or different parties. Borgen ("Perspectives for Mission," 186) lists these scriptures under what he calls the "Abrahamic jurisdiction" and the "Sinaitic jurisdiction". Unfortunately, however, both Borgen's and Vos' proposals, while suggestive, remain preliminary, sketchy, and undeveloped.

157 In a previous study of Rom 9:30–10:8, I (*The Word is Near You*, 181–2) suggested that Paul's interpretation of Lev 18:5 and Deut 30:12–14, summarized under the key phrases "by the works of law" and "by faith" respectively, would seem to imply a distinction within the Old Testament concept of the Law. Instead of talking about such a dialectic within the Law, I now rather suggest that we should speak about two distinctive jurisdictions manifested in the Law *and* the Scripture.

3:13–14). This means that each of the two jurisdictions of “trust” and “works of Law” has a specific meaning of its own relative to the Christ event. In order to elaborate on this proposal, I turn to a closer analysis of Gal 3:11–12. Here, the propositions made by Paul, followed by references to scriptural texts, can be displayed as follows:

Gal 3:11:

<u>Proposition</u>:
a: And because no one is justified before God in the law, it is evident that

<u>Attestation from Scripture</u>:
b: the just one from trust shall live (Hab 2:4 LXX)

Gal 3:12:

<u>Proposition</u>:
a: The Law, however, is not from trust, but

<u>Attestation from the Law of Moses</u>:
b: the one having done them shall live in them (Lev 18:5 LXX)

At this juncture of his argument, then, Paul juxtaposes two jurisdictions he sees at work in Scripture, i.e. the “Abrahamic jurisdiction” and the “Mosaic jurisdiction”. In Gal 3:11a, Paul continues the line of thought from the preceding v. 10, that within the “jurisdiction of Law”, only the curse applies. This makes it evident that righteousness and life are attained and manifested within the “Abrahamic jurisdiction” (cf. Gen 15:6 and Hab 2:4). The difference and distinction between the two jurisdictions is expressed both in the propositions and in the scriptural references attached to them. As I mentioned above (2.1), the proposition in 3:11a is an exegetical paraphrase of Ps. 142:2 LXX, “for no one living is righteous before you”. This statement cannot be taken in an absolute way, because those of trust are justified (cf. Gen 15:6; Hab 2:4). Thus, the exegetical clarification ascribed to the Psalm passage by Paul means that it should be interpreted in a more restricted sense about the jurisdiction of the Law, that is, “because in the Law no one (living) is justified before God.”[158] Such a paraphrase of Ps 142:2 LXX may also support the causal translation of the first ὅτι clause as a continuation of the preceding v. 10, with Hab 2:4 taken as the conclusion: “And because (ὅτι) in the law no one is justified before God, it is evident that (δῆλος ὅτι) the just one from trust shall live”.[159] The general formulation of Hab 2:4 in Gal 3:11b is a further example of how Paul employs scriptural generalizations as a

158 So, Dahl, *Studies in Paul*, 170 n. 18.
159 For this translation and the scholarly discussion of it, cf. e.g. de Boer, *Galatians*, 202–3.

paradigm similar to his way of referring to Gen 15:6 in Gal 3:6 and different from a marked self-contained citation. As to the wording, the main discussion has revolved around the question whether the prepositional phrase ἐκ πίστεως refers back to and modifies the subject ὁ δίκαιος or points forward to the verb ζήσεται, or both? In Paul's letters and in the immediate context of Gal 3:11b, ἐκ πίστεως is never assocated with life, while it is repeatedly connected with cognates of the verb δικαιόω (cf. 2:16, 17; 3:8, 24; 5:5) or the substantive δικαιοσύνη (cf. 2:21; 3:6). Thus, it is probable that Paul reads the verse as "the one who is righteous by faith shall live." However, another question remains: does the verb ζήσεται refer to eschatological life or to a certain conduct or manner of living? The observation that the words in Gal 3:11b correspond to formulations in Gal 3:11a and the following citation of Lev 18:5 in Gal 3:12b corroborates the understanding that ζήσεται refers to a distinct mode of living. This correspondence of words between Gal 3:11a, Gal 3:11b, and Gal 3:12b can be displayed as follows (the corresponding expressions have been underscored):

Gal 3:11a: ὅτι δὲ <u>ἐν νόμῳ</u> οὐδεὶς <u>δικαιοῦται</u> παρὰ τῷ θεῷ [...]
Gal 3:11b: ὅτι <u>*ὁ δίκαιος*</u> <u>*ἐκ πίστεως*</u> <u>*ζήσεται*</u>· (Hab 2:4 LXX)
Gal 3:12b: *ὁ ποιήσας αὐτὰ* <u>*ζήσεται*</u> <u>*ἐν αὐτοῖς*</u>. (Lev 18:5 LXX)

The negative formulation οὐδεὶς δικαιοῦται corresponds to the positive scriptural expression ὁ δίκαιος, and ἐν νόμῳ corresponds to ἐκ πίστεως.[160] Likewise, ἐκ πίστεως ζήσεται in the formulation of Hab 2:4 corresponds to ζήσεται ἐν αὐτοῖς in the citation of Lev 18:5. The conclusion that can be drawn on the basis of these parallel formulations is that to live "in the law" (v.11a) and "in them (i.e., the observance of the law by doing them; v. 12b)" and to "live from trust" are understood as living within two mutually exclusive jurisdictions qualified by righteousness and trust and by observance of the law, respectively.[161]

This explanation of what ζήσεται means, referring to a certain mode of living within two mutually exclusive jurisdictions, is confirmed by the proposition Paul makes in Gal 3:12a: ὁ δὲ νόμος οὐκ ἔστιν ἐκ πίστεως. As we have observed above (in section 2.2), Paul here employs the exegetical texhnique of abandoning one meaning of a scripture in contrast to its proper meaning, in order to distinguish between what it means "to live" according to the jurisdiction of Law (summar-

---

160 Cf. Watson, "By Faith (of Christ): An Exegetical Dilemma and its Scriptural Solution," in *The Faith of Jesus Christ: Exegetical, Biblical, and Theological Studies*, ed. M.F. Bird and P.M. Sprinkle (Peabody, MA: Hendrickson, 2009), 161.

161 For a similar interpretation of ζήσεται in Gal 3:11b in the light of the context, see de Boer, *Galatians*, 207–8.

ized by the formula ἐξ ἔργων νόμου and stated in Lev 18:5) as distinct from the jurisdiction of trust (summarized by the formula ἐκ πίστεως expressed in Gen 15:6 about Abraham's trust in God's promise and in Scripture as such according to Hab 2:4).

In sum, Paul's formulations and juxtaposition of Hab 2:4 and Lev 18:5 (in which he only borrows words from the scriptures without any indication of a marked quotation) do not then reflect a tension or contradiction in Scripture as such, but refer rather to two distinctive jurisdictions in the Torah and Scripture. Thus, as we shall see below, this distinction between these two jurisdictions is presupposed by Paul with regard to the specific role they have in their own right relative to the event of Christ.

Paul's logic, that those under the "Mosaic jurisdiction" can only incur its curse, might further be explained by his application of the citations of Deuteronomy (not only Deut 21:23 in Gal 3:13, but also Deut 27:26 in Gal 3:10) to the crucifixion of Christ. In accordance with Paul's emphatic and vivid formulation in Gal 3:1 that the crucified Jesus Christ had been publicly "proscribed", Christ is precisely exhibited openly as the one who suffered the curse by virtue of being "hanged on the tree" (cf. Deut 21:23 in Gal 3:13), and who for this reason was exposed in public as a lawbreaker within the "Mosaic jurisdiction" (cf. Deut 27:26 in Gal 3:10). Thus, in both Gal 3:10 and 3:13, words from the Law about a curse are cited, offering the legal evidence for the proposition formulated by Paul.[162] In the following quotations, words from the Law are in italics:

Gal 3:10:

Proposition:

> For all who rely on "the works of *law*" are under *a curse*; [...]

Legal evidence from the Law of Moses:

> For it is written,
> *Cursed is everyone who does not observe and obey all the things written in the book of the law.* Deut 27:26

162 It is to be noted that the adjective ἐπικατάρατος occurs both in Deut 27:26 cited in Gal 3:10 and in Deut 21:23 cited in Gal 3:13. Thus, the hermeneutical rule of *gezerah shavah* seems to be at work, which means that when two passages of Scripture have a phrase in common the interpretation of each might be illuminated by the other.

Gal 3:13:

Proposition:

> Christ redeemed us from *the curse* of the *law*, by becoming *a curse* for us [...].

Legal evidence from the Law of Moses:

> For it is written,
> *Cursed be every one who hangs on a tree.* Deut 21:23

In Gal 3:13, Deut 21:23 LXX is applied to the case of the crucifixion of Christ, and interpreted within the context of the curse of the law, which means he is seen as a cursed lawbreaker. Deut 21:22–23 states that the one who is hanged on a tree is a criminal who himself has committed a crime punishable by death: "And if a man has committed a crime punishable by death and he is put to death, and you hang him on a tree, his body shall not remain all night upon the tree, but you shall bury him on the same day, for a hanged man is accursed by God [...]." This accords with Paul's thematic statement in Gal 3:1 and the ambigious meanings of προγράφω there; when Jesus Christ has been openly exposed as having been crucified, he is not only seen as one who had been sentenced and executed as a lawbreaker, but also as one hanged publicly as a manifestation of his having been cursed by the Law. Paul's vivid usage of such terminology of a public exposure of the crucified Jesus Christ before the eyes of the Galatians, then, accords with what is stated as a general legal rule about a lawbreaker in Deut 27:26, cited in Gal 3:10: this person is accursed as a lawbreaker according to the jurisdiction of the Law. In the light of the immediate context of Gal 2:21, Paul's portrait of the crucified Jesus Christ as a "proscribed" criminal was meant to deter the Galatians from being subjected to the jurisdiction of the Law, and thus being put under the threat of a curse of the Law for all who fail to do it.[163] Both as a previous persecutor of the Church and later as an apostle, Paul himself had probably maintained the historical circumstance that Jesus Christ was executed and publicly exposed on the cross as a cursed criminal. This historical reference and view is already presupposed in the pointed formulation in Gal 2:21: "[...] if justification were through the law, then Christ died for nothing." According to the jurisdiction of the Law, Christ's death was then merely the common punishment of one who was sentenced to death and hanged for the sake of deterrence by exposing his body as a cursed criminal according to the

163 For a similar reading of the application of Deut 27:26 to Jesus Christ, see Dahl, *Studies in Paul*, 171–2; Borgen, "Openly Portrayed," 350.

regulations of Deut 27:26 and Deut 21:23. Instead of succumbing to the threat of such a curse by siding with the teaching of Paul's opponents, the Galatians should stick to what he had proclaimed. Thus, in Paul's mind the "Mosaic jurisdiction" attested in scriptures such as Deut 21:23 and Deut 27:26 might be taken to apply to Christ's vicarious death as a lawbreaker. Accordingly, as an apostle, Paul changed his position, and interpreted Christ's crucifixion differently, as he also stated in the proposition in Gal 3:13: Christ redeemed us from the curse of the Law, by becoming a curse "*for us*". Paul's "new perspective" became then: Although Jesus Christ was innocent, he became, by virtue of being crucified, a curse "for us". Furthermore, by virtue of the notion that Christ Jesus was accursed vicariously "for us", a legal redemption from the Law has occurred, and this has made it evident that those who subjected themselves to the jurisdiction of the Law were themselves under the condemnation of those who do not keep all of it. In order to anticipate any further objections to his message, Paul elaborates why the two jurisdictions in the Torah and Scripture were both designed in their own right to pertain to the event of Christ. In order to bolster such a claim, I turn to a closer analysis of Gal 3:14.[164]

5.2 The Crucified Christ interpreted within the Context of the "Abrahamic Jurisdiction"

Since Gal 3:14 draws the consequences of the sequence of Abraham's trust and blessing (Gal 3:6–9) and the redemptive event of Christ's being "hanged upon a tree" (Gal 3:10 – 13), Paul considers a dynamic interaction taking place between the two jurisdictions involved in the Christ event. Thus, the "Abrahamic jurisdiction" is seen as being eschatologically put into effect when Christ died vicariously within the "Mosaic jurisdiction", so much so that the death of Christ is interpreted as confirming the oath of promise God gave to Abraham and his descendant, encompassing even the blessing of the nations that takes place in Abraham's "seed", the crucified Christ.

In Gal 3:14, Paul begins to develop the meaning of the Christ event within the "Abrahamic jurisdiction" centered on God's oath of promise given to Abraham and to his descendant. With regard to the function of Gal 3:14 in its literary context, I have suggested above (cf. section 1) that the first conclusion (cf. the first ἵνα in 3:14a) elaborates further on the conflated scriptures in Gal 3:8b and on

164 Cf. also 2 Cor 5:21: "For *our sake* (ὑπὲρ ἡμῶν) He [God] made him to be sin who knew no sin […]."

Paul's interpretative claim that "those of trust are blessed together with the faithful Abraham" (3:9). This promise of blessing, identical with the oath of promise first given to Abraham and later reiterated to his one descendant, Isaac, has been fulfilled and now even given to the nations "in Christ Jesus " (3:14a). Moreover, the consequence of this event, that Christ as a hanged man is accursed "for us" (3:13), not only means redemption from the curse incurred by those living within the "Mosaic jurisdiction", but also (cf. the second ἵνα) that the blessing of Abraham is identified as the Spirit that has been received by means of "trust" (3:14b).[165]

Gal 3:14a continues Paul's argument from the conflated citation in Gal 3:8b through an exegetical paraphrase of God's oath of promise (Gen 22:18 / Gen 26:3–4), making clear that the promised blessings acrue to the benefit of the nations "in Jesus Christ". Dahl has made the claim that apart from Rom 8:32, Gal 3:14a contains the clearest Pauline allusion to the oath of promise in Genesis 22. Thus, Dahl suggested that the statement, "εἰς τὰ ἔθνη ἡ εὐλογία τοῦ Ἀβραὰμ γένηται ἐν Χριστῷ Ἰησοῦ", represents an exegetical paraphrase of the oath of promise given to Abraham post-*Akedah:* "ἐνευλογηθήσονται ἐν τῷ σπέρματί σου πάντα τὰ ἔθνη τῆς γῆς" (Gen 22:18 LXX). According to Dahl, the expression "ἡ εὐλογία τοῦ Ἀβραάμ" derives from Gen 28:4, while the words "ἐν τῷ σπέρματί" in Gen 22:18 have been replaced by "ἐν Χριστῷ Ἰησοῦ".[166] Dahl's suggestion is warranted by the fact that Gal 3:16 makes such an interpretation explicit through the identification of Abraham's seed with Christ.[167] The observation that Gal 3:14a and 3:16 refer back to the promises spoken to Abraham also suggests that a citation of Gen 22:18 is already echoed in Gal 3:8a. Although the reference to Abraham's seed, ἐν τῷ σπέρματί, is absent from the conflated citation in Gal 3:8b, it is probable that Paul also seems to presuppose such a wording, since he picks up the theme of Abraham's blessing from Gal 3:9 and continues his elaboratation of it in Gal 3:14a. So, both the references to "τὰ ἔθνη" and to the εὐλογία of Abraham (cf. the noun in 3:14a referring back to the verb form ἐνευλογεῖν / εὐλογεῖν in 3:8–9) in 3:14a link up with the argument in 3:8–9.[168] This link probably also means that the phrase "in Christ Jesus" in

---

165 I take the idiom "trust" to refer here to the polyvalence of πίστις in Gal 3:1–14, referring both to Abraham's "trust"'/ "faithfulness" and to God's "faithfulness" in keeping his oath to Abraham. Cf. Hays, *The Faith of Jesus Christ*, xliv-xlviii; de Boer, *Galatians*, 148–50.

166 Dahl, "The Atonement," 137–51. Cf. also Levenson, *The Death and Resurrection*, 222.

167 Dahl, *Studies in Paul*, 131.

168 Cf. Morland, *The Rhetoric of Curse in Galatians*, 220; J.R. Wisdom, *Blessing for the Nations and the Curse of the Law: Paul's Citation of Genesis and Deuteronomy in Gal. 3:8–10*, WUNT 2 (Tübingen: Mohr Siebeck, 2001), 197.

Gal 3:14a serves as an *analepsis* to the words "in you" referred to in Gal 3:8.[169] Moreover, the biblical phrase καὶ ἐνευλογηθήσονται [ἐν τῷ σπέρματί σου] πάντα τὰ ἔθνη, about the blessings to the nations mediated through Abraham's descendant, occurs not only in Gen 22:18, but also in Gen 26:4, reminiscent of the oath of promise first spoken to Abraham in Gen 22:18. Both passages consider that the oath of promise to Abraham, securing blessings for the nations, are going to be conferred on Isaac's descendants, because Abraham had proved himself to be faithful to God when he was willing to sacrifice Isaac.[170] Given that the citation in Gal 3:8b evokes not only Gen 12:3 and 22:18, but plausibly 26:3–4 as well, it seems that Paul considers these Genesis passages as a *continuum* in the Abraham cycle, in which the oath of promise is seen as a reaffirmation of the earlier blessings promised in Gen 12:3, encompassing blessings to all nations in Abraham's descendant, Christ.[171] The conjunction of these scriptures in Jewish exgetical tradition and the further allusions to the promises given to both Abraham *and* his seed in Gal 3:16, 3:22b and 3:29 might support this suggested reading of Gal 3:8b.

Apparently, Paul assumes in Gal 3:14 that the blessing coming to the nations in terms of the Spirit is understood as a fulfillment of God's oath of promise to Abraham. When the second purpose clause (in 3:14b) seems to be appended in order to explicate the first one (in 3:14a), the blessing of Abraham would then be equated with the promise of the Spirit received by trust.[172] But the question is: How can Paul associate the Spirit with the promise to Abraham? This equation of the Spirit and the promise has puzzled scholars, so that (for example) Hays asks:

> Even if we grant Paul his argument that the promise to Abraham is fulfilled in Christ, what authorizes his further inference that the *Spirit* is the fulfillment of this promise? In Gal 3:14 it is clear that "the blessing of Abraham" is somehow equated with "the promise of the Spirit". But how can Paul pose this equation? Nowhere in the OT does the promise to Abraham

---

169 Cf. M.V. Novenson, *Christ Among the Messiahs: Christ Language in Paul and Messiah Language in Ancient Judaism* (Oxford: OUP, 2012), 125: "Here, significantly, ἐν Χριστῷ Ἰησοῦ takes the place of ἐν σοί in Gal 3:8, as the adverbial phrase expressing the means by which the blessing comes."

170 Grüneberg, *A Philogical and Exegetical Study of Gen 12:3*, 239.

171 Cf. Levenson, *The Death and Resurrection*, 211: "Once Jesus has displaced Isaac it follows that the promises and blessings that had been associated with the beloved son par exellence in Genesis must be available instead through the Christian messiah. This is, in fact, the implication of Paul's first clause in Gal 3.14."

172 Cf. Watson, *Paul and the Hermeneutics of Faith*, 192.

> have anything to do with the Spirit. [...] Yet Paul speaks of the presence of the Spirit as an obvious evidence that the promise is now fulfilled. Is this a purely arbitrary assertion?[173]

Similarly, Williams comments:

> By "the promise of the Spirit" he means the promised Spirit, the Spirit promised in the past and now poured out upon the Jesus-people. But promised where? In Scripture, Paul would surely say. But where in Scripture? And to whom? Such questions await an answer.[174]

Various solutions have been proposed, such as searching for an answer in data in other parts of the letter to the Galatians, or in the Hebrew Bible apart from Genesis, or in Jewish expositions of relevant passages in the Abraham narrative in Genesis. I shall briefly review some of the proposed explanations. With regard to evidence in the letter of Galatians itself, Williams argues that God's promise of descendants implicitly contains the promise of the Spirit, since Paul claims in Gal 4:29 that Abraham's true sons are born according to the Spirit.[175] This suggestion points in a viable direction, but fails to convince, because Paul actually claims here that this promise encompasses all of his descendants, including those who were not born according to the Spirit.

Furthermore, Hays has suggested an allusion to Isa 44:3 LXX: "[...] because I will provide water in their thirst to those who walk in a dry land; I will put my Spirit on your offspring and my blessings on your children."[176] It is indeed true, as Hays point out, that this passage shares the elements of the Spirit, the seed, and blessing with Galatians 3:14.[177] But although much of the same vocabulary appears here as elsewhere in Galatians 3 – 4, there are no indications elsewhere in Galatians that Paul had this passage in mind.[178]

A more viable approach seems to be to understand Gal 3:14 in the light of Jewish expositions of the Abraham narrative in Genesis. Thus, Thiessen has recently suggested:

> When claiming that God has promised the *pneuma* to Abraham and to his seed (Gal 3:14 – 16), Paul intends his readers to recognize that Gen 15:5 and 22:16 – 18, in promising

---

173 Hays, *The Faith of Jesus Christ*, 181.

174 Williams, *Galatians*, 94.

175 Williams, "Promise in Galatians: A Reading of Paul's Reading of Scripture," *JBL* 107.4 (1988): 709 – 20.

176 Translation according to NETS.

177 See Hays, *The Faith of Jesus Christ*, 182 – 3.

178 On this point, I concur with the view of Thiessen, *Paul and the Gentile Problem*, 132.

> that Abraham's seed would be like the stars of heaven, contained the implicit promise of the *pneuma*, the stuff of the star / angels.[179]

In order to undergird this suggestion, Thiessen refers to both a Jewish understanding of the stars as pneumatic angelic bodies and to a Stoic conception of the stars as pneumatic celestial bodies.[180] Against this background, he assumes that when Paul read Gen 15:5 with its promise of seed like the stars of heaven, he saw an obvious reference to Christ, who, as *the* seed of Abraham, bestowed his own *pneuma* upon the Galatian believers, and so "gave birth to a host of pneumatic seed, among the Galatians—thus bringing the Abrahamic blessing upon and into the gentiles."[181] Thiessen's proposal is problematic, primarily because he seems to read too much into the Pauline text. For example, the lack of reference to Gen 15:5 in Galatians 3 speaks strongly against Thiessen's view that he intends his readers to recognize such a text. If there is a Jewish expository tradition that he wants the Galatians to invoke, it would rather depart from Gen 15:6, which Paul clearly cites (Gal 3:6) and of which he makes an exegetical paraphrase throughout Gal 3:6 – 29, along with other scriptures from Gen 22:18 / 26:4 (Gal 3:8 – 9, 14, 16, 29). Moreover, the fact that textual evidence of an equation of stars and seed in the Pauline text is elusive, makes Thiessen's suggestion highly questionable, not least his conjecture that Paul might have implied a reference to a conception of *pneuma* that the Galatians would have heard along the lines that can be inferred from Jewish and Stoic ideas of stars as pneumatic beings.

In section 3.2 above, I argued that Jewish expositions of Gen 15:6, rather than one particular text in Scripture, enabled Paul to make the association between Abraham and the Spirit.[182] Although Philo does not use either of the words "promise" and "blessing" in this context, he affirms that Abraham himself partakes of the Spirit on the basis of his trust in God (Gen 15:6), and implicitly states that the Spirit will subsequently come to the non-Jews, when they become proselytes in accordance with this standard role model of Abraham. Thus, in a context in which Philo makes a key statement about Abraham as the "founder" of the Jewish nation (cf. *Virt.* 212) and "the standard of nobility for all proselytes (*Virt.* 219), he writes that Abraham, as a result of "believing God", received the Spirit (*Virt.* 217). In a recent study of Gal 3:1 – 14, Borgen too points to the text in Philo, *Virt.* 212 – 219, as relevant:

179 Thiessen, *Paul and the Gentile Problem*, 159.
180 Cf. his review of the relevant data in Thiessen, *Paul and the Gentile Problem*, 135 – 47.
181 Thiessen, *Paul and the Gentile Problem*, 159.
182 Cf. Bekken, "Abraham og Ånden," 265 – 76, esp. 274 – 5.

As a comment on the question of Abraham and the Spirit in Gal 3:14 seen in context, the passage in Philo's treatise *On the Virtues* 212–219 seems to be relevant. Here Abraham, being the first proselyte and the founder of the Jewish nation, is seen as a standard, a model for proselytes. Like him they have set out with a vision for a beatiful settlement, in a state of true life and vitality, with truth as director and president (*Virt.* 219).[183]

However, since both my own and Borgen's observations on Gal 3:14 are brief and might be somewhat conjectural, they should be elaborated upon in the context of Paul's reasoning in Gal 3:1–14, as well as in the light of another Jewish motif that seems to be a concealed substructure behind this verse, namely, the expectation that Abraham's piety would live on among his descendants and thus confer upon them the benefits he was promised. The question is whether these two strands of thought might offer further help to understand Gal 3:14 and the correlation therein between the notion of Abrahams's blessing to the nations in Jesus Christ and the promise of the Spirit. The brief answer I shall suggest is in the affirmative.

The examination of the literary organization of Galatians 3 (see section 1 above) suggests that the scriptures about and to Abraham and his descendants (3:6–9) served as a warrant for the Galatians' experience of having received and being transformed by the Spirit (3:2–5). Thus, the link between 3:2–9 and 3:14 in terms of the promise that Abraham's blessing was going to be conferred on his descendants, even among non-Jews who had become Jewish proselytes, is supplied by the experience that the Spirit was given to those who had emulated Abraham's behavior of trust. In Paul's view, based on an exegetical paraphrase of Gen 15:6, the Galatian converts received the Spirit as an approval of being justified by trust, and by implication understood as valid Jewish proselytes, apart from observance of the Mosaic jurisdiction (3:2, 5, 10). Thus, they had emulated Abraham when he believed God, who reckoned it to his merit, and became the first proselyte (3:2, 5–6). Moreover, by evoking Abraham's reception of the promise of Spirit by trust, Paul can draw the "inference of best explanation", namely, that the Galatian converts themselves are legitimate sons of Abraham (3:7). Thus, Paul deduces this status of valid descent from Abraham from their partaking in the blessing that is inherent in the oath of promise to Abraham (3:8b), so that they can be said to have been blessed together with faithful Abraham (3:9). Consequently, when Paul in Gal 3:14b identifies the blessing of Abraham with the promise of the Spirit in the case of the Galatian converts, he sums up the argument from Gal 3:6–9 that the Galatians' reception of the Spirit proved their status as both legitimate sons of Abraham and valid heirs of the oath of promise to

183 Cf. Borgen, "Perspectives for Mission," 189.

Abraham. This line of thought also accords with Gal 4:29, which states that Abraham's sons are born according to the promise of Spirit, i.e., like Isaac.

The motif of the merits of Abraham conferred upon his true descendants, which finds expression in the oath of promise, might have some bearing on the interpretation of other elements in Gal 3:14 too. In chapter 2, I commented on the thought pattern, evinced also by Philo, that there is a direct relationship between the piety of Abraham living on in his descendants and the blessings that are expected to be conferred upon them. Accordingly, when Philo can speak distinctively about Abraham as the most ancient member of the Jewish nation, it is Abraham as a foundational model of piety that is emphasized. Thus, in *Abr.* 3 – 6 Philo explains that Abraham is worthy to be emulated, since he belongs to the second triad of men (together with Isaac and Jacob), "whose virtues happen to have been recorded in the the most holy writings" (§4). Thus, Philo's aim of writing the commentary on Abraham's life is to make clear that his words and deeds embody the unwritten and universal Law and exemplify the virtue of piety which can achieved and replicated by means of adherence to the written and particular Law of Moses (*Abr.* 5 – 6, 276). Moreover, Philo underlines that Abraham is worthy of emulation in his rejection of polytheism, trust in the One God, and the virtues he gained when he received and was transformed by the Spirit (*Virt.* 212 – 219). On the basis of these means of marking identity, that is, on the condition that they prove themselves legitimate successors of the piety demonstrated by Abraham and the other ancestors of the nation (Isaac and Jacob), God's providential blessing continues to be bestowed on his descendants.[184] It is significant that Philo, in his exposition of Gen 26:3 – 4 in *QG* 4:180, refers explicitly back to the oath of promise to Abraham in Gen 22:16 – 18, in order to emphasize the requirement of reproducing Abraham's promise-worthy behavior, in order for Isaac and his descendants to be appropriate recipients of the promised gifts that were expected to be conferred upon them.

In a corresponding way, Paul's reasoning in Gal 3:8b–9, 14, 22b, and 29 seems to be structured on this idea of emulating Abraham's piety as a condition for being party to the promised blessings. In Gal 3:8b–9, Paul reflects this strand of thought, when he defines Abraham's sons as those who have acquired the same trust and blessing as Abraham, and therefore are valid recipients of the promise and heirs of his blessings, or, as Paul puts it, "those of trust are blessed together with the faithful Abraham".

184 Cf. particularly the passages referred to in chapter 2, such as *Spec.* 4:180 – 181, *Virt.* 79, *Praem.* 166, and *QG* 4:180.

Affirmations about the Spirit which the Galatians received by trust in analogy to Abraham in Gal 3:2–6 provide the framework of Paul's discussion of the promise of the Spirit in Gal 3:14. In that case, Gal 3:14b refers back to the incident and draws the analogy to the way in which Abraham received the Spirit by trust (cf. Gal 3:5–6). In a manner that corresponds to Philo, then, continuing his argument from Gal 3:2–9, Paul claims that the reception of the Spirit through trust by "we", i.e., by both the Galatian converts and the Jews, demonstates that the piety of Abraham and his blessings continue to live on among his descendants as an affirmation of their partaking in the oath of promise that results from Abraham's faithfulness, and now comes to fruition in his seed, Jesus Christ. As Hays comments on Gal 3:14: "Paul then takes the blessing of Abraham himself as a prefiguration of the blessing which will be fulfilled, as Gen 22:18 indicates, only in the 'seed'."[185] At this juncture, however, I suggest we should add to Hays' observation that it is not only the promise in Gen 22:18 that indicates such a mediated version of Abraham's piety and blessing in his seed, but also the oath of promise reiterated to his seed in Gen 26:3–4. In addition to Philo, Sir 44:20–21 also alludes to both these texts, which may provide a referential background for Paul's reasoning in 3:14. Thus, it is conceivable that Paul's rivals in Galatia had used these texts in order to argue that it was by observing the Mosaic Law (*sic* like Abraham himself) that the Galatian converts proved themselves appropriate recipients of these promises mediated through Abraham's seed. Paul's immediate response is that, as descendants of Abraham, they are partakers of the promises to Abraham that come to the nations "in Jesus Christ", the seed of Abraham, and that this is demonstrated by their reproducing the same piety and blessing that characterized Abraham, that is, by receiving the Spirit through trust (τοῦ πνεύματος λάβωμεν διὰ τῆς πίστεως, 3:14b). For Paul, the reception of the Spirit by trust and the reception of promised blessings are guarantees of the same phenomena, i.e., the legitimate status of the Galatian converts as valid proselytes, descendants of Abraham, and heirs of the promise. That is the main reason why Paul links the experience of the Galatian converts to the model of Abraham. Just as Abraham had believed in God, they received the Spirit by trust as a sign of being approved by God as valid proselytes, and thus also heirs to the blessings God gave to Abraham and his descendants by the oath that results from Abraham's faithfulness. As I shall argue below, the reference to Abraham's blessing as mediated to the nations "in Jesus Christ" in Gal 3:14a

---

185 Hays, *Echoes of Scripture in the Letters of Paul*, 180. For a similar emphasis that the blessings will be bestowed on the nations in the seed of Abraham according to the promise in Gen 22:18, cf. Witherington III, *Grace in Galatia*, 228.

points forward to 3:16 and 3:29 and Paul's allusion to both versions of the oath of promise in Genesis.

The Galatian converts' experience of having received the Spirit through trust on the analogy of Abraham provides the framework of Paul's discussion of the promise (cf. 3:2–6 and 4:1–7). Here, the reception of the Spirit "in Jesus Christ" mentioned in Gal 3:14b refers back to Gal 3:1–5, and thus can be understood as an elaboration on the theme of the crucifixion of Jesus Christ in the light of the oath of promise, and vice versa. Thus, I suggest that Paul's argument goes as follows: Since Jesus Christ as Abraham's offspring was crucified and thus was exposed publicly as a cursed criminal "*for us*", this meant that the *curse* of the Law was legally removed from Abraham's offspring. Since Paul presupposes that those under the "Mosaic jurisdiction" could only incur its curse, and not its blessings (cf. Deut 28:1–14), the crucifixion of Jesus Christ "*for us*" meant at the same time a legal redemption and actual freedom from the Law of Moses itself. According to Paul, "we", i.e., both Jews and Galatian converts who believed, had received the blessings according to the "Abrahamic jurisdiction" in terms of the Spirit. For Paul, then, the Christ event meant that God in his faithfulness had kept his oath of promise to Abraham and his "seed", seen as an adequate reward for Abraham's trust.

At this point, it seems that another scriptural idea might lurk in the background of this reasoning, i.e., the notion that the "Sinaitic Law" nests within the covenant God at first established with Abraham. In passages in Scripture such as Exod 32:10 – 13; Lev 26:39 – 45; Ps 105:26 – 42, and in the ensuing Jewish tradition, we find that when Israel obeys the commandments and was promised to receive future blessings, but instead failed to observe the commandments and became subject to the sanctions of punishment, the antecedent promise that ensued on the established past obedience of Abraham remained in effect for Abraham's kin and offered a source of enduring blessings for the errant people. Accordingly, when they made a remedy for their sins, either through repentance or using the available means of atonement (e.g., the rituals of sacrifices, especially on the Day of Atonement, Yom Kippur), they were transferred back to the Abrahamic promise of blessing that was never brokered. J.D. Levenson has summarized this dynamic interplay between what he call the Abrahamic and Sinaitic covenants as follows:

> As the narrative of the Torah goes, the Sinaitic covenant thus nests within the Abrahamic, or patriarchal one. For when Israel comes to Sinai and unanimously accepts the covenant that God offers them, they are already in a covenantal relationship that was never brokered but simply announced to their father Abraham generations earlier. The overall effect of this arrangement is to preserve the notes of both conditionality and unconditionality: Israel's willingness to obey God's laws and commandments, now presented as stipulations of

> the covenant, is indispensable, and yet when the Israelites fall into disobedience, the antecedent Abrahamic covenant (reiterated to Isaac and Jacob) remains in effect and offers a reservoir of grace for the errant people.[186]

Paul's argument in Gal 3:10 – 14 becomes more coherent against the background of such a Jewish thought pattern. As I have argued, Paul's argument in Gal 3:8 – 9 is indebted to the exegetical tradition based on a conjunction of Gen 15:6 and Gen 22:18 / 26:4, namely, that Abraham's trust has become the basis for God's oath of promise given to him and his descendant, with the result that the promised blessings benefit his descendants who have aquired the same piety as the ancestor. Paul's appropriation of this idea to the situation in Galatia meant that he took the Christ event and the reception of Spirit as a manifestation of the fact that the piety and blessing of Abraham had already been conferred upon his descendants, both Jews and Galatian converts, who had come to believe and received the Spirit on the analogy of Abraham himself. It seems to me that Paul's argument in Gal 3:10 – 14 rests on the following two premises:

1. Since Jesus Christ was seen by Paul as the "seed" of Abraham (cf. 3:16, 29), his execution by crucifixion was interpreted as confirming what God had promised by an oath to Abraham.

2. While in the Hebrew Bible and the ensuing Jewish tradition a remedy was provided for those who failed to keep the commandments of the Law, as a transition from the "curse of the Law" to the blessings of the Abrahamic covenant, the crucifixion of Jesus Christ radically changed Paul's view of the role of the Torah in that regard. Since Jesus Christ was crucified and hanged on a tree as a cursed criminal "for us", and not supposedly "for his own crimes", it was the effects of his death within the "Mosaic jurisdiction" that instead provided the remedy and made the transition to the blessings possible. Thus, according to Paul's new perspective, there was a distinctive difference between the "Sinaitic" and "Abrahamic" covenants with regard to the way one could reach the blessings. Whereas the "Mosaic jurisdiction" in its Deuteronomic theology envisages Israel's blessing as conditioned on what one may do in the future, and never as a reward for what one has already done, the "Abrahamic jurisdiction", centered on Abraham's trust and God's promise, asserts that the unconditional blessing which ensues upon Abraham's trust is already an established fact in the past, not a future possibility. These blessings continue to be conferred on his descendants who demonstrate the kind of similarity to Abraham by sharing his trust in God and reception of the Spirit.

---

186 Levenson, *Inheriting Abraham*, 56.

On the basis of these presuppositions, it becomes easier to grasp Paul's argument *e contrario* in Gal 3:6–14: only the curses of the Law could be incurred by those living within the "Mosaic jurisdiction" (Gal 3:10–14). The blessings, however, after the arrival of Abraham's ultimate "seed", Jesus Christ, were to be offered only to Abraham's descendant within the "Abrahamic jurisdiction", centered on the scriptural words about and to Abraham and his offspring in terms of trust in God and the oath of promise (Gal 3:6–9, 14).

I shall round off this section by summarizing what I have argued is a coherent interpretation Gal 3:10–14 in the context of 3:1–14. The theme of Christ's execution as a crucified criminal (3:1) pertains to both the "Mosaic jurisdiction" and the "Abrahamic jurisdiction" attested in the Torah and Scripture. If the former jurisdiction was still maintained as valid (2:21), and the Galatian converts still insisted on accepting and living within it, the consequence was that Christ died only as a cursed criminal, liable to punishment on account of transgressions. The effect of Christ's death was then to be considered as void; it would be of no benefit to them. As a corollary, they were in danger of affirming that Christ was brought to the cross and publicly exposed as an accursed criminal for his own crimes (Gal 3:10), thereby themselves incurring the curse of the Law. For Paul, the historical circumstance that Jesus Christ, as the "seed" of Abraham (Gal 3:14a), was publicly exposed as being hanged on a tree as an accursed criminal (Gal 3:1, 10, 13) "for us", meant not only a redemption from the curse of the Law and thus from the "Mosaic jurisdiction" itself, but also a transition to the "Abrahamic jurisdiction" with its promise of blessing for the Abrahamic descendants of Jews and converts, based on the assurance of God's oath of promise given as an adequate reward for the promise-worthy trust of Abraham (3:8–9, 14). Accordingly, Paul interpreted the death of Christ as a confirmation of the oath of promise (Gen 22:18; 26:3–4), grounded in both God's initial promise (Gen 12:3) and Abraham's trust (Gen 15:6). His death as Abraham's ultimate "seed" thus brought forth the promised blessing of the Spirit to all his descendants, including both the Jews and even the Galatian converts who had trust, after the role model of Abraham himself (Gal 3:5–9, 13–14).

In short, Paul's message of the crucified Christ is incompatible with the enduring validity of the Law, but in harmony with the covenant with its inherent promise of God's commitment to Abraham and his descendant. Paul continues to elaborate this argument in the following verses, Gal 3:15–29, to which I now turn.

6 Gal 3:15 – 29: The Dynamic of the "Abrahamic Jurisdiction" and the "Mosaic Jurisdiction"

6.1 Abraham's Covenant and Promise relative to the Law of Moses (Gal 3:15 – 18)

In Gal 3:15 – 18 Paul continues his argument from Gal 3:8 – 14 that the "Abrahamic jurisdiction" centered on God's promise to Abraham also applies to his one offspring, and consequently cannot be dependent on the "Mosaic jurisdiction" and observance of Law. Paul asserts that the Law cannot nullify the covenant and the promise which goes along with it. As a proof, he argues that the Abrahamic covenant and promise had priority over the Sinaitic Law, which came much later, so that the inheritance Abraham was promised could not have been attained by the Law. Moreover, if the Law of Moses was a codicil determiming the conditions for the validity for the covenantal promise, the promise would have been rendered void.

My main contribution in this section is shaped by the following assumptions: 1. The "covenant" mentioned in Gal 3:15 – 18 alludes to Gen 15:9 – 18, in which the covenantal promise that constitutes it was solemnly ratified by God at the "covenant between the pieces". Moreover, the promises Paul explicitly mentions in the proposition that is introduced in Gal 3:16a (τῷ δὲ Ἀβραὰμ ἐρρέθησαν αἱ ἐπαγγελίαι καὶ τῷ σπέρματι αὐτοῦ) refer specifically to the oath of promise, which first was given to Abraham (Gen 22:16 – 18), and subsequently reiterated to Isaac and his descendants (Gen 26:3 – 4). In Gal 3:16b, the phrase *καὶ τῷ σπέρματί σου* refers to Gen 26:3 as the cited intertext, of which Paul gives a paraphrasing exegesis to warrant his claim about Jesus Christ as the ultimate offspring through whom the blessings promised to Abraham and Isaac are fulfilled. Thus, Paul can speak of the promise in the singular (3:17 – 18) as well as of the promise in the plural (3:16), since the oath of promise to the descendants of Abraham and Isaac (Gen 26:3 – 4) contains a plurality of promises and at the same time is a reaffirmation of the already existing covenantal promise (Gen 15:1 – 8).

2. In Gal 3:15, 17, Paul makes use of two hermeneneutical concepts, that is, the argument *a minore ad maius* and the principle of order and rank, respectively, by which he is able to argue the priority and primacy of the promise to Abraham in relation to the Law.

3. In Gal 3:18, the assertion that the inheritance comes from the covenantal promise and not from the Law resonates with a contemporary Jewish negotiation on Abraham's promise of blessing relative to the Law. It is my suggestion that some of these assumptions, which I shall deal with below, can be illuminated

by evidence in the Pauline text itself as well as in Philonic and rabbinic data. I believe that the implications of this evidence have not yet been fully worked out and exploited for an interpretation of this text.

6.1.1 The Promises ratified by the Abrahamic Covenant and affirmed by God's Oath

Three main questions have been discussed with regard to the referent of διαθήκη within the context of Gal 3:15 – 18: What is the legal connotation of this term, when is it ratified, and to which specific texts does it refer to, in that case? Various answers have been suggested, beginning from the premise that διαθήκη refers to Greco-Roman or Jewish Law. In what follows, I shall restrict myself to the solutions delivered recently by S.W. Hahn and B.R. Trick. In the case of the Jewish Law, Hahn concludes that διαθήκη refers to the legal instrument of the Abrahamic covenant, equivalent to the oath of promise to Abraham in Gen 22:16 – 18:

> It was demonstrated above that διαθήκη in Gal 3:15 should be taken as "covenant", which accords well with the actual statements of the verse and the "covenant logic" of the context. In particular, the διαθήκη Paul has in mind in vv. 15, 17 is the covenant oath sworn by God at the Akedah to Abraham and his "seed" (Gen 22:16 – 18). The example of a "human covenant" (Gal 3:15) itself may have been prompted by the record of a human covenant immediately preceding the Akedah (Gen 21:22 – 34). A pattern of allusion to the Akedah and its context is evident throughout Gal 3:6 – 18.[187]

Correspondingly, Trick shares Hahn's view that the διαθήκη referred to in Gal 3:17 is the instrument ratified by God after the event of the *Akedah* according to Gen 22:16 – 18, but he differs from Hahn when he takes it to refer to the Greco-Roman Law and its concept of a "testamentary adoption":

> According to Gal 3:17, however, God does ratify the Abrahamic διαθήκη well before the giving of the law. When does this ratification occur? The obvious answer is Gen 22 when, as a result of Abraham's obedience in the *Aqedah*, God swears by himself that he will fulfill all that he has promised to Abraham and his seed (Gen 22:16 – 17).[188]

Both Hahn's and Trick's suggestions fail to convince, for several reasons. In the first place, if we take at face value that Paul expressly introduces a chronology adopted by LXX and Josephus, we may assume that Paul has the διαθήκη "cut between the pieces" (Gen 15:9 – 18) in mind when he talks about a legally

187 Hahn, "Covenant," 99.
188 Trick, *Abrahamic Descent*, 177.

valid covenant in Gal 3:15–18.[189] Thus, in Gal 3:17, Paul presupposes the problem of contrast discussed in rabbinic data between the number of years referred to in Gen 15:13 (400 years) and Exod 12:41 (430 years). The first number was reckoned from the birth of Isaac, while the latter was reckoned from the covenant according to Genesis 15:18. At this point, then, it seems that Paul invokes the rabbinic solution, when he refers to the latter number of 430 years reckoned from God's "covenant between the pieces" with Abraham.[190] Hence, when Paul in Gal 3:17 emphasizes that the Law came 430 years after (*μετὰ* τετρακόσια καὶ τριάκοντα ἔτη) the Abrahamic covenant that was ratified beforehand (διαθήκην *προ*κεκυρωμένην), it is obvious that the ratification of God's covenant cannot have taken place after Isaac was born or after the *Akedah*.[191]

Secondly, the identification of the ratified covenant with an oath presupposes what Hahn takes for granted and states explicitly, namely that "a covenant *was always ratified by an oath*" (his emphasis).[192] Against such a view, I would bring to attention a somewhat overlooked essay by E.J. Bickerman, in which the distinction he makes between a ratified covenant and the oath seems relevant.[193] Here, Bickerman made the compelling argument that an oath is not a ratification of a covenant, but a distinctive reaffirmation of an earlier promise inherent in the covenant. Just as the covenant could confirm an earlier promise, the characteristic of an oath is to be an additional affirmation of the antecedent promise, i.e., in order to make the commitment indissoluble, an even better way "to strengthen the positive dispositions of the one who took the oath."[194] So, for example, there is a distinction between the *berith* with Abraham as it is described in Genesis 15, and the oath God "swears" by himself in the words spoken to the patriarch in Genesis 22. The *berith* cut with Abraham (Gen 15:1–18) is made in order to emphasize that God cannot go back on the promise made to Abraham and his descendants, whereas the oath God later swears to Abraham and Isaac (Gen 22:16–18; 26:3–4) reaffirms his commitment to fulfill the initial promise. This line of thought, as I shall argue below, dovetails well with Gal 3:15–18, which makes a clear distinction between the promise to Abra-

---

189 So, e.g., Daube, *The New Testament and Rabbinic Judaism*, 440–1; Dahl, *Studies in Paul*, 169 n. 17.

190 On Paul's use of rabbinic exegetical traditions in Galatians 3, cf. Dahl, *Studies in Paul*, 169 n. 17.

191 *Pace* Trick (*Abrahamic Descent*, 179), who contends that Isaac was "born before the ratification of the διαθήκη".

192 Hahn, "Covenant," 85.

193 Bickerman, "'Cutting a Covenant'," 1–31.

194 Bickerman, "'Cutting a Covenant'," 24.

ham ratified by God through the instrument of a covenant (3:17 – 18) and the reaffirmation of the promise to Abraham and to his seed (3:16, 22b).

Third, although both Hahn and Trick refer to the event of the *Akedah* as the background for the Abrahamic covenant, they differ about which specific source text lies behind Paul's reference to the διαθήκη and the singular promise as well as the plurality of promises in Gal 3:16 – 18. Since Hahn reads Gen 22:15 – 18 as a covenant episode, he argues for an allusion to this text behind Gal 3:15 – 18: "Indeed, it can be shown that this Abrahamic covenant episode fits the context of Paul's remarks in Gal 3:6 – 18 better than the other two covenant-making episodes, Gen 15:17 – 21 and 17:1 – 27."[195] His main argument is that only the divine oath in Gen 22:15 – 18 displays three main characteristics singled out in the Pauline text, i.e., (1) that the covenant ratified by God with a solemn oath (Gal 3:17 – 18), (2) is given to Abraham and his seed (Gal 3:16, 18), and (3) concerns the blessing secured for the Gentiles (Gal 3:14). While the third element is absent from Genesis 15, the element of a ratification by God is missing in Genesis 17. Three observations, however, speak against seeing Gen 22:16 – 18 as the "Abrahamic covenant episode" behind Gal 3:15 – 18: First, Gen 22:16 – 18 is not referred to as a ratified covenant by God, but as an oath that God swears. Second, the key phrase καὶ τῷ σπέρματι αὐτοῦ in Gal 3:16 is absent from Genesis 22. Third, in Gal 3:16, Paul seems to juxtapose the promises spoken *to* Abraham *and to* his seed (*τῷ* δὲ Ἀβραὰμ ἐρρέθησαν αἱ ἐπαγγελίαι *καὶ τῷ* σπέρματι αὐτοῦ), an element which is also missing in Gen 22:16 – 18, since there only Abraham is highlighted as the recipient of the oath of promise.

Although Trick affirms the importance of Gen 22:18 for the understanding of the argument in Gal 3:16 – 18, he finds that for Paul's phrase καὶ τῷ σπέρματι αὐτοῦ in Gal 3:16, "God's expressed intention in Gen 17:7 to establish a διαθήκη with Abraham and his seed better fits the context in Galatians and suggests Gen 17:8 as Paul's source."[196] Three objections can be raised against this suggestion too: First, although it has been suggested that Paul's allusion to a plurality of promises corresponds to several promises in Gen 17:1 – 9, it is, however, a fact that the clause καὶ τῷ σπέρματι αὐτοῦ in both Gen 13:15 and 17:8 refers primarily to a single promise, viz. the promise of land. This makes Trick's assumption that the Abrahamic διαθήκη and the conditional promises in Genesis 17 are ratified by the oath of promise in Gen 22:16 – 18 unconvincing, not least since neither of the elements of a ratification, a covenant, nor the promise of land are alluded to in this text. As Moberly claims, "The notable feature about Gen. xxii 16 is that

195 Hahn, "Covenant," 90.

196 Trick, *Abrahamic Descent*, 176.

the divine oath is uniquely not connected with the giving of the land, as the entire concern of *vv.* 16 – 18 is with Abraham's descendants."[197]

Secondly, unlike Gal 3:17, in Gen 17:7 the "covenant" is not said to be established by a ratifying rite on God's part, but refers only to such a validation on Abraham's part in terms of the binary obligation of circumcision. Again, to follow the reasoning suggested by Bickerman, when God swears to Abraham that he will fulfill the promises spoken to him, the oath itself functions, not as a ratification of a covenant, but rather as the strongest affirmation of the promise inherent in the covenant, which has already been ratified and established by God. Moreover, since Trick suggests that the Abrahamic covenant in Genesis 17 provides a referential background, I find his suggestion that this covenant is to be understood as a "testamentary adoption" unwarranted, since there seems to be no evidence that the Abrahamic covenant was associated with a legal instrument of this kind, either in Genesis 17 and 22 or in the early interpretative reception of Gal 3:15 – 18. In addition, as far as I can see, Trick does not provide evidence from either Jewish, Greek, or Roman Law that would have corroborated his thesis, namely, that a will or a testament in terms of a "testamentary adoption" was ratified by an oath. Therefore, it is my impression, to say the least, that this proposal entails a forced interpretation of Paul's argument throughout Galatians 3 – 4.

Thirdly, in Gal 3:16, Paul emphasizes that the promises were not spoken only to Abraham, but *to* Abraham *and to* his seed. This element too is absent from Genesis 17.

To sum up: Hahn's and Trick's suggestions fail to convince, because the evidence does not provide "the inference of best explanation" with regard to the the main questions that introduced this section, i. e., the legal meaning of διαθήκη, the time of its ratification, and the specific texts referred to in the context of Gal 3:15 – 18. This negative conclusion indicates the need for a further investigation. In what follows, a fresh approach is presented, suggesting that the promise that constitutes the covenant ratified by God "between the pieces" is seen as having been reaffirmed by the oath spoken by God to Abraham and his offspring. Thus, while the text alluding to the promissory covenant is Gen 15:1 – 18, at this juncture the specific text referring to the oath of promise is Gen 26:3 – 4. As I shall argue, both these texts higlight the characteristics of Gal 3:15 – 18 and provide a coherent reading of Paul's line of thought in the immediate context of Gal 3:8 – 29.

197 Moberly, "The Earliest Commentary on the Akedah," 315.

As I pointed out above, it seems that Paul invokes an exegetical tradition attested in later rabbinic discussions that the number of 430 years is reckoned from God's "covenant between the pieces" with Abraham. This is particularly emphasized when Paul says in Gal 3:17 that the Law came 430 years *after* (*μετὰ* τετρακόσια καὶ τριάκοντα ἔτη) the Abrahamic covenant that was ratified *beforehand* (διαθήκην *προ*κεκυρωμένην). The corallary Paul draws, namely that a promise on the terms of a ratified covenant cannot be nullified, indicates that the covenant was established as a legal sanction of the promise. Paul therefore infers that a ratified covenant with Abraham could not be annulled by the Law of Moses, since it was legally binding and irrevocable on God's part.

With regard to Paul's exegetical paraphrase of the phrase cited in Gal 3:16—"[...] but it says, 'And to your offspring,' that is, to one person, who is Christ (ὡς ἐφ' ἑνός· *καὶ τῷ σπέρματί σου*, ὅς ἐστιν Χριστός)"—to what specific scripture does Paul here refer? While I argued against Hahn and Trick that the Abrahamic covenant had already been legally ratified through the ritual when God walks "between the pieces" long before the divine oath spoken to Abraham according to Genesis 22, I shall propose that the promises referred to in Gal 3:16 refer specifically to the oath of promise that was reiterated and spoken to Isaac and his descendants in a way reminiscent of Gen 26:3 – 4. Thus, Paul's argument is that the promise first ratified by the "covenant between the pieces" has been reaffirmed by the oath of promise spoken first to Abraham and subsequently reiterated to Isaac, and is taken by Paul to apply, not to the plurality of Isaac's descendants, but solely to Christ. Such a conjecture might gain in probability because it satisfies the following conditions: First, the "promises" must refer primarily to the oath of promise, since this is the only promise spoken both *to* Abraham *and to* his descendant, Isaac. Second, the phrase *καὶ τῷ σπέρματί σου*, which Paul interprets about Christ, must be part of the citation. Third, the citation that is evoked should conform to the coherent argument in the immediate context of Gal 3:6 – 29. In what follows, I shall offer some observations that point in favor of Gen 26:3 – 4 as the only reference which complies with these requirements.

In the first place, Gen 26:2 – 5, 24 render the *only* divine promises spoken to Isaac, which explicitly reiterate the oath of promise reminiscent of Gen 22:16 – 18.[198] This fact might thus explain the juxtaposition of Abraham and his offspring as the recipients of the promises mentioned in Gal 3:16a: "τῷ δὲ Ἀβραὰμ ἐρρέθησαν αἱ ἐπαγγελίαι καὶ τῷ σπέρματι αὐτοῦ." If we take this proposition at face value, it may thus refer to the oath of promise spoken not *just* to

198 Cf. Moberly, "The Earliest Commentary on the Akedah," 322.

Abraham, but *to* Abraham *and to his seed* (τῷ δὲ Ἀβραάμ [...] καὶ τῷ σπέρματι αὐτοῦ), namely, to the pledge explicitly reiterated to Isaac according to Gen 26:3: "[...] and will bless you; for to you and to your descendants [...] I will fulfill the oath that I swore to your father Abraham." This is corroborated by the fact that this passage is the only text in which both Abraham and Isaac are mentioned as recipients of the oath of promise. Similarly, the double addressees of the promises in Gal 3:16 are separetely marked out by the conjunction καί and twice by the article in dative, corresponding to the formulations about the recipients of the promise in Gen 26:3 (the underlined words in the following citation of this verse emphasize that the oath of promise is spoken *to* Abraham and *to* Isaac): "σοὶ γὰρ καὶ τῷ σπέρματί σου δώσω πᾶσαν τὴν γῆν ταύτην καὶ στήσω τὸν ὅρκον μου, ὃν ὤμοσα Αβρααμ τῷ πατρί σου."

Second, the argument that the phrase "καὶ τῷ σπέρματί σου" in Gal 3:16 is not applied in Gen 22:18,[199] because the phrase used in this passage is "ἐν τῷ σπέρματί σου" rather than "τῷ σπέρματί σου",[200] speaks in favor of Gen 26:3 as its reference. This observation is supported by another feature too: Paul's exegetical paraphrase of the expression "καὶ τῷ σπέρματί σου" in Gen 26:3 thus presupposes a retrospective reading about the generic singular of all of Isaac's offsprings ("as of many"). As we have pointed out, at this juncture Paul makes use of the exegetical technique of confirming one specific reading of the text over against an alternative one. Thus, Paul affirms his own correct reading in terms of a specific singular descendant ("that is, to one person"), pointing forward to Christ, rather than to all among the subsequent generations of Abraham who are descended from Isaac.[201] Such an understanding of Gal 3:16 contrasts with that of J.D. Levenson, who thinks Paul here interprets scripture ("καὶ τῷ σπέρματί σου" taken from Gen 13:15 and 17:8) to mean that Isaac has disappeared from Paul's horizon altogether and has been superseded by Christ.[202] Hence, the figure of Isaac seems only to be presupposed by Paul in such a way that the promise to Isaac concerns his descendants, which Paul iden-

199 The position of καί and the preposition ἐν in Gen 22:18 (*καὶ ἐνευλογηθήσονται ἐν τῷ σπέρματί σου*) seems to rule out this text as the source behind Gal 3:16. Similarly, Trick, *Abrahamic Descent*, 176 n. 184, *pace* scholars such as, e.g., C.J. Collins, "Galatians 3:16: What Kind of Exegete Was Paul?" *TynBul* 54.1 (2003): 82 – 6; J. Becker, *Die Briefe an die Galater, Epheser und Kolosser*, NTD (Göttingen: Vandenhoeck & Ruprecht, 1998), 53; Schoeps, *Paul*, 180 – 1.

200 So Daube, *The New Testament and Rabbinic Judaism*, 438.

201 I believe that the terminology of "figural interpretation" as defined by Auerbach (*Mimesis*, 73) is perhaps more adequate than "typology" in order to describe the connection Paul presupposes between Isaac's offspring and Christ, who is thought of as Abraham's offspring.

202 Levenson, *Death and Resurrection*, 213.

tifies as the specific singular descendant Christ, who confirms the oath of promise to Isaac. Moreover, an allusion to Gen 26:3 – 4 in Gal 3:16 does not come out of the blue, but, as I have suggested above, might already have been evoked in the conflated quotation of words from Gen 12:3 (*ἐνευλογηθήσονται ἐν σοί*), 22:18, and 26:4 (*καὶ ἐνευλογηθήσονται [...] πάντα τὰ ἔθνη*) as the potential source behind Gal 3:8b (προευηγγελίσατο τῷ Ἀβραὰμ ὅτι *ἐνευλογηθήσονται ἐν σοὶ πάντα τὰ ἔθνη*). Paul's philogical exegesis in 3:16 of the phrase "καὶ τῷ σπέρματί σου" as referring to Christ thus makes explicit the warrant for his elaboration of ἐν σοί in 3:8b to apply to the prepositional phrase ἐν Χριστῷ Ἰησοῦ in 3:14 about Jesus Christ, as the specific descendant by whom Abraham's blessing and the oath of promise are fulfilled.

Third, while the expression "καὶ τῷ σπέρματί σου" does appear also in Gen 13:15, 15:18, 17:8 and 24:7, and in each of these texts is related primarily to the single promise of land, it is specifically referred to in Gal 3:16 in connection with a plurality of promises and the descendant-mediated version of blessing contained in the oath of promise reiterated to Isaac according to Gen 26:3 – 4.[203] Given the putative confusion of the promises to Abraham and his offspring in the proposition of Gal 3:16a, it is natural to link Gal 3:16b and the subsequent paraphrase of the phrase "καὶ τῷ σπέρματί σου" to Gen 26:3 as intertext.[204] Rather than referring to the promise of land, which "plays no part in the argument of Galatians",[205] the phrase "καὶ τῷ σπέρματί σου" in Gal 3:16 serves as a "metalepsis",[206] citing a small piece of the precursor text Gen 26:3 – 4, by which Paul

203 Cf. P.R. Williamson, *Sealed with an Oath: Covenant in God's unfolding Purpose*, NSBT (Nottingham: Apollos, 2007), 198: "Significantly, when Yahweh reiterates the promise of territorial inheritance to Isaac, it is included within the parameters of the oath sworn to Abraham in the context of the Aqedah incident (Gen 26:3 – 5)."

204 A parallel may be Gen 26:3 as the intertext alluded to in T. Ab. 3:6:

> And the Commander-in-chief blessed Isaac and said:
>
> > "The Lord God will grant to you his
> > promise which he promised to your father
> > Abraham; he will grant to you the
> > precious oath (made to) your father and
> > your mother."

See the analysis (unfortunately, without commenting on Gal 3:16) of T.Ab. 3:6 by D.C. Allison, *Testament of Abraham*, CEJL (Berlin; New York: De Gruyter, 2003), 119, and Conway, *The Promises of God*, 94 – 5.

205 Bruce, *Galatians*, 172.

206 For a definition of the literary concept and technique of "metalepsis", cf. Hays, *Echoes of Scripture in the Gospels*, 11:

> Metalepsis is a literary technique of citing or echoing a small bit of a precursor text in such a way that the reader can grasp the significance of the echo only by recalling or

picks up the line of thought from Gal 3:14 about Christ as the means of the blessings offered to Abraham's offsprings. This seems also to be the implication of Paul's use of the phrase "the blessing of Abraham" (ἡ εὐλογία τοῦ Ἀβραάμ) in Gal 3:14, which derives from Gen 28:4, a passage concerning Isaac's confirmation of his descendant Jacob and the Jewish people collectively as his and Abraham's rightful heirs of the promise. For Paul, this oath of promise about Abraham's blessing in terms of the Spirit is now regarded as conferred on Abraham's descendants "in Christ Jesus", replacing "in your offspring" in Gen 22:18 and Gen 26:4.[207] As I shall point out in the next section, this view seems to be corroborated by Paul's reference to Isaac and his offspring in Gal 4:1 – 2, 21 – 31 as well. In the latter passage, Paul says that the Galatian converts were adopted into the family of Sarah (4:28, 31) in line with God's promise, and became adopted children according to their reception of the Spirit, resembling the natural-born child Isaac (4:29).

Finally, as the phrase "καὶ τῷ σπέρματί σου" in Gen 26:3 refers to Isaac's offsprings, so Paul also interprets the single descendant Christ as a collective person, encompassing those who belong to him. Hence, in the next section (6.3), we shall see that the reference to Gen 26:3 – 4, perhaps already presupposed in Gal 3:8b and elaborated further by means of the method of exegetical paraphrase in Gal 3:14 and 3:16 about Christ, is taken further in Gal 3:26 – 29, where the identification of both Christ and those who belong to him as Abraham's offspring is made explicit.

As I shall argue below, the line of thought in Gal 3:17 – 18, i.e., the priority and independence of the promises over against the Law of Moses, conforms to the context of a Jewish discussion on Abraham, in which the oath of promise was conceived in *continuum* with motifs such as Abraham's covenant, circumcision, descendants, and his adherence to the Law of Moses. In order to understand fully the referential background of Paul's implied reference to Gen 26:3 – 5, in which he takes his place in a Jewish discourse of his own day, it is significant that this passage was embedded in such an exegetical tradition and context.

---

recovering the original context from which the fragmentary echo came and then reading the two texts in dialogical juxtaposition.

207 Cf. Levenson, *Death and Resurrection*, 211; Dahl, *Studies in Paul*, 131.

6.1.2 The Hermeneutical Principles of *a Minore ad Maius* and Order and Rank

It is a commonplace among scholars that Paul applies the hermeneutical principle of *a minore ad maius* in Gal 3:15–18.[208] Another argument at work, which has not been taken into account in the interpretation of this passage, concerns the hermenuetical principle of order and rank, which is attested by Philonic and rabbinic evidence. As I shall suggest, both these principles are interwoven in order to enforce Paul's dissociation of the "Mosaic jurisdiction" from the "Abrahamic jurisdiction". Both principles illustrate and underscore Paul's main point in this passage, which I take to run as follows: First, just as it is a legal norm and binding precedent that a human covenant, once ratified, could not be changed or annuled, how much more does not this legal norm apply on the level of a "divine jurisdiction". Second, the fact that the Law of Moses came four hundred thirty years after the divine covenant that was ratified "between the pieces" proves that the Law had a subordinate order and rank relative to the promise. Therefore, the Law could not annul the ratified covenant and the oath of promise, through which God's promises had been solemnly guaranteed and reaffirmed.

Although it is commonly held that Paul makes use of the argument *a minore ad maius* in Gal 3:15–18, the suggestion has not been made that a reference to the principle of a legal analogy conceived as a binding precedent might be involved in such an argument. Some observations on Paul's vocabulary may corroborate that this is the case in Gal 3:15–18 too.

In Gal 3:15 the expression κατὰ ἄνθρωπον λέγω has usually been taken as introducing an argument *ad hominem* and as an illustration or example, meaning: "let me take an example from everyday life." A more viable understanding of the preposition κατά would take it to refer to a legal context, introducing the legal procedure and norm according to which something takes place.[209] The con-

---

208 See, e.g., deSilva, *The Letter to the Galatians*, 307; Trick, *Abrahamic Descent*, 162; de Boer, *Galatians*, 219; Tolmie, *Persuading the Galatians*, 124–5; Hahn, "Covenant," 87–8; H.-J. Eckstein, *Verheissung und Gesetz: Eine Exegetische Untersuchung zu Galater 2,15–4,7*, WUNT (Tübingen: Mohr Siebeck, 1996), 172; H. Schlier, *Der Brief an die Galater*, KEK (Göttingen: Vandenhoeck & Ruprecht, 1971), 144.

209 Cf., e.g., BAGD. John 18:31 offers an illustration. In connection with the lawsuit against Jesus, Pilate orders the Jewish leaders and specifies the Law according to which Jesus should be judged: "Take him yourselves and judge him according to your law (κατὰ τὸν νόμον)." 1 Cor 9:8–9 provides another example. As one of the three other Pauline instances (cf. the legal undertones also in Rom 3:5 and 6:19) in which we find the cognate phrase "κατὰ ἄνθρωπον", the preposition again introduces the legal norm on which Paul deduces his argument : "Do I say this in accordance with human authority (κατὰ ἄνθρωπον ταῦτα λαλῶ)? Does not the law also say the same? For it is written in the law of Moses, 'You shall not muzzle an ox while it is treading out the grain'."

trasting of a human authority with the Law of Moses as the source of the legal norm that we find here may have some bearing on Paul's reasoning in Gal 3:15–17. In Gal 3:15, the legal norm involved deals with the procedure of a human "covenant". Since Paul does not specify which kind of human "covenant" he has in mind, the meaning of the legal procedure he refers to can be broader and more general, rather than referring to a specific case. The legal procedure and norm are crystal clear, however: once the "covenant" is ratified, it cannot be altered or annulled.

The reference to this legal procedure as one that cannot be annulled might speak in favor of taking it as a binding precedent on which a decision of any subsequent legal case is to be based. Moreover, the specific legal terminology, with "satellite" words set alongside the legal procedures of a human and divine covenant, also supports this idea. Such legal terminology is represented by the words κυρόω, προκυρόω, ἀκυρόω, ἀθετέω, and ἐπιδιατάσσομαι.[210] The touchstone behind a precedent is the need for legal consistency, "treating like cases alike", in an attempt to demonstrate how a legal issue in a similar case can relate to the current dispute or case at hand. The prime analogy of such a precedent on a "lesser" human level is then compared with a compatible legal issue on a "greater" divine level. This emerges from the comparison of the entities implied by Paul's use of the adverb ὅμως in conjunction with the noun ἄνθρωπος in the gentive (3:15) and the prepositional expression ὑπὸ τοῦ θεοῦ (3:16). The meaning of the argument *a fortiori* is fairly clear: where a binding precedent exists even with regard to a human covenant, how much more is this true according to the jurisdiction in the case of God's covenant with Abraham.

I now turn to another aspect of Paul's reasoning at work in this passage, viz. the hermeneutical principle of order and rank. With regard to the problem of narrative sequence in the Torah, we have already observed in a previous chapter how both Philo and the rabbis are involved in a discussion about the narrative order and place of Genesis as part of the Torah. The basic question was: Why did the Law of Moses open with Genesis, containing only narratives and no laws, instead of starting off with Exodus 12, which contains the first laws given to Israel? As we have seen, a variety of answers were offered in the attempt to articulate and relate the role and function of the narratives in Genesis to the later laws of the Torah.[211] Other similar examples on the interrelation between "narrative and nomos" in the Torah can be conveyed in the case of the rabbis, but there

---

210 For the legal connotations of these terms, cf. Betz, *Galatians*, 157–8.

211 See S.D. Fraade, "Nomos and Narrative Before *Nomos and Narrative*," *Yale Journal of Law and the Humanities* 17.1 (2005): 82–6; Kugel, "Jubilees, Philo, and the Problem of Genesis," 305–11.

are also precedents in exegetes such as Philo and Paul in the first century CE.[212] Thus, going beyond previous research, I shall suggest that Paul's reasoning in Gal 3:17,[213] related to the problem of sequence and rank in the Pentateuchal account, has analogies in Philo and the rabbinic literature.[214]

In the interpretation of the Penteteuchal sequence of events, Philo and the rabbinic literature sometimes even draw on the same exegetical motifs and traditions. For example, the question why Adam was created last is asked several times in rabbinic writings *(e.g.,* Gen. Rab. 8:1; Lev. Rab.14:1; t. Sanh. 8:7*)*. Particularly interesting is the parallel in structure and content between *Opif.* 77, (a) "One should ask the reason why man comes last in the world's creation, for, as the sacred writings show, (b) he was the last whom the Father and Maker fashioned", and t. Sanh. 8:7 and 9: (b) "Man was created last. (a) And why was he created last?" Both texts raise the question in point (a), while point (b) states the fact that man according to the biblical text was created last. The reason why man came last in the sequence of creation although he was higher in rank is stated in both texts: As a giver of a banquet does not summon to supper before the meal is prepared, the Ruler and King of all creation has prepared all things for man before he was created. At this point, the two texts share an exegetical motif (*Opif.* 78; t. Sanh. 8:9), in which the picture of a banquet is employed to provide the answer, and thus goes beyond the text of Genesis 1. The basic principle which is presupposed in such discussions of sequence and rank is that the last in a sequence is of subordinate rank relative to the first in the order. This idea is implicitly mentioned and presupposed in *Opif.* 87:

> There is a point, however, as to which ignorance must be avoided. The fact of having been the last to come into existence does not involve an inferiority corresponding to his place in the series.

A similar idea is attested in the rabbinic rule, attested in Sipre Num § 73, in a comment on Num 10:3 – 4. Here, the German translation provided by K.G. Kuhn runs: "Jeder, der im Bibeltext vorangeht, geht [auch] in Wirklichkeit voran."[215]

---

212 Cf. A. Samely, "Between Scripture and Its Rewording: Towards a Classification of Rabbinic Exegesis," *JJS* 42.1 (1991): 39 – 67, esp. 48 – 9.

213 See also my essay "Philo's Relevance for the Study of the New Testament," 231 – 2.

214 For the similarities between Philo and the rabbinic litterature, cf. Borgen, *An Exegete for His Time*, 85 – 9. At this point, however, Borgen fails to draw on Paul as another parallel of this exegetical feature.

215 K.G. Kuhn, *Der Tannaitische Midrasch Sifre zu Numeri*, Rabbinische Texte (Stuttgart: Kohlhammer, 1959), 188.

Paul's reasoning in Gal 3:17 seems to follow the same line of thought. Accordingly, he appears to argue from the exegetical principle of order and rank, implying that in the sequence of narrative events described in the Torah, the Law given at Sinai came *later* and thus was subordinate in rank and unable to make invalid the promise *previously* given to Abraham and ratified by the covenant God made with him: "My point is this: the law, which came four hundred and thirty years *later*, does not annul a covenant *previously* ratified by God, so as to nullify the promise" (Gal 3:17). Thus, it seems that Paul elaborates on his argument *a minore ad maius* from Gal 3:15, but his intention at this juncture is to emphasize the precedence and superiority of the promise ratified through God's "covenant between the pieces" over against the Law of Moses.

Rom 4:11–12 follows a similar kind of problem-solving exegesis and reasoning to Gal 3:15–18. In Rom 4:3, Paul quotes Gen 15:6: "Abraham believed God, and it was reckoned to him as righteousness." On this basis, Paul asked in Rom 4:10: "How then was it reckoned to him?" This "how" (πῶς) refers not to the process of how this did happen, but to its "when": "Was it before or after he had been circumcised?" The answer was: "It was not after, but before he was circumcised. He received the sign of circumcision as a seal of the righteousness that he had by faith while he was still uncircumcised" (Rom 4:10 – 11). Thus, in Rom 4:12 Paul maintained that the basic and superior principle which had priority for Jews and converts alike was righteousness by faith. The Law of Moses regarding circumcision had therefore an inferior and subordinate place relative to the principle of righteousness of faith, and was meant primarily as a judicial approval ("seal") for those Jews who followed the example of Abraham and believed. The purpose of this order and rank between the principles of faith and the law of circumcision was that Abraham was meant to be the father of both Jews and proselytes, who followed the model of Abraham who trusted in God, and thus were embraced by the promise, without distinction.[216]

To return to Gal 3:17, to Paul the Law was legally unauthorized, not only to annul the promise, but also in anyway to supplement it, in such a way that the blessings promised to Abraham were thought of as conditioned on the Law, not on the promise. The argument of the latter position, which finds expression in Gal 3:18, is again centered on the "Abrahamic jurisdiction" in terms of the promised blessing conferred on Abraham, relative to the Law and the "Mosaic jurisdiction".

216 Cf. Bekken, "Philo's Relevance for the Study of the New Testament," 232.

6.1.3 Abraham's Promise and Blessing relative to the Law

In Gal 3:17, Paul separates the promise from the Law, on the ground that the Sinaitic Law was revealed 430 years later. He makes this contrast to reassure the Galatian readers that the promise had priority over against the Law. Obviously, as Betz states, he "intends to render impossible the assumption that the revelation of the Torah on Mount Sinai could imply a cancellation of the promise made to Abraham."[217] In Gal 3:18, then, Paul proceeds to provide an explanation (cf. γάρ) for this assumption by introducing the term κληρονομία. The intention is fairly plain. Paul continues to drive a wedge between the law and promise, by making it clear that the Law could not come between the promise and the blessing of inheritance: "if, then, the inheritance comes from the law, it no longer comes from the promise; but God granted it to Abraham through the promise." Paul's view has been compared and placed in contradistinction to the Jewish tradition from which either Paul himself or his opponents presumably took their bearings. For example, L. Hartman comments as follows on Gal 3:17:

> As a matter of fact Paul's statements fly in the face of any decent Judaism of those days, and should be shocking also to the opponents. But by isolating the Abraham covenant from the others, Paul succeeds in driving a wedge between law and promise.[218]

At this juncture, Hartman presupposes and refers to Betz, who represents quite a common view in Pauline scholarship when he writes that "Paul polemically separates what Judaism tries to hold together".[219] According to scholars such as Hartman and Betz, Paul also disregards another view held by many Jews of his day, viz. the Jewish position that Abraham actually kept the law of Moses.[220] If that is the case, the question arises, as again Betz puts it, "whether this contrasting of Abraham with the Torah of Moses is Paul's own invention or whether there were antecedents."[221] As a fresh answer, I shall suggest that Paul's contrast between Abraham and the Law relative to the promise actually has an analogy in the Jewish discourse on Abraham.

Scholars have drawn a contrast between the reading of Genesis in Paul and that in Philo and the author of Jubilees. So, for example, Watson claims:

> In their different ways, Philo and the author of *Jubilees* read the Genesis narrative along the lines that Paul rejects. Given the Pauline antithesis, it is possible to place their readings on

217 Betz, *Galatians*, 158.
218 Hartman, "Galatians 3:15–4:11," 139.
219 Betz, *Galatians*, 159.
220 Hartman, "Galatians 3:15–4:11," 139 n. 25; Betz, *Galatians*, 159.
221 Betz, *Galatians*, 139.

> one side and his on the other. To that extent, the two types of reading are incommensurable: what is affirmed by the one is denied or downplayed by the other.[222]

As I pointed out in the introductory chapter, Watson's comment is unuanced and fails to account for the modifications referred to by Philo himself in a discussion with his interlocutors. *Pace* Watson and others, Philo's distinction between two jurisdictions within the Torah has some affinity with Paul, so that we might claim that both authors stand on the same side in opposition to those who interpret Abraham's relation to the promise relative to the Law along the lines of the author of Jubilees, Philo's interlocutors, and the later rabbis. This entails that there was a distinction in the concept of Torah between two jurisdictions, i.e., the "Abrahamic jurisdiction" centered on Abraham and his trust in the promise, and the "Mosaic jurisdiction", revealed through Moses at Sinai. In *Abr.* 275 – 276, we have seen that Philo seems to have read the Abrahamic narrative in terms of a *continuum* in Genesis about Abraham's trust in the promise and the oath of promise spoken to him (Gen 15:6 and Gen 22:16 – 18; 26:3 – 4) as a manifestation of the divine Law in Nature (Gen 26:5) over against his interlocutors, who presumably interpreted the same texts as a portrayal of Abraham who was compliant with the Law of Moses. Philo's interlocutors, the author of Sirach 44 and Jubilees 24, rabbis, and possibly Paul's rivals in Galatia argue that Abraham's obedience to the law was a *sine qua non* for the fulfillment of God's oath of promised blessings. In a way corresponding to Paul, Philo emphasizes that the Law of Moses was not set in writing until later (cf. *Abr.* 5). This means that both Philo and Paul maintained that Abraham's trust cannot have been anything but trust in God's promise, set in opposition to the "works of Law" and the notion that Abraham actually followed the Law of Moses.

As I pointed out in chapter four, Gen 26:5 was taken as evidence for the assumption that Abraham was blessed both in his youth and in old age because of his observance of the Torah before its revelation at Sinai. It is significant that the versions according to the Kaufman and Parma mss. and the Yerushalmi both refer to Abraham's blessings both in his youth as well as in his old age, in other words, both before and after his circumcision. Here, I render y. Qidd. 4:12:

> And so you find with regard to Abraham, our father, that he kept the Torah even before it had come into the world, as it is said, "because Abraham obeyed my voice and kept my charge, my commandments, my statutes, and my Torahs" (Gen 26:5). So also [the Torah] made him great and blessed him when he was young, and gave him a future and a hope when he was old. When he was young, what does it say? "Now Abraham was very

222 Watson, *Paul and the Hermeneutics of Faith*, 223.

> rich in cattle, in silver, and in gold". And when he was old, what does it say? Now Abraham was old, well along in years, and the Lord had blessed Abraham in all things" (Gen 24:1).

It is worth noting that the versions in the Tosefta and the Bavli according to the Vienna manuscripts are comparatively distinct. Again, Gen 26:5 is taken as a witness, but this time as a rationale for the view that Abraham was blessed more in his old age than in his youth, since he fulfilled the Law in his old age:

> And the Omnipresent blessed when in his old age more than in his youth. And why all this? Because he kept the entire Torah even before it had come, since it says, "Since Abraham obeyed my voice and kept my charge, my commandments, my statutes and my Torahs" (Gen 26:5)–My Torah is not said, but rather, my Torahs–this teaches that to him were revealed the mysteries of the Torah in all their details (t. Qidd. 5:21).

On the basis of Paz's observations[223] on these later modifications in the version attested in Tosefta and the Bavli, Hayes has recently made the following comments:

> Paz argues that this version responds to the claim–problematic to some rabbinic minds–that Abraham was blessed prior to observing the Law as signaled by his uncircumcision (45). By emphasizing the greater blessing that came with full Torah observance (circumcision and all of the commandments, statutes, and teachings; Gen 26:5), these versions of the tradition (which Paz argues are later modification) disable the Christian reliance on Abraham as proof that the Law is not needed to procure divine blessing.[224]

At this juncture, both Paz and Hayes seem to maintain the common view that sees the rabbinic interpretation of Abraham as Torah observant as a polemic directed against the Pauline interpretation of Abraham as prenomian.[225] For example, Hayes disregards the evidence in Philo, *Abr.* 276, where Philo attests competing understandings of Abraham and the divine Law. In chapter four, I came to the conclusion that Abraham's obedience to a pre-Sinaitic Torah in the rabbinic sources might resemble a Jewish polemic against a prenomian tendency in the understanding of Abraham that predated Paul, and that was in fact held by Philo himself. Given this background, the rabbinic sources seem to make sense in their own right within the framework of a Jewish debate on the prom-

223 Cf. Paz, "Prior to Sinai," 42 – 8.

224 C. Hayes, *Divine Law*, 341.

225 Cf., e. g., the scholars and literature referred to by J.P. Schultz, "Two Views of the Patriarchs: Noahides and Pre-Sinai Israelites," in *Texts and Responses: Studies Presented to Nahum N. Glatzer on the Occasion of His Seventieth Birthday by His Students*, ed. M.A. Fishbane and P.R. Flohr (Leiden: Brill, 1975), 43 – 59, esp. 56.

ised blessing to Abraham relative to his obedience of the Law. At any rate, the rabbinic sources may be cautiously taken to attest a Jewish debate, against which Paul could claim that Abraham received the promise of blessing prior to, and apart from, his observance of the Law.

It can be seen that the Jewish debate concerning Abraham's blessings relative to his circumcision and obedience to the Law is relevant for the undestanding of Gal 3:17–18. Paul too took part in a corresponding inner-Jewish negotiation on Abraham, which seems to have operated with a conception of Abraham as an observer of the Law of Moses. Paul's twist on the Jewish tradition in v. 17–18, then, should be seen against the background of such a Jewish discussion on Abraham, in which the oath of promise was conceived in *continuum* with motifs such as Abraham's covenant, circumcision, descendants, and his adherence to the Law of Moses. It is significant that Gen 26:3 – 5 was embedded within such an exegetical tradition and context. Both Philo and Paul, however, seem to reverse the order evinced in Sir 44:19 – 21, and claim that the oath of promise given to Abraham (*sic* Gen 22:16 – 18; Gen 26:3 – 4) was given prior to, independently of, and separated from the Law of Moses (cf. the use of Gen 26:5). Like Philo, Paul, then, dissociated Abraham from Law-observance, and aligned him with the oath of promise as a reaffirmation of the earlier promise to Abraham. In contrast to Philo, however, and contrary to a Jewish tradition that saw the oath of promise to Abraham (Gen 22:16 – 18) and his descendant (Gen 26:3 – 4) as contingent on his Law-observance (Gen 26:5), Paul disregarded the Law of Moses as the means to the fulfillment of the Abrahamic promise of blessing. This interpretation of the distinction Paul makes between the Abrahamic promise and the Law of Moses provides a coherent reading of Gal 3:15 – 18 that fits well into the context of Gal 3:6 – 14. The fact that the citation in Gal 3:8b evokes not only Gen 12:3 and 22:18, but possibly 26:4 as well, might imply that Paul considers these scriptures as a *continuum* in the Abraham cycle, in which the oath of promise is regarded as a reaffirmation of the earlier blessings promised in Gen 12:3 and Genesis 15, encompassing blessings to Abraham himself, his descendants, and the nations through his descent. The detailed exegetical argument that Paul develops in Gal 3:15 – 25 as a backing for his reasoning in Gal 3:6 – 14 shows that such a claim was controversial in the Jewish context in which Paul's letter to the Galatians should be read.

In Gal 3:18, Paul explains the reason why the promise of blessing in terms of inheritance could not come from the Law. In the first place, if that was the case, the inevitable corallary would be that the Law had annulled the promise. Next, the promise was grounded in the gifts that God made to Abraham: τῷ δὲ Ἀβραὰμ δι' ἐπαγγελίας κεχάρισται ὁ θεός, which I translate as: "God has conferred the gift (of inheritance) to Abraham through promise". This phrase should be compared with a similar phrase in *Abr.* 273: [...] τὴν δι' ὅρκου βεβαίωσιν ὧν ὑπέσχετο δωρεῶν, which I translate as follows: "[...] the confirmation through oath of the gifts which He [God] promised." If we take the promise in Paul's text to include the oath of promise to Abraham, the meaning is the same in both Philo and Paul: The initial promise of gifts has already been given to Abraham in terms of the covenantal promise. Now this promise has been confirmed by the oath of promise given to Abraham. The ambiguity of the term ἐπαγγελία to include both the covenant promise and its reaffirmation through the promises to Abraham corresponds well to the way in which Paul can speak of the promise both in the singular (3:17–18) and in the plural (3:16), since the oath of promise to Abraham and his descendant (Gen 26:3 – 4) contains a plurality of promises and is a reaffirmation of the already existing covenantal promise (Gen 15:1– 8). The train of thought in Gal 3:17– 18 amounts to the conclusion that the gifts promised to Abraham are mediated apart from and independently of the Law. Now, when the time of the "Abrahamic jurisdiction" has come to pass, namely, the realization of the promise of blessing in terms of the trust that God grants Abraham by oath in return from Abraham's trust / faithfulness, and in terms of the reception of the Spirit in Abraham's seed, Christ, this proves that it could neither be revoked nor supplemented by the "Mosaic jurisdiction".

Again, Paul's reasoning in Rom 4:13 – 15 provides a parallel, and explains why the promise of blessing could not run through the Law; the Law brings only transgression and makes one liable to wrath. The argument functions, as in Gal 3:10 – 13, as an argument *e contrario*, which clarifies why the Law cannot lead to the realization of the future promise of blessing in terms of the inheritance of the world that was envisaged by God's oath of promise. If that was the case, the inevitable conclusion would follow that the trust displayed by Abraham was null and the subsequent oath of promise provided by God was void. Thus, the Law would not only bring the promise to a definitive halt, but would also "empty" trust as the basic criterion of appropriate response to God's promise. Instead, it would make the promise contingent on Abraham's past obedience of the pre-Sinaitic Law, and correspondingly Israel's blessings dependent on their adherence to the Sinaitic Law in the future. Evoking the exegetical tradition with respect to the conjunction of Gen 15:6—Gen 22:16 – 18—Gen 26:3 – 4, Paul presupposes that the future blessings are grounded wholly on the terms of Abraham's obedience of trust *and* the subsequent reward of God's oath of promise as an established and reaffirmed fact (cf. Gal 3:8b–9, 14), not as a future possibility contingent upon Abraham's or Israel's adherence to the Law.

In order to summarize my reading of Gal 3:15 – 18 in the context of Gal 3:1– 14, I shall endevour to convey my observations by the means of a paraphrase of Paul's line of thought: My siblings, I speak according to a human norm: No one may add to or cancel even a human being's will, when it has been ratified. On the basis of such a binding precedent, a decision on a subsequent case can be made; my point is this: how much more does not this legal norm apply on the level of a "divine jurisdiction"? Thus, when the previously given promise to Abraham is ratified by God in the "covenant between the pieces", no one can nullify it. Moreover, the promise was confirmed through the oath of promise, not *just* spoken to Abraham, but *to* Abraham *and to his offspring*, which does not apply to many descendants, but to the one individual offspring Christ, encompassing his descendants. Furthermore, since the Law of Moses came four hundred thirty years after the covenant established "between the pieces", this proves that the Law had a subordinate order and rank relative to the priority of the promise, and so it cannot cancel either the original promise or God's confirmation of it by the oath of promise granted to Abraham and to his descendant. The corollary is that the inheritance, the gift promised to Abraham by oath, i.e., the Spirit, is not posited on his observance of the Law of Moses, for God granted it to Abraham on the basis of his trust and continues to confer this gift on his descendants who emulate Abraham's promise-worthy piety of trust.

When Paul emphasizes the precedence and priority of the promise of inheritance that applies to those of trust over against the Law of Moses and those who do according to its commandments, the question of the specific role of the Torah relative to the promise becomes urgent. In the course of Paul's argument, an answer to this question comes in the proceeding passage, Gal 3:19 – 25, to which I now turn.

6.2 The Dynamic of the Two Jurisdictions of Torah and Scripture (Gal 3:19 – 25)

This section argues that Paul elaborates further why the "Abrahamic jurisdiction" has precedence, that is, order, rank, and validity over against the subsequent "Mosaic jurisdiction" made effective by the Sinaitic Law. For Paul, it is imperative to show that both jurisdictions in the Torah stand in a dynamic relation to each other, so much so that Paul interprets the Sinaitic Law as having a time-limited and specific function which contributes to the purpose of implementing the "Abrahamic jurisdiction". Again, I shall provide fresh data which may illuminate some of the enigmatic statements and arguments in Gal 3:19 – 25 within a Jewish context evinced by Philo.

In Gal 3:19 – 25, Paul continues to establish the argument that the Law of Moses does not annul the promise of blessing, since it is of a subordinate rank and is not intended to abrogate the promise. If that is the case, he first raises the inevitable question: "Why then the Law?" (v. 19a). A twofold answer is provided in v. 19b, of which the first part is answered in vv. 21–22, while the last part is elaborated further in vv. 23–24. I shall begin with an analysis of 3:19c–20 in its Jewish context, which in turn may shed light on what Paul goes on to say about the relation between the dynamic of the Law that is integral to the promise of God in this passage.

In vv. 19c–20, Paul interrupts himself with a parenthetical explicative comment on the mediation of the Sinaitic Law: "and it was ordained through angels by (the) hand of a mediator. Now a mediator is not one; but God is one." This enigmatic statement is one of the most difficult ones in Galatians, to say the least, and many interpretations have been offered in order to explain its obscure details.[226]

Paul's reference to the concept of a mediator as mutually exclusive to the notion of the one God represents the chief problem in this text. The following options seem the most viable:

1. A mediator presupposes the notion of a duality of parties, between whom the mediator goes, which contrasts with the oneness of God.[227]

2. A mediator implies that multiple parties were involved, including the one God, implying a procedure of mediation in contrast to the communication, immediacy, and action of the one God.[228] "Since the concept of mediator presupposes by definition a plurality of parties,"[229] it is not at all necessary to argue for the one option against the other. Some further observations of the text in its Jewish context suggest that Paul had both conceptions in mind.

It is my conjecture that Paul not only presupposes an angelic mediation of the Law, but also employs a concept of agency attested in Greco-Roman and Jewish texts, in which a commissioned agent could be understood as an intermediary between several parties. Accordingly, agents could send another agent on their behalf, authorized to act on his own authority. Thus, according to Paul,

---

226 For surveys of previous research and interpretations, see Keener, *Galatians*, 283–4; S. Nordgaard, "Paul and the Provenance of the Law: The Case of Gal 3,19–20," *ZNW* 105.1 (2014): 64–79; C. Heil, "'Angeordnet durch Engel durch die Hand eines Mittlers' (Gal 3,19): Das paulinische Konzept von der Vermittlung der Tora," in *Vermittelte Gegenwart: Konzeptionen der Gottespräsenz von der Zeit des Zweiten Tempels bis Anfang des 2. Jahrhunderts n.Chr.*, ed. A. Taschl-Erber and I. Fischer (Tübingen: Mohr Siebeck, 2016), 229–43; T. Callan, *The Law and the Mediator: Gal. 3:19b–20* (PhD diss., Yale University, 1976).

227 Thus, e.g., Trick, *Abrahamic Descent*, 195–7; Longenecker, *Galatians*, 142; Lightfoot, *Galatians*, 146.

228 For example, Tolmie, *Persuading the Galatians*, 136; T. Callan, "Pauline Midrash: The Exegetical Background of Gal 3:19b," *JBL* 99.4 (1980): 566; Betz, *Galatians*, 171.

229 Betz, *Galatians*, 171.

Moses was commissioned by the angels, sent on their behalf as a legally authorized mediator / agent, as an intermediary between the angels and the people. Basically, then, Moses, as a commissioned agent, stood in the same legal relation to God as the angels, since it was God who had commissioned the angels with the Law in the first place, and Moses then returns and reports to God. Hence, Paul can state that the Law was arranged by three parties: by God who "orders" the Law to be given "through" the agency of the angels *and* "by the hand of" Moses. This divine arrangement of the Law mediated through angelic envoys, one of whom was Moses, contrasts with the one God, who spoke directly to Abraham and Isaac when he communicated the promise. For this reason, the immediacy of the promise on God's part corresponds to the nature of the one God, while the mediation of the Law through many agents highlights its provisional function and main purpose. If it was *God alone*, as in the process by which the promise came to be, who gave the Law to Israel, other mediators would be superfluous. Accordingly, the Law of Moses is given later as an addition, through a plurality of mediators. It is provisional, and has a time-limited charge and authority for the sake of its purpose, and is valid only until the oath of promise spoken directly to Abraham and Isaac comes to fruition. The angelic meditation of the Law through their agent Moses manifests its inferiority to the immediacy of the promise. Some inferences from the notion of agency and Jewish traditions of the mediation of the Law at Sinai may provide an explanation in favor of this reading. I shall draw specifically upon Philo's text in *Somn.* 1:141 – 143 as the lens for my interpretation of Gal 3:19 – 20 that may help us to bring its textual elements into focus as a consistent and coherent whole.

Gal 3:19c seems to be misunderstood, when some exegetes separate God from giving the Law at Sinai.[230] The *passivum divinum* in terms of the passive construction of the verb διατάσσω and the preposition διά with the genitive indicate that God is the logical subject and thus the originator of the Law.[231] In Second Temple literature, there are two modes in the way the Law was given at Sinai, either through an angelic mediation, on the agency and authority of the angels who revealed the Law at God's command, or immediately to Moses as the messenger, who then received the Law directly from the mouth of God.[232] The former motif is usually taken to be attested in Jubilees, Philo, Josephus, and also in early Christian texts such as Gal 3:19 – 20; Hebr 2:2; and Acts

230 Thus, for example, de Boer, *Galatians*, 288; Martyn, *Galatians*, 366.
231 Cf. Heil, "'Angeordnet durch Engel durch die Hand eines Mittlers' (Gal 3,19)," 232; Williams, *Galatians*, 99; Dahl, *Studies in Paul*, 173.
232 Najman, *Seconding Sinai*, 60 – 3.

7:53,[233] while the latter motif is evinced in the book of Sirach, the Qumran literature, and is later evidenced in Origen and rabbinic literature.[234] My reading of Gal 3:19 – 20 presupposes that Paul might be familiar with both traditions, but that he wants to modify them for the sake of his argument. While the angelic tradition in Gal 3:19c seems to be evoked as familiar, Paul has been seen as "unique in explicitly linking the mediation of Moses with that of a multiplicitly of angels. (How he envisages this concretely is not clear.)"[235] *Pace* such an idiosyncratic view on Paul's part, I shall suggest that the association of Moses with a plurality of angels in the giving of the Law at Sinai is an exegetical motif known to Philo, and which might help to clarify Paul's conception too. Paul's use of the angelic tradition, however, deviates from the tradition in another sense. Unlike, for example, the author of Jubilees, who based the authority of the Law on its angelic mediation, Paul rather seems to downgrade the Law by emphasizing its provisional authority, valid until the realization of the promise made to Abraham and Isaac.[236] If so, this means that Paul contrasts the way in which the Law and the promise were given, on the ground that *the former was mediated by several mediators such as the angels and Moses* as a provisional charge, over against *the latter communicated directly by God, without employing messengers,* as an enduringly legal expression of God's will.

As a further explanation of this interpretation, I shall use some details in *Somn.* 1:141 – 143 as a referential background against which I interpret Gal 3:19c–20. These texts should be brought into conversation and given more attention beyond the fact that they implicitly and generally seem to refer to Moses as a mediator, μεσίτης.[237] *Somn.* 1:141 – 143 reads:

> [...] ὁ δὲ ἱερὸς λόγος ἀγγέλους εἴωθε καλεῖν προσφυεστέρῳ χρώμενος ὀνόματι· καὶ γὰρ τὰς τοῦ πατρὸς ἐπικελεύσεις τοῖς ἐγγόνοις καὶ τὰς τῶν ἐγγόνων χρείας τῷ πατρὶ διαγγέλλουσι. παρὸ καὶ ἀνερχομένους αὐτοὺς καὶ κατιόντας εἰσήγαγεν, οὐκ ἐπειδὴ τῶν μηνυσόντων ὁ πάντη ἐφθακὼς θεὸς δεῖται, ἀλλ' ὅτι τοῖς ἐπικήροις ἡμῖν συνέφερε μεσίταις καὶ διαιτηταῖς λόγοις χρῆσθαι διὰ τὸ τεθηπέναι καὶ πεφρικέναι τὸν παμπρύτανιν καὶ τὸ μέγιστον ἀρχῆς αὐτοῦ κράτος. οὗ λαβόντες ἔννοιαν ἐδεήθημέν ποτέ τινος τῶν μεσιτῶν λέγοντες· "λάλησον σὺ ἡμῖν, καὶ μὴ λαλείτω πρὸς ἡμᾶς ὁ θεός, μή ποτε ἀποθάνωμεν." οὐ γὰρ ὅτι κολάσεις, ἀλλ' οὐδ' ὑπερβαλλούσας καὶ ἀκράτους εὐεργεσίας χωρῆσαι δυνάμεθα, ἃς ἂν αὐτὸς προτείνῃ δι' ἑαυτοῦ μὴ χρώμενος ὑπηρέταις ἄλλοις.

233 Cf., e.g., Jub. 1:27–29; 2:1; *Abr.* 115; *Ant.* 15:136.
234 Cf., e.g., Sir 45:5; 4Q377 2 II; Mek. Šabb. 1; Sipre Zuta 12; Sipre Pisqa 42; Origen's commentary on Song 1:2. For a discussion of these texts and relevant secondary literature, see H. Najman, *Past Renewals*, 131 – 42.
235 Callan, "Pauline Midrash," 553.
236 Najman, *Past Renewals*, 129 – 30.
237 Callan, "Pauline Midrash," 555.

> [...] but the sacred record is wont to call them "angels" or messengers, employing an apter title, for they both convey the biddings of the Father to His children and report the children's need to their Father. In accordance with this they are represented by the lawgiver as ascending and descending: not that God, who is already present in all directions, needs informants, but that it was a boon to us in our sad case to avail ourselves of the services of "words" acting on our behalf as mediators, so great is our awe and shuddering dread of the universal Monarch and the exceeding might of His sovereignty. It was our attainment of a conception of this that once made us address to one of those mediators the entreaty: "Speak thou to us, and let not God speak to us, lest haply we die" (Ex. xx. 19). For should He, without employing ministers, hold out to us with His own hand, I do not say chastisements, but even benefits unmixed and exceeding great, we are incapable of receiving them. *Somn.* 1:141–143

Before I look at some details in this text, I offer some notes on the Greco-Roman and Jewish concept of agency in general. M.M. Mitchell has studied the conventions on diplomacy and envoys in the Greco-Roman context and found a correspondence between the halakhic principles of agency and Greco-Roman diplomatic conventions about envoys.[238] For example, she refers to the characteristics of agency in Jewish halakhah,[239] such as "(a) the unity between the agent and his sender, (b) although the agent is subordinate; (c) the obedience of the agent to the will of the sender; (d) the task of the agent in the lawsuit; (e) his return and reporting back to the sender; and (f) his appointing of other agents as an extension of his own mission in time and space."[240] This concept is broader and comprises other forms of authorized activity than just that of the actual commissioning of an envoy. It may refer to a permanent or a time-limited agency, to a transfer of authority from father to son within a familial setting, or to other kinds of authorization of various professions and functions, as well as to social conventions like that of a proper reception of the envoy, etc.[241]

In the period of the Roman empire, a large number of ambassadors and other commissioned agents were present in Rome, either as professional agents, such as an ambassador, commissioner or other forms of full-time representation,

---

238 M.M. Mitchell, "New Testament Envoys in the Context of Greco-Roman Diplomatic and Epistolary Conventions: The Example of Timothy and Titus," *JBL* 111.4 (1992): 641–62.

239 Mitchell, "New Testament Envoys," 645 n. 11.

240 At this point, Mitchell draws specifically on the study of P. Borgen, "God's Agent in the Fourth Gospel," in *Religions in Antiquity: Essays in Memory of E. R. Goodenough*, ed. J. Neusner, SHR (Leiden: Brill, 1968), 137–48, esp. 143–4.

241 J.-A. Bühner, *Der Gesandte und sein Weg im 4. Evangelium: Die kultur- und religionsgeschichtlichen Grundlagen der Johanneischen Sendungschristologie sowie ihre traditionsgeschichtliche Entwicklung*, WUNT 2 (Tübingen: Mohr Siebeck, 1977), 189–98; Mitchell, "New Testament Envoys," 647–51.

or because they were sent on a provisional and specific commission. Philo himself can illustrate how the principles of agency reflect the conventions of agency in the Greco-Roman world and in a Jewish context. He reports that he once was part of a Jewish delegation of five envoys, sent on behalf of the Jews in Alexandria to appear before the Emperor, in order to negotiate with Gaius on the issue of equal rights between Jews and Greeks in Alexandria. Thus, as the leader of the delegation representing the Alexandrian Jewish community to Emperor Gaius Caligula, Philo states in general the relation between the envoys and those who have sent them: "the suffering of envoys (πρέσβεις) recoils on those who have sent him" (*Legat.* 369).[242] Here, Philo implicitly reflects the principle that a proper reception of the envoy entails the proper reception of those who sent him, and thus the converse implications of the rejection of an envoy.[243] In this connection, he uses the Greek technical terms πρέσβυς and πρεσβευτής for the human envoys. The latter term πρεσβευτής is used in the paragraph next to the one just quoted from *De Legatione ad Gaium:* "Surely it was a cruel situation that the fate of all the Jews everywhere should rest precariously on us five envoys (πρεσβευταί)" (§ 370).[244] Philo can also use the diplomatic term πρεσβευτής about angels, acting as ambassadors between humans and God. Angels are described as "the servitors and lieutenants of the primal God whom he employs as ambassadors (πρεσβευταί) to announce the predictions which he wills to make to our race" (*Abr.* 115). A similar understanding of the role of the angels, as intermediaries between God, the Father, and his children, comes to expression in *Somn.* 1:141: "[...] but the sacred record is wont to call them 'angels' or messengers, employing an apter title, for they both convey the biddings of the Father to His children and report the children's need to their Father." Here, we can see how the mediation of the angels involved their being sent as envoys, who in turn report to the sender. Moreover, this text exemplifies the idea of commissioning and the role of agency within a familial setting as its background. Thus, the existing relationship between the Father and his children is the basis for what the angels

242 Philo here draws on the diplomatic principle that "an agent is like the one who sent him". For its use in rabbinic data, cf. Mek. Exod 12:3, 6; m. Ber. 5:5; b. B. Meṣ. 96a.

243 The same basic rule of agency lies behind Paul's description of his meeting with the Galatians, when they saw his role as an envoy to be that of a "messenger", representing God or Christ Jesus himself: "[. . .] you [. . .] received me as a messenger of God, as Christ Jesus" (Gal 4:14). For the the translation of ἄγγελος, taken not to mean "angel", but rather "messenger", cf. Mitchell, "New Testament Envoys," 646 n. 17: "I prefer the latter, 'messenger,' here, since it is so clearly bound up with the assumption that the envoy should be properly received, and because there is nothing in the passage to suggest that Paul likens himself to the supernatural envoys, angels."

244 Compare also Philo, *Flacc.* 97, 98, and *Legat.* 182. On the use of the term πρεσβευτής / *legatus,* cf. D. Kienast, "Presbeia," *PWSup* 13: 546 – 52.

do as go-betweens for God and his children. J.-A. Bühner refers to the legal role of the agents within the institution of a family household as the background of these ideas.[245]

Philo also employs the idea of the angels as God's messengers to the concept of the Logos as an ambassador sent from the heavenly God and King to human beings on earth. We should also note that Philo says that the Logos, the Archangel, acts as ambassador and communicates between God, the Father, and mortals, as a ruler to his subjects: "This same Logos both pleads with the immortal as suppliant for afflicted mortality and acts as ambassador (πρεσβευτής) of the ruler to the subject" (*Her.* 205). Thus, Philo's affirmation of the "two-ways role" of the Logos suggests that *Somn.* 1:141–143 applies this function to "words" (μεσίταις καὶ διαιτηταῖς λόγοις), one of the mediators of which (τινος τῶν μεσιτῶν), with an obvious reference to Moses, was the representative intermediary by whom the Law was mediated at Sinai:

> it was a boon to us in our sad case to avail ourselves of the services of "words" ("λόγοι") acting on our behalf as mediators, so great is our awe and shuddering dread of the universal Monarch and the exceeding might of His sovereignty. It was our attainment of a conception of this that once made us address to one of those mediators the entreaty: "Speak thou to us, and let not God speak to us, lest haply we die" (Ex. 20:19). *Somn.* 1:142–143

The use of the term for an intermediary (μεσίτης) at this particular event might indicate that Moses was authorized for a specific time-limited mission. The role of Moses as an intermediary and the reference to Exod 20:19 suggest that this was an event which also involved the other party to the transaction. Thus, Philo says that the one mediator acted on behalf of the people, who were terrified by the circumstances and begged Moses to speak to them, instead of God. It is also noteworthy that Philo seems to say something about the necessity and purpose of the mediation of the Law through a messenger. A hypothetical tension is drawn between the negative outcome if God alone directly spoke the "words" to the people, which would mean that the people would die, and thus be unable to receive the punishments as well as the benefits that came with the Law. For this reason, the mediation of the Law through messengers such as Moses became necessary: "For should He, without employing ministers, hold out to us with His own hand, I do not say chastisements, but even benefits unmixed and exceeding great, we are incapable of receiving them" (*Somn.* 1:143).

Against this background, using *Somn.* 1:141–143 as a lens, I offer some brief observations on Gal 3:19–20. In the first place, both Philo and Paul share the

---

245 Bühner, *Der Gesandte*, 195–9.

Jewish exegetical motif of an angelic mediation of the Law, along with the notion of Moses as one of the mediators. H. Schlier asks: "may it be that the Pauline *μεσίτης* ['mediator'] of Gal 3:19 is a hidden concept of Moses as akin to the *ἄγγελος* ['angel' or 'messenger']?"[246] Betz comments on this question: "If this were true, one could understand why the angels who ordain the Law are associated with Moses as a mediator."[247] *Somn.* 1:141 – 143 affirms the assumptions made by these scholars. Thus, although both Philo and Paul make use of general statements on the mediator, Moses is assumed to be the one mediator through whom the the angels / messengers communicated the Law.

Next, in his mediatorial function, Moses must take account of all the parties, God, the angels, and the people. This assertion is based on the answers one gives to the following question: What in v. 19 warrants the general statement and definition in v. 20a (ὁ δὲ μεσίτης ἑνὸς οὐκ ἔστιν) about whose and what sort of mediator Moses was in contrast with God (ὁ δὲ θεὸς εἷς ἐστιν)? The particular enigma in v. 20 is how one understands "one" in both clauses of the verse. With regard to v. 20a, the problem is how to explain the genitive, either as a subjective genitive indicating whose mediator Moses was not ("the mediator [Moses] is not *of one*"), or as a qualitative genitive defining what sort of mediator Moses was not ("the mediator [Moses] is not *one*").[248] There might be a possibility that Paul plays on the ambiguity, so that both meanings are involved. In the first case, the purpose must be to say as a general statement that the presence of a mediator presupposes a multiplicity of parties. This corresponds to the *scenario* envisaged in *Somn.* 1:141 – 143, in which a mediator (*sic* Moses) was seen as a representative of more than one party, that is, of the angels / messengers and of behalf of the people of Israel.

On the other hand, if the genitive is numerical and qualitative, the intention is to say that Moses was not only one in the sense of being simple, and as such contrasts with the simplicity of God. If so, Paul's comment on Moses's mediation of the Law as a mediator in Gal 3:20 who is not *one* who can operate on his own, and therefore mutually exclusive of the concept of the *one* God, might be a modification of Moses's role as an intermediary. Previous scholarship seems to have overlooked the point that the expression "by the hand of a mediator" in v. 19c applied to Moses may suggest such an interpretation.[249] As we have already pointed out, a principle in Jewish and Greco-Roman diplomatic relations was that an agent could appoint other agents as an extension of their own commis-

246 Schlier, *Der Brief an die Galater*, 161.
247 Betz, *Galatians*, 170.
248 Callan, "Pauline Midrash," 566.
249 See Keener, *Galatians*, 282; Das, *Galatians*, 362; Moo, "Galatians," 235.

sion.[250] Thus, the expression ἐν χειρί could be a rendering of the Hebrew ביד (literally "through the hand of"), which in the Jewish terminology of agency would mean that an envoy appointed on behalf of another agent was authorized to operate legally on his own.[251] If this is the sense in Gal 3:19c, then, it is all the more understandable that Paul needs to explicate in his parenthetical statement in v. 20 what he means. The line of thought is, then, that the commission and authority of the angels has been extended to another mediator to carry out the task, viz. Moses. Paul's denial that Moses is one can thus be taken in this sense of being simple, that is, authorized to accomplish the charge on his own. Moses's role as a mediator contradicts such an implication. Philo's reasoning in *Somn* 1:143 provides an analogy; here, Philo also contrasts the need for ministers with the case if the immediacy of God alone were involved in the giving of the Law to Israel: "For should He, without employing ministers, himself hold out to us on his own [...]. " Thus, both Philo and Paul seem to presuppose that God was not immediately involved in the giving of the Law, although he was the originator and giver of the Law, and that Moses as an intermediary worked for a plurality of partners, that is, for the angels comissioned by God. Hence, the two prepositional phrases, "through angels, by the hand of a mediator" in 3:19c, imply that Moses was in the immediate service of the angels rather than of God.

Finally, the contrast Philo draws in *Somn.* 1:143 between the agency of an intermediary—by implication, Moses portrayed as acting as a "mediator" (μεσίτης) on behalf of a plurality of messenger-beings—and the singularity of God, who is in no need of any messengers, may shed light on the specific purpose of the Law that Paul has in mind in Gal 3:19 – 24. As we noted above, Philo reflected on why God alone could not interact with Israel and why it was necessary to deploy messengers: "For should He, without employing ministers, hold out to us with His own hand, I do not say chastisements, but even benefits unmixed and exceeding great, we are incapable of receiving them" (*Somn.* 1:143). Thus, it seems here that Philo, like Paul, provides a rationale for the mediation of the Sinaitic Law through ministers such as angels and Moses, and not directly by God, because of the frailty and sin of the people who received it. A similar view, in which God's immediacy is distanced from the giving of Law of Moses because of its function of inflicting punishments, resonates with Philo's distinction between

250 Mitchell, "New Testament Envoys," 645.

251 Cf. Bühner, *Der Gesandte*, 198 n. 16: "In der juristischen Sprache des Judenthums meint יד nich nur aktuelle Verfügungsgewalt, sondern die grundlegende Berechtigung zum Handeln in eigener rechtlicher Verantwortung."

the Decalogue mediated by God alone and the special laws given by Moses.[252] Thus, for example, in *Decal.* 19, Philo stresses "that those which He [God] gave in His own person and by His own mouth alone include both laws and heads summarizing the particular laws, but those in which he spoke through the prophet [Moses] all belong to the former class." In *Decal.* 175 – 178, Philo further emphasizes that God did not intertwine the Decalogue with penalties, as is the case with the "special" laws of Moses.[253] Thus, God

> judged it was most in accordance with His being to issue His saving commandments free from any admixture of punishment, that men might choose the best, not involuntarily, but of deliberate purpose, not taking senseless fear but the good sense of reason for their counselor. *Decal.* 177[254]

At this juncture, Philo resonated with Stoic philosophy that ascribed educational aims to law and the importance of free choice, through which the law is chosen for its own sake to restrain vice and give incentive to virtues.[255]

In a way that corresponds to Philo, the mediation of the Law through a mediator meant for Paul that it served a distinct function relative to the promise given to Abraham and to his offspring, which was spoken directly by God him-

---

252 This accords with what Philo affirms in his "Exposition of the Law", that disobedience relative to the special laws of Moses incurs punishments and curses. Cf. *Praem.* 4, 126 – 162; *Mos.* 2:52 – 65. See Bekken, *The Word is Near You*, 35 – 7.

253 Cf. on this subject, Y. Amir, *Die hellenistische Gestalt des Judentums bei Philon von Alexandrien*, Forschungen zum Jüdisch-Christlichen Dialog (Neukirchen: Neukirchener Verlag, 1983), 153 – 7.

254 Philo asserts, however, that δίκη, the surveyor of human affairs, would enforce the commandments by inflicting punishment on sinners in virtue of her natural hatred of evil (*Decal.* 177). In both the "Exposition of the Law" and the historical writings, Philo refers to δίκη as the divine agency enforcing on the wicked those punishments (*Praem.* 136) that Deuteronomy and Leviticus warn will be inflicted on those who disregard the "Mosaic jurisdiction" (*Praem.* 127 – 151). Cf. the analogy in Rom 13:4, in which the governing authorities are seen as the servants of God, executing wrath from Justice (ἔκδικος) on the wrongdoer. The same idea and cognate is to be found in Rom 12:19 and Heb 2:2. Moreover, an illustration of this principle is provided by Philo's account of Flaccus. Here, Philo concludes that when Flaccus was killed by the agents of Emperor Gaius, the retribution of his crimes against the Jewish people was carried out with mathematical precision according to the principle of δίκη: "For it was the will of δίκη that the butcheries which she wrought on his single body should be as numerous as the number of the Jews whom he unlawfully put to death" (*Flacc.* 189). On this subject, cf. Bekken, *The Lawsuit Motif*, 188 – 9.

255 On the Stoic influence on Philo's conception of the Jewish Law, see now M.R. Niehoff, *Philo of Alexandria: An Intellectual Biography* (New Haven; London: Yale University Press, 2018), 151 – 4.

self. For this reason, the giving of the Law itself through mediators showed that it was only an inferior and provisional arrangement until "the offspring should come, to whom the promise applies". Unlike Philo, however, Paul held that the Law was not intended to mediate benefits, but rather was given solely "for the sake of transgressions" (Gal 3:19), and to hand everything over to the sway of sin (cf. Gal 3:22a: "But the scripture has imprisoned all things under the power of sin [...]"), which can be taken to imply transgressions liable to punishments.[256] Although Paul, unlike Philo, does not adduce here a supporting prooftext in his statements about the negative purpose of the Sinaitic Law, his argument seems to follow a hermeneutical perspective shared by Philo, namely, that the Law could not have been mediated by God directly, but only through a plurality of messengers such as angels and by the hand of Moses, if the purpose of the Law was to be bearable for the people who received it.

In Pauline scholarship, the reasoning about the negative function of the Law has been taken to be "un-Jewish" and "Paul's most original contribution to the interpretation of the Scriptures."[257] However, a comparison of Paul with Philo with regard to their rationale for the mediation of the Law may indicate that Paul's argument would not perhaps have been conceived to be so idiosyncratic in a Jewish context as scholars have surmised. Both the similarity and the contrast are illuminating and should be highlighted. Both authors seem to share the view of a distance of the Law relative to God, expressed by the exegetical motif of an angelic mediation of the Law, and envisaging Moses as one of the mediators among them. On Philo's part, the rationale behind this dissociation of God from the procedure of mediating the Law was to offer the people the possibility of receiving both the chastisements and the benefits of the Law. Unlike Philo, Paul, in view of an ongoing argument, separates God from the Law, and emphasizes the "negative" role of the Law, "for the purpose of transgression", in order to keep the blessings which emerge from God's promise separate from the Law. As I shall now endeavor to demonstrate, Paul saw this role on the part of the Torah as integral to the promise spoken without a mediator and directly by God himself to Abraham and to his descendant.

If both the promise and the Law derive from the same God, and the Law was intended to serve a merely negative function, a second problem then arises, which Paul sharply formulates in the question: "Is the law then opposed to the promises of God?" (Gal 3:21). Whether or not a *dictum* has been raised here in opposition to Paul, he is nevertheless at this stage driven to clarify his

---

256 Dahl, *Studies in Paul*, 134.
257 Dahl, "Paul's Letter to the Galatians," 59.

stance on the Law in relation to the promise. The issues implied seem to have been whether the Law is the means to the fulfillment of the promise, and, if this is not the case, is it at all to be seen as integral to the promise? The basic question beneath these issues is perhaps: Does God actually contradict himself in the way he handles the Law and the promise? Very different answers have been given by scholars to some of these questions that are implied in Gal 3:21. For example, Betz regards the question as mirroring a charge by Paul's critics that he separates the promise to Abraham from the Torah of Moses, "but Paul's strong denial μὴ γένοιτο ('by no means') shows that he wants to avoid such a separation."[258] Likewise, although he does not explicate exactly what this entails, Dunn claims that "the role of the law is consistent with, integrated into that of the promise."[259] Most recently, K.O. Sandnes argues against the view held by Betz and Dunn, suggesting that it "owes more to Romans than to Galatians."[260] Hence, Sandnes suggests that Gal 3:21 is to be regarded as a *dictum* which emerges from the position of his opponents:

> They urged that according to Paul, God made contradictory statements, since Paul, in fact, denied what to them was the concise summary of the law (Lev 18:5). To them, Paul related selectively to the law, not taking the whole into account, and thereby left God inconsistent. God had given a law that was in opposition to the promise God had given to Abraham. To Paul this was essential; to his antagonists this was disastrous.[261]

Sandnes's view of an opposition between Law and promise as "essential" is to a large extent based on the position taken by de Boer.[262] Unlike Sandnes, however, de Boer rejects the view that implies that Paul has presented a contradictory God. Rather, Paul's intention is to reaffirm a separation between the promises and the Law:

> Paul's question is not: "Is the law *of God* then against the promises of God?" [...] Paul's theological and rhetorical purpose in this passage is precisely to dissociate God from the law; he has no interest in bringing God's promises to Abraham and the law into a positive relationship [...]. Paul's answer therefore does not show that he wants to avoid a separation of the promises and the law (so Betz 173); on the contrary, it shows that he wants emphatically to reaffirm that separation.[263]

258 Betz, *Galatians*, 173.
259 Dunn, *Galatians*, 192.
260 Sandnes, *Paul Perceived*, 82.
261 Sandnes, *Paul Perceived*, 83.
262 Sandnes, *Paul Perceived*, 82 notes 105, 111, and 112.
263 de Boer, *Galatians*, 232.

In a similar vein, Barclay says that "the Torah is thus neither integral to, nor a means toward, the fulfillment of the Abrahamic blessing."[264] Moreover, Barclay claims:

> But because the Torah was neither integral to the story of the promise, nor effective in securing its fulfillment, it is portrayed as standing in an indirect relation to the "one God", whose singular purpose was carried by the gift of the promise, anticipating Christ (3:16, 18).[265]

Mitchell has rightly critized Barclay's reading of the relationship between the Law and the promise:

> This is for me the most 'shocking' part of JB's reading. How can the Torah not be 'integral to the story of the promise' (p. 404) when it is γραφή (= νόμος / תורה) that pre-preached the gospel in the promise to Abraham (3.8, προευαγγελίζεσθαι)? Can one say that Paul has 'removed the Torah from the trajectory of the promise' (p. 407) in light of Paul's outright denial that the law is against the divine promises in 3.21a: ὁ οὖν νόμος κατὰ τῶν ἐπαγγελιῶν [τοῦ θεοῦ]; μὴ γένοιτο?[266]

In his answer to Mitchell, Barclay maintains his view that the Torah is not included or "integral" in the story line of the promises:

> His [Paul's] distancing rhetoric forces him to raise and answer (in the negative) the question of whether promise and law are somehow opposed, but non-opposition does not mean combination into an 'integral' or singular phenomenon.

In view of this ongoing scholarly discussion on the relationship between the Law and promise in terms of an opposition or a separation, or whether the Law was or was not integral to the story of the promise, I shall suggest that Gal 3:21 – 24 elaborates further on Paul's distinction between two conceptions within the Torah and Scripture, namely, between an "Abrahamic jurisdiction" centered on Abraham's trust and God's promise, and a "Mosaic jurisdiction". Again, in view of the preceding reasoning in Gal 3:6 – 20, the latter has a distinctive function disjoined from the former, but nevertheless has an integral or dynamic interaction with it, in order to bring the former to its fruition.

---

264 Barclay, *Paul and the Gift*, 401.
265 Barclay, *Paul and the Gift*, 404.
266 Mitchell, "Gift Histories," *JSNT* 39.3 (2017): 318. Her objection might be relevant to the view defended by Sandnes and de Boer too.

In the first place, some of the text-witnesses to Gal 3:19 and 3:21 may provide clues to which legal conceptions are collocated in Paul's reasoning about the Law and the promise. Although it is probably a later modification of the earlier witness chosen by Nestle-Aland's 28th edition, it is noteworthy that Dahl takes the variant reading νόμος τῶν πράξεων by text-witnesses such as P46 F G in Gal 3:19 as indicating a distinction within Paul's concept of the Law.[267] In Gal 3:21, the words rendered in square brackets [τοῦ θεοῦ], although missing in the best text-witnesses P 46 and Vaticanus, are included in Nestle-Aland's 28th edition. Thus, regardless of the text-critical assesments of the variants in Gal 3:19 and 3:21, they may provide additional evidence of a distinction in Paul's concept of the Law and Scripture, i.e., between a "Mosaic jurisdiction", in terms of the word νόμος centered on the "deeds" that it prescribes, and an "Abrahamic jurisdiction", aligned with Abraham's trust and God's promise. The variant text-witnesses may thus actually bring us closer to the real issue at stake in Gal 3:21: The question is not whether the Law and the promise present a contradictory God, but rather: Is there a conflict in the Torah and Scripture between the "Mosaic jurisdiction" and the "Abrahamic jurisdiction"? As I have argued already throughout this chapter, such a question resonates well with Paul's argument in Gal 3:6 – 20, but also in the context of a Jewish controversy on the question of the relationship between Abraham and the Law of Moses.

The conjunction οὖν in Gal 3:21 signals that a conclusion is drawn from the preceding verses. This means that Paul's fundamental deliberations on the Law of Moses relative to the promise in Gal 3:15 – 18 provide the backbone of the question that is now raised: If the blessing of inheritance comes from God's covenant with its inherent promise, and not from the Law (3:17– 18), or if indeed the Law was given for the purpose of transgression (3:19a) and was temporarily subordinated to the superiority of the promise of Abraham's offspring, Christ, to whom the promises applied (3:16, 19b), or if the Law of Moses could not even be spoken directly by God as was the promise (3:19c, 20), do not all these circumstances amount to asking whether the Law is against the promises of God? Thus, from its immediate context one might infer that Paul's question in Gal 3:21 envisages a separation between the Law of Moses and God's promise, but such a conclusion is met with an outright denial on Paul's part: μὴ γένοιτο. Some further observations on Gal 3:19 – 24 in the view of Paul's argument in Gal 3:6 – 14 support the notion that Paul proceeds to explain how the two jurisdictions attested in the Torah and Scripture intersect in a dynamic interaction. This means that the Law

267 Dahl, *Studies in Paul*, 176. For a further discussion of the text variants in Gal 3:19, cf. S.C. Carlson, *The Text of Galatians and its History*, WUNT 2 (Tübingen: Mohr Siebeck, 2015), 192 – 3.

is considered to be in harmony with the promise to Abraham and to his offspring, and therefore contributed to its fulfillment, on the basis of Abraham's trust, and hence not by "works of Law" as a way of life in compliance with the regulations prescribed by the Mosaic Law.

Vocabulary derived from the jurisdiction of Law abounds in Gal 3:19 – 24, as it has in Gal 3:1 – 13. If these passages are read together, it seems that Paul presents many of the same elements, which describe the course of the legal procedure in terms of a crime (1) characterized as a transgression of the law, (2) followed by an arrest of the guilty person, accompanied by imprisonment and custody, until the case came up (3) before a judicial authority, in which a (4) verdict of guilt could result in (5) a sentence and subsequent (6) punishment in the form of an execution and public display of the criminal. These are conventional features of a legal proceeding well attested in Jewish and Greco-Roman legal sources.[268] As I have argued above, in Gal 3:1 – 13, elements 4, 5, and 6 were applied by Paul to highlight the crucifixion of Jesus Christ in keeping with how an alleged lawbreaker was dealt with according to the jurisdiction of the Law (Gal 3:1, 10, 13). Since the execution of Christ was a legal action that took place vicariously "*for us*", Paul could turn a criminal report on Jesus Christ on its head, so that the death of Jesus Christ was seen to have fulfilled the promised blessings to Abraham for both Jews and the ἔθνη (Gal 2:21; 3:13 – 14). As I shall further point out, in Gal 3:19 – 24, elements 1, 2, and 3 of a legal procedure are deployed to present the temporal character of the Law as a provisional, interim jurisdiction valid for the time between Moses and Christ. In a way corresponding to the line of thought in Gal 3:10 – 14, Paul emphasizes that the negative purpose of the Law was not to be a temporary substitute for the promise nor a Law code added in order to regulate it, but rather an arrangement that positively pertained to the realization of the promise in Christ.

In order to justify his outright denial of the possibility of a conflict between the Law and God's promises (Gal 3:21a), Paul inserts an explanatory statement about the Law in the form of a hypothetical clause in an unreal condition: "For if a law had been given that could make alive, then righteousness would indeed come through the law" (Gal 3:21b). At this juncture, Paul seems to pick up his line of thought from 3:11 – 12, drawing on the terminology of law, life,

---

268 Cf. B. Palme, "Roman Litigation: Reports of Court Proceedings," in *Law and Legal Practice in Egypt from Alexander to the Arab Conquest: A Selection of Papyrological Sources in Translation, with Introductions and Commentary*, ed. J.G. Keenan, J.G Manning, and U. Yiftach-Firanko (Cambridge: CUP, 2014), 482 – 6; A.Z. Bryen, *Violence in Roman Egypt: A Study in Legal Interpretation* (Philadelphia: University of Pennsylvania Press, 2013), 126 – 64; Kelly, *Petitions, Litigation, and Social Control in Roman Egypt*, 75 – 122.

and righteousness, which brings to mind his citations of Lev 18: 5 and Hab 2:4. The echo of Lev 18:5, which speaks about "doing the Law" (τὸ νόμον ποιῆσαι), corresponds well with the Western readings of 3:21, which speaks about the "Law of deeds" (νόμος τῶν πράξεων). Thus, as in 3:11–12, Paul here seems to presuppose a distinction between the jurisdiction of the Law, which was incapable of providing life and righteousness, and the jurisdiction based on trust (this is affirmed by the citation of Hab 2:4 in 3:11). Although the Law fails to give life and righteousness, it is obvious that the meaning of the Law was to serve a different purpose compatible with God's promises, since Paul explicitly claims that the Law is not against them. The idea that the function of the Law is integral to the promises is then further developed in 3:21–22.

The intention of the Law was not to give life and righteousness, and it "was added for the sake of transgressions, until the offspring would come to whom the promise had been made" (3:19). I take the phrase παράβασις ("transgression") here to mean that the Law was given both "because of transgression" caused by the sin or "crime" committed" (cf. the term ἁμαρτία in 3:22), and for the purpose of making known the crime as "violations" of a law and liable to punishment.[269] Such an interpretation seems to be backed up by the figure of speech of imprisonment in 3:22: "Scripture has imprisoned all things under sin". This

269 The latter meaning, in which a transgression liable to punishment presupposes the existence of a Law, is explicitly conveyed in Rom 4:15: "For the law brings wrath; but where there is no law, neither is there violation." Paul seems to presuppose the view that prior to the Law there can be no infraction of it, so that it was the Law that brought humans into a state of legal accountability. We can perhaps understand the subtle nuance of Paul's reasoning by taking into account what Philo says in *Abr.* 6. According to this passage, the patriarchs lived in a time before the particular laws (of Moses) had been set in writing, conceived of as a period of legal leniency:

> They committed no guilty action of their own free will or purpose, and where chance led them wrong they besought God's mercy and propitiated Him with prayers and supplications, and thus secured a perfect life guided aright in both fields, both in their premeditated actions and in such as were not of freely-willed purpose.

A similar line of thought can be found in Jub. 33:15–17. On Paul's use of legal arguments in order to describe the pre-Sinaitic period of the patriarchs and on this basis assert freedom from the Law, cf. G.A. Anderson, "The Status of the Torah in the Pre-Sinaitic Period: St. Paul's Epistle to the Romans," in *Biblical Perspectives: Early Use and Interpretation of the Bible in Light of the Dead Sea Scrolls: Proceedings of the First International Symposium of the Orion Center for the Study of the Dead Sea Scrolls and Associated Literature, 12–14 May, 1996*, ed. M.E. Stone and E.G. Chazon (Leiden; Boston; Köln: Brill, 1998), 1–23, esp. 4, 10, 14; Dahl, *Studies in Paul*, 175; O. Linton, "Paulus och Juridiken," *STK* 21.3 (1945): 173–92.

image seems to imply, as F.F. Bruce suggested, that "the written law is the official who locks the law-breaker up in the prisonhouse of which sin is the jailor".[270] It is worth noticing here that the Scripture is the subject of this statement. This means that Scripture is seen as a wider concept, encompassing the jurisdiction of the Law,[271] not as a self-contained entity, but an instrument that was subordinated to the Abrahamic jurisdiction in terms of the promise (cf. Gal 3:8, 17–18).[272] Thus, although the Law plays a negative role, since it unable to generate life and righteousness and capable only of defining transgressions and keeping them shut up under sin, it does have a positive part in the realization of the Abrahamic promises. The distinctive function of the Law as an interim arrangement in the service of the fulfillment of the promises emerges also from the temporal indicators and the ἵνα-clauses in 3:22b and 3:24b, similar to the ones in 3:14b. The temporal function of the Law is explicit in Gal 3:19 – 25: it had a role *until* and *before* the promised "offspring" (3:19b), "Christ" (3:23 – 24), and "trust" (3:25) "came". Just as the authority of the Law is thus affirmed, so too its task of serving a purpose is highlighted: "so (ἵνα) that what was promised [...] might be given to those who trust" (3:22b), and "so (ἵνα) that we might be justified by trust" (3:24b). The cumulative effect of these statements in the context of Gal 3:10 – 25 explains that the verdict of the Law that resulted in the crucifixion of Christ as a criminal (cf. also Gal 2:21– 3:1) served the fulfillment of God's promises.

The Law as a provisional jurisdiction that played a preparatory function also finds expression through the analogy of a παιδαγωγός, who was to be an educator and guardian watching over those who are minors until they came of age at a defintive time.[273] The statements "παιδαγωγὸς [...] εἰς Χριστόν" (3:24a), and "οὐκέτι ὑπὸ παιδαγωγόν ἐσμεν " (3:25) show that the metaphor of a παιδαγωγός defines the timelimit of the Law; its period is expressly "no longer" when the time

270 Bruce, *Galatians*, 180.

271 It is plausible that ἡ γραφή here refers back to the specific citation of Deut 27:26 in Gal 3:10, since Paul also elsewhere applies the definitive article together with "Scripture" in the singular. Thus, e. g., Keener, *Galatians*, 287; Longenecker, *Galatians*, 144; Burton, *Galatians*, 195 – 6.

272 *Pace* Barclay ("The Gift and its Perfections: A Response to Joel Marcus and Margaret Mitchell," *JSNT* 39.3 [2017]: 341), who makes an excessively clear-cut distinction between the promise and the Torah, as if the Torah was not part of Scripture. Contrast Hartman, "Galatians 3:15 – 4:11," 141; Bruce, *Galatians*, 180; Betz, *Galatians*, 175; Dahl, *Studies in Paul*, 174.

273 For a survey of the Jewish and Graeco-Roman referential background of this analogy in Gal 3:24 – 25, cf. Keener, *Galatians*, 290 – 3; J. Schröter, *From Jesus to the New Testament*, trans. W. Coppins. Baylor-Mohr Siebeck Studies in Early Christianity (Waco, TX: Baylor University Press, 2013), 174 – 6.

of the "Abrahamic jurisdiction" of trust and promise in terms of Abraham's "offspring", Christ, has come to take its authoritative place.[274]

Gal 3:22b evokes and picks up the reference to the promises to Abraham and to his descendant, Christ, from Gal 3:14, 16, 17, and 18: ἵνα ἡ ἐπαγγελία ἐκ πίστεως Ἰησοῦ Χριστοῦ δοθῇ τοῖς πιστεύουσιν. The main theological issue involved in this verse can be formulated as follows: What would it mean in the immediate context to speak about πίστις Ἰησοῦ Χριστοῦ as the ground on which "the promise" is given to those who trust? In what follows, I shall offer a fresh answer to this question in some brief comments on this verse in the light of an analogy in Philo which has not yet attracted scholarly attention. My starting point is the discussion of the phrase πίστις Ἰησοῦ Χριστοῦ, and I begin with some observations by M.D. Hooker on this phrase in the context of Galatians 3.

Hooker argues both grammatically as well theologically for a reading of πίστις Ἰησοῦ Χριστοῦ best taken to convey a subjective genitive, meaning the faith / faithfulness of Christ.[275] For my purpose, her discussion on Christ's faithfulness relative to Abraham and "those who trust" seems particularly relevant in the context of Gal 3:22b. Hooker argues that the phrase ἐκ πίστεως Ἰησοῦ Χριστοῦ "refers to the grounds on which the promise stands".[276] As she explains, however, two interpretations of this claim are possible:

> Should we take the phrase ἐκ πίστεως Ἰησοῦ Χριστοῦ with ἡ ἐπαγγελία (understood as the original promise) or with δοθῇ (understanding ἐπαγγελία as 'that which was promised')? [...] It could mean that what was promised on the basis of Christ's faith might be given to those who believe; or that what was promised might be given, on the basis of Christ's faith, to those who believe. Now the promise was made to Abraham *and his seed* (v. 16), but it was made on the basis of *Abraham's* faith; it is fulfilled in Christ, who is Abraham's seed and therefore shares his faith. If the phrase does refer to Christ's faith, then, it seems that it is more likely that Paul is saying that the promise is now ratified on the basis of Christ's faith.[277]

If we take the phrase as a subjective genitive, Hooker admits that either interpretation is possible. Although the phrase ἐκ πίστεως Ἰησοῦ Χριστοῦ could be taken

274 In Rom 7:1–6 and 9:30 – 10:4 Paul also emphasizes the time limit of the Law of Moses relative to the Christ event.

275 For a review of the intense debate and literature over the last thirty years concerning this phrase and the question whether a subjective or objective genitive is meant in Gal 2:16 and 3:22b, cf. B. Schliesser, "'Christ-Faith' as an Eschatological Event (Galatians 3.23 – 26): A 'Third View' on Πίστις Χριστοῦ," *JSNT* 38.3 (2016): 277–300; T. Morgan, *Roman Faith and Christian Faith: Pistis and Fides in the Early Roman Empire and Early Churches* (Oxford: OUP, 2015), 270 – 1 n. 39.

276 M.D. Hooker, "Πίστις Χριστοῦ ," *NTS* 35.3 (1989): 329.

277 Hooker, "Πίστις Χριστοῦ ," 329.

to refer to Christ's trust, a reference to the corresponding trust of Abraham seems to be implied in Paul's argument. Hence, I shall argue that both interpretations are implied and make sense if we take the promise referred to in Gal 3:8b and elabrated upon throughout 3:14 – 29 (cf. 3:14b, 16,17, 18, 19, 21, 22b, and 29) to encompass an allusion to the oath of promise spoken first to Abraham (Gen 22:16 – 18) and subsequently to Abraham's offspring, Christ (Gen 26:3 – 4), on the basis of their common trust. Thus, if this suggestion holds true, Paul's train of thought concerning the organic linearity of the believers' trust that connects them to Abraham and Christ goes along these lines: The oath of promise was given both *to* Abraham *and to* his seed, Christ (3:16). This means that the promised blessing, which was originally made to Abraham on the basis of his trust (3:6, 9), was reaffirmed to his very descendant, Christ, on the ground of the trust he shared with his ancestor (since Paul in 3:7 defines Abraham's sons by sharing the same trust, it follows logically that Christ displayed the same conduct of trust). Thus, the promise of blessings was also available and affirmed to those believers who emulated both Abraham's and Christ's trust. It seems to me that if we begin with Hooker's conclusion about the subjective genitive, the logic of such an argument follows nicely, and may strengthen the case for a subjective genitive in Gal 3:22b. As I shall show, such a reading of Gal 3:22b fits well in the immediate context and the coherent argument of Gal 3:6 – 29, and may be corroborated in the light of an analogy and the exegesis of Gen 26:3 – 4 provided by Philo in *QG* 4:180, to which I first turn.

In the following citation of *QG* 4:180, based on the translation of the Loeb edition, I have inserted the extant Greek fragments of the text in parenthesis:

> What is the meaning of the words, “I will establish my oath, which I swore to thy father? First, this must be said, that the words of God do not differ from oaths. And by whom does God swear, if not by himself? And He is said to swear, because of our weakness, for we think that just as in the case of man an oath differs from words, so also is it in the case of God (’Αδιαφοροῦσιν ὅρκων λόγοι θεοῦ καὶ κατὰ τίνος ἂν ὤμοσεν ὁ θεός, ὅτι μὴ ἑαυτοῦ; λέγεται δὲ ὀμνύναι διὰ τὴν ἡμετέραν ἀσθένειαν τῶν ὑπολαμβανόντων ὡς ἐπ’ ἀνθρώπου διαφέρειν λόγων ὅρκους, οὕτως ἐπὶ θεοῦ). [...] And in the second place, He wishes to praise the son as one worthy of his father's nobility, for He would not firmly establish the blessings made to the father with an oath, for the sake of the son, if He did not witness the same virtue in him (’Επαινεῖ δὲ καὶ τὸν υἱὸν ὡς πατρῴας ἄξιον εὐγενείας.[278] Οὐ γὰρ ἂν βεβαιότερον ἱδρύετο τὰς μεθ’ ὅρκων γεγενημένας ἐπὶ τοῦ πατρὸς εὐλογίας[279] τῷ υἱῷ, εἰ μὴ καὶ τούτῳ τὴν αὐτὴν ἀρετὴν προσεμαρτύρει). Cease, therefore, now from praising nobility

278 In the light of the context, I follow here the Loeb edition (transl. R. Marcus) and its insertion of the word εὐγενείας in place of the Greek fragment, which has εὐεργίας.

279 The Greek fragment has here εὐλογίας, which makes better sense in referring to the promise of blessings inherent in the oath of promise to Abraham in Gen 22:16 – 18. Cf. also *Abr.* 273.

> separately by itself and learn from the divine Scriptures what true (nobility) is, and repent. For this (passage) clearly teaches us to define and judge and discern the well-born (as being) not those who have sprung from good fathers or grandparents and are content with that alone, but those who are themselves emulators of their (fathers') piety.

In Philo's exegetical paraphrase of Gen 26:3, some features stand out.[280] First, although God's oath is identical with God's words, it is given as a concession to human beings, because of their distinction between these two entities. Philo's identification of God's words with the oath he spoke to Abraham occurs elswhere in his works too.[281]

Second, although the oath is not defined here as an confirmation, as in *Abr.* 273, the same cognate is used, namely in terms of its inherent blessings (εὐλογίαι) as something established as all the more secure and steadfast (cf. βέβαιος). Thus, there is an allusion to both Gen 22:16 – 18 and Gen 26:4, in which these blessings are made originally to Abraham and reiterated so as to be made fresh to his son.

Third, the reiterating of the oath to Abraham's son (Isaac) was dependent on God's consideration of his being found "worthy" (ἄξιος) of Abraham's nobility. This is further explained (cf. γάρ) by the proposition that the promise of blessings would not have been established to Abraham's descendant, if it were not for the fact that the son qualified as a promiseworthy recipent, that is, as one who emulated the virtue of his father. Accordingly, the adjective ἄξιος refers to Isaac as a fitting beneficiary of the oath of promise, as a true descendant of Abraham.[282]

Finally, to Philo the general lesson to be learned from this scripture was the principle that genealogical affinity to an ancestor alone was not sufficient, but that ethnicity should also be discerned and defined on the basis of a spiritual kinship between the fathers and their descendants and, on their part, in terms of their emulation of the piety of the ancestors. As we have pointed out earlier, we find this criteria of true spiritual kinship grounded in shared piety elsewhere

---

280 Unfortunately, Conway (*The Promises of God*, 117, 119) only refers to this text as evidence of Philo's use of the ὅρκος / ὄμνυμι lexemes for a divine pledge, without offering any further comments.

281 *Leg.* 3:204; *Sacr.* 93; *Decal.* 84. See Bekken, *The Lawsuit Motif*, 126 – 36; Conway, *The Promises of God*, 116 – 7.

282 Philo's use of "worth"-language (ἄξιος and its cognate verb ἀξιόω) evokes the value of congruity and equality, in accordance with which God's gifts are distributed appropriately to those "fitting" / "worthy" to receive them. For this reason, for example, Philo can ask, when considering Abraham's offspring, whether they are the "worthy heir" (ἄξιος κληρόνομος) of divine blessings (*Her.* 33). Cf. Barclay, *Paul and the Gift*, 223 – 9.

in Philo's works. Although genealogy matters for Philo, he makes an exception from this norm and so relativizes physical descent, in order to include proselytes from various ethnic backgrounds in the Jewish *politeia* as well as to warn apostates who do not live up to the requirement of piety. Piety is what counts, more than blood.[283] Thus, although it is not explicitly emphasized by Philo, the implicit line of thought is that the oath of promise in terms of their blessings must be handed down to each generation on the basis of virtues on the part of the descendants that correspond to those of their patriarchs. As we have seen, Philo's reference to Gen 26:5 and Abraham as a foundational model for the Jewish nation to emulate also corroborates the kind of reasoning implied here in the interpretation of Gen 26:3–4.

In a comparison of Gal 3:22b with *QG* 4:180, I shall briefly make the case that Paul follows a reasoning not unlike Philo's interpretation of the same underlying source, namely, the oath of promise in Gen 26:3–4. If we work back from Gal 3:22, we may trace some of the threads in Gal 3:6–21 that are tied up here.[284] As I have argued above (4.2), an allusion to Gen 26:4 might already have been evoked in the composite quotation of words from Gen 12:3 (*ἐνευλογηθήσονται ἐν σοί*), 22:18, and 26:4 (*καὶ ἐνευλογηθήσονται* [...] *πάντα τὰ ἔθνη*) in Gal 3:8b (προευηγγελίσατο τῷ Ἀβραὰμ ὅτι *ἐνευλογηθήσονται ἐν σοὶ πάντα τὰ ἔθνη*). The elaboration of the oath of promise to Abraham in Gal 3:14a, in the exegetical paraphrase of its expression "ἐν τῷ σπέρματί σου" that Abraham's blessing "might come in Christ Jesus", points forward to Gal 3:16, which then continues the philological exegesis and the affirmation that the "seed" of Abraham is Christ. As we have seen in the quotation from Hooker's reading of the promise in Gal 3:22b, she refers back to Gal 3:16 and its fulfillment in Christ as the background of Gal 3:22b: "Now the promise was made to Abraham *and his seed* (v. 16), but it was made on the basis of *Abraham's* faith; it is fulfilled in Christ, who is Abraham's seed and therefore shares his faith."[285] In her reasoning on how the promise is fulfilled, Hooker goes on to explain how this is spelt out in Gal 3:23–25: "The time has come for faith to 'be revealed'; thus we are no longer thinking only of Abraham's faith, but of faith made possible in and through Christ". The same point is emphasized further on in her essay: "Now the promise is fulfilled – for Abraham's seed, and for those in him – on the basis of faith. Logic

283 Cf. Gruen, "Philo and Jewish Identity," 189–95.

284 Cf. for the train of thought in the preceding verses leading up to Gal 3:22, R.B. Matlock, "Saving Faith: The Rhetoric and Semantics of πίστις in Paul," in *The Faith of Jesus Christ: Exegetical, Biblical, and Theological Studies*, ed. M.F. Bird and P.M. Sprinkle (Peabody, MA: Hendrickson, 2009), 81–3.

285 Hooker, "Πίστις Χριστοῦ ," 330.

suggests that in v. 22 Paul is referring to the faith of Christ himself."[286] The implicit logic of Hooker's argument is reasonable: if Christ is the offspring of Abraham, then his trust / faithfulness must bear a resemblance to Abraham's trust / faithfulness. But whereas Hooker thinks that the original promise was that given to Abraham and later fulfilled in Christ, a specific reference to Gen 26:3 – 4 as the original promise supports such a reasoning, and makes even better sense in the immediate context. This means that the promise in Gal 3:22b refers back to the oath of promise that was not *just* spoken to Abraham (3:8), but *to* Abraham "*and to his seed*", i.e., to Christ (3:16), on the basis of his trust / faithfulness, emulating that of Abraham. In a recent article on the theme of Πίστις Χριστοῦ, Hooker makes a general comment which is relevant to understanding this organic linearity between Abaham and Christ in terms of sharing the characteristic of trust:

> To describe someone as 'the son of so-and so' was to argue that he had the characteristics of so-and so. To be a true son meant not only to be obedient to one's father, but to be fully in accord with one's fathers's will and purposes. Such a son would trust his father and prove trustworthy.[287]

This line of thought resonates well with both Philo's interpretation of Gen 26:3 – 4 in *QG* 4:180 and the immediate context in Gal 3:6 – 9. According to Philo, the oath of promise made to the father (Abraham) was reiterated for the sake of the son (Isaac), because the son was considered by God as a worthy recipent of it, namely, as one who emulated the virtue of his father. Thus, Isaac was a fitting beneficiary of the oath of promise and exemplified what it meant to be a true descendant of Abraham. Moreover, in *QG* 4:180, Philo deduced from the oath of promise applied to the son the principle that genealogical affinity to an ancestor alone was not sufficient, but that kinship should also be discerned on the ground of spiritual bonds between the fathers and their descendants. Thus, the implicit line of thought was that the oath of promise in terms of their blessings was mediated to the descendants on the basis of virtues that corresponded to that of their fathers. In short, the patriarchal promise was the means of discerning identity.

In a parallel way to Philo, Paul may have taken the oath of promise reaffirmed to Isaac as a prefiguration of Christ, who resembled the character trait of Abraham in his trust / faithfulness and so became a worthy beneficiary of the oath of promise, through whom the promised blessings were further mediat-

286 Hooker, "Πίστις Χριστοῦ ," 330.
287 Hooker, "Another Look at πίστις Χριστοῦ ," *SJT* 69.1 (2016): 60.

ed to those who emulated the promise-worthy behavior of trust. This means that the phrase ἐκ πίστεως Ἰησοῦ Χριστοῦ should be taken both with ἡ ἐπαγγελία (understood as the original oath of promise) and δοθῇ (seen as "that which was promised ").[288] If so, Paul's argument departs from the proposition that the oath of promise was spoken not *just* to Abraham, but *to* Abraham *and to his seed* (τῷ δὲ Ἀβραὰμ [...] καὶ τῷ σπέρματί αὐτοῦ), i.e. Christ (3:16). As I have argued above (4.2), Paul understands the descendant-mediated version of the promise (cf. Gen 22:18 / 26:4), ensuing upon Abraham's trust (cf. Gen 15:6), as a reaffirmation of the existing promise to Abraham (cf. Gen 12:3). Thus, the oath of promise represented the measure of God's trust added to the trust in God which Abraham antecedently possessed (3:8 – 9). For this reason, a promise of blessing which was grounded solely in God's will is transformed to an oath of promise (Gal 3:8b) based upon *both* God's trust / faithfulness (Gal 3:8a) *and* Abraham's trust/ faithfulness (Gal 3:9). In fact, my interpretation of the expression πιστῷ Ἀβραάμ is supported by the phrase ἐκ πίστεως Ἰησοῦ Χριστοῦ in Gal 3:22b. Logic suggests that the latter phrase is referring to the trust / faithfulness of Christ, the Abrahamic offspring, so that the oath of promise was given to him on the basis of a promise-worthy behavior emulating Abraham. Thus, as the oath of promise which was originally made to Abraham (Gen 22:16 – 18), on the ground of his trust (Gen 15:6), this was also the case later, when it was reiterated to his offspring (Gen 26:3 – 4); it was on the ground of trust that Christ received it, showing himself to be Abraham's true offspring.[289] It is as if Paul in Gal 3:22b asserts that the promise has been posited on the same terms, but now extended to encompass the trust of Christ as the premise for its realization. As in Gal 3:10 – 14, where he juxtaposed Deut 27:26 and the oath of promise in Gen 26:4, Paul once again seems to presuppose exactly these same scriptures in order to underscore the same point in Gal 3:22: the "Mosaic jurisdiction" subserves the fulfillment of the promise. The meaning of both passages can thus be paraphrased as follows: The Scripture testifies to the fact that Christ's trust / faithfulness (3:22b), namely, Christ's trustful self-giving on the cross (cf. 1:4; 3:13), by being subjected to the jurisdiction of Law "under the power of sin" (3:22a) and

288 *Pace* Hays (*The Letter to the Galatians*, 269), who neglects the question whether there is an interpreted text such as Gen 26:3 – 4 in Jewish exegesis at Paul's own time which might explain such an understanding of the phrase ἐκ πίστεως Ἰησοῦ Χριστοῦ in Gal 3:22b.

289 A similar train of thought centered in a "organic linearity" between Abraham, Christ and the believers is also to be found in Romans 4, although to a lesser extent than in Galatians 3, cf. Barclay, *Paul and the Gift*, 479 – 92; M.D. Hooker, "'Heirs of Abraham': The Gentiles' Role in Israel's Story: A Response to Bruce Longenecker," in *Narrative Dynamics in Paul: A Critical Assessment*, ed. B.W. Longenecker (Louisville, KY: Westminster John Knox Press, 2002), 89 – 90.

"by becoming a curse for us" (3:13), had the outcome that what was promised might be given on the basis of trust (3:22b), including even the ἔθνη who have experienced the blessing of the Spirit mediated through Christ (Gal 3:9, 14a).

Again, the patrilineal correspondence between the conduct of Christ's trust and those who belong to him is presupposed in this application of the promise in a manner analogous to what we have seen in Philo, *QG* 4:180. This line of thought resonates with Paul's claim that those of trust are Abraham's sons (3:6–7) and therefore partakers of the oath of promise to Abraham (3:8–9), with its inherent righteousness and blessings that are conferred on "those of trust". In Paul's use of the first person plural "we" in 3:14a, there is a reference back to the reception of the Spirit by the Galatian converts: "so that we might receive the promise of the Spirit through trust". In fact, the questions raised at the start of Paul's argument in 3:2–5 are now answered. Their reception of the Spirit affirms the fulfillment of the oath of promise to Abraham, posited on the terms of trust, and thus serves as a legitimation of this experience. Furthermore, the reference to Christ in 3:14a is cataphoric and points forward to Gal 3:16: "But the promises were spoken to Abraham and to his seed", which Paul, through philogical exegesis, applies to Christ. This application suggests that the original oath of promise to both Abraham and to his seed was fulfilled in Christ and was received on the ground of trust, that is to say, both Abraham's and Christ's trust. In 3:29, Paul further identifies Christ with Abraham's offspring, which he takes to mean that those who are in Christ belong to the descendants of Abraham and therefore are heirs of the promise granted to Abraham and to his seed.

To sum up: Paul, not unlike Philo, appropriates the oath of promise (Gen 22:18; 26:4) as a warrant for the claim that the Galatian converts have the status of being legitimate descendants from Abraham and so valid party to the promise of blessings spoken to Abraham and to his descendant. For Paul, the promised blessing, confirmed by an oath of promise from God given as a reward for Abraham's trust, had now been conferred on Abraham's offspring in the gift of the Spirit, and mediated solely on the basis of the same trust that characterized Abraham and his true descendant, Christ.

In the next section, I shall study how Paul finally wraps up this line of thought, which sees the Galatian converts as legitimate offsprings and heirs of Abraham.

6.3 Abaraham's Offspring: Participation in Christ, Adopted Sons of God, and Heirs of the Promise (Gal 3:26 – 29)

As I have argued so far, when Paul in Gal 3:6 – 25 makes a special mention of the Galatian converts, it is because they at the outset are not Abraham's natural descendants. Thus, a special provision seems to be needed, if they are to be understood as valid Abrahamic descandants and so party to the promise. In the course of Paul's ongoing argument, their experience of having received the Spirit by trust, emulating the model of Abraham, warrants that they are not only legitimate proselytes approved by God but also validated as Abraham's sons and partakers of the promise that goes with it. I have also argued that Paul provides backing for this warrant, since he was facing opponents who probably stuck to a genealogical and legal definition of Abraham's descendants and held that those Jews and proselytes were partakers of the promise posited on circumcision and observance of the Law as an emulation of Abraham's promise-worthy behavior. Thus, in contrast to these opponents, Paul centers these terms on Abraham's trust in the context of an inner-Jewish debate on Abraham, of which the Galatian conflict and a similar discussion attested in Philo's writings may be conceived as independent examples. In the context of this Jewish discourse, Abraham is accentuated as the paradigm of the proselyte as well as the founder of the Jewish nation, identified as those who emulate the piety of the ancestor. For Paul, not unlike Philo, this characterization of Abraham allowed him to posit trust in God and the corresponding responsiveness on God's part in terms of the oath of promise as disjoined from the subsequent revelation of the Law through Moses. According to Paul, God's trust / faithfulness, manifested in Christ, who was cursed within the jurisdiction of the Law, was proof that He kept his pledge to Abraham. Hence, the death and crucifixion of Christ meant that the jurisdiction of the Law had a temporarily, but legitimate function and place in Scripture, which contributed to the realization of the oath of promise and so to putting the "Abrahamic jurisdiction" into effect. As I shall further suggest, Gal 3:26 – 4:7 shows how Paul provides additional weight to this argument when he goes on to apply it to the situation of his addressees. Again, it would appear that Philo's writings might shed fresh light on Paul's appropriation of Abraham as the role model to warrant his claim about the Galatian proselytes as valid descendants and heirs of God's oath of promise spoken to Abraham and to his seed.

My approach will be as follows: In the analysis of Gal 3:26 – 4:7 I shall particularly address Paul's arguments concerning the status of the Galatian converts characterized as Abraham's offspring "in Jesus Christ", "sons of God", and "heirs according to the promise", respectively. As a corollary, I shall only offer some brief remarks on other key ideas in this passage in so far as this is relevant for the purpose of my discussion.

6.3.1 Abraham's Offspring "in Christ"

As I argued above (6.1), the phrase "καὶ τῷ σπέρματί σου" in Gal 3:16 refers to the oath of promise spoken to Isaac concerning the blessings that will be conferred upon his offspring (Gen 26:3 – 4), conceived as a collective entity. By means of philogical exegesis, Paul made the claim that the one "seed" Jesus Christ is the ultimate confirmation of these promises "to Abraham and to his offspring". In the course of Paul's train of thought, this interpretation makes explicit the warrant for the exegetical paraphrase in Gal 3:14a, where it is presupposed that the phrase "in Christ Jesus" replaces the expression "ἐν τῷ σπέρματί σου " in Gen 22:18 / 26:4. Thus, in Paul's mind, the σπέρμα envisioned in Gen 26:3 – 4, about whom the promises were made was never meant to refer to the generic singular of the collectivity of the Jewish people as the descendant of Isaac ("as of many"), but to Christ as a specific singular ("to one person") conceived as a collective person, including those who belong to him. As we shall see, such an understanding of Paul's exegetical interpretation of σπέρμα with regard to Christ is further upported by Gal 3:29, in which the identification of both Christ and those who belong to him as Abraham's offspring is made explicit.

In Gal 3:26 – 29 the theme of being "in Christ Jesus" or "in Christ" is crucial for the applications made to the Galatian proselytes, and helps to determine the connotation of the designation "Abraham's offspring" (3:29).[290] Paul's philological exegesis in Gal 3:16 about Christ is cataphoric and is further picked up in Gal 3:29: "And if you belong to Christ, then you are Abraham's offspring, [...]." By means of the protasis, Paul summarizes Gal 3:26 – 28. The phrase "And if you belong to Christ" (3:29a) thus apparently means the same as "for all of you are one in Christ" (3:28), namely, the community that participates in and is carried by Christ. The apodosis in Gal 3:29a ("then you are Abraham's offspring") draws the conclusion (cf. the conjunction ἄρα) and makes explicit the identification of Christ and the Galatian converts as Abrahamic offspring. The collective understanding of Christ as identical with Abraham's offspring is also supported by the way the apodosis picks up the thesis stated in 3:7 about Abraham's sons, which suggests that Paul considers this to be proven. Moreover, the phrase "if you be-

---

290 For Gal 3:29 as an *inclusio* that frames the whole passage Gal 3:6 – 29, cf. Keener, *Galatians*, 318; deSilva, *The Letter to the Galatians*, 340; Hartman, "Galatians 3:15 – 4:11," 144; Betz, *Galatians*, 201; Mussner, *Der Galaterbrief*, 266.

long to Christ" in 3:29 is anaphoric and refers back to Christ as a collective person in the immediate context of 3:26 – 28:

> [...] for *in Christ Jesus* you are all sons of God through trust. As many of you as were baptized *into Christ* have clothed yourselves with Christ. There is no longer Jew or Greek, there is no longer slave or free, there is no longer male and female; for all of you are one *in Christ Jesus*.

In the statement "for all of you are one in Christ Jesus," Paul evidently understands Christ as a collective person who unites "all sons of God" (3:26) across the diversity, the differences, and the dual categories in terms of nationality (Jew – Greek), social position (slave – free), and sex (male – female) (3:28). Such affirmations mean that to be "in Christ" has a social dimension with communal implications. Thus, to participate in the collective person of Christ means to live within the commuity of Abraham's descendants, on the basis of transformed life conditions concerning unity that go beyond the various distinctions within it.[291] As I have pointed out earlier (chapter 2), although Philo was sensitive to the issue of lineage, his affirmation that spiritual kinship was superior to blood-line meant that the proselytes' different ethnic origins became relativized in view of the spiritual bonds and the equality established between them and the Jews within the Jewish *politeia*.[292] For Paul, in a similar manner, Jewish identity on the part of the Galatian converts goes beyond genealogical kinship and physical descent from Abraham. In fact, not unlike Philo, Paul's negotiation of Abraham amounts to a figurative conception of Abraham and his kin that lays stress on the ancestor as a model of proselytes and Jews who emulate his trust in God. E. Gruen has most recently expressed a similar understanding of the meaning of Abraham's "seed" in Galatians:

> In the Epistle to the Galatians, the Apostle underscores the meaning unambigiously. He identifies the sons of Abraham as the men of faith. Plainly the metaphor of "seed" or descent, which one might expect to be the quintessential marker of racial or ethnic identity, can, for Paul, serve to signal a continuity of belief.[293]

This idea may have some bearing on the distinction between Jew and Greek in Gal 3:28 too. It seems not to be by accident that we find this relativization of physical descent and ethnic origins between Jew and Greek in the context of a

---

291 D. Aune, "Galatians 3:28 and the Problem of Equality in the Church and Society," in *From Judaism to Christianity: Tradition and Transition: A Festschrift for Thomas T. Tobin, S. J., on the Occasion of His Sixty-Fifth Birthday*, ed. P. Walters, NovTSup (Leiden: Brill, 2010), 153 – 83.
292 Cf. Berthelot, "Judaism as 'Citizenship'," 125 – 9.
293 Gruen, "Paul and Jewish Ethnicity," 360.

discussion of the question of who belongs to Abraham's true kinship. The fact that Paul's argument in this section of the letter culminates with an emphaisis on Abraham's descendants who are incorporated in Christ confirms that this was a key issue in the controversy. Paul's answer, then, seems to be that biological descent and ethnic differences are now made irrelevant in the light of what it means to belong to the unity of Christ, in whom a new basis is established for the kinship ties within the lineage of Abraham. Implicitly, the ethnic implications of Paul's statement on the unity of Jew and Greek also makes sense in an inner-Jewish context, in which the question of the equality between the native Jews and proselytes was a concern. In fact, Philo's emphasis on the equal rights on the part of the proselytes as citizens of the Jewish *politeia* might provide a Jewish context for Paul's statement in Gal 3:28. As I shall point out below, the question whether the proselytes fully belonged to the true descendants of Abraham would also appear to pertain to the distinctions between the dual categories "slave – free", and "male – female".

6.3.2 Abraham's offspring as Adopted Sons of God

In Gal 3:26, a new element emerges, addressed directly to the Galatian proselytes: "you are God's sons". Together with the motifs of "trust" and "in Christ", pointing to the terms on which the the status of the Galatian converts is now identified, Paul adduced the motif of sonship as the reason (γάρ) why "we are no longer under any pedagogue" (3:25). Here, the reference to a "pedagogue" signals that the role and period of the "Mosaic jurisdiction" is expressly "no longer" an option for the Galatian proselytes, now that the time of the "Abrahamic jurisdiction" has dawned and taken effect by virtue of the arrival of Christ (3:24) and the revelation of trust (3:25).[294] Thus, the mention of Galatian proselytes as "sons of God" in Christ, who are emancipated from the "Mosaic jurisdiction", anticipates Gal 4:3 – 7:

> So with us; while we were minors, we were enslaved to the elemental spirits of the world. But when the fullness of time had come, God sent his Son, born of a woman, born under the law, in order to redeem those who were under the Law, so that we might receive adoption as children. And because you are children, God has sent the Spirit of his Son into our hearts, crying, "Abba! Father!" So you are no longer a slave but a son, and if a son, then also an heir, through God.

---

294 In the preceding context, cognates of πίστις are explicitly aligned with references to either Abraham (Gal 3:5, 6, 8, 9, 14) or Christ (Gal 3:14, 22b, 24) and in antithesis to νόμος (Gal 3:2, 5, 12, 23, 24, 25).

This text represents an application of a human analogy introduced in 4:1–2 about a minor heir, who is in a situation comparable to the position of a slave before he comes of age and so can legally be heir and master of the inheritance he is entitled to:

> My point is this: heirs, as long as they are minors, are no better than slaves, though they are the masters of everything; but they remain under guardians and trustees until the date set by the father.

The points of comparison between the analogy and the application can be displayed as follows:

Analogy	**Application**
Present status:	*Past status and problem:*
a minor	while we were minors
no better than slaves	we were enslaved
under guardians and trustees	under the elemental spirits of the world
Resolution by the father:	*Resolution and intervention by God:*
until the date set by his father	until the date set by his father
	God sent his Son
	for the purpose of adoption (as sons)
Consequences:	*Present consequences:*
master of everything	no longer slave
heir of the father	(adopted) son and therefore heir
	transformation by the Spirit
	filial intimacy and closeness
	worship / prayer to God as father

As many scholars have pointed out, it is not possible to match every detail in Gal 4:1–7 with a specific legal situation of Paul’s own time.[295] This conclusion, however, seems not to be crucial for the interpretation of the application Paul makes of the analogy at large. It is perhaps more important to examine some of the elements in Gal 4:1–7 in its Jewish context. Although I shall pay particularly attention to the motif of the Abraham as an adopted son of God in terms of being the paradigmatic proselyte, there are also some indications that Paul presupposed an interpretation and contrast between Abraham’s two sons, Ishmael and Isaac, that can be envisaged in Philo’s writings. In what follows, I shall particu-

295 Cf., e.g., Keener, *Galatians*, 321–5; Witherington III, *Grace in Galatia*, 282; Betz, *Galatians*, 202–4.

larly draw on relevant Philonic texts in order to shed new light on Gal 3:26 and 29 in the context of Gal 4:1–7. A comparison of these Philonic texts with Paul makes it apparent that they provide a background for Paul's emphasis on being Abraham's offspring in terms of the legal right of heirship that is ascribed to an adopted son of God.

In the first place, *Virt.* 214–219 and *Sobr.* 55–58 supplies a referential backround for Paul's application of the analogy in a context where he speaks about the contrast between the past and present existence of the Galatian proselytes (cf. 3:1–5; 4:8–9).

In earlier scholarly work on the Pauline text in comparison with Philo, these texts have not been exploited sufficiently for the purpose of a comparison. For example, J.M. Scott compares *Sobr.* 56 with *Virt.* 211–219 from the angle of a "divine adoption of the proselyte",[296] but in the case of Paul, he only compares the former with the notion of υἱοθεσία in Gal 4:5, and asserts that "the two texts are otherwise hardly comparable":

> For in *Sobr.* 56 Abraham is seen as the adopted son of God as the result of his prototypical conversion to monotheism, whereas in Gal 4:5 believers are seen as adopted as a result of the Second-Exodus redemption at a particular *heilsgeschichtliche* moment.[297]

The result is that Scott takes only the Jewish tradition based on 2 Sam 7:14 as the specific Jewish background of "adoption of sons",[298] which, he asserts, "provides the logical and necessary starting point for any further investigation of the sonship of believers in Paul."[299] V. Rabens has compared *Sobr.* 56–58 with Paul, but with an emphasis on Rom 8:12–17.[300] Although Rabens follows Scott's

296 Cf. J.M. Scott, *Adoption as Sons of God: An Exegetical Investigation into the Background of ΥΙΟΘΕΣΙΑ in the Pauline Corpus*, WUNT 2 (Tübingen: Mohr Siebeck, 1992), 88–96.
297 Scott, *Adoption as Sons of God*, 176, n. 195.
298 Cf. Scott, *Adoption as Sons of God*, 186: "The Exodus typology of the passage sets the sending of the Son (v. 4) in a traditional, messianic framework, which suggests that the υἱοθεσία of the sons (v. 5) should be interpreted in light of the Jewish expectation of divine adoptive sonship in the messianic time based on 2 Sam 7:14." *Pace* Scott, in view of some scholars there are few indications of an exodus typology in Gal 4:1–2; so, e.g., Keener, *Galatians*, 321; Das, *Paul and the Stories*, 125–45; Moo, "Galatians," 259; J.K. Goodrich, "Guardians, Not Taskmasters: The Cultural Resonances of Paul's Metaphor in Galatians 4.1–2," *JSNT* 32.3 (2010): 254–69.
299 Scott, *Adoption as Sons of God*, 269. For the criticism leveled against Scott's work, see T.J. Burke, *Adopted into God's Family: Exploring a Pauline Metaphor*, NSBT (Nottingham: Apollos, 2006), 55–8; E.M. Heim, *Adoption in Galatians: Contemporary Metaphor Theories and the Pauline Huiothesia Metaphors*, BibInt (Leiden; Boston, 2017), 168–9.
300 Cf. V. Rabens, *The Holy Spirit and Ethics in Paul: Transformation and Empowering for Religious-Ethical Life*, WUNT 2 (Tübingen: Mohr Siebeck, 2010), 219–37; idem, "*Pneuma* and the Be-

analysis of *Sobr.* 56, he too neglects the relevance in the context of Gal 4:6 of the motif of Abraham as a prototypical proselyte. Thus, for Rabens it seems sufficient to point out that both Philo and Paul can apply the concept of adoption to describe the filial intimacy and family relation between Abraham and God.[301] Martyn and, most recently, Borgen remedy the need for taking the motif of Abraham as the model for proselytes into more account as the background for Gal 4:1–7. Martyn, commenting on Gal 4:3, suggests that Paul takes the reference to "the elements of the cosmos" to apply to the elements that the Galatians in their former life as polytheists worshiped as divinities. In that regard, Martyn refers to Paul's opponents, who may have referred to the traditions of Abraham as the paradigmatic proselyte, "in which the patriarch is said to have made the journey to the knowledge of God by an astrological contemplation of the elements, being the first to observe the holy feasts at the correct times (e.g., *Jubilees* 16)."[302] His suggestion that Paul draws on a portrait of Abraham's transition from Chaldean idolatry to monotheism as a paradigmatic proselyte seems more cogent in the light of the coherent argument in Galatians and other Jewish interpretations of Abraham. Without referring to Martyn, however, Borgen's conclusion to his brief observations on *Virt.* 212–222 in comparison with Gal 4:1–7 can be taken as support for such a proposal:

> The basic structure of the rather long passage in Philo's *Virt.* 212–222 is the same as that found in the shorter passage of Paul in Gal 4:1–7: (1) Cosmic and earthly powers are at work in evil and destructive ways; (2) God and humans act, and a radical change takes place; and (3) the result is that persons experience good fellowship and community life. In both passages the Spirit is at work.[303]

The studies of Martyn and Borgen, drawing on Philonic material on Abraham as the paradigmatic proselyte, are solid and invite further scrutiny. Since neither of these scholars exploit *Sobr.* 55–58 in comparison with Gal 4:1–7, their observations should be advanced to include this text, with particular attention to its description of Abraham as the prototypical proselyte, who makes a journey from polytheism to the one true God and thereupon becomes an adopted son of God. The fact that the most recent studies of the metaphor of adoption in Paul

holding of God: Reading Paul in the Context of Philonic Mystical Traditions," in *The Holy Spirit, Inspiration, and the Cultures of Antiquity: Multidisiplinary Perspectives*, ed. J. Frey and J.R. Levison, Ekstasis (Berlin/New York: De Gruyter, 2014), 293–329.

301 Rabens, "*Pneuma* and the Beholding of God," 297, n. 17.

302 Martyn, *Galatians*, 400.

303 Borgen, "Perspectives for Mission," 189–91.

also neglect the Philonic texts as relevant for its use in Gal 4:5 warrants such a study.[304]

Against the background of previous scholarship, a viable suggestion is that Philo and Paul interpret the conversion of the proselytes within the conceptual framework of adoption. Thus, both authors seem to presuppose a composite portrait of Abraham as the paradigmatic proselyte who experiences God's liberation from a past setting of idolatry, which results in a radical transformation by the Spirit and adoption as a son within God's family. In my brief account of each of these aspects I shall begin with some observations on the Philonic texts, before I comment on their relevance for the interpretation of Gal 3:26 and 29 in the context of Gal 4:1–7.

(1) The Past Existence of Abraham and the Galatian Proselytes

As I mentioned in the second chapter, both Philo and the rabbis envisaged adoption as a procedure with features corresponding to the process of conversion. Thus, as an exception from the natural, genealogical facts, the two ideas of adoption and conversion made it possible to transform a non-Jew into a Jew.[305] The first stage in this process implied the severing of the ties with the native, biological, family and its deities. For example, Philo writes in *Virt.* 214–217a that Abraham was a Chaldean by birth, whose father was an astrologer, one of those who believe "the stars and the whole heaven and universe are gods" (*Virt.* 212). Having a conception of these things, and being under divine inspiration, Abraham left behind the power and delusion of such false creeds, and broke up from his country, race and paternal home

> knowing that if he stayed the delusions of the polytheistic creed would stay within him and render it impossible for him to discover the One, who alone is eternal and the Father of all things, conceptual and sensible, whereas if he removed, the delusion would also remove from his mind and its false creed be replaced by the truth. *Virt.* 214.

Moreover, Abraham's religious and social breach with the pagan context became the fundamental identifying mark and "the standard of nobility" for all proselytes, who, "abandoning the ignobility of strange laws and monstrous customs which assigned divine honours to stock and stones and soulless things in general, have made a journey to a better settlement, in a commonwealth full of

304 Cf. Burke, *Adopted into God's Family*; R.B. Lewis, *Paul's 'Spirit of Adoption' in its Roman Imperial Context*, LNTS (London; New York: Bloomsbury T & T Clark, 2016); Heim, *Adoption in Galatians.*

305 Cf. Berthelot's study, "Entre Octroi de la Citoyenneté et Adoption."

true life and vitality, with truth as its director and president" (*Virt.* 219). Although Philo does not refer explicitly to Abraham as a proselyte in *Sobr.* 55 – 58, there are many features in the description of Abraham in this text that coincide with his portrait of Abraham as the the prototypical proselyte in *Virt.* 212–219. Thus, *Sobr.* 56 says that Abraham "alone is nobly born, for he has registered God as his father (μόνος γὰρ εὐγενὴς ἅτε θεὸν ἐπιγεγραμμένος πατέρα) [...]." Here, Abraham is characterized by his nobility, which makes him the model of εὐγένεια for proselytes (cf. *Virt.* 219). Moreover, when Philo says that Abraham "has registered God as his father", he uses the same verb (ἐπιγράφω) that he employs elsewhere to describe how pagans ascribe paternity to many divinities.[306] As Scott notes: "Hence the same expression in *Sobr.* 56 refers to the fact that, in contrast to the polytheists, Abraham ascribes the paternity not to many gods, but to the one true God, the creator of all."[307] This understanding is also supported by the causal link Philo draws in *Sobr. 56* and *Virt.* 218 – 219 between being "well-born" (εὐγενής) and ascribing paternity to God by putting trust in Him as a Father (cf. Gen 15:6 in *Virt.* 216). Accordingly, *Sobr.* 57 characterises Abraham as a "sole freeman", who is released from vain opinion (κενὴ δόξα), which corresponds to the polytheistic doctrines that Abraham had to leave behind, because otherwise, "the polytheistic creed would stay within him and render it impossible for him to discover the One, who alone is eternal and the Father" (*Virt.* 214). As we have seen in chapter two, this portrait of Abraham as a former Chaldean polytheist who makes a journey to the true God is explicitly expressed in *Abr.* 69 – 70:

> For the Chaldeans were especially active in the elaboration of astrology and ascribed everything to the movements of the stars. [...] But while exploring numerical order as applied to the revolution of the sun, moon and other planets and fixed stars, and the changes of the yearly seasons and the interdependence of phenomena in heaven and on earth, they concluded that the world itself was God, thus profanely likening the created to the Creator. Then opening the soul's eye as though after profound sleep, and beginning to see the pure beam instead of the deep darkness, he followed the ray and discerned what he had not beheld before, a charioteer and pilot presiding over the world and directing in safety his own work, assuming the charge and superintendence of that work and of all such parts of it as are worthy of the divine care.

The points of comparison between the analogy and the application in Gal 4:1–3 displayed above show that an important issue is the notion of slavery and the analogy of a slave changed into a son. Thus, Gal 4:3 seems to tell about the

306 Cf. *Decal.* 8; *Migr.* 69; *Conf.* 144; *Fug.* 144.
307 Scott, *Adoption as Sons of God*, 93.

past existence of non-Jews who become proselytes, and who earlier "were enslaved to the elemental spirits of the world".[308] As applied to the Galatian proselytes, Gal 4:3 can be taken to refer to their position before God as similar to that of the slave before they were liberated and became adopted as sons of God. Just as Philo writes in *Virt.* 214 and Abr. 69 – 70 about the delusional power of pagan gods in elementary and season-based phenomena in nature, from which Abraham departed as the first proselyte, Paul similarly refers to the pagan background of the Galatian proselytes, who once had been "enslaved to beings that by nature are not gods"(4:8). Just as Abraham replaced the false creed in which he was reared (*Abr.* 69) by the truth (*Virt.* 214), and thus came to be the first person spoken of as believing in God (*Virt.* 216 referring to Gen 15:6), so the Galatian proselytes too seem to have turned away from calendrical and season observances dependent on phenomena in nature, and to have come to trust in God (Gal 3:5 – 6; Gen 15:6), and thus received knowledge of the true God. Thus, the temporal formulas "then" (τότε) and "now" (νῦν) in Gal 4:8 – 10 serve to contrast this former and present life of the Galatian proselytes:

> Formerly, when you did not know God, you were enslaved to beings that by nature are not gods. Now, however, that you have come to know God, or rather to be known by God, how can you turn back again to the weak and beggarly elemental spirits? How can you want to be enslaved to them again? You are observing special days, and months, and seasons, and years.

However, the concept of "slavery under the elements" in 4:3 may also include a reference to the "slavery" of those who are subjected to the "Mosaic jurisdiction". As, for example, Betz suggests, being under the "tutors" and "administrators" (4:2) as the masters of the slaves must be comparable to being under the slavery of the Law: "Being 'under them' is not different from being 'under the Law' (3:22 – 25)."[309] As we noted earlier, this conjecture corresponds to Paul's idea that the emancipation from slavery and being made a son are the result of a redemption from the Law: "God sent his Son, born of a woman, born under the law, in order to redeem those who were under the Law, so that we might receive adoption as children" (4:4 – 5). Since this statement is applied in the first person plural to "we", it probably refers to the "slavery" of Jews and those among the Galatian converts who yield to the observance of the "Mosaic jurisdiction", such as the cultic regulations referred to in Gal 4:9 – 10 might imply: "How

308 For a recent survey of the various approaches to the phrase στοιχεῖα τοῦ κόσμου, cf. Keener, *Galatians*, 325 – 33.
309 Betz, *Galatians*, 205.

can you want to be enslaved to them again? You are observing special days, and months, and seasons, and years."[310] If, then, Paul's application of 4:1 in 4:3 (cf. οὕτως καὶ ἡμεῖς) in the expression "while we were minors" (ἦμεν νήπιοι) may have special reference to the slavery under the Law, a few comments on the hyperbolic distinction between the "minor" child "no different from a slave" in 4:1 and on Paul's application of it in 4:3 may be relevant. In *Sobr.* 8 – 9, commenting on the story of Ismael in Genesis 21, Philo states:

> [...] when Ishmael had apparently lived about twenty years, Moses calls him a child by comparison with Isaac, who is full grown in virtues. [...] Still all the same, grown up as he was, he is called a child, thus marking the contrast between the sophist and the sage. For wisdom is Isaac's inheritance and sophistry Ishmael's, as we propose to shew in the special treatise, when we deal with the characteristics of the two. For the mere infant bears the same relation to the full-grown man as the sophist does to the sage, or the school subjects to the sciences which deal with virtues.

The fact that Paul makes use of other exegetical traditions related to the contrast between Ishmael and Isaac in Gal 4:21 – 31 corroborates the conjecture that Paul makes use of an exegetical motif attested in Philo about the contrast between Abraham's two types of sons, Ishmael and Isaac in Gal 4:1.[311] This exegetical tradition seems to have escaped notice in the scholarly discussion on this text, with the apparent exception of Dahl, who refers to the similarity between Philo's and Paul's appropriation of the contrast between Ishmael and Isaac as the minor child and the grown-up man, respectively. On the basis of this observation and the contrast drawn by Paul in Gal 4:21 – 31 between Ishmael and Isaac, Dahl claims: "If the similarity at this point is more than a coincidence, it would prove that the allegory in 4:21 ff. was already in Paul's mind when he

310 Keener, *Galatians*, 363 – 4; Das, *Galatians*, 423 – 5; de Boer, *Galatians*, 275 – 6.

311 When Paul in Gal 4:29 presents the two births as a contrast between flesh and spirit, it becomes more evident that he draws on expository traditions. In support of this understanding, one can refer to the corresponding contrast between body and soul made by Philo in the exposition of Gen 16:3 in *QG* 3:21: "For with the concubine the embrace was of bodies a bodily one for the sake of begetting children. But with the wife the union was one of the soul harmonized by heavenly (Greek fragment: divine) love." Cf also *QG* 3:60: "[...] moreover, it is said that 'in the other year' she will bear Isaac, for that birth is not one of the life of the time which now exists but of another great, holy, sacred and divine one." A similar and more elaborate view is expressed in *Migr.* 141, where Sarah speaks (Gen 21:7):

> For I bare a son, she continues, not as Egyptian women do in their bodily prime but as the Hebrew souls do, in my old age at a time, that is, when all things that are mortal and objects of sense-perception have decayed, while things immortal and intellectually discerned have grown young again, meet recipients of honour and esteem.

wrote Gal 4:1 ff."[312] Unfortunately, his elaboration of this point with reference to Paul is only suggestive, and should therefore be taken further.

If Dahl's supposition is correct, namely, that the similarity between Gal 4:1–3 and Gal 4:21–31 is not a mere coincidence, how, then, can the exegetical tradition about Ishmael and Isaac in 4:1–3 serve as argument in the context of Galatians? For my purpose here, I shall offer only a brief, but fresh suggestion towards an answer. If we presuppose that Paul builds upon the exposition attested in Philo, he actually says that the same relationship exists between the minor child, Ishmael, and the grown up man, Isaac. This means that while he is an infant, Isaac's position is not much different from that of the slave-son, Ishmael, which implies that he is not yet come of age, that is, given his freedom as an legitimate heir. In Gal 4:3–7, then Paul applies to the case of his addressees this situation of Isaac as a minor child and slave, who will later be changed into a man come of age and a son authorized to aquire all that he is entitled to as an heir. Here, he compares the situation of Isaac, relative to Ishmael, to the case of Abraham's offspring, Christ and those who belong to him. This is confirmed by the fact that many features from Gal 4:21–31 have been taken over and depend on the passage in 3:5–4:7. Once the Abrahamic true sons, in the manner of Isaac and his offspring, have been identified with Christ and those who belong to him as a collective person, and authorized as the heirs of the promise by trust, it follows that their situation can be compared and contrasted with Ishmael, the minor child, as the slave symbol. This emphasis on Ishmael as a slave is given force in Paul's appropriation of other expository traditions in Gal 4:21–31, in which the slave-son Ishmael, like his mother Hagar, belong to the context of Jewish proselytes, and become models for those who belong to the slavery under the Law.[313] Thus, Paul sees the contrast between Ishmael and Isaac in Gal 4:21–31 as illustrating the relationship between those Jewish proselytes who are enslaved under the Sinaitic covenant and Law, like Ishmael, and those of Abraham's offspring, like Isaac and his descendants, who are true sons and heirs of Abraham's covenant by virtue of the Spirit and the prom-

312 Dahl, "Paul's Letter to the Galatians," 64.

313 Both Paul and Philo see Hagar and Ishmael as prototypes of both slavery and Jewish proselytes. Thus, according to Philo, Hagar needs to realize that "of free and really high-born souls He who is free and sets free is the Creator, while slaves are makers of slaves" (*Fug.* 212). According to Paul, the slave girl Hagar is the type of the Sinai covenant, who gives birth to slaves, as well as of Jerusalem, the center of the people of the Law, who lives in slavery together with her children. The way of thinking about slavery is the same, although the applications are quite antithetical. To Philo, the Hebrew life as a Jewish proselyte is founded on the Law of Moses, and is freedom, while to Paul it means slavery.

ise. With regard to the situation of the Galatian proselytes, Paul's purpose here as elsewhere in the letter is to oppose any endeavour to yield to those who spread propaganda in favor of the jurisdiction of the Law of Moses. If such propagators of the Law claimed that the Galatian proselytes had to obey the commandment of circumcision, a logical outcome was they had to become "citizens" of the Jewish community, who lived according to the "Mosaic jurisdiction", and had Jerusalem as their religious, legal, and political center and "mother-city".[314] Paul reworks this role of Jerusalem by drawing a sharp distinction between the present Jerusalem, who lives "in slavery with her children" (4:25), and the Jerusalem above, who "is free, and [...] is our mother" (4:26). Thus, what Paul says in Gal 4:23 – 25 continues the same line of thought as in Gal 3:22 – 25, 28, and 4:1 – 7. Moreover, if Gal 3:5 – 4:7 anticipates 4:21 – 31 it also makes the proposal that the allegory in the latter text was first put forward by Paul's opponents more unlikely.[315]

(2) Abraham's and the Galatian Proselytes' experience of God's Liberation and Transformation

We saw above that Philo says in *Sobr.* 57 that Abraham is a "sole freedman", released from the polytheistic doctrines of his Chaldean past. This designation of Abraham as "free" (ἐλεύθερος) or one who is made free (ἐλευθεροποιός) corresponds to the action taken by God, who brought about this release and change. Hence, Philo here takes God as the agent who has set Abraham free: "for he is released (ἐλευθεροποιός) from the most tyrannous of mistresses, vain opinion, whom God the liberator has cast down from her citadel on the hill and humbled all her pride". In the context of *Sobr.* 55 – 58, this aspect of God as a liberator correlates with the measures of goodness and mercy, corresponding to the name of God as distinct from "Lord": "For while the words 'Lord and God' proclaim Him master and benefactor of the world which is open to our senses, to that goodness

314 For the role of Jerusalem and the legal aspects involved when proselytes were granted Jewish "citizenship" based on common law, see, e.g., J. Leonhardt-Baltzer, "Diaspora Jewish Attitudes to *Metropoleis:* Philo and Paul on Balanced Personalities, Split Loyalties, Jerusalem, and Rome," in *The Urban World and the First Christians*, ed. S. Walton, P.R. Trebilco, and D.W.J. Gill (Grand Rapids: Eerdmans, 2017), 86 – 98, and S. Pearce, "Jerusalem as 'Mother-City' in the Writings of Philo of Alexandria," in *Negotiating Diaspora: Jewish Strategies in the Roman Empire*, ed. J.M.G. Barclay, LSTS (London: T & T Clark, 2004), 19 – 36.

315 *Pace* C.K. Barrett, "The Allegory of Abraham, Sarah, and Hagar in the Argument of Galatians," 154 – 170, esp. 162 – 3.

which our minds perceive He is saviour and benefactor only, not master or lord (*Sobr.* 55).” At this juncture, Philo seems to share a Jewish tradition in which the names of God are interpreted in a manner similar to what the rabbis call the “measures” for His ways of dealing with humanity, namely kindness and punishment or mercy and judgment,[316] although Philo interpreted the names differently from the rabbis; for him, “God” (θεός) represented the beneficent and and gracious aspect of God, while “Lord” (κύριος) stood for the ruling or punishing aspects of God. It is reasonable to believe that Philo attests an early stage of a debate attested among the rabbis concerning the measures of God and the relationship between fear and love, or judgement and mercy.[317] Nevertheless, Philo seems here to bring this tradition to bear on his description of Abraham as the prototypical proselyte relative to God. Thus, the metaphorical use of the slave–master relationship within a household is employed by Philo to underscore Abraham's relation to God, in which God is not conceived as a slavemaster (δεσπότης), but is rather seen as his savior and benefactor and as a friend of Abraham: “[...] He is saviour and benefactor only, not master or lord. For wisdom is rather God's friend than His slave (φίλον γὰρ τὸ σοφὸν θεῷ μᾶλλον ἢ δοῦλον).” The underlying thought here seems to be the Greek topos that the status of a slave is not compatible with being a friend of the master in the household, such as we find for example in Plato, *Leg.* 757a, using the same terminology as Philo: “For slaves will never be friends with masters (δοῦλοι καὶ δεσπόται οὐκ ἄν ποτε γένοιντο φίλοι)”.[318] Rather than being a slave under a distant master within a household, Philo draws on the metaphor of adoption into a family fellowship, in which Abraham experiences God, not only as a friend, but also as a Father who offers his sonship: “he has registered God as his Father and become by adoption His only son” (μόνος γὰρ εὐγενὴς ἅτε θεὸν ἐπιγεγραμμένος πατέρα καὶ γεγονὼς εἰσποιητὸς αὐτῷ μόνος υἱός).[319] While in *Sobr.* 57, Abraham

---

316 Although they do not deal with *Sobr.* 55–58, N.A. Dahl and A. Segal have adduced much material from Philo's writings that attests the use of this tradition. Cf. N.A. Dahl and A. Segal, “Philo and the Rabbis on the Names of God,” *JSJ* 9.1 (1978): 3–11. In contrast to Dahl and Segal, however, D. Winston (*Logos and Mystical Theology in Philo of Alexandria* [Cincinnati, OH: Hebrew Union College Press, 1985, 21–2]) maintains “that it was indeed Philo's utter dependence on the LXX which had caused him to reverse the Palestinian tradition.”

317 According to Dahl (*Studies in Paul*, 168, n. 15), Philonic evidence would have confirmed the work of H. Ljungmann, *Guds barmhärtighet och dom* (Lund: Gleerup, 1950), who has explored the rabbinic data on the use of the names for God in Scripture.

318 For the same idea, cf. also Plato, *Parm.* 133d; Aristotle, *Pol.* 1253b6, 1278b35.

319 Here, Philo employs the noun εἰσποιητός, which is based on the verb εἰσποιεῖν. For the use of the same verbal form for adoption, cf. Plato, *Leg.* 878a. For a survey of the technical terms for “adoption”, see B. Byrne, *'Sons of God' – 'Seed of Abraham': A Study of the Idea of the Sonship of*

is made free (ἐλευθεροποιός) by the action taken by God who brought about this change, *Virt.* 217 also states that Abraham's radical transformation was brought about by the initiative of God, namely by his experience of the transformative Spirit:

> Thus whenever he was possessed, everything in him changed to something better, eyes, complexion, stature, carriage, movements, voice. For the divine spirit which was breathed upon him from on high made its lodging in his soul, and invested his body with singular beauty, his voice with persuasiveness, and his hearers with understanding.

In *Virt.* 218 – 219, Philo proceeds to summarize his description of Abraham's transformation from the preceding paragraphs *Virt.* 214 – 217:

> Would you not say that this lone wanderer without relatives or friends was of the highest nobility, he who craved for kinship with God and strove by every means to live in familiarity with Him, he who while ranked among the prophets, a post of such high excellence, put his trust in nothing created rather than in the Uncreated and Father of all, he who as I have said was regarded as a king by those in whose midst he settled, a sovereignty gained not with weapons, nor with mighty armies, as is the way of some, but by the election of God, the friend of virtue, who rewards the lovers of piety with imperial powers to benefit those around them? He is the standard of nobility for all proselytes, [...]

Correspondingly, Paul says God has brought about a radical change in the Galatian proselytes. As we have pointed out above (cf. 3.2), Paul presupposes in Gal 3:2 – 5 that, in an experience corresponding to Abraham's, they have experienced a transformation through receiving the Spirit by trust and God's power manifestations:

> Did you receive the Spirit [...]Having started with the Spirit [...] Did you experience so much [...] Well then, does God supply you with the Spirit and work miracles [...] by your believing what you heard? Just as Abraham [...]

Moreover, in Gal 4:4 – 5, Paul probably draws on the analogy of Isaac, as the minor child (4:1 – 2), to the situation of Christ, who almost lived in the same slave-position as Ishmael under the Law. Paul emphasizes that Christ, sharing the same predicament of the humans, who earlier "were enslaved to the elemental spirits of the world" (4:3), was commisioned as God's son to accomplish the redemptive activity of God. Hence, in order to bring God's liberation and redemp-

God of All Christians in Paul Against the Jewish Background, AnBib (Rome: Biblical Institute, 1979), 79 – 80.

tion from the Law, it was necessary that Christ was born of a woman and came to live under the jurisdiction of the Law:

> But when the fullness of time had come, God sent his Son, born of a woman, born under the law, in order to redeem those who were under the law, so that we might receive adoption as children. Gal 4:4 – 5

With regard to the overall purpose of the letter to the Galatians, this affirmation about God's redemptive activity serves Paul's argument that the Galatian proselytes should retain their freedom in Christ (cf. 5:1) and not subject themselves to the jurisdiction of the Law and become citizens of the Jewish community, with Jerusalem as religious and juridical capital.[320]

(3) Abraham and the Galatian Proselytes as Sons Adopted into God's Family

As I said above, the first stage in the process of conversion and adoption implied the severing of the ties with the native family and its deities. This first stage is interwoven with a second move, which meant that the proselyte or adopted person received a new family and new kinship bonds. Both these aspects seem to be intertwined in Philo's description of Abraham as an adopted son of God and as the model for other proselytes. As we have noted, Philo emphasizes Abraham's closeness to God as his saviour and benefactor. Accordingly, he was not a slave under a distant master. The state of being an adopted son is seen as equivalent to ascribing paternity to God as a Father and being a friend of God, to whom God confides his thoughts and plans, and on whom he confers his riches, and benedictions. Thus, this experience of being an adopted son results in extreme happiness and the adequate human reaction of benedictions, in terms of praise and thanksgiving given in return:[321]

---

320 With regard to the role of Jerusalem reflected in the conflict in Galatians, the scholarly discussion has revolved around the question whether "Jerusalem" is a metonym for the Jewish-Christian church (so, e.g., Martyn, *Galatians*, 457 – 9) or a reference to Judaism and Torah-observance in general (cf., e.g., Das, *Galatians*, 498 – 9; Witherington III, *Grace in Galatia*, 333 – 4). Paul's comments on the role of "Jerusalem" both in Gal 2:1 – 10 and 4:21 – 31 suggest a more specific target, however, namely, against the position that the Jewish proselytes were to be tied to the "present Jerusalem" and thus be integrated within the Jewish community and submit themselves to the jurisdiction of the Law of Moses. This assumption is, in general, supported by Paul's statement that that the Sinai covenant stands in the same rank and line as Jerusalem (4:25), the center of the Jews of the Law of Moses.

321 On Philo's distinction between God being blessed (εὐλογητός), as an affirmation of a divine quality and reality, and God being blessed (εὐλογημένος) as the result of a divine action, that is,

> What, then, of him who has been deemed worthy of blessings so great, so transcendent, so multitudinous? What should he do but requite his Benefactor with the words of his lips with song and with hymn? That is, it seems, the inner meaning of the saying, "blessed be the Lord, the God of Shem." For it is meet that he who has God for his heritage should bless and praise Him, since this is the only return that he can offer, and all else, strive as he will, is quite beyond his power. *Sobr.* 58

In the context of *Virt.* 214 – 219, one finds that Abraham's journey from leaving his native country, his race, and paternal home was inspired by his search for a new society, a more holy one; he was searching for kinship and a life in familiarity with God. Accordingly, in *Virt.* 217 – 219 Philo states that it was God who induced him to do so by the means of the Spirt who dwellt in him:

> For the society also which he sought was not the same as they sought, but oftener under inspiration another more august. Thus whenever he was possessed, everything in him changed to something better, eyes, complexion, stature, carriage, movements, voice. For the divine spirit which was breathed upon him from on high made its lodging in his soul, and invested his body with singular beauty, his voice with persuasiveness, and his hearers with understanding. Would you not say that this lone wanderer without relatives or friends was of the highest nobility, he who craved for kinship with God and strove by every means to live in familiarity with Him?

It is noteworthy that it is in this process of obtaining a divine home, kinship, and familiarity with God that Philo accentuates Abraham's pre-eminence, by placing the demonstative pronoun οὗτος ("this one") first in the sentence, as the "standard of nobility (εὐγένεια) for all proselytes" (οὗτος ἅπασιν ἐπηλύταις εὐγενείας ἐστὶ κανών, *Virt.* 219). Philo then concludes his description of Abraham as the model of proselytes by reference to the communal life in which he set out to be settled: "[Abraham] made a journey to a better settlement, in a commonwealth full of true life and vitality, with truth as its director and president" (*Virt.* 219). Although, as we have pointed out earlier, Philo never explicitly ascribes to the proselytes the status of adopted sons of God, such an idea may nevertheless be implicit and presupposed in these texts. Accordingly, when Philo in *Sobr.* 56 also emphasizes that Abraham is εὐγενής, it would seem that Abraham's adoption as son of God is an aspect that belongs to the portrait of him as the model for proselytes.

---

as the result of humans being blessed by God, cf. *Migr.* 108. For Philo, benediction (εὐλογία) means prayer in terms of "praise" or "thanksgiving", cf. *Praem.* 79; *Fug.* 73; *Migr.* 70. For a discussion of these texts in a Jewish context, cf. E.J. Bickerman, "Blessing and Prayer," in idem, *Studies in Jewish and Christian History, Volume Two*, AJEC (Leiden; Boston: Brill, 2007), 585 – 95, esp. 587, 593.

As Philo thought of Abraham's transformation enacted by the Spirit in terms of his being brought into an intimate son-Father relationship and kinship with God, Paul too describes him in corresponding categories. Gal 4:5 – 6 evinces this train of thought:

> [...] in order to redeem those who were under the law, so that we might receive adoption as sons. And because you are sons, God has sent the Spirit of his Son into our hearts, crying, "Abba! Father!"

Since both Gal 3:27 and 4:6 indicate that Paul takes the Galatians' sonship for granted, there has been much discussion of the relationship between this status and their reception of the Spirit: is sonship the presupposition of the gift of the Spirit, or vice versa?[322] An answer to this question must take its point of departure in the experience that the Galatians had received the Spirit and in Paul's interpretation of this experience. As I have argued so far, the Galatian converts' reception of the Spirit provides a specific historical case of becoming proselytes after the manner of Abraham, regarded as the paradigmatic proselyte. Accordingly, in Gal 3:5 – 6, Paul compares their transformation by the Spirit and the power manifestations enacted by God with Abraham's experience. Moreover, the gift of the Spirit is evidence that they are Abraham's true sons, which Paul deduces from the fact that only Abraham's descendants can receive the promised blessing in terms of the Spirit (3:7 – 9, 14). Here in Gal 4:5 – 6, it would seem that this line of thought is taken one step further. Becoming adopted sons of God is more important than being Abraham's sons. Again, in Paul's mind, the Spirit is also evidence that the Galatian proselytes belong to God's new family as adopted sons of God. His use of the metaphor of adoption as son, in a manner similar to Philo's description of Abraham, describes the sovereign act by which God has liberated the Galatian proselytes from being subjected to cosmic powers as slaves and brought them into a new family relationship with God as their *pater familias*. Since the Galatian proselytes have already experienced the gift of the Spirit, "having started with the Spirit" (3:3), it is more likely that their sonship as adopted sons of God is evidenced by the Spirit, rather than that the gift of Spirit was somehow dependent on their status as God's sons. If this is correct, we may paraphrase the meaning of 4:5 – 6 as follows:

> Because you are adopted sons of God, which is evident through your gift of the Spirit, you also certainly know by this experience that God gave you the Spirit of sonship, which has

322 Cf. Hartman, "Galatians 3:15 – 4:11," 148; Betz, *Galatians*, 209; Bruce, *Galatians*, 198; Lightfoot, *Galatians*, 169.

enabled and inspired us so we can address God as our Father. By receiving the Spirit of his own true Son, we have evidence that we participate in the family of God as adopted sons together with Abraham and his seed.

As we have seen, many of the key elements we have found in Philo's characterization of Abraham are the same as in Paul's argument throughout 4:1 – 7: being slave or free, God's intervention as liberator, resulting in transformation by the Spirit, adoption and sonship of God, an intimate relationship with God, in which they share confidential knowledge, and which enables adequate and inspired forms of addressing God as the heavenly Father. These shared elements may support the hypothesis that both Philo's and Paul's conception of adoption as son of God is related to an understanding of Abraham, who sought kinship with God (cf. *Virt.* 218). The logical outcome of the affirmation about Abraham as the model of proselytes might then be that the proselytes also have received a new kinship with God.[323]

I have claimed above that the ethnic distinction between Jew and Greek should be understood in the context of Jewish proselytism, and that it has been relativized in Paul's mind in the light of the superiority of a spiritual kinship with Abraham and the emphasis on unity within the Jewish community. Like Philo, Paul too takes the national lineage of Abraham's descent seriously.[324] For this reason, they both had to solve the problem of the non-Jewish lineage of the Jewish proselytes. Unlike Philo, who defends the inclusion of the proselytes by granting them fellowship and citizenship within the Jewish community on the basis of virtues in accordance with the Law of Moses, Paul carves out a room for the Jewish converts by linking them to Abraham through their trust in Christ and reception of the Spirit, so that he can claim that they too were descendants of Abraham in spite of their foreign lineage. This affirmation takes us to the last

323 It is noteworthy that Paul ascribes the status of being God's adopted child not only to the non-Jews, but also to Israel, according to Rom 9:4 – 5, which says that to the Israelites "belong the adoption (ἡ υἱοθεσία), the glory, the covenants, the giving of the law, the worship, and the promises, to them belong the patriarchs [...]." While this conception of Israel as God's children derives from the Tanach, several scholars have pointed out that Paul's use of the terminology of adoption may be influenced by the Roman concept; see, for example, Berthelot, "Entre Octroi de la Citoyenneté et Adoption," 37 – 50; L.S. Kim, "Another Look at Adoption in Romans 8:15 in Light of Roman Social Practices and Legal Rules," *BTB* 44.3 (2014): 133 – 43; F. Lyall, "Roman Law in the Writings of Paul: Adoption," *JBL* 88.4 (1969): 458 – 66.

324 The importance of this topic finds expression when Paul identifies his own origins and lineage. Thus, in these passages, he may identify himself as an Israelite from the offspring of Abraham (Rom 11:1; 2 Cor 11:22), the Israelites as his own brothers and kinsmen (Rom 9:3 – 5; 11:14), and himself as one who was circumcised, from the race (γένος) of Israel, of the tribe of Benjamin, a Hebrew born of Hebrews (Phil 3:5). Cf. Gruen, "Paul and Jewish Ethnicity," 42 – 3.

part of this section and to some brief comments on the motif of Abraham's offspring being envisaged as adopted sons and heirs of God.

6.3.3 Abraham's Offspring as Heirs of the Promise

This motif is expressed in Gal 3:29 by means of the following proposition: "then you are Abraham's offspring, heirs according to the promise." The phrase "heirs" (κληρονόμοι) in the plural is picked up in the singular "heir" (κληρονόμος) in Gal 4:7: "So you are no longer a slave but a son, and if a son then also an heir (κληρονόμος), through God." The principle behind both these statements would be that the status of being sons, Abraham's sons and God's sons respectively, guarantees the inheritance. In this section, I shall offer a few observations on the concept of adoption relative to the legal right of inheritance.The metaphor of adoption implied two basic principles that seem to be reflected in 4:1–7. Firstly, the adopted son was seen as having equal status with that of the natural son in a household. Although the fact of adoption itself showed that he did not belong to the biological family by birth, he could be considered to rank with the family, almost as if he was a natural son. Secondly, the corollary of being in the capacity of an adopted son was the lawful right to inherit. As an illustration and evidence of these connotations of adoption, I quote from two Egyptian papyri and two texts in Philo's writings. Although *P. Oxy.* 1206 and *P. Lips.* 28 are of a late date (335 CE and 381 CE respectively), the attestation by Philo may indicate that the notions about adoption were comparatively common and constant in the first centuries in the Eastern Mediterranean. With regard to the practice of adoption in Roman Egypt, however, recent studies suggest that it is perhaps based on the people's law ("Volksrecht") rather than on Greek and Roman Law.[325] The advantage of drawing on relevant papyri texts on adoption is that they may go beyond formal or metaphorical concepts and give us a glimpse into the real life situations and social aspects of the lifeworld in which the agents who are described are embedded.

P. Oxy. 1206 (335 CE) is the earliest surviving adoption contract. It describes how a husband and wife, Heracles and Isarion, have given away their two-yearolf son for adoption to the adopting father Horion:

325 On the discussion of adoption contracts in Greek papyri from later Roman Egypt, cf. S.R. Huebner, "Adoption and Fosterage in the Ancient Eastern Mediterranean," in *The Oxford Handbook of Childhood and Education in the Classical World*, ed. J.E. Grubbs, T. Parkins, and R. Bell (Oxford: OUP, 2014), 521–3.

l. 6 ὁμολογοῦμεν ἡμῖς [μὲν ὅ τ]ε Ἡρακλῆς καὶ ἡ γ[υ]νὴ Εἰσάριον
l. 7 ἐκδεδωκέναι σοὶ τῷ Ὡρίωνι τὸν ἐξ [ἡμ]ῶν υἱὸν Πατερ[μοῦθ]ιν ὡς ἐτῶν
l. 8 δύο εἰς υείοθεσίαν, ἐμὲ δὲ τὸν [Ὡρίων]α ἔχειν το[ῦτ]ον γνήσιον
l. 9 υἱὸν πρὸς τὸ μένειν αὐτῷ τὰ ἀπ[ὸ τ]ῆς διαδοχῆς τῆς κληρονομίας
l. 10 μου δίκαια, καὶ οὐκ ἐξέστε μοι τοῦτον ἀπώσασθαι οὔτε εἰς
l. 11 δουλαγωγείαν ἄγειν διὰ τὸ εὐγενῆ αὐτὸν εἶν[α]ι κ[αὶ] ἐξ εὐγενῶν
l. 12 γονέων ἐλευθέρων [...].

(l. 6 We acknowledge, Heracles and his wife Isarion on the one side,
l.7. that we have given away to you, Horion, for adoption our son Patermouthis, aged about two years,
l. 8 and I, Horion, on the other side, that I have taken him as my true son
l. 9 so as to establish for him the rights of succession to my estate,
l. 10 and it shall not be lawful for me to disavow him or
l. 11 reduce him to slavery, because he is well-born and of well-born
l. 12 and free parents [...]. Trans. *Loeb*, 31[326])

According to the second adoption contract, *P. Lips.* 28 (381 CE), a grandmother, Aurelia Teeus, gives her grandson for adoption to her son, Silvanus, who is a younger brother of the adoptee's late father. The text reads:

l. 14 κατ̣[ὰ] τ[ο]ῦτο [ὁμο]λο̣[γοῦ]με[ν ἐ]γὼ μὲν ἡ Τεεὺς π̣[αρ]α̣δεδωκέναι σοὶ [τ]ῷ Σιλβανῷ τὸν μνημονευθέντα παῖδ[α] π̣ρ[ὸς υἱ]οθεσίαν [...] πρ[ὸ]σ τὸ εἶναι σοῦ υἱ[ὸ]ν γησιον καὶ πρωτότοκον ὡς ἐξ ἰδίου αἵματος γεννηθέντα σοι, [...].
l. 16 ἐγὼ δὲ ὁ Σιλβανὸς παρειληφέναι παρὰ σοῦ τῆς μητρός μου Τεεῦτος τὸν προκείμενον υἱὸν Παπνουθίου(*) πρὸς υἱοθεσίαν ὅνπερ θρέψω καὶ ἱματιζῶ(*) εὐγενῶς καὶ γνησίως ὡς υἱὸν γνήσιον καὶ φυσικὸν ὡς ἐξ ἐ[μ]οῦ γενόμενον [...].
l. 21 εἶναι δ' αὐτὸν καὶ τῶν ἐμῶν πραγμάτων κληρονόμον υἱοθετηθέντα μοι ὡς προείρηται [...].

(l. 14 In accordance with this, I, Teeus, turn over to you, Silvanus, the aforementioned child for adoption [...], with the intention that he is to be your legitimate and firstborn son, as if he were engendered by you from your own blood [...].
l. 16 On my part, I, Silvanus, receive from you, my mother, for adoption the aforementioned son of Papnouthios, whom I shall feed and clothe in decent and appropriate fashion as my own legitimate and physical son, as though he were born from me, [...].
l. 21 Further, he who has been adopted by me is to be heir of my property as stipulated above [...]. Trans. Rowlandson[327])

326 LCL 266; cf. also A. Hunt, ed. and trans., *The Oxyrhynchus Papyri: Part IX* (Oxford: OUP, 1912), 242 – 4.
327 J. Rowlandson, ed., *Women & Society in Greek & Roman Egypt: A Sourcebook* (Cambridge: CUP, 1998), 297.

In *Congr.* 22–23, Philo draws a comparison between Hagar's status as a proselyte and an adopted child. The comparison would seem to suggest that both a proselyte and an adoptee are persons on the borderline. The proselyte stands on the borderline from being a foreigner who originally was not an ordinary citizen. Correspondingly, an adoptee is on the borderline between not being a natural child and being one who has received a new family with the right to inherit. Hagar's situation on the borderline is expressed in fundamental terms by means of an etymological interpretation of her name, translated by the Greek term παροίκησις. Thus, Hagar means "sojourner", "one who dwells beside", i.e., a person on the borderline between foreigners and citizens (μεθόροι ξένων καὶ ἀστῶν): "The sojourner in so far as he is staying in the city is on par with the citizens, in so far as it is not his home, on par with foreigners" (*Congr.* 23). The borderline place of Hagar is then compared to the status of an adopted person: "In the same way, I should say, adopted children, in so far as they inherit from their adopters, rank with the family; in so far as they are not their actual children, with outsiders" (*Congr.* 23). This portrait of Hagar as a borderline person, who is a pagan Egyptian woman by birth and who has become a proselyte within the household of Abraham, pertains also to her son Ishmael, who stands on the borderline between being Abraham's legitimate son and Sarah's son by adoption:

> And therefore I shall not defer to lead to you a bride who will supply you with what is lacking in myself. And if our prayers for the birth of children are answered, the offspring will be your legitimate (γνήσιος) children, but surely mine also by adoption (θέσις). But to avoid any suspicion of jealousy on my part take if you will my handmaiden, outwardly a slave, inwardly of free and noble race, proved and tested by me for many years from the day when she was first brought to my house, an Egyptian by birth, but a Hebrew by her rule of life. *Abr.* 250–251

Although Philo never explicitly applies the concept of adoption to proselytes,[328] it is noteworthy that he interprets both Hagar and her son Ishmael in association with the concept of adoption in the context of Jewish proselytism.[329] This interpretation of Ishmael as adopted into Abraham's family seems to go beyond other statements, however, in which children of mixed marriages who have been

328 In his references to the concept of adoption, Philo never uses the Greek word υἱοθεσία, but instead uses other terms such as θέσις or εἰσποιέω, or the phrase υἱὸν ποιέω. Cf. *Abr.* 250; *Mos.* 1:19, 32–33, 149; *Flacc.* 9; *Legat.* 23.

329 For a study of Philo's conception of the figures of Hagar and Ishmael as proselytes, cf. P. Borgen, "Some Hebrew and Pagan Features in Philo's and Paul's Interpretation of Hagar and Ishmael," in *The New Testament and Hellenistic Judaism*, ed. P. Borgen and S. Giversen (Aarhus: Aarhus University Press, 1995), 151–64.

adopted into the family of a Hebrew father are mentioned along with Egyptians who have become Jewish proselytes.[330]

I believe that these texts and principles of adoption provide a referential background for Gal 4:5 – 7, and can shed light on some aspects of this text to which scholars have not paid enough attention. With regard to the first principle, both *P. Oxy.* 1206 (l. 8 – 9: δύο εἰς υεἱοθεσίαν, ἐμὲ δὲ τὸν [Ὡρίων]α ἔχειν το[ῦτ]ον γνήσιον υἱόν) and *P. Lips.* 28 (l. 14: πρ[ὸς υἱ]οθεσίαν [...] πρ[ὸ]σ τὸ εἶναι σοῦ υἱ[ὸ]ν γηνσιον καὶ πρωτότοκον ὡς ἐξ ἰδίου αἵματος γεννηθέντα σοι [...]; l. 16: πρὸς υἱοθεσίαν ὅνπερ θρέψω καὶ ἱματιζῶ εὐγενῶς καὶ γνησίως ὡς υἱὸν γνήσιον καὶ φυσικὸν ὡς ἐξ ἐ[μ]οῦ γενόμενον [...]) attest that the adopted son was regarded as having equal status with that of the natural son in a household. According to the latter text, while the legal fiction of adoption itself manifested that the adoptee did not belong to the biological family by birth, he could even be considered "as if he were engendered by you from your own blood" and "as legitimate and physical son (ὡς υἱὸν γνήσιον καὶ φυσικὸν), as though he were born from me." The same view is implicit in Philo's comment on Ishmael's adoption into Abraham's family by Sarah. As an adopted (θέσις) child, Ishmael had the same status relative to Sarah, almost as if he was her natural son, as he had to Abraham as his legitimate (γνήσιος) born son. On this basis, he had a legitimate place in rank with Abraham's family, almost as if he was considered an insider with a status equal to a natural born son of both Abraham and Sarah.

This implication of the conception of adoption might have some bearing on our interpretation of Gal 4:5 – 6. Since this is the only place in the Pauline literature where we find the expression "the Spirit of his Son", it is reasonable to ask why we find this phrase here, and how the Spirit is related to Christ. As I shall suggest, both questions may relate to the implicit understanding of adoption that we just have observed. Above, I took the relationship between sonship and gift of the Spirit to mean that their sonship as adopted sons of God is evidenced by the Spirit. At this point, I shall add another aspect to my earlier paraphrase of Gal 4:5 – 6: "By the gift of the Spirit, you know what this adoption and sonship imply, namely, that you became a legitimate son by means of receiving the Spirit of his own true 'natural' Son. Hence, although an adopted son, you have evidence that you participate in the family of God as if you were considered to have equal status with God's own legitimate Son." This sense of being an adopted son implies that Paul crafts a new genealogy for his Galatian proselytes by resorting to the concept of adoption, claiming that they, as adopted sons of God, are ascribed the full rights of a son together with God's natural Son. The

330 Cf. *Mos.* 1:147.

fact that they share the same Spirit of God's Son is evidence of this status. This conclusion challenges some assumptions in recent research. While it is true, as D.R. Moore-Crispin and B. Witherington III maintain,[331] that υἱοθεσία should be translated "full rights of sons" as in the translation of NIV, such a contextual sense may be implicit in the notion of adoption, which means that the adopted child became "just as one from blood". Moreover, Hodge and Thiessen assume that the concept of the Spirit entails a material aspect, which opposes the distinction made between the "physical" and "spiritual" kinship:

> In Romans 8:14–17 and Galatians 4:1–7, [Paul] seems to be playing on characteristics of pneuma assumed by a range of his contemporaries, especially in his representation of pneuma as a binding agent which unites the gentiles to Christ. [...] In this way, this procreative pneuma creates a new kinship, and does so materially. This conception of pneuma as a physical, transformative agent challenges the oppositional relationship between "physical" and "spiritual" kinship which Pauline scholars often assume. Adoption through the spirit is one of a variety of ways to conceive of relatedness; the spirit makes that relation both tangible and material. In Paul the Spirit serves as a version of "shared blood" in that it provides a tangible, organic connection between Christ and the gentiles.[332]

Building upon Hodge's assumptions, Thiessen makes a similar claim:

> The spiritual / physical or spiritual / material distinction implies an unreal / real distinction —one that wrongly believes that Paul opposes biological descent (flesh and blood) to a fictive descent (a spiritual kinship based on faith). In contrast, the distinction with which Paul works is not physical versus spritual (in the sense of non-material), but sarkic—fleshly, as opposed to pneumatic—materially conceived [...][333]

Whether or not Hodge and Thiessen are right in their view that the Spirit functions like "shared blood", Paul's use of the concept of adoption itself affirms that it was impossible for a non-Jew to become a Jew in a biological sense. Thus, the concept of adoption was a legal fiction that presupposed that the adoptee was at the outset, as Philo says, "in so far as they are not their actual children" an outsider and foreigner with regard to their natural descent (*Congr.* 23). Therefore, it was due to this biological fact that the topic of the non-Jewish lineage of proselytes took on immediate importance, so that he could envisage adoption as a fitting concept to deal with the "Gentile problem". Thus, exactly because the metaphorical concept of adoption reasonated with the idea of a spiritual kinship

---

331 D.R. Moore-Crispin, "Galatians 4.1–9: The Use and Abuse of Parallels," *EQ* 61.3 (1989): 216; Witherington III, *Grace in Galatia*, 283.
332 Johnson Hodge, *If Sons, Then Heirs*, 75–6.
333 Thiessen, *Paul and the Gentile Problem*, 115.

distinctive from physical descent, it gave Paul an opportunity to exploit this concept to craft a new lineage for proselytes, by connecting them to Abraham as the model proselyte, who was transformed by the Spirit and became an adopted son of God. As we shall see next, it was in spite of their improper physical origin and foreign ancestry that Paul, on the basis of the spiritual kinship with Abraham and the concept of adoption by virtue of the shared Spirit of God's Son, could establish the Galatian proselytes as legitimate heirs and partakers of God's promise. In this case too, the reception of the Spirit with particular reference to the role of Christ is taken as evidence and affirmation of this reality of heirship.

Both the papyri referred to above and Philo attest to the second principle involved in the concept of adoption, namely, the right of the adopted child to become a legitimate heir. This can be seen in the following citations:

> *P. Oxy.* 1206, l.8 – 10: [...] ἐμὲ δὲ τὸν [Ὡρίων]α ἔχειν το[ῦτ]ον γνήσιον υἱὸν πρὸς τὸ μένειν αὐτῷ τὰ ἀπ[ὸ τ]ῆς διαδοχῆς τῆς κληρονομίας μου δίκαια ([...] and I, Horion, on the other side, that I have taken him as my true son so as to establish for him the rights of succession to my estate.)
>
> *P. Lips.* 28, l. 21: εἶναι δ' αὐτὸν καὶ τῶν ἐμῶν πραγμάτων κληρονόμον υἱοθετηθέντα μοι ὡς προείρηται [...] (Further, he who has been adopted by me is to be heir of my property as stipulated above [...])
>
> *Congr.* 23: καὶ οἱ θετοὶ παῖδες, ᾗ μὲν κληρονομοῦσι τὰ τῶν θεμένων, τοῖς γνησίοις, ᾗ δ' οὐ γεγέννηνται πρὸς αὐτῶν, τοῖς ὀθνείοις (and adopted children, in so far as they inherit from their adopters, rank with the family; in so far as they are not their actual children, with outsiders.)

In all these texts, cognates of κληρο- are used in the form of a noun (κληρονόμος /κληρονόμια) or verb (κληρονομέω) to describe the adopted child's right to inherit. Since the term for "heir" (κληρονόμος) was originally applied to someone who had been assigned a κλῆρος, either by lot or by being given it as a portion or share,[334] it is relevant again to mention its use in *Sobr.* 56. Here, as in *Congr.* 23, Philo applies the principle that an adopted son is a legitimate heir of the adopting father to the relationship between God and Abraham: "But the man who has this inheritance (κλῆρος) has advanced beyond the bounds of human happiness; for he alone is nobly born, inasmuch as he has God attributed to him as his Father, and being his adopted only son, he is not rich, but allwealthy". It is noteworthy that this reference to the inheritance of Abraham in terms of being assigned a share in God's wealth, is to be found in a context that understands Abraham as an adopted son. This motif corroborates my earlier suggestion that Paul in Gal 3:6 – 29 and 4:1 – 10

334 Cf. BDAG on κλῆρος.

relates to the image of Abraham as the model of both proselytes and the Jews. Both these passages regard the Abrahamic offspring, including the Galatian proselytes, as legitimate adopted sons of God, and this proves that they are rightful heirs of the promise of God given to Abraham and his seed. Thus, in both texts, Paul focuses on their status of sonship, which guarantees their inheritance.

As I have argued throughout this chapter, the exegetical motif of the Spirit, which the Galatians received through trust in God (Gen 15:6) on the analogy of Abraham in Gal 3:2–6, is further interpreted as the fulfillment of the promised blessing of the Spirit in Gal 3:14. In that case, Gal 3:14b refers back to the incident and analogy of how Abraham received the Spirit by trust (cf. Gal 3:5–6) and this is taken as the promised blessing that those of trust would share together with Abraham, as the fulfillment of God's trust granted to Abraham in terms of the oath of promise (Gal 3:8–9). This we can deduce from Paul's reference to Abraham's blessing in 3:14, taken as the fulfillment of the promise cited in 3:8b with special reference to the promised gift of the Spirit. In that case, Abraham's status as the model of proselytes in terms of his transformation by the Spirit was taken as a prefiguration of the fulfillment of the oath of promise in Gen 22:18 and Gen 26:3–4, namely that the promised blessing of the Spirit "might come in Christ Jesus", Abraham's true seed (3:16). It is a conceivable assumption that Paul's rivals in Galatia had argued that the Galatian proselytes proved themselves to be appropriate recipients of these promises given to Abraham's descendants only if they observed the Mosaic Law, in a manner like Abraham himself. This assertion is supported by the observation that the author of Sirach, Philo's interlocutors, and later rabbis maintained a similar view. In Gal 3:16, 18, 22, 29, Paul counters this line of thought with the concepts of κληρονομία and ἐπαγγελία, arguing that the inheritance is affirmed to be mediated according to the oath of promise granted to Abraham and to his seed (3:16, 19), and not through the Law, which came later (3:18). Thus, by means of his appropriation of the oath of promise (cf. particularly his allusion to Gen 26:3 applied to Christ in 3:16), Paul also makes the point in Gal 3.22b that the promise is mediated to those who share the same family likeness with Abraham, that is, the conduct of trust manifested in Abraham's seed, Christ. In 3:29, then, Paul reaches the conclusion of this train of thought, by pointing out that those who belong to Christ are the true offspring of Abraham, and so heirs according to the promise (κατ' ἐπαγγελίαν κληρονόμοι). This conclusion draws together the argument from 3:5–16, namely, that the gift of the Spirit confirms that the promised blessing of Abraham has come to fruition in Christ, the seed of Abraham. This in turn proves for Paul that the Galatian proselytes are not just legitimate sons of Abraham (3:7), but also valid heirs of the oath of promise spoken to Abraham and to his seed (3:8–9, 14, 16). One can then ask how the Spirit is related to Christ and the topic of sonship and inheritance. Another answer to this question is given in the context of Gal 4:1–7.

While the Spirit in the context of Gal 3:1–29 is seen as a token of the promised blessing and inheritance of Abraham, taking effect through the crucifixion of Christ, Gal 4:6–7 takes this argument one step further, and is meant to set a full-stop to the argument about the Spirit-experience and the status and the situation of the Galatians. This text explains the Spirit as the Spirit of God's Son (τὸ πνεῦμα τοῦ υἱοῦ) in terms of affirming the assigned status of sonship and heirship. In other words, the Spirit validates the Galatian proselytes as adopted sons of God, who through experiencing the Spirit of sonship show that they belong to God's family and already are legitimate heirs of God's promise to Abraham. Moreover, when, in a way that corresponds to Abraham, they experienced God's liberation from the false creeds of polytheism and were adopted by God, they received a status in relation to God not as slaves, but as sons: they were given the status of heirs of God. Accordingly, when they received the Spirit, they were assigned a share in the sonship of Christ and in the blessings that the life in the Spirit involved.

To sum up this section: Gal 4:7 is an *inclusio* referring back to the thesis in 3:7 on Abraham's sons and the promise, which is now considered as proven. In fact, the questions raised at the beginning of Paul's argument in 3:2–5 are now answered. It was neceesary for Paul to affirm that the Galatian proselytes were Abraham's sons through Christ, Abraham's true offspring. Only thus could the proselytes expect to be heirs. But it was more fundamental to trace their lineage back to God, as the ultimate ancestor. This is why Paul makes use of the metaphor of adoption. It is only through sharing the Spirit of Abraham, who was also in Christ, God's son, that they could become adopted sons of God, like Abraham, and thus rightful heirs of the promise God had uttered to Abraham and to his seed, Christ. In Christ, then, the Galatian proselytes became both Abraham's offspring and sons of God, to whom the promise of heirship was given.

7 Conclusions

The analysis of Paul's argument in Galatians 3 leads to the following conclusions:

1. Gal 3:6–29 is a small "exegetical treatise", in which words from the main quotation of Gen 15:6 in 3:6 have been given an exegetical paraphrase in the course of the passage. In paraphrasing Scripture, by which a biblical phrase has been replaced or supplemented by other interpretative terms, Paul has incorporated exegetical motifs that deviate or go beyond a mere repetition or restate-

ment of the biblical text. The parallels in Philo and other Jewish data also show that Paul has steeped his argument in conventional forms such as exegetical structures and terminology of his own day.

2. Philo and Paul share exegetical traditions and motifs, in which Gen 15:6 has been paraphrased about Abraham's reception of the Spirit as the paradigm of Jewish proselytes. The comparison of the Galatian converts' experience to this crucial event in Abraham's life meant that, thanks to their reception of the Spirit through trust in the manner of Abraham, the Galatians were to be understood as legitimate proselytes apart from circumcision and a life within the jurisdiction of Mosaic Law. Paul's argument was most probably developed in a debate with his opponents, who drew the opposite conclusion from the same exegetical motif and data, namely, that if the Galatian converts further were to emulate the virtue of piety of Abraham, they needed to be circumcised and thus become adherents of the jurisdiction of Law revealed through Moses.

3. Paul presupposed that Abrahamic sonship meant that the ancestor was the common father of Jews and converts, not of non-Jews in general. By paraphrasing Gen 15:6 in Gal 3:7, Paul took Abraham's trust as the identifying mark of being his genuine descendant and thus the ground for the Abrahamic kinship into which the converts have been integrated. Paul's delimitation of the true descendants of Abraham, identified as "those of trust", had probably its context in an intra-mural Jewish debate, in which Paul faced people who maintained a genealogical definition based on physical descent from the patriarchs and who would require of proselytes circumcision and subsequently observance of the Law of Moses as an expression of emulating the virtue of piety Abraham acieved through his trust in God.

4. In Gal 3:8 – 9, Paul advances the exegetical paraphrase of Gen 15:6 by a refashioning of the conduct of God in the image of Abraham. At this juncture, Paul seems to adopt a pattern of thought, attested by Philo, in which a reciprocity was drawn between Abraham's trust and the conduct of trust / faithfulness expected in return from God, namely, to keep the oath of promise granted to Abraham and his descendant (cf. Gen 22:18; 26:3 – 4). Like Philo, Paul takes the oath of promise as granted as God's response to Abraham's trust in general before the Law was revealed through Moses. Thus, the oath of promise was not posited on the *Akedah* or Abraham's obedience to the Law of Moses, but rather grounded wholly in both Abraham's trust *and* God's reaffirmed trust to keep his promise of blessings. Abraham's πίστις in God's promise meant to share the πίστις of God, identified by his conduct of being trustworthy / faithful (πιστός). In Paul's view, it was this correspondence between Abraham's trust *and* God's responsiveness to Abraham's trust by means of the oath of promise that enabled

Abraham's blessings to reach his descendants, encompassing "those of trust" even among the "nations".

5. The Jewish debate attested in Philo's writings on Abraham may provide a context for a corresponding debate reflected in Galatians, and suggest that there were Jewish antecedents and analogies to Paul's reasoning in his own time. The imaginary interlocutors referred to by Philo maintained a position similar to the author of Jubilees and the later rabbis with regard to the secondary character of the Sinaitic Law: they probably saw Abraham as a pre-Sinaitic observer of the jurisdiction of Moses. Philo, himself, however, obviously felt it necessary to correct and modify such a position, and claims that this could not have been the case, since the Sinaitic laws had not yet been set in writing (cf. *Abr.* 5 and 275). These modifications suggest that Philo operates with a distinction between two jurisdictions in the concept of the Torah, whereby Abraham's trust in God and His promises are regarded as manifesting adherence to the unwritten divine Law in Nature that is antecedent to, and distinct from, the special laws that were later promulgated at Sinai. According to Philo, the Sinaitic legislation only sets forth as legislation the archetypical divine Law and exemplifies the same virtues that is manifested in the legal figure of Abraham.

Philo's distinction between two sets of laws or jurisdictions within the Torah, the more general attested by Abraham and the particular later revealed by Moses, has some affinity with Paul. Although he does not apply legal terminology to Abraham, Paul too seems to have made a distinction in the concept of the Torah between what we may call an "Abrahamic jurisdiction", centered on Abraham's trust and God's promise, and the "Mosaic jurisdiction" revealed later at Sinai. Since Paul seems to create the phrase ἐκ πίστεως ("those of trust") based on the model of Abraham, in contrast to the expression ἐκ ἔργων νόμου ("those of works of law"), it is likely that Paul takes his place in a Jewish negotiation on Abraham relative to the Law of Moses. Thus, Paul construes Abraham's trust in God's promise, rather than observance of the Law of Moses, as the basic mark of identification and of what constitutes the status of Abrahamic descendants. Paul's questions concerning Abraham's reception of the Spirit in contrast to obedience to the "works of Law" in Gal 3:2, 5, and the exegetical argument in Gal 3:10–25 regarding the relationship between Abraham's trust in the promise and the Law of Moses, are formulated in order to counter anticipated objections to his basic arguments, for which they provide further backing.

6. In Gal 3:10–14, Paul elaborates on the descendant-mediated blessings that result from the correspondence between Abraham's trust and God's oath of promise (Gal 3:6–9), on the one hand, and the redemptive event of Christ's crucifixion as being "hanged upon a tree" (Gal 3:10–13), on the other hand. Thus, Paul approaches the Christ event from the perspective of a dynamic inter-

action between the "Abrahamic" and the "Mosaic" jurisdictions. Three aspects of the interpretation of the Christ event stand out. In the first place, by picking up the line of thought in Gal 2:21 and 3:1, Paul emphasized the outcome of Christ's crucifixion: If the Law of Moses was still in force, Christ had died for nothing, as one who was sentenced to death and hanged as an accursed criminal for the sake of deterrence, according to the regulations of Deut 27:26 and 21:23. Instead of succumbing to the threat of such a curse, by siding with the teaching of Paul's opponents, the Galatians should stick to what he had proclaimed. Second, as an apostle of Jesus Christ, Paul had altered his perspective on the fact of the crucifixion: The execution and impalement on the cross demonstrated that the crucified Christ became a curse "*for us*". Third, Paul makes it clear that Christ's death as a crucified criminal also pertains to the "Abrahamic jurisdiction". When Christ, as Abraham's ultimate "seed", died vicariously within the context of the "Mosaic jurisdiction", God's oath of promise to Abraham and his descendant remained valid and actually were put into effect, and thus offered a reservoir of blessing for those who had not kept all of God's commandments (Gal 3:10), even encompassing the blessing of the "nations" (Gal 3:14) .

7. In Gal 3:15 – 18, Paul asserts that the oath of promise was not contingent on the Law of Moses, since the promise previously given to Abraham was ratified by God in the "covenant between the pieces", so that no one can nullify it. Moreover, Paul succeeded in showing that the oath of promise was not *just* spoken to Abraham (Gen 22:16 – 18), but *to* Abraham *and to his offspring* (Gen 26:3 – 4), which applies, not to many descendants, but to the one individual offspring, Christ, encompassing his descendants. The fact that the Law of Moses came four hundred and thirty years after the covenant established "between the pieces" proves that the Law had a subordinate order and rank relative to the priority of the promise. Accordingly, it cannot cancel either the original promise or God's reaffirmation of it in the oath of promise to Abraham and his descendant. The corollary is that the inheritance, the gift promised to Abraham and his descendant, which is identified by Paul as the Spirit, does not depend on observance of the Law of Moses, for God continues to confer his gift solely through the promise received by trust (Gal 3:14).

8. In Gal 3:19 – 25, Paul argues that the Law of Moses does not annul the promise of blessing, since the Law is of a subordinate rank and is therefore integral to the promise of God. Paul makes use of an exegetetical motif that suggested that the Law, in contrast to God's promises, was given only at third hand from God. Thus, in a way analogous to Philo, Paul makes use of the Jewish tradition that the Law was arranged by three parties: by God who "orders" the Law to be given "through" the agency of the angels *and* "by the hand of" Moses. This divine arrangement of the Law mediated through angelic envoys,

who included Moses, forms a contrast to the one God, who spoke directly to Abraham and Isaac when he gave the oath of promise. For this reason, the immediacy of the promise on God's part corresponds to the nature of the one God, while the mediation of the Law through many agents highlights its temporal and provisional function. It is valid until the realization of the promise made to Abraham and his offspring.

9. Paul's emphasis on the descendant-mediated version of the promise (cf. Gen 22:17–18 / 26:3–4), ensuing upon Abraham's trust (cf. Gen 15:6), applies to the interpretation of the phrase ἐκ πίστεως Ἰησοῦ Χριστοῦ in Gal 3:22b. In the context of Gal 3:6–21, logic suggests that this phrase refers to the trust of Christ, the Abrahamic offspring, so that the oath of promise was given to him on the basis of conduct like that of his ancestor Abraham. Thus, as the oath of promise which was originally made to Abraham (Gen 22:16–18), on the ground of his trust (Gen 15:6), proved that he was trustworthy, the same is also true when it was later reiterated to his offspring (Gen 26:3–4). Again, the patrilineal correspondence between the conduct of Abraham, Christ, and his descendants is presupposed in this application of the oath of promise, in a manner analogous to what we have seen in Philo, *QG* 4:180. This line of thought also resonates with Paul's claim that those of trust are Abraham's sons (3:6–7) and therefore partakers of the oath of promise to Abraham (3:8–9), with its inherent righteousness and blessings which are conferred on "those of trust".

10. Since the Galatian converts were not Abraham's natural descendants, Paul was sensitive to the problem of their foreign lineage and therefore made a special provision for them in order for them to be recognized as valid Abrahamic descendants and so numbered as heirs of the promise. In the course of Paul's ongoing argument, their experience of having received the Spirit and of God's working of powers through trust after the model of Abraham guarantees that they are proselytes approved by God and therefore validated as Abraham's sons and partakers of the oath of promise. The conclusion in Gal 3:29 is therefore an *inclusio* referring back to the thesis in 3:7 about Abraham's sons and the promise, which is now considered as proven. In order to affirm the status of the Galatian proselytes as legitimate Abraham's sons through Christ, Paul explicitly made clear that Jesus Christ was Abraham's offspring, and that the Galatian converts thus were heirs to the blessing promised to Abraham and to his offspring by oath. Finally, in Gal 4:1–7, Paul adds another guarantee of their status as heirs, based on the concept of Abraham as an adopted son of God. Like Abraham, through sharing the Spirit of God, who was also in Christ, God's son, Abraham's sons too shared in the sonship of God, and thus were to be considered rightful heirs of the promise that God had once spoken to Abraham and to his one "seed", Christ. When this is applied to the status of the Galatian proselytes,

they are considered to be both Abraham's offspring and sons of God, to whom the promise of heirship was given.

Chapter 6: Final Summary of the Study

The aim of the present study has been to offer a new reading of Paul's appropriation of Abraham in Gal 3:6–29 against the background of Jewish data, especially drawn from the writings of Philo of Alexandria, which either have not been appropriated or ought to be brought more centrally into scholarly discussion. Let me now bring together and briefly summarize the main conclusions reached in each part of this study.

The focus of chapter two is on Philo's portrayal of Abraham as the paradigmatic model, regarded as the first proselyte and the founder of the Jewish nation. This was determinative of his understanding of Jewish ethnic identity and of what he considered as identifying "marks" of a genuine Abrahamic descendant or of becoming a proselyte. The ethnic differentiation between the Jewish *ethnos* and other peoples that exists because of ethnic origins and lineage means that Philo does not make an ethnic blending of a born Jew and a convert. This is why he never says that proselytes get a new lineage as Abraham's descendants or become members of the Jewish *ethnos*. The proselytes receive a Jewish identity in terms of the character traits they share with Abraham as their model convert, such as receiving the Spirit and the transformation they achieve in terms of a virtue of piety when they come to believe in the one God. Hence, Philo would seem to have made a special provision for the incorporation of proselytes who choose to live according to these core virtues and common laws embodied in the Law of Moses, which is understood to promote the very same virtue of piety Abraham achieved, the founder of the Jewish proselyte nation. As a corollary of this ethnic differentiation, Philo tends rather to speak of the new spiritual kinship and fellowship bond between Jews and proselytes within the Jewish *politeia*.

Moreover, referring explicitly back to the oath of promise to Abraham in Gen 22:16–18, Philo emphasizes the emulation of Abraham's character and nature in order to safeguard the promised blessings on the part of the descendants. The interpretation of these passages presupposes a direct relationship between the virtue of piety and conduct of Abraham and God's blessings that are expected to be received by the generations that succeed the ancestor. The scriptural line of thought behind Philo's reasoning seems to be the dynamic interaction between the "Mosaic jurisdiction" and the antecedent "Abrahamic jurisdiction", which means that when the laws of Moses are broken, the Abrahamic promise of blessings remains in effect and offers a reservoir of restoration to the errant people.

In chaper three, the analysis of *Abr.* 262–273 suggests that Philo presupposes a pattern of thought whereby he interprets Gen 15:6, detached from its narrative

https://doi.org/10.1515/9783110722109-007

context, in conjunction with Gen 22:16–18 from the perspective of a parallelism between Abraham's conduct of trust and the conduct of trust / faithfulness expected in return from God. In lieu of taking the oath of promise as a reward for the *Akedah*, Philo interprets Gen 22:16–18 about the πίστις God grants Abraham in return as a response for his trust (πίστις; Gen 15:6) in general. This correspondence conforms to a trend well attested in Jewish Haggadah.

Chapter four explores further the exegetical tradition that reads Gen 15:6, 22:16–18, and 26:3–5 in *continuum* as a series of Abrahamic events that belong together. So, Philo detaches Abraham's trust (Gen 15:6) from his putative observance of the Law of Moses, and rather one-sidedly relates it to the promises given to Abraham (Gen 22:16–18). In contradistinction to an application of Gen 26:5 that conceived Abraham's virtue of piety and the Law of Moses as inseparable, a position that he explicitly states is held by some others of his day, Philo reads it about Abraham's observance of the divine Law in Nature, without dissolving the relation that exists between the divine Law in Nature and the Law of Moses. This exegetical manoeuver suggests that Philo made a distinction within the concept of the Torah between an "Abrahamic jurisdiction", in which Abraham's trust in the promise is seen as epitomizing the divine Law in Nature, and the "Mosaic jurisdiction", taken to reflect and promote the virtues that Abraham had achieved through what he had said and done. This distinction is the result of Philo's concern to appropriate Abraham in his Hellenistic and Jewish context, without compromising the distinction between these two "jurisdictions" in the Torah and their cosmic significance in a Greco-Roman and Jewish context. Since the Law of Moses contains the record and jurisdiction of what Abraham and the patriarchs achieved through their instinctive words and deeds, it is, as a written Law code, unlike any other human legislation that operates among Greeks and Romans. It is the best possible approximation to the cosmic divine Law in Nature.

In part two, and my final chapter, I seek to demonstrate that Gal 3:6–29 provides a small "exegetical treatise" in which the exegetical paraphrase of Gen 15:6 has incorporated various exegetical traditions and motifs and molded these into conventional forms.

A comparison with Philo suggests that Paul's exegetical paraphrase of Gen 15:6 has incorporated the exegetical motif about Abraham's reception and transformation of the Spirit through his becoming the first Jewish proselyte. By comparing the Galatian converts' experience to this crucial event in Abraham's life, Paul argued that the Galatians were to be understood as legitimate proselytes apart from circumcision and a life within the jurisdiction of Mosaic Law (Gal 3:2, 5–6). This argument was most probably developed in an intra-mural Jewish debate with his opponents, who drew the opposite conclusion from this exegetical motif and experience, namely, that the Galatian converts in order to emulate Abraham's virtue of piety needed to be circumcised and become adherents of the commandments of the Mosaic Law.

By paraphrasing Gen 15:6 about the identifying mark of Abrahamic sonship (Gal 3:7), Paul, then, emphasizes that foundational character of descent from Abraham has its origin in Abraham's trust in God. This delimitation of the genuine descendants of Abraham probably occurs in a context in which Paul faced people who maintained a genealogical definition based on physical descent from the patriarchs, and who would require of the proselytes circumcision and Law observance as the expression of the emulation of Abraham's trust in God.

Gal 3:8–9 can be seen as a further exegetical paraphrase of Gen 15:6, as a refashioning of the conduct of God in the image of Abraham. At this point, Paul seems to build upon a pattern of thought, attested in Philo, in which a reciprocity was drawn between Abraham's conduct of πίστις (Gen 15:6) and the corresponding πίστις on God's part in blessing Abraham and his descendants, as had been promised by oath (cf. Gen 22:18; 26:3–4). Like Philo, Paul takes the oath of promise as a reward for Abraham's trust in general, and not as a gift for the *Akedah* (not withholding his son Isaac) or his putative obedience to the Law of Moses. Thus, the oath of promise was grounded wholly in Abraham's trust and in God's trust to keep the promise. In Paul's view, it was this correspondence of trust / faithfulness on the part of both Abraham *and* God that enabled the promise of blessings to reach his descendants, encompassing "those of trust" among the "nations".

The Jewish debate attested in Philo's writings about Abraham's relationship to the Law of Moses may provide a context for a corresponding debate reflected in Galatians, and suggest that there were Jewish antecedents and analogies to Paul's reasoning in his own time. Thus, Philo's distinction between two jurisdictions in the concept of the Torah, centered on Abraham's trust in the promise and on observance of the Law of Moses, respectively, has some affinity with Paul. Without explicitly applying legal terminology to Abraham as Philo did, Paul too seems to operate with a distinction in the concept of the Torah and Scripture, in which he separated the "Abrahamic jurisdiction" from the the "Mosaic jurisdiction". Since Paul seems to create the phrase ἐκ πίστεως ("those of trust") on the model of Abraham's trust in God, in contrast to the expression ἐκ ἔργων νόμου ("those of works of law"), centered on obedience to the Law of Moses, it is likely that Paul takes his place in a similar Jewish debate on Abraham. Thus, in a corresponding way as Philo, Paul construes Abraham's virtue of piety, centered on his trust in God's promise as opposed to his being a Jewish observer of the Torah, as the "legal" norm for what constitutes lineal descent from Abraham and the status of being a party to the promise. Paul's questions concerning Abraham's reception of the Spirit through trust apart from obedience to the "works of Law" (Gal 3:2, 5), and the exegetical argument concerning Abraham's trust in the promise relative to the Law of Moses (Gal 3:10–25), are made in order to counter anticipated objections to his basic arguments and to provide further backing for them.

In Gal 3:10–14, Paul elaborates on the descendant-mediated blessings that result from Abraham's trust and God's promise (Gal 3:6–9) and the redemptive event of Christ's crucifixion as being "hanged upon a tree" (Gal 3:10–13). Thus, Paul interprets the Christ event from the perspective of a dynamic interaction taking place between the "Abrahamic" and "Mosaic" jurisdictions. As an apostle, Paul had altered his perspective on the Christ event in three ways: First, his execution and public exposure as a crucified criminal within the jurisdiction of the Law of Moses demonstrated that his death became a curse "for us". Second, Christ's death as a crucified criminal was also applied to the "Abrahamic jurisdiction": When Christ as Abraham's ultimate "seed" died vicariously, this confirmed what God had promised Abraham by oath, in that the promised blessings were put into effect, even encompassing the blessing of the "nations" in Jesus Christ (Gal 3:13–14). Third, albeit the descendant-mediated version of the promise in terms of the oath of promise was not *just* spoken to Abraham (Gen 22:16–18), but *to* Abraham *and to his offspring* (Gen 26:3–4), Paul did not take it to apply to the many descendants of Abraham and Isaac, but rather specifically to the one individual "seed" Christ, encompassing his offspring (Gal 3:15–18).

In Gal 3:19–25, Paul continues to establish the argument that the Law of Moses does not annul the promise of blessing, since it was of a subordinate order and rank and therefore was integral to the promise of God. Paul thus makes use of an exegetical motif that suggested that the Law, in contrast to God's promises, was given only at third hand from God. The divine arrangement of the Law mediated through angelic envoys, who included Moses, contrasts with the one God, who spoke the oath of promise directly to Abraham and Isaac. For this reason, the immediacy of the promise on God's part corresponds to the nature of the one God, while the mediation of the Law through many agents highlights its temporal and provisional function: it is valid until the realization of the promise made to Abraham and his offspring.

Since the Galatian converts are not Abraham's natural descendants, a special provision was made for them, so that they could inherit the status of descent from Abraham and thus become heirs of the promise. In the course of Paul's ongoing argument, their experience of having received the Spirit by trust after the model of Abraham guarantees that they are proselytes approved by God and therefore validated as Abraham's sons and partakers of the oath of promise. With regard to the Galatian proselytes as Abraham's sons through Christ, Paul made it explicitly clear that since Jesus Christ was Abraham's offspring, they were heirs to the blessing promised to Abraham and to his offspring (Gal 3:29). Furthermore, like Abraham, through sharing the Spirit of God, who was also in Christ, God's son, the Galatian proselytes too share in this sonship of God, which meant they were considered to be both legitimate descendants from Abraham and sons of God, to whom the promise of heirship was given (Gal 4:1–7).

Bibliography

Abbreviations follow mainly the rules according to *The SBL Handbook of Style*, 2nd ed. Atlanta, GA: SBL Press, 2014.

A Sources and Reference Works

1 The Bible: Texts and Translations

Biblica Hebraica. Stuttgartensia. Edited by R. Kittel et al. Stuttgart: Deutsche Bibelstiftung, 1977.

Novum Testamentum Graece. 28th ed. Edited by K. Aland et al. Stuttgart: Deutsche Bibelgesellschaft, 2012.

Septuaginta, Vols. 1–2. 8th ed. Edited by A. Ralphs. Stuttgart: Deutsche Bibelstiftung, 1935.

A New English Translation of the Septuagint: A New Translation of the Greek into Contemporary English – An Essential Resource for Biblical Studies. Edited by A. Pietersma and B.G. Wright. New York; Oxford: OUP, 2007. (NETS)

Holy Bible: New Revised Standard Version containing the Old and New Testaments. Peabody, MA: Hendrickson, 1989.

2 Jewish Texts

a. Apocrypha and Pseudepigrapha

The Apocrypha and Pseudepigrapha of the Old Testament, Vols. 1–2. Edited by R.H. Charles. Oxford: Clarendon Press, 1913.

The Old Testament Pseudepigrapha, Vols. 1–2. Edited by J.H. Charlesworth. London: Darton, Longman & Todd, 1983–85.

The Greek Versions of the Testaments of the Twelve Patriarchs. Edited by R.H. Charles. Oxford: Clarendon Press, 1908.

b. Philo

If not stated otherwise, the Greek texts of Philo's writings are quoted according to *Loeb Classical Library* (Cambridge, MA: Harvard University Press).

Philon: Les Œuvres de Philon d'Alexandrie. Philo translated by R. Arnaldez, J. Caseaux, and S. Daniel et al. Paris: Cerf, 1961–79.

Philo von Alexandria: Die Werke in deutscher Übersetzung. Edited by L. Cohn et al. Berlin: De Gruyter, 1962–64.

https://doi.org/10.1515/9783110722109-008

Philonis Alexandrini Opera quae supersunt. Edited by L. Cohn, P. Wendland, S. Reiter, and I. Leisegang. Berlin: Reimer, 1962.

c. Qumran

Die Texte aus Qumran: Hebräisch und Deutsch. Edited by E. Lohse. München: Kösel-Verlag, 1971.

The Dead Sea Scrolls Translated: The Qumran Texts in English. Edited by F. García Martínez. Leiden: Brill, 1994.

d. Rabbinic Literature

The Aramaic Bible: The Targums. Edited by K. Cathcart, M. Maher, and M. McNamara. Edinburgh: T & T Clark, 1987–.

The Bible in Aramaic: The Pentateuch according to Targum Onkelos. Edited by A. Sperber. Leiden: Brill, 1959.

The Targums of Onkelos and Jonathan ben Uzziel on the Pentateuch: With the Fragments of the Jerusalem Targum. Translated by J.W. Etheridge. New York, NY: KTAV Publishing House, 1968.

The Mishnah: Translated from the Hebrew with Introduction and brief Explanatory Notes. Translated by H. Danby. New York: OUP, 1933.

The Babylonian Talmud. Edited by I. Epstein. London: The Soncino Press, 1935–52.

The Palestinian Talmud. Printed by D. Bomberg. Venice, 1523–24.

The Tosefta: Translated from the Hebrew. Edited by J. Neusner. New York: KTAV Publishing House, 1977–86.

Mekilta de-Rabbi Ishmael. Edited and translated by J.Z. Lauterbach. Philadelphia, PA: Jewish Publication Society, 1949.

3 Greek and Latin Sources

In general, the ancient *Greek and Latin texts* are referred to according to *Loeb Classical Library* (Cambridge, MA: Harvard University Press). In the case of papyri, the documents are provided by the papyrological database available at the following url: www.papyri.info. In some cases, modifications of these translations have been made.

4 Lexica and Grammars

Bauer, W. and F.W. Danker. *A Greek-English Lexicon of the New Testament and Other Early Christian Literature.* Third ed. Chicago, IL: The University of Chigago Press, 1979. (BDAG)

Blass, F. and A.F. Debrunner. *A Greek Grammar of the New Testament and other Early Christian Literature: A Translation and Revision of the ninth–tenth German edition*

incorporating supplementary notes of A. Debrunner by R.W. Funk. Chicago, IL; London: The University of Chicago Press, 1961.
Borgen, P., K.S. Fuglseth, and R. Skarsten. *The Philo Index: A Complete Greek Word Index to the Writings of Philo of Alexandria.* Grand Rapids: Eerdmans; Leiden: Brill, 2000.
Kittel, G. and G. Friedrich, eds. *Theologisches Wörterbuch Zum Neuen Testament.* Stuttgart: W. Kohlhammer Verlag, 1933–79.
Lampe, G.W.H., ed. *A Patristic Greek Lexicon.* Oxford: Clarendon Press, 1961.
Liddell, H., G.R. Scott, and H.S. Jones. *A Greek-English Lexicon.* Oxford: Clarendon Press, 1958. (LSJ)
Rehkopf, F. *Septuaginta-Vokabular.* Göttingen: Vandenhoeck & Ruprecht, 1989.

B Secondary Literature

Adams, S.A and S.M. Ehorn, eds. *Composite Citations in Antiquity: Volume One: Jewish, Greco-Roman, and Early Christian Uses.* LNTS 525. London: Bloomsbury T & T Clark, 2016.
Adams, S.A and S.M. Ehorn, eds. *Composite Citations in Antiquity: Volume Two: New Testament Uses.* LNTS 593. London: Bloomsbury T & T Clark, 2018.
Allison, D.C. *A Critical and Exegetical Commentary on The Epistle of James.* ICC. London: Bloomsbury T & T Clark, 2013.
Allison, D.C. *Testament of Abraham.* CEJL. Berlin; New York: De Gruyter, 2003.
Amir, Y. *Die hellenistische Gestalt des Judentums bei Philon von Alexandrien.* Forschungen zum Jüdisch-Christlichen Dialog. Neukirchen: Neukirchener Verlag, 1983.
Anderson, G.A. "The Status of the Torah in the Pre-Sinaitic Period: St. Paul's Epistle to the Romans." Pages 1–23 in *Biblical Perspectives: Early Use and Interpretation of the Bible in Light of the Dead Sea Scrolls: Proceedings of the First International Symposium of the Orion Center for the Study of the Dead Sea Scrolls and Associated Literature, 12–14 May, 1996.* Edited by M.E. Stone and E.G. Chazon. Leiden; Boston; Köln: Brill, 1998.
Arnim, H.F.A. *Stoicorum Veterum Fragmenta.* 4 Vols. Leipzig: Teubne, 1903–24.
Arnold, B.T. *Genesis.* NCBC. Cambridge: CUP, 2009.
Attridge, H.W. *The Epistle to the Hebrews: A Commentary on the Epistle to the Hebrews.* Hermeneia. Philadelphia: Fortress Press, 1989.
Auerbach, E. *Mimesis: The Representation of Reality in Western Literature.* Translated by W.R. Trask. Princeton: Princeton University Press, 1953.
Augustine's Commentary on Galatians. Translated by E. Plumer. Oxford: OUP, 2003.
Aune, D. "Galatians 3:28 and the Problem of Equality in the Church and Society." Pages 153–83 in *From Judaism to Christianity: Tradition and Transition: A Festschrift for Thomas T. Tobin, S. J., on the Occasion of His Sixty-Fifth Birthday.* Edited by P. Walters. NovTSup 136. Leiden: Brill, 2010.
Austin, J.L. *How to Do Things with Words: The William James Lectures.* Cambridge, MA: Harvard University Press, 1962.
Baden, J.S. *The Promise to the Patriarchs.* Oxford: OUP, 2013.
Barclay, J.M.G. "The Gift and its Perfections: A Response to Joel Marcus and Margaret Mitchell." *JSNT* 39.3 (2017): 331–44.
Barclay, J.M.G. *Paul and the Gift.* Grand Rapids: Eerdmans, 2015.

Barclay, J.M.G. "Paul, the Gift and the Battle Over Gentile Circumcision: Revisiting the Logic of Galatians." *ABR* 58 (2010): 36–56.
Barclay, J.M.G. *Obeying the Truth: A Study of Paul's Ethics in Galatians*. Edinburgh: T & T Clark, 1988.
Barrett, C.K. "The Allegory of Abraham, Sarah, and Hagar in the Argument of Galatians." Pages 154–70 in *Essays on Paul*. London: SPCK, 1982.
Bauckham, R. *James: Wisdom of James, Disciple of Jesus the Sage*. London; New York: Routledge, 1999.
Becker, J. *Die Briefe an die Galater, Epheser und Kolosser*. NTD. Göttingen: Vandenhoeck & Ruprecht, 1998.
Begleiter, B. *Imagining a Patriarch: Images of Abraham in Early Jewish and Christian Exegesis*. PhD diss., Yale University, 2004.
Bekken, P.J. *The Lawsuit Motif in John's Gospel from New Perspectives: Jesus Christ, Crucified Criminal and Emperor of the World*. NovTSup 158. Leiden; Boston: Brill, 2015.
Bekken, P.J. "Philo's Relevance for the Study of the New Testament." Pages 226–68 in *Reading Philo: A Handbook to Philo of Alexandria*. Edited by T. Seland. Grand Rapids: Eerdmans, 2014.
Bekken, P.J. *The Word is Near You: A Study of Deuteronomy 30:12–14 in Paul's Letter to the Romans in a Jewish Context*. BZNW 144. Berlin; New York: De Gruyter, 2007.
Bekken, P.J. "Abraham og Ånden: Paulus' anvendelse av Genesis 15:6 i Galaterbrevet 3:6 belyst ut fra jødisk materiale." *Tidsskrift for Teologi og Kirke* 71.4 (2000): 265–76.
Ben-Porat, Z. "The Poetics of Literary Allusion", *PTL: A Journal for Descriptive Poetics and Theory of Literature* 1 (1976): 105–128.
Bernstein, M.J. *Reading and Re-Reading Scripture at Qumran: Volume 2*. STDJ 107 / 2. Leiden: Brill, 2013.
Berthelot, K. "Judaism as 'Citizenship' and the Question of the Impact of Rome." Pages 107–29 in *In the Crucible of Empire: The Impact of Roman Citizenship Upon Greeks, Jews and Christians*. Edited by K. Berthelot and J.J. Price. Interdisciplinary Studies in Ancient Culture and Religion 21. Leuven: Peeters Publishers, 2019.
Berthelot, K. "Adoption as a Conceptual Tool to Think About Conversion: A Study in Philo, Paul, and Rabbinic Literature." Paper preseneted at the Annual Meeting of the SBL. Boston, 2017.
Berthelot, K. "Entre Octroi de la Citoyenneté et Adoption: Les Modèles Pour Penser la Conversion Au Judaïsme à l'Époque Romaine." *Pallas* 104 (2017): 37–50.
Betz, H.D. *Galatians: A Commentary on Paul's Letter to the Churches in Galatia*. Hermeneia. Philadelphia: Fortress Press, 1979.
Bickerman, E.J. "'Cutting a Covenant'." Pages 1–31 in *Studies in Jewish and Christian History: A New Edition in English Including the God of the Maccabees, Introduced by Martin Hengel: Volume One*. Edited by A. Tropper. AJEC 68 / 1. Leiden: Brill, 2007.
Bickerman, E.J. "Blessing and Prayer." Pages 585–95 in *Studies in Jewish and Christian History: A New Edition in English Including the God of the Maccabees, Introduced by Martin Hengel:* Volume Two. Edited by A. Tropper. AJEC 68 / 2. Leiden; Boston: Brill, 2007.
Bickerman, E.J. "Utilitas Crucis." Pages 726–93 in *Studies in Jewish and Christian History: A New Edition in English Including the God of the Maccabees, Introduced by Martin Hengel: Volume Two*. Edited by A. Tropper. AJEC 68 / 2. Leiden; Boston: Brill, 2007.

Bird, M.F. An Anomalous Jew: Paul Among Jews, Greeks, and Romans. Grand Rapids: Eerdmans, 2016.
Birnbaum, E. "The Biblical Interpretations of Philo: On the Life of Abraham." Pages 916–50 in *Outside the Bible: Ancient Jewish Writings Related to Scripture.* Edited by L.H. Feldman, J.L. Kugel, and L.H. Schiffman. Lincoln, NE: Jewish Publication Society, 2013.
Birnbaum, E. *The Place of Judaism in Philo's Thought: Israel, Jews, and Proselytes.* SPhiloM. Atlanta: Scholars Press, 1996.
Birnbaum, E. and J. Dillon. *Philo of Alexandria, On the Life of Abraham: Introduction, Translation, and Commentary.* PACS. Leiden; Boston: Brill, 2020.
Borgen, P. "Perspectives for Mission: Galatians 3:1–14 in Context." Pages 181–92 in *The Church and Its Mission in the New Testament and Early Christianity: Essays in Memory of Hans Kvalbein.* Edited by D.E. Aune and R. Hvalvik. WUNT 404. Tübingen: Mohr Siebeck, 2018.
Borgen, P. "Openly Portrayed as Crucified: Some Observations on Gal 3:1–14." Pages 345–53 in *Christology, Controversy and Community: New Testament Essays in Honour of David R. Catchpole.* Edited by D.G. Horrell and C.M. Tuckett. NovTSup 99. Leiden: Brill, 2000.
Borgen, P. *Philo of Alexandria: An Exegete for His Time.* NovTSup 86. Leiden; New York: Brill, 1997.
Borgen, P. "Some Hebrew and Pagan Features in Philo's and Paul's Interpretation of Hagar and Ishmael." Pages 151–64 in *The New Testament and Hellenistic Judaism.* Edited by P. Borgen and S. Giversen. Aarhus: Aarhus University Press, 1995.
Borgen, P. "Philo of Alexandria: A Critical and Synthetical Survey of Research Since World War II." Pages 98–154 in *ANRW* II:21:1. Berlin; New York: De Gruyter, 1984.
Borgen, P. *Paul Preaches Circumcision and Pleases Men and Other Essays on Christian Origins.* Trondheim: Tapir Publishers, 1983.
Borgen, P. "God's Agent in the Fourth Gospel." Pages 137–48 in *Religions in Antiquity: Essays in Memory of E. R. Goodenough.* Edited by J. Neusner. SHR 14. Leiden: Brill, 1968.
Borgen, P. *Bread from Heaven: An Exegetical Study of the Concept of Manna in the Gospel of John and the Writings of Philo.* NovTSup 10. Leiden: Brill, 1965.
Bormann, L. "Abraham as 'Forefather' and His Family in Paul." Pages 207–33 in *Abraham's Family: A Network of Meaning in Judaism, Christianity, and Islam.* Edited by L. Bormann. WUNT 415. Tübingen: Mohr Siebeck, 2018.
Bousset, W. *Die Religion des Judentums im Späthellenistischen Zeitalter.* HNT 21. Tübingen: Mohr Siebeck, 1926.
Brock, S. "Two Syriac Verse Homilies on the Binding of Isaac." *Le Muséon* 99 (1986): 61–129.
Bruce, F. F. *The Epistle of Paul to the Romans:An Introduction and Commentary.* London: Tyndale Press, 1963.
Bruce, F. F. *The Epistle of Paul to the Galatians: A Commentary on the Greek Text.* NIGTC. Grand Rapids: Eerdmans, 1982.
Bryen, A.Z. *Violence in Roman Egypt: A Study in Legal Interpretation.* Philadelphia: University of Pennsylvania Press, 2013.
Bultmann, R. *Theology of the New Testament: Volume 1.* Translated by K. Grobel. New York: Scribners, 1951.

Bultmann, R. "πιστεύω κτλ." *TDNT* 6: 1–11.
Burke, T.J. *Adopted into God's Family: Exploring a Pauline Metaphor.* NSBT 22. Nottingham: Apollos, 2006.
Burton, E.D.W. *A Critical and Exegetical Commentary on the Epistle to the Galatians.* ICC. Edinburgh: T. & T. Clark, 1921.
Bühner, J.-A. *Der Gesandte und Sein Weg Im 4. Evangelium: Die Kultur- und Religionsgeschichtlichen Grundlagen der Johanneischen Sendungschristologie Sowie Ihre Traditionsgeschichtliche Entwiklung.* WUNT 2 / 2. Tübingen: Mohr Siebeck, 1977.
Byrne, B. *'Sons of God' – 'Seed of Abraham': A Study of the Idea of the Sonship of God of All Christians in Paul Against the Jewish Background.* AnBib 83. Rome: Biblical Institute, 1979.
Callan, T. *The Law and the Mediator: Gal. 3:19b–20.* PhD diss., Yale University, 1976.
Callan, T. "Pauline Midrash: The Exegetical Background of Gal 3:19b." *JBL* 99.4 (1980): 549–67.
Calvert-Koyzis, N. *Paul, Monotheism and the People of God: The Significance of Abraham Traditions for Early Judaism and Christianity.* JSNTSup 273. London; New York: T & T Clark, 2004.
Carlson, S.C. *The Text of Galatians and Its History.* WUNT 2 / 385. Tübingen: Mohr Siebeck, 2015.
Carpenter, M. *Kontakia of Romanos, Byzantine Melodist: On Christian Life.* Columbia, MS: Iniversity of Missouri Press, 1973.
Chapman, D.W., and E.J. Schnabel. *The Trial and Crucifixion of Jesus: Texts and Commentary.* WUNT 344. Tübingen: Mohr Siebeck, 2015.
Cohen, S.J.D. *The Beginnings of Jewishness: Boundaries, Varieties, Uncertainties.* Hellenistic Culture and Society. Berkeley; Los Angeles; London: University of California Press, 1999.
Coles, R.A. "4060. Official Correspondence.". In *The Oxyrhynchus Papyri: Volume LX.* London: The British Academy, 1994.
Collins, C.J. "Galatians 3:16: What Kind of Exegete Was Paul?" *TynBul* 54.1 (2003): 75–86.
Collins, J.J. "Apocalyptic Eschatology in Philosophical Dress in the Wisdom of Salomon." Pages 93–108 in *Shem in the Tents of Japhet: Essays in Encounter of Judaism and Hellenism.* Edited by J.L. Kugel. JSJSup 74. Leiden; Boston; Köln: Brill, 2002.
Conway, K.P. The Promises of God: The Background of Paul's Exclusive Use of 'Epangelia' for the Divine Pledge. BZNW 211. Berlin: De Gruyter, 2014.
Cook, J.G. *Crucifixion in the Mediterranean World.* WUNT 327. Tübingen: Mohr Siebeck, 2014.
Cranford, M. "The Possibility of Perfect Obedience: Paul and an Implied Premise in Gal 3:10 and 5:3." *NovT* 36.3 (1994): 242–58.
Cribiore, R. *Writing, Teachers, and Students in Greco-Roman Egypt.* ASP 36. Atlanta, GA: Scholars Press, 1996.
Cross, F. M. *From Epic to Canon: History and Literature in Ancient Israel.* Baltimore; London: Johns Hopkins University Press, 1998.
Dahl, N.A. "Når Paulus spør." Pages 47–59 in *Kirken i Tiden; Troen i Folket.* Edited by N.K. Lie. Oslo: Verbum, 1993.
Dahl, N.A. "The Atonement: An Adequate Reward for the Akedah?" Pages 137–51 in *Jesus the Christ: The Historical Origins of Christological.* Edited by D.H. Juel. Minneapolis: Fortress Press, 1991.

Dahl, N.A. *Jesus the Christ: The Historical Origins of Christological Doctrine.* Edited by D.H. Juel. Minneapolis: Fortress Press, 1991.

Dahl, N.A. Studies in Paul: Theology for the Early Christian Mission. Minneapolis: Augsburg, 1977.

Dahl, N.A. "Paul's Letter to the Galatians: Epistolary Genre, Content and Structure." Unpublished manuscript. Yale University, 1973.

Dahl, N.A. *Das Volk Gottes: Eine Untersuchung Zum Kirchenbewusstsein Des Urchristentums.* Skrifter Utg. Av Det Norske Videnskaps-Akademi i Oslo. II. Hist.-Filos. Klasse, 1941 / 2. Oslo: J. Dybwad, 1941.

Dahl, N.A. and A. Segal. "Philo and the Rabbis on the Names of God." *JSJ* 9.1 (1978): 1–28.

Das, A.A. *Paul and the Stories of Israel: Grand Thematic Narratives in Galatians.* Minneapolis: Fortress Press, 2016.

Das, A.A. *Galatians.* ConcC. St. Louis, MO: Concordia Publishing House, 2014.

Daube, D. *The New Testament and Rabbinic Judaism.* Peabody, MA: Hendrickson, 1994.

Davies, W.D. *Jewish and Pauline Studies.* London: S.P.C.K., 1984.

Davis, B.S. "The Meaning of ΠΡΟΓΡΑΦΗ In the Context of Galatians 3.1." *NTS* 45.2 (1999): 194–212.

de Boer, M.C. "Observations on the Significance of the Old Testament in Galatians." Pages 211–26 in *The Scriptures of Israel in Jewish and Christian Tradition: Essays in Honour of Maarten J.J. Menken.* Edited by B.J. Koet, S. Moyise, and J. Verheyden. NovTSup 148. Leiden; Boston: Brill, 2013.

de Boer, M.C. *Galatians: A Commentary.* NTL. Louisville, KY: Westminster John Knox Press, 2011.

deSilva, D.A. *The Letter to the Galatians.* NICNT. Grand Rapids: Eerdmans, 2018.

Dibelius, M. *Der Brief des Jakobus.* KEK, Abt. 15. Göttingen: Vandenhoeck & Ruprecht, 1956.

Donaldson, T.L. "Paul, Abraham's Gentile 'Offspring,' and the Torah." Pages 135–50 in *Torah Ethics and Early Christian Identity.* Edited by S.J. Wendel and D.M. Miller. Grand Rapids: Eerdmans, 2016.

Donaldson, T.L. "Paul Within Judaism: A Critical Evaluation from a 'New Perspective' Perspective." Pages 277–301 in *Paul Within Judaism: Restoring the First-Century Context to the Apostle.* Edited by M.D. Nanos and M. Zetterholm. Minneapolis: Fortress Press, 2015.

Donaldson, T.L. *Paul and the Gentiles: Remapping the Apostle's Convictional World.* Minneapolis: Fortress Press, 2006.

Donaldson, T.L. "The 'Curse of the Law' and the Inclusion of the Gentiles: Galatians 3.13–14." *NTS* 32.1 (1986): 94–112.

Dunn, J.D.G. *The New Perspective on Paul.* Grand Rapids: Eerdmans, 2008.

Dunn, J.D.G. *The Epistle to the Galatians.* BNTC. London: A & C Black, 1993.

Dunn, J.D.G. *Jesus, Paul and the Law.* Louisville, KY: John Knox, 1990.

Eckstein, H.-J. *Verheissung und Gesetz: Eine Exegetische Untersuchung zu Galater 2,15–4,7.* WUNT 86. Tübingen: Mohr Siebeck, 1996.

Eco, U. *A Theory of Semiotics.* Bloomington: Indiana University Press, 1976.

Ego, B. "Abraham als Urbild der Toratreue Israels: Traditionsgeschichtliche Überlegungen zu einem Aspekt des biblischen Abrahambildes.". Pages 25–40 in *Bund und Torah: zur theologischen Begriffsgeschichte in alttestamentlicher, frühjüdischer und urchristlicher*

Tradition. Edited by F. Avemerie and H. Lichtenberger. WUNT 92. Tübingen: Mohr Siebeck, 1996.
Feldman, L.H. "Philo's Version of the Akedah." SPhiloA (2002), 66–86.
Fraade, S.D. "Nomos and Narrative Before *Nomos and Narrative*." *Yale Journal of Law and the Humanities* 17.1 (2005): 81–96.
Fraade, S.D. *From Tradition to Commentary: Torah and Its Interpretation in the Midrash Sifre to Deuteronomy*. Albany, NY: State University of New York Press, 1991.
Fredriksen, P. "How Later Contexts Affect Pauline Content, or: Retrospect is the Mother of Anachronism." Pages 17–51 in *Jews and Christians in the First and Second Centuries: How to Write Their History*. Edited by P.J. Tomson and J.J. Schwartz. CRINT 13. Leiden: Brill, 2014.
Fredriksen, P. "Judaizing the Nations: The Ritual Demands of Paul's Gospel." *NTS* 56.2 (2010): 232–52.
Fredriksen, P. *From Jesus to Christ: The Origins of the New Testament Images of Jesus*. New Haven; London: Yale University Press, 1988.
Gadamer, H.-G. *Gesammelte Werke: Bd. 1: Hermeneutik I: Wahrheit und Methode: Grundzüge einer philosophischen Hermeneutik*. Tübingen: Mohr Siebeck, 2010.
Ginzberg, L. *The Legend of the Jews: 7. Vols*. Philadelphia: The Jewish Publication Society of America, 1968.
Goodenough, E.R. *By Light, Light: The Mystic Gospel of Hellenistic Judaism*. New Haven: Yale University Press, 1935. Repr., Amsterdam: Philo Press, 1969.
Goodman, M. "Epilogue." Pages 509–12 in *Abraham, the Nations, and the Hagarites: Jewish, Christian, and Islamic Perspectives on Kinship with Abraham*. Edited by M. Goodman, G.H. van Kooten, and J.T.A.G.M. van Ruiten. TBN 13. Leiden; Boston: Brill, 2010.
Goodrich, J.K. "Guardians, Not Taskmasters: The Cultural Resonances of Paul's Metaphor in Galatians 4.1–2." *JSNT* 32.3 (2010): 251–84.
Grässer, E. *Der Glaube im Hebräerbrief*. Marburg: N.G. Elwert Verlag, 1965.
Gregory, B.C. "Abraham as the Jewish Ideal: Exegetical Traditions in Sirach 44:19–21." *CBQ* 70.1 (2008): 66–81.
Griffiths, J.I. *Hebrews and Divine Speech*. LNTS 507. London: Bloomsbury, 2015.
Grosse, E.U. *Text und Kommunikation: Eine linguistische Einführung in die Funktionen der Texte*. Stuttgart: Kohlhammer, 1976.
Gruen, E.S. "Philo and Jewish Identity." Pages 179–95 in *Strength to Strength: Essays in Honor of Shaye J. D. Cohen*. Edited by M.L. Satlow. BJS 363. Providence, RI: Brown University, 2018.
Gruen, E.S. "Paul and Jewish Ethnicity." Pages 351–67 in *Talmudic Transgressions: Engaging the Work of Daniel Boyarin*. Edited by C.E. Fonrobert, I. Rosen-Zvi, A. Shemesh, and M. Vidas. Leiden; Boston: Brill, 2017.
Grüneberg, K.N. *Abraham, Blessing and the Nations: A Philological and Exegetical Study of Gen 12:3 in its Narrative Context*. BZAW 332. Berlin; New York: De Gruyter, 2003.
Gülich, E. and W. Raible. *Linguistische Textmodelle*. UTB. München: Fink, 1977.
Hahn, F. "Genesis 15,6 im Neuen Testament." Pages 90–107 in *Probleme biblischer Theologie*. München: Kaiser, 1971.
Hahn, S.W. "Covenant, Oath, and the Aqedah: Διαθήκη in Galatians 3:15–18." *CBQ* 67.1 (2005): 79–100.

Hansen, G.W. *Abraham in Galatians: Epistolary and Rhetorical Contexts*. JSNTSup 29. Sheffield: Sheffield Academic Press, 1989.
Hartman, L. "Galatians 3:15–4:11 as Part of a Theological Argument on a Practical Issue." Pages 127–58 in *The Truth of the Gospel (Galatians 3:15–4:11)*. Edited by J. Lambrecht. MSBen.BE 12. Rome: Benedictina, 1993.
Hartman, L. *Asking for a Meaning: A Study of 1 Enoch 1–5*. ConBNT 12. Lund: Gleerup, 1979.
Hartman, L. *Prophecy Interpreted: The Formation of Some Jewish Apocalyptic Texts and of the Eschatological Discourse Mark 13 Par*. ConBNT 1. Lund: Gleerup, 1966.
Harvey, A.E. "The Opposition to Paul." Pages 321–33 in *The Galatians Debate: Contemporary Issues in Rhetorical and Historical Interpretation*. Edited by M.D. Nanos. Peabody, MA: Hendrickson, 2002.
Hay, D.M. "Pistis as 'Ground for Faith' in Hellenized Judaism and Paul." *JBL* 108.3 (1989): 461–76.
Hayes, C. *What's Divine About Divine Law? Early Perspectives*. Princeton; Oxford: Princeton University Press, 2015.
Hayes, C. *Gentile Impurities and Jewish Identities: Intermarriage and Conversion from the Bible to the Talmud*. Oxford: OUP, 2002.
Hays, R.B. *Echoes of Scripture in the Gospels*. Waco, TX: Baylor University Press, 2016.
Hays, R.B. *Reading Backwards: Figural Christology and the Fourfold Gospel Witness*. Waco, TX: Baylor University Press, 2014.
Hays, R.B. *The Faith of Jesus Christ: The Narrative Substructure of Galatians 3:1–4:11*. 2nd ed. BRS. Grand Rapids: Eerdmans; Dearborn, MI: Dove Booksellers, 2002.
Hays, R.B. *The Letter to the Galatians: Introduction, Commentary, and Reflections*. NIB. Nashville: Abingdon, 2000.
Hays, R.B. *Echoes of Scripture in the Letters of Paul*. New Haven: Yale University Press, 1989.
Heil, C. "'Angeordnet Durch Engel Durch die Hand Eines Mittlers' (Gal 3,19): Das Paulinische Konzept von der Vermittlung der Tora." Pages 229–43 in *Vermittelte Gegenwart: Konzeptionen der Gottespräsenz von der Zeit Des Zweiten Tempels Bis Anfang Des 2. Jahrhunderts n. Chr.* Edited by A. Taschl-Erber and I. Fischer. WUNT 367. Tübingen: Mohr Siebeck, 2016.
Heim, E.M. *Adoption in Galatians: Contemporary Metaphor Theories and the Pauline Huiothesia Metaphors*. BibInt 153. Leiden; Boston, 2017.
Hellholm, D. "Amplificatio in the Macro-Structure of Romans." Pages 123–51 in *Rhetoric and the New Testament: Essays from the 1992 Heidelberg Conference. FS Wilhelm Wuellner*. Edited by S.E. Porter and Th.H. Olbricht. JSNTSup 90. Sheffield: JSOT Press, 1993.
Hellholm, D. "Substitutionelle Gliederungsmerkmale und die Komposition des Matthäusevangeliums." Pages 11–76 in *Texts and Contexts: Biblical Texts in Their Textual and Situational Contexts. Essays in Honor of Lars Hartman*. Edited by T. Fornberg and D. Hellholm. Oslo: Scandinavian University Press, 1995.
Hellholm, D. *Das Visionenbuch des Hermas als Apokalypse: Formgeschichtliche und texttheoretische Studien zu einer literarischen Gattung. Band I: Methodologische Vorüberlegungen und makrostrukturelle Textanalyse*. ConBNT 13 / 1. Lund: Gleerup, 1980.
Himmelfarb, M. *A Kingdom of Priests: Ancestry and Merit in Ancient Judaism*. Philadelphia: University of Pennsylvania Press, 2006.
Holladay, C.R. *Acts: A Commentary*. NTL. Louisville, KY: Westminster John Knox Press, 2016.

Hooker, M.D. "Another Look at πίστις Χριστοῦ." *SJT* 69.1 (2016): 46–62.
Hooker, M.D. "'Heirs of Abraham': The Gentiles' Role in Israel's Stoty: A Response to Bruce Longenecker." Pages 85–96 in *Narrative Dynamics in Paul: A Critical Assessment.* Edited by B.W. Longenecker. Louisville, KY: Westminster John Knox Press, 2002.
Hooker, M.D. "Πίστις Χριστοῦ." *NTS* 35.3 (1989): 321–42.
Horsley, R.A. "The Law of Nature in Philo and Cicero." *HTR* 71.1–2 (1978): 35–59.
Huebner, S.R. "Adoption and Fosterage in the Ancient Eastern Mediterranean." Pages 510–31 in *The Oxford Handbook of Childhood and Education in the Classical World.* Edited by J.E. Grubbs, T. Parkins, and R. Bell. Oxford: OUP, 2014.
Huizenga, L.A. *The New Isaac: Tradition and Intertextuality in the Gospel of Matthew.* NovTSup 131. Leiden: Brill, 2009.
Hunt, A., ed. and trans. *The Oxyrhynchus Papyri: Part IX.* Oxford: OUP, 1912.
Jacobs, I. "The Midrashic Background for James II. 21–3." *NTS* 22.4 (1976): 457–64.
Johanson, B. *To All the Brethren: A Text-Linguistic and Rhetorical Approach to I Thessalonians.* ConBNT 16. Stockholm: Almqvist & Wiksell, 1987.
Johnson Hodge, C. *If Sons, Then Heirs: A Study of Kinship and Ethnicity in the Letters of Paul.* Oxford: OUP, 2007.
Juel, D.H. *Messianic Exegesis: Christological Interpretation of the Old Testament in Early Christianity.* Philadelphia: Fortress Press, 1988.
Kamesar, A. "The Literary Genres of the Pentateuch as Seen from the Greek Perspective: The Testimony of Philo of Alexandria." SPhA 9 (1997): 143–89.
Keener, C.S. *Galatians: A Commentary.* Grand Rapids: Baker Academic, 2019.
Keener, C.S. *Galatians.* NCBC. Cambridge: CUP, 2018.
Kelly, B. *Petitions, Litigation, and Social Control in Roman Egypt.* Oxford: OUP, 2011.
Kienast, D. "Presbeia." *PWSup* 13: 499–628.
Kim, L.S. "Another Look at Adoption in Romans 8:15 in Light of Roman Social Practices and Legal Rules." *BTB* 44.3 (2014): 133–43.
Kobler, F. *Letters of Jews through the Ages, 2. Vols.* Philadelphia: Jewish Publication Society, 1978.
Köster, H. "νόμος φύσεως: The Concept of Natural Law in Greek Thought." Pages 521–41 in *Religions in Antiquity: Essays in Memory of E. R. Goodenough.* Edited by J. Neusner. SHR 14. Leiden: Brill, 1968.
Köster, H. "Die Auslegung der Abraham-Verheissung in Hebräer 6." Pages 95–109 in *Studien zur Theologie der alttestamentlichen Überlieferungen.* Edited by R. Rendtorff and K. Koch. Neukirchen: Neukirchener Verlag, 1961.
Kratz, R.G. "Die Verheissungen an die Erzväter: Die Konstruktion ethnischer Identität Israels." Pages 35–66 in *The Politics of the Ancestors: Exegetical and Historical Perspectives on Genesis 12–36.* Edited by M.G. Brett and J. Wöhrle. FAT 124. Tübingen: Mohr Siebeck, 2018.
Kugel, J.L. "Jubilees, Philo, and the Problem of Genesis." Pages 295–311 in *The Hebrew Bible in Light of the Dead Sea Scrolls.* Edited by N. David, A. Lange, K. De Troyer, and S. Tzoref. FRLANT 239. Göttingen: Vandenhoeck & Ruprecht, 2012.
Kugel, J.L. "Exegetical Notes on 4Q225 'Pseudo-Jubilees'." *DSD* 13.1 (2006): 73–98.
Kugel, J.L. *Traditions of the Bible: A Guide to the Bible as It Was at the Start of the Common Era.* Cambridge, MA: Harvard University Press, 1998.
Kugel, J.L. *The Bible As It Was.* Cambridge, MA: Harvard University Press, 1997.

Kugel, J.L. *In Potiphar's House: The Interpretive Life of Biblical Texts.* San Francisco: Harper, 1990.
Kuhn, K.G. *Der Tannaitische Midrasch Sifre zu Numeri.* Rabbinische Texte. Stuttgart: Kohlhammer, 1959.
Kujanpää, K. *The Rhetorical Functions of Scriptural Quotations in Romans: Paul's Argumentation by Quotations.* NovTSup 172. Leiden; Boston: Brill, 2019.
Leonhardt-Baltzer, J. "Diaspora Jewish Attitudes to *Metropoleis:* Philo and Paul on Balanced Personalities, Split Loyalties, Jerusalem, and Rome." Pages 86–98 in *The Urban World and the First Christians.* Edited by S. Walton, P.R. Trebilco, and D.W.J. Gill. Grand Rapids: Eerdmans, 2017.
Levenson, J.D. *Inheriting Abraham: The Legacy of the Patriarch in Judaism, Christianity, and Islam.* Library of Jewish Ideas. Princeton: Princeton University Press, 2012.
Levenson, J.D. *The Death and Resurrection of the Beloved Son: The Transformation of Child Sacrifice in Judaism and Christianity.* New Haven; London: Yale University Press, 1995.
Levin, C. "Die Väterverheissungen: Eine Bestandaufnahme." Pages 125–43 in *The Post-Priestly Pentateuch: New Perspectives on its Redactional Development and Theological Profiles.* Edited by F. Giuntoli and K. Schmid. FAT 101. Tübingen: Mohr Siebeck, 2015.
Levison, J.R. *The Spirit in First Century Judaism.* AGJU 29. Leiden; New York: Brill, 1997.
Lewis, N. "Notationes Legentis." *BASP* 33 (1996): 61–66.
Lewis, N., and R. Meyer. *Roman Civilization: A Sourcebook: Roman Empire, Vol. 2.* Records of Civilization Sources & Study. New York: Columbia University Press, 1990.
Lewis, R.B. *Paul's 'Spirit of Adoption' in its Roman Imperial Context.* LNTS 545. London; New York: Bloomsbury T&T Clark, 2016.
Lightfoot, J.B. *Saint Paul's Epistle to the Galatians: A Revisited Text with Introduction, Notes, and Dissertations.* London; New York: Macmillan and Co., 1896.
Lindsay, D.R. *Josephus and Faith: Pistis and Pisteuein as Faith Terminology in the Writings of Flavius Josephus and in the New Testament.* AGJU 19. Leiden: Brill, 1993.
Linton, O. "Paulus och Juridiken." *STK* 21.3 (1945): 173–92.
Ljungman, H. *PISTIS: A Study of Its Presuppositions and Its Meaning in Pauline Use.* Acta: Skrifter Utgiven Av Kungl. Humanistiska Vetenskapssamfundet i Lund. Lund: Gleerup, 1964.
Ljungman, H. *Guds barmhärtighet och dom.* Lund: Gleerup, 1950.
Longenecker, R.N. *Galatians.* WBC. Nashville: Thomas Nelson, 1990.
Lührmann, D. "Pistis Im Judentum." *ZNW* 64.1 (1973): 29–36.
Lyall, F. "Roman Law in the Writings of Paul: Adoption." *JBL* 88.4 (1969): 458–466.
Maartens, J.W. "The Meaning and Function of the Law in Philo and Josephus." Pages 27–40 in *Torah Ethics and Early Christian Identity.* Edited by S.J. Wendel and D.M. Miller. Grand Rapids: Eerdmans, 2016.
Maartens, J.W. *One God, One Law: Philo of Alexandria on the Mosaic and Greco-Roman Law.* SPhAMA 2. Boston; Leiden: Brill, 2003.
Marmorstein, A. *The Doctrine of Merits in Old Rabbinical Literature.* 1920. Repr., New York: KTAV Publishing House, 1968.
Martyn, J.L. *History and Theology in the Fourth Gospel.* Third ed. NTL. Edinburgh: T & T Clark, 2003.
Martyn, J.L. *Galatians: A New Translation with Introduction and Commentary.* AB. New York: Doubleday, 1997.

Matlock, R.B. "Helping Paul's Argument Work? The Curse of Galatians 3.10–14." Pages 154–79 in *The Torah in the New Testament: Papers Delivered at the Manchester–Lausanne Seminar of June 2008*. Edited by M. Taites and P. Oakes. LNTS 401. London: T & T Clark, 2009.
Matlock, R.B. "Saving Faith: The Rhetoric and Semantics of πίστις in Paul." Pages 73–89 in *The Faith of Jesus Christ: Exegetical, Biblical, and Theological Studies*. Edited by M.F. Bird and P.M. Sprinkle. Peabody, MA: Hendrickson, 2009.
McFarland, O. *God and Grace in Philo and Paul*. NovTSup 164. Leiden: Brill, 2015.
Meeks, W.A. "Corinthian Christians as Artificial Aliens." Pages 129–38 in *Paul Beyond the Judaism / Hellenism Divide*. Edited by T. Engberg-Pedersen. Louisville, KY: Westminster John Knox Press, 2001.
Menken, M.J.J. "Composite Citations in the Gospel of Matthew." Pages 34–61 in *Composite Citations in Antiquity: Volume Two*. Edited by S.A. Adams and S.M. Ehorn. LNTS 593. London: Bloomsbury T & T Clark, 2018.
Menken, M.J.J. *Studies in John's Gospel and Epistles: Collected Essays*. CBET 77. Leuven; Paris; Bristol, CT: Peeters, 2015.
Migne, J.P. *Commentaria in Epistolae Ad Galatas*. PL. Paris, 1844–64.
Mitchell, M.M. "Gift Histories." *JSNT* 39.3 (2017): 304–23.
Mitchell, M.M. "New Testament Envoys in the Context of Greco-Roman Diplomatic and Epistolary Conventions: The Example of Timothy and Titus." *JBL* 111.4 (1992): 641–62.
Moberly, R.W.L. "אמן." Pages 427–33 in *New International Dictionary of Old Testament Theology & Exegesis*. Edited by W.A. Van Gemeren. Carlisle: Paternoster Press, 1996.
Moberly, R.W.L. "Abraham's Righteousness (Genesis XV 6)." Pages 103–30 in *Studies in the Pentateuch*. Edited by J.A. Emerton. VTSup 41. Leiden: Brill, 1990.
Moberly, R.W.L. "The Earliest Commentary on the Akedah." *VT* 38.3 (1988): 302–23.
Moo, D.J. "Galatians.". In *Galatians*. BECNT. Grand Rapids: Baker Academic, 2013.
Moore-Crispin, D.R. "Galatians 4.1–9: The Use and Abuse of Parallels." *EQ* 61.3 (1989): 203–23.
Morgan, T. *Roman Faith and Christian Faith: Pistis and Fides in the Early Roman Empire and Early Churches*. Oxford: OUP, 2015.
Morland, K.A. *The Rhetoric of Curse in Galatians: Paul Confronts Another Gospel*. Emory Studies in Early Christianity 5. Atlanta, GA: Scholars Press, 1995.
Moxnes, H. "Who Are the Children of Abraham in Romans 4? Retelling the Memory of Abraham 'Our Ancestor'." Pages 193–210 in *The Church and Its Mission in the New Testament and Early Christianity: Essays in Memory of Hans Kvalbein*. Edited by D.E. Aune and R. Hvalvik. WUNT 404. Tübingen: Mohr Siebeck, 2018.
Moxnes, H. *Theology in Conflict: Studies in Paul's Understanding of God in Romans*. NovTSup 53. Leiden: Brill, 1980.
Muir, S. "Vivid Imagery in Galatians 3:1—Roman Rhetoric, Street Announcing, Graffiti, and Crucifixions." *BTB* 44.2 (2014): 76–86.
Mussner, F. *Der Galaterbrief*. HThKNT. Freiburg (im Breisgau): Herder, 1974.
Myre, A. "La Loi de la Nature et la Loi Mosaic Selon Philon d'Alexandrie." *ScEs* 28 (1976): 163–81.
Myre, A. "La Loi et la Pentateuque Selon Philon d'Alexandrie." *ScEs* 25 (1973): 208–25.
Myre, A. "La Loi l'Ordre Cosmique et Politique selon Philon d'Alexandrie." *ScEs* 24 (1972): 217–47.

Najman, H. *Past Renewals: Interpretative Authority, Renewed Revelation, and the Quest for Perfection in Jewish Antiquity.* JSJSup 53. Leiden; Boston: Brill, 2010.
Najman, H. *Seconding Sinai: The Development of Mosaic Discourse in Second Temple Judaism.* JSJSup 77. Leiden: Brill, 2003.
Najman, H. "A Written Copy of the Law of Nature: An Unthinkable Paradox." SPhiloA 15 (2003): 54 – 63.
Najman, H. "The Law of Nature and the Authority of Mosaic Law." SPhiloA 11 (1999): 55 – 73.
Neutel, K. "'Neither Jew Nor Greek': Abraham as a Universal Ancestor." Pages 291 – 305 in *Abraham, the Nations, and the Hagarites: Jewish, Christian, and Islamic Perspectives on Kinship with Abraham.* Edited by M. Goodman, G.H. van Kooten, and J.T.A.G.M. van Ruiten. TBN 13. Leiden: Brill, 2010.
Neyrey, J.H. "Bewitched in Galatia: Paul and Cultural Anthropology." *CBQ* 50.1 (1988): 72 – 100.
Niehoff, M.R. *Philo of Alexandria: An Intellectual Biography.* New Haven; London: Yale University Press, 2018.
Niehoff, M.R. *Jewish Exegesis and Homeric Scholarship in Alexandria.* Cambridge: CUP, 2011.
Niehoff, M.R. "Homeric Scholarship and Bible Exegesis in Ancient Alexandria: Evidence from Philo's 'Quarrelsome' Colleagues." *CQ* 57.1 (2007): 166 – 82.
Nikiprowetzky, V. *Le Commentaire De L'Écriture Chez Philon D'Alexandrie.* Leiden: Brill, 1977.
Nordgaard, S. "Paul and the Provenance of the Law: The Case of Gal 3,19 – 20." *ZNW* 105.1 (2014): 64 – 79.
Noth, M. *Gesammelte Studien Zum Alten Testament.* München: C. Kaiser, 1957.
Novenson, M.V. *Christ Among the Messiahs: Christ Language in Paul and Messiah Language in Ancient Judaism.* Oxford: OUP, 2012.
Oeming, M. "Der Glaube Abrahams: Zur Rezeptionsgeschichte von Gen 15,6 in der Zeit des zweiten Tempels." *ZAW* 110.1 (1998): 16 – 33.
Ophir, A, and I. Rosen-Zvi. *Goy: Israel's Multiple Others and the Birth of the Gentile.* Oxford: OUP, 2018.
Ostwald, M. "*Was There a Concept* Agraphos Nomos *in Classical Greece?*" Pages 70 – 104 in *Exegesis and Argument: Studies Presented to Gregory Vlastos.* Edited by E.N. Lee, A.P.D. Mourelatos, and R.M. Rorty. Assen: Van Gorcum, 1973.
Ostwald, M. *Nomos and the Beginnings of the Athenian Democracy.* Oxford: Clarendon Press, 1969.
Paavola, S. "Abduction as a Logic and Methodology of Discovery: The Importance of Strategies." *Foundation of Science* 9.3 (2004): 267 – 83.
Palme, B. "Roman Litigation: Reports of Court Proceedings." Pages 482 – 86 in *Law and Legal Practice in Egypt from Alexander to the Arab Conquest: A Selection of Papyrological Sources in Translation, with Introductions and Commentary.* Edited by J.G. Keenan, J.G Manning, and U. Yiftach-Firanko. Cambridge: CUP, 2014.
Paz, Y. "Prior to Sinai: The Patriarchs and the Mosaic Law in Rabbinic Literature in View of Second Temple and Christian Literature." Jerusalem: Hebrew University of Jerusalem [Hebrew], 2009.
Pearce, S. "Notes on Philo's Use of the Terms ἜΘΝΟΣ and ΛΑΟΣ." SPhiloA 28 (2016): 205 – 26.

Pearce, S. "Jerusalem as 'Mother-City' in the Writings of Philo of Alexandria." Pages 19–36 in *Negotiating Diaspora: Jewish Strategies in the Roman Empire.* Edited by J.M.G. Barclay. LSTS 45. London: T & T Clark, 2004.
Peirce, C.S. *Collected Papers of Charles Sanders Peirce: 8. Vols.* Edited by C. Hartshorne and P. Weiss. Cambridge, MA: Harvard University Press, 1960.
Rabens, V. "*Pneuma* and the Beholding of God: Reading Paul in the Context of Philonic Mystical Traditions." Pages 293–329 in *The Holy Spirit, Inspiration, and the Cultures of Antiquity: Multidisiplinary Perspectives.* Edited by J. Frey and J.R. Levison. Ekstasis 5. Berlin; New York: De Gruyter, 2014.
Rabens, V. *The Holy Spirit and Ethics in Paul: Transformation and Empowering for Religious-Ethical Life.* WUNT 2 / 283. Tübingen: Mohr Siebeck, 2010.
Reinhartz, A. "The Meaning of *Nomos* in Philo's *Exposition of the Law.*" *SR* 15.3 (1986): 337–45.
Rosen-Zvi, I. "Pauline Traditions and the Rabbis: Three Case Studies." *HTR* 110.2 (2017): 169–94.
Rosen-Zvi, I. and A. Ophir. "Paul and the Invention of the Gentiles." *JQR* 105.1 (2015): 1–41.
Rowlandson, J., ed. Women & Society in Greek & Roman Egypt: A Sourcebook. Cambridge: CUP, 1998.
Runia, D.T. "Philo and the Gentiles." Pages 28–45 in *Attitudes to Gentiles in Ancient Judaism and Early Christianity.* Edited by D.C. Sim and J.S. McLaren. LNTS 499. London: Bloomsbury T & T Clark, 2013.
Runia, D.T. "The Structure of Philo's Allegorical Treatise *De Agricultura*," SPhA 22 (2010): 87–109.
Runia, D.T. *Philo of Alexandria: On the Creation of Cosmos According to Moses: Introduction, Translation, and Commentary.* PACS. Leiden: Brill, 2001.
Runia, D.T. *Philo in Early Christian Literature: A Survey.* CRINT. Assen: Van Gorcum, 1993.
Runia, D.T. "Further Observations on the Structure of Philo's Allegorical Treatises," *VC* 41.2 (1987): 105–138.
Runia, D.T. "The Structure of Philo's Allegorical Treatises: A Review of Two Recent Studies and Some Additional Comments." *VC* 38.3 (1984): 209–56.
Samely, A. *Rabbinic Interpretation of Scripture in the Mishnah.* Oxford: OUP, 2002.
Samely, A. "Between Scripture and Its Rewording: Towards a Classification of Rabbinic Exegesis." *JJS* 42.1 (1991): 39–67.
Sanders, E.P. *Paul and Palestinian Judaism: A Comparison of Patterns of Religion.* Philadelphia: Fortress, 1977.
Sandmel, S. *Philo's Place in Judaism: A Study of Conceptions of Abraham in Jewish Literature.* New York: KTAV Publishing House, 1971.
Sandmel, S. "Philo's Environment and Philo's Exegesis." *JBR* 22.4 (1954): 248–53.
Sandmel, S. "Philo's Place in Judaism." *HUCA* 25 (1954): 209–37.
Sandnes, K.O. *Paul Perceived: An Interactionist Perspective on Paul and the Law.* WUNT 412. Tübingen: Mohr Siebeck, 2018.
Sandnes, K.O. *A New Family: Conversion and Ecclesiology in the Early Church with Cross-Cultural Comparisons.* SIHC 91. Bern: Peter Lang, 1994.
Sass, G. *Leben aus den Verheissungen: Traditionsgeschichtliche und biblisch-theologische Untersuchungen zur rede von Gottes Verheissungen im Früjudentum und beim Apostel Paulus.* FRLANT 164. Göttingen: Vandenhoeck & Ruprecht, 1995.

Saussure, F. de. *Cours de Linguistique Géneralé.* Paris: Payot, 1916.
Schlatter, A. *Der Glaube Im Neuen Testament.* Stuttgart: Calwer, 1927.
Schlier, H. *Der Brief an die Galater.* KEK. Göttingen: Vandenhoeck & Ruprecht, 1971.
Schliesser, B. "'Christ-Faith' as an Eschatological Event (Galatians 3.23–26): A 'Third View' on Πίστις Χριστοῦ." *JSNT* 38.3 (2016): 277–300.
Schliesser, B. *Abraham's Faith in Romans 4: Paul's Concept of Faith in Light of the History of Reception of Genesis 15:6.* WUNT 2 / 224. Tübingen: Mohr Siebeck, 2007.
Schoeps, H.J. *Paul: The Theology of the Apostle in the Light of Jewish Religious History.* Translated by H. Knight. Philadelphia: The Westminster Press, 1961.
Schreiner, T.R. *Galatians.* Zondervan Exegetical Commentary Series: New Testament. Grand Rapids: Zondervan, 2010.
Schröter, J. *From Jesus to the New Testament.* Translated by W. Coppins. Baylor-Mohr Siebeck Studies in Early Christianity 1. Waco, TX: Baylor University Press, 2013.
Schultz, J.P. "Two Views of the Patriarchs: Noahides and Pre-Sinai Israelites.". Pages 43–59 in *Texts and Responses: Studies Presented to Nahum M. Glatzer on the Occasion of His Seventieth Birthday by His Students.* Edited by M.A Fishbane and P.R. Flohr. Leiden: Brill, 1975.
Scott, J.M. *Adoption as Sons of God: An Exegetical Investigation into the Background of ΥΙΟΘΕΣΙΑ in the Pauline Corpus.* WUNT 2 / 48. Tübingen: Mohr Siebeck, 1992.
Seierstad, I.P. *Budskapet: Et utvalg av gammeltestamentlige artikler.* Oslo: Universitetsforlaget, 1971.
Shroyer, M. "Alexandrian Jewish Literalists." *JBL* 55.4 (1936): 261–84.
Siegert, F. *Drei hellenistische – jüdische Predigten I. Ps.-Philon, "Über Jona", "Über Simson" und "Über die Gottesbezeichnung, wohltätig verzehrendes Feuer": Übersetzung aus dem Armenischen und sprachliche Erläuterungen.* WUNT 20. Tübingen: Mohr Siebeck, 1980.
Silva, M. "Abraham, Faith, and Works: Paul's Use of Scripture in Galatians 3:6–14." *WTJ* 63.2 (2001): 251–67.
Spiegel, S. *The Last Trial: On the Legends and Lore of the Command to Abraham to Offer Isaac as a Sacrifice: The Akedah.* New York: Pantheon Books, 1967.
Sprinkle, P. *Law and Life: The Interpretation of Leviticus 18:5 in Early Judaism and Paul.* WUNT 2 / 241. Tübingen: Mohr Siebeck, 2008.
Stanley, C.D. "Composite Citations: Retrospect and Prospect." Pages 203–209 in *Composite Citations in Antiquity: Volume One.* Edited by S.A. Adams and S.M. Ehorn. LNTS 525. London: T&T Clark, 2016.
Stanley, C.D. *Arguing with Scripture: The Rhetoric of Quotations in the Letters of Paul.* London: T & T Clark, 2004.
Stein, E. *Philo und der Midrasch: Philos Schilderung der Gestalten Des Pentateuch Verglichen mit der Des Midrasch.* BZAW 57. Giessen: De Gruyter, 1931.
Stendahl, K. *Paul Among Jews and Gentiles.* Philadelphia: Fortress Press, 1976.
Sterling, G.E. "The School of Moses in Alexandria: An Attempt to Reconstruct the School of Philo." Pages 141–66 in *Second Temple Jewish Paideia in Context.* Edited by G. Boccaccini and J. Zurawski. BZNW 228. Berlin: Walter de Gruyter, 2017.
Sterling, G.E. "'A Law To Themselves': Limited Universalism in Philo and Paul." *ZNW* 107.1 (2016): 30–47.

Sterling, G.E. "When the Beginning is the End: The Place of Genesis in the Commentaries of Philo." Pages 428–46 in *The Book of Genesis: Composition, Reception, and Interpretation*. Edited by C.A. Evans et al. Leiden: Brill, 2012.

Sterling, G.E. "'Prolific in Expression and Broad in Thought': Internal References to Allegorical Commentary and Exposition of the Law." *Euphrosyne* 40 (2012): 55–76.

Sterling, G.E. "'Philo Has not Been Used Half Enough': The Significance of Philo of Alexandria for the Study of the New Testament." *PRSt* 30.3 (2003): 251–69.

Stowers, S.K. "What is 'Pauline Participation in Christ'?" Pages 352–71 in *Redefining First-Century Jewish and Christian Identities: Essays in Honor of Ed Parish Sanders*. Edited by F.E. Udoh et al. CJA 16. Notre Dame: University of Notre Dame Press, 2008.

Taubenschlag, R. *Opera Minora: II. Band*. Warsaw: Panstwowe Wydawnictwo Naukowe, 1959.

Thiessen, M. "Paul, the Animal Apocalypse, and Abraham's Gentile Seed." Pages 65–78 in *The Ways That Often Parted: Essays in Honor of Joel Marcus*. Edited by L. Baron, J. Hicks-Keeton, and M. Thiessen. Atlanta, GA: SBL Press, 2018.

Thiessen, M. "Paul, Essentialism, and the Jewsih Law: In Conversation with Christine Hayes." *Journal for the Study of Paul and His Letters* 7.1–2 (2017): 80–85.

Thiessen, M. *Paul and the Gentile Problem*. Oxford: OUP, 2016.

Tolmie, F.D. Persuading the Galatians: A Text-Centred Rhetorical Analysis of a Pauline Letter. WUNT 2 / 190. Tübingen: Mohr Siebeck, 2005.

Trick, B.R. *Abrahamic Descent, Testamentary Adoption, and the Law in Galatians: Differentiating Abraham's Sons, Seed, and Children of Promise*. NovTSup 169. Leiden; Boston: Brill, 2016.

Urbach, E. E. *The Sages: Their Concepts and Beliefs*. Cambridge, MA: Harvard University Press, 1987.

van der Lans, B. "Belonging to Abraham's Kin: Genealogical Appeals to Abraham as a Possible Background for Paul's Abrahamic Argument." Pages 307–318 in *Abraham, the Nations, and the Hagarites: Jewish, Christian, and Islamic Perspectives on Kinship with Abraham*. Edited by M. Goodman, G.H. van Kooten, and J.T.A.G.M. van Ruiten. TBN 13. Leiden; Boston: Brill, 2010.

Van Seter, J. *Abraham in History and Tradition*. New Haven: Yale University Press, 1975.

Vos, J.S. "Die Hermeneutische Antinomie bei Paulus (Galater 3.11–12; Römer 10.5–10)." *NTS* 38.2 (1992): 254–70.

Wan, S.-K. "Abraham and the Promise of Spirit: Points of Convergence Between Philo and Paul." Pages 209–224 in *Things Revealed: Studies in Early Jewish and Christian Literature in Honor of Michael E. Stone*. Edited by E.G. Chazon, D. Satran, and R.A. Clements. JSJSup 89. Leiden; Boston: Brill, 2004.

Watson, F. *Paul and the Hermeneutics of Faith*. 2nd ed. London: Bloomsbury T & T Clark, 2016.

Watson, F. "By Faith (of Christ): An Exegetical Dilemma and its Scriptural Solution." Pages 147–63 in *The Faith of Jesus Christ: Exegetical, Biblical, and Theological Studies*. Edited by M.F. Bird and P.M. Sprinkle. Peabody, MA: Hendrickson, 2009.

Wazana, N. "'For an Impaled Body is a Curse of God' (Deut 21:23): Impaled Bodies in Biblical Law and Conquest Narratives." Pages 69–98 in *Law and Narrative in the Bible and in Neighbouring Ancient Cultures*. Edited by K.-P. Adam, F. Avemarie, and N. Wazana. FAT 2 / 54. Tübingen: Mohr Siebeck, 2012.

Weinfeld, M. *Deuteronomy and the Deuteronomic School*. Oxford: Clarendon Press, 1972.

Wendt, H. "Galatians 3:1 as an Allusion to Textual Prophecy." *JBL* 135.2 (2016): 369–89.
Wenham, G.J. *Genesis 16–50*. WBC. Dallas: Word Books, 1994.
Wenham, G.J. *Genesis 1–15*. WBC. Waco, TX: Word Books, 1987.
Westermann, C. *Genesis 12–36*. BK. Neukirchen-Vluyn: Neukirchener Verlag, 1981.
Westermann, C. *The Promises to the Fathers: Studies on the Patriarchal Narratives*. Translated by D.E. Green. Philadelphia: Fortress Press, 1980.
Wilcox, M. "'Upon the Tree' – Deut 21:22–23 in the New Testament." *JBL* 96.1 (1977): 85–99.
Wilf, S. *The Law Before the Law*. Plymouth: Lexington Books, 2008.
Williams, S.K. *Galatians*. ANTC. Nashville: Abingdon Press, 1997.
Williams, S.K. "Promise in Galatians: A Reading of Paul's Reading of Scripture." *JBL* 107.4 (1988): 709–20.
Williamson, P.R. *Sealed with an Oath: Covenant in God's unfolding Purpose*. NSBT 23. Nottingham: Apollos, 2007.
Williamson, P.R. *Abraham, Israel and the Nations*. JSOTSup 315. Sheffield: Sheffield Academic Press, 2000.
Williamson, R. *Philo and the Epistle to the Hebrews*. ALGHJ 4. Leiden: Brill, 1970.
Wilson, T.A. *The Curse of the Law and the Crisis in Galatia: Reassessing the Purpose of Galatians*. WUNT 2 / 225. Tübingen: Mohr Siebeck, 2007.
Wilson, W.T. *Philo of Alexandria, On Virtues: Introduction, Translation, and Commentary*. PACS. Leiden; Boston: Brill, 2011.
Windisch, H. *Die Frömmigkeit Philos und ihre Bedeutung für das Christentum: Eine religionsgeschichtliche Studie*. Leipzig: J.C. Hinrichs, 1909.
Winston, D. *Logos and Mystical Theology in Philo of Alexandria*. Cincinnati, OH: Hebrew Union College Press, 1985.
Winston, D. "Philo's Ethical Theory." Pages 381–88 in *ANRW 21.1: Part 2, Principat 21.1*. Edited by H. Temporini and W. Haase. Berlin: De Gruyter, 1984.
Wisdom, J.R. *Blessing for the Nations and the Curse of the Law: Paul's Citation of Genesis and Deuteronomy in Gal. 3:8–10*. WUNT 2 / 133. Tübingen: Mohr Siebeck, 2001.
Witherington III, B. *Grace in Galatia: A Commentary on St Paul's Letter to the Galatians*. Edinburgh: T & T Clark, 1998.
Wolfson, H. A. Philo: Foundations of Religious Philosophy in Judaism, Christianity, and Islam: 2 Volumes. Cambridge, MA; London: Harvard University Press, 1947.
Wright, N.T. *The Climax of the Covenant: Christ and the Law in Pauline Theology*. Edinburgh: T & T Clark, 1991.
Zetterholm, K.H. "Isaac and Jesus: A Rabbinic Reappropriation of a 'Christian' Motif?" *JJS* 67.1 (2016): 102–120.

Index of Ancient Sources

1 Hebrew Bible / Old Testament

https://doi.org/10.1515/9783110722109-009

2 Apocrypha and Old Testament Pseudepigrapha

3 Hellenistic Jewish Authors

4 Dead Sea Scrolls

5 New Testament

6 Rabbinic Literature

7 Christian Authors

8 Greek and Latin Authors

9 Papyri

Index of Modern Authors

https://doi.org/10.1515/9783110722109-010